SPITFIRE SIN

A True Life of Relentless A

SPITFIRE SINGH

A True Life of Relentless Adventure

The Biography of AVM Harjinder Singh

MIKE EDWARDS MBE

BLOOMSBURY

NEW DELHI • LONDON • OXFORD • NEW YORK • SYDNEY

First published, 2016
This export edition published 2017

BLOOMSBURY PUBLISHING INDIA PVT. LTD.
New Delhi London Oxford New York Sydney

ISBN 978-93-86141-61-3

10 9 8 7 6 5 4

Published by Bloomsbury Publishing India Pvt. Ltd.
2nd Floor, Building No. 4
DDA Complex LSC, Pocket 6 & 7, Sector C
Vasant Kunj, New Delhi 110070

Printed and bound in India by Replika Press Pvt. Ltd.

Dedication

For my long suffering wife, Clare,
who has put up with yet another of my projects.
For my daughters Ella and Gracie.
When asked, 'Where is dad?', no longer the answer,
'tip tapping on his computer as always!' ... or is it?

Contents

Preface

'Indians will not be able to fly and maintain military aeroplanes.
It's a man's job; and all you have done is bring the greatest disgrace
on yourselves.'

– Air Marshal Sir John Steele
Air Officer Commander-in-Chief, India, 1931 to 1935

Delhi, 2012

Being in the Marshal's living room is like being permitted access
within his memory banks. Bookcases creak with the browned covers
of old books, intermingling with the splashes of bright colour, almost
gaudy in comparison, of newer volumes. Statues, plaques, ornaments and
other exotic gifts are on every shelf, but the main focus in the room is an
action-packed painting behind him of an enormous, silver biplane on
operations over the brown, rocky, moonscape, scrubland of Afghanistan
in the 1940s. As he talks you can see the crystal clear eyes glaze over, his
voice's tone cuts through the background noise as he is back to his days as
a young man. We are riding along with him as we taste time travel.

In the living room at his home, the 93 year-old Marshal of the
Indian Air Force (IAF), Arjan Singh, DFC, is dressed in a comfortable
light linen shirt and trousers. Gone is the blue uniform with the braid,
stripes and medals from our previous meeting. The short walk from the
air-conditioned car is enough to have my shirt sticking to my skin under

the suit jacket. Once inside the house, the air-conditioning unit keeps the
hot, humid, Delhi temperatures at bay, but its gentle whir requires me,
and Group Captain Maheshwar, to lean forward to hear the softly-spoken
Marshal talk. Together, we listen and stare wide-eyed at this opened
doorway into history.

He takes us back to when he was the thrusting young buck, joining
the one and only Indian Air Force squadron. In that gentle, whispery
voice of his, he recounts how his expectations were brought crashing
to earth as he was made to clean and polish the Wapiti for days before
he was even considered to fly it. The Indian Sergeant was not only in-
charge of the technicians, he also had the big biplanes in his care and he
was not going to let the young Pilot Office Arjan Singh near the plane
until he was satisfied that this newcomer would pay enough respect to his
aircraft. Marshal Arjan Singh admits that this Sergeant, another Singh,
could be quite fearsome to the young officers joining and he, for one, was
certainly frightened of him at first. The more experienced pilots showed
no fear of Sergeant Harjinder Singh, just the utmost respect towards him.
We talk more about Harjinder Singh and how he flew as the Squadron
Commander's rear gunner as well as cosseting these machines on the
ground as if his own meagre funds had purchased them! The Marshal
can recall the first flight with Harjinder Singh as his own tail gunner
and directs his personal Staff Officer to the correct logbook, from his
bookcase, and even the correct page of that log, all from memory!

Harjinder had been summoned with all of the other 200 IAF personnel,
to be on the receiving end of that 'pep' talk in 1934 from Sir John Steele.
Harjinder had already defied the odds to be where he was. This shocking
talk only hardened the edge to Harjinder's resolve and set his life, already
one of controversy, on the path of relentless adventure. A life over lawless
Afghanistan, to the jungles of Burma against the Japanese, to the Empire's
heart in UK and to the unthinkable battlefields against men he saw as
cousins and brothers.

The Marshal deftly demonstrates his ease with time travel by effortlessly
bringing us right back to present day. He asks me if I knew that Harjinder
was responsible for the vintage aircraft I was flying last time we met. I am
a novice of time travel compared to the Marshal, travelling back only a few
months but the images and memories are vivid; I know they always will
be even if I get to rival the age of this icon in front of me.

When we first met, the Marshal's tall slender frame was immaculately uniformed. Wisps of fine white hair poked out from the Indian Air Force badged turban. The bushy snow-white beard under his aquiline nose bearing the scars from 1941. Was it an incredibly well-aimed bullet, or just sheer bad luck that shot through the Hawker biplane's fuel pipe, leading to a lucky escape from both, the inevitable crash, and, equally inevitably, the vicious tribesmen hunting him down?

As usual, the parade in Delhi was at the Hindon Air Force base. The crowds looked out over the parade ground onto the line of modern aircraft facing them. Behind these dormant aircraft was a gigantic cloth backdrop in Air Force blue, gently rustling in the ever-so-slight breeze. This massive splash of colour in the brown landscape formed a stunning backdrop to the parade ground and hid from sight the taxiway and runway beyond. The TV news cameras were rolling with the live broadcast and the camera shutters clicked and snapped as the 80th anniversary celebrations edged towards their conclusion. All bar one of those parked aircraft had the dull grey colours of the IAF, designed to blend in with their environment. The big, Russian-built Sukhoi Su-30 fighter, the dart like Mirage fighter and the rotund C-130 Hercules were all there.

The British Jaguar ground-attack aircraft looked uncomfortable on its ungainly undercarriage, not happy to be on the ground; this aircraft only looks natural, and very business-like, in the air. The new boy in the IAF, the British-built Hawk trainer took its rightful place. Both those British-built aircraft came under the BAE umbrella and are both powered by British Rolls-Royce engines. Those are the present-day links to Britain that stretch through 80 years of IAF history.

Right in the centre of those warrior-like aircraft, diminutive, and completely dwarfed, was another British aeroplane. This collection of wood, metal and fabric is the Grandmother, or even the Great Grandmother, of those menacing machines. Even the companies that built this aircraft, and its engine, are the distant ancestors of the British-based multinational giant responsible for the present-day brutes surrounding her. This old lady made herself felt by virtue of her bright yellow colour, and her aging, graceful beauty, making the green, white and saffron IAF roundels leap out at you from the pages of history. She is a tiny 1940s Tigermoth, open-cockpit biplane, all wire and fabric. Referred to by all simply as the 'Tiger'. Her name is apt in terms of her existence in India, but there is not a hint of the striped hunter, with unbridled power, that, according to the news, still prowls the countryside not too distant from the perimeter wire.

The gentle breeze that nuzzled the open ground carried enough heat to raise a sweat, even at that early hour, and brought a promise of furnace heat by mid-day. The sky was a hard, cloudless, piercing blue. The constant Delhi dust-filled haze blurred the horizon making the border from ground to sky indistinct, giving the heavens a painted, unreal, retro cinema studio feeling. The 250 Sky-warriors, Airmen and women of the IAF, started to march off the parade ground. As the echoes of the applause began to fade a strange sight unfolded. From behind the blue fabric backdrop, six Air Force technicians made an unexpected appearance. Their marching was awkward, self-conscious, as if aware that the eyes of everyone in the crowd had swivelled to focus solely on them. To the amazement of the crowd, the tail of this old yellow biplane was lifted shoulder high by the last two. Once steady on their shoulders the technicians marched off the parade ground, pushing the Tiger nose-first, giving the impression of the old lady chasing after the Sky-warriors as the military band struck up with the music of the British group, the Pet Shop Boys, at full volume. The musical choice of 'It's a Sin' seemed a strange one. A comment on the Tiger being manhandled away, or aviation in general?

Out of sight behind the temporary blue backdrop of the parade ground, standing on the sun-browned grass, was a group of pilots in green flying suits together with two British Engineers in borrowed black, IAF Engineers' overalls. The small stature of the overall's original owner left James, the senior of the two Brits, with a strangely high pitched voice as he mumbled something about not the way to treat a week-old vasectomy operation. Under the supervision of these two engineers, the Tiger has spent sixteen months being restored from the skeletal, semi-abandoned machine left in an Air Force hangar in Delhi into this 'better-than-new' stunning machine. Only two weeks before, I had taken the Tiger on its post-restoration test flights in an equally blue sky, but on a cold, crisp, British September day.

From the group of pilots, two walked forward from behind the screen, over the dusty grass to the Tiger. We stepped up onto the black walkway on the bottom wing and swung our legs into the two separate cockpits. I climbed into the back seat with Wing Commander 'Kool' Kulresthra, an Indian Air Force Test pilot, in the front 'passenger' seat. There had not even been time to train him on this aircraft type so, with helmet, goggles and gloves covering the majority of my skin, I masqueraded as an IAF pilot even down to the small Indian tricolour badges proudly worn on my shoulders!

Reaching around in the seat, to take the straps from the technicians, caused stabs of pins and needles from my still stiff back and shoulder muscles. The previous morning, at the nearest metro station to Hindon, I stood waiting for the IAF transport, having caught the first train of the morning. No transport was waiting for me at the station and only after a barrage of missed calls and sms messages did I have the salvation of a technician being sent on a motorbike to collect me. Time was short so I utilised the time changing into my green flying suit on the steps of the metro station.

If a white face, a Gora, on the metro attracts attention anyway, a semi-naked one getting changed makes you the highlight of the early morning rush hour! The little Hero Honda bike snaked through the traffic, getting me to the aircraft side with only seconds to spare for the flypast rehearsal.

With Delhi's media attending in force to see the old lady take her place in the 80th anniversary flypast, I wasn't going to let anything spoil the Tiger's moment of glory, so, after our rehearsal, I opted to sleep on the floor in a nearby room. The sleeping arrangements had been a success even if the body didn't think much of it now.

The flypast to celebrate 80 years of the IAF was awe inspiring. The transport aircraft flew down the length of runway from right to left of the crowd. Then the fighter formations came head on, directly at the crowd, throwing anti-missile flares out before they pulled up to split, screaming to the left and right in a crescendo of noise as their engines' roar caught up with their darting images.

The question that spun around in my head was do I start the Tiger's engine immediately and risk it overheating as we wait, or do I risk delaying, only to find that the engine won't start on cue? Not an uncommon occurrence with this 70-year-old engine. The Tiger has no brakes, so wooden chocks are placed in front of the wheels to stop it rolling forward when, or was that if, the engine started. We tried to wait, we tried to be patient, and trust the newly-restored engine, but the need to do *something* was just too great!

From the back cockpit I raised my left hand, forefinger in a rotating motion pointing directly up into the glassy blue heavens which was the signal to start the engine, to get on with our mission. One technician, chosen because his shoulders look like they could carry the world upon them, stepped forward and placed his hand on the propeller. The Tiger has no starter motor, so this was engine starting 1930's style. Four times the propeller was turned to suck fuel from the fuel tank in the top wing into the cylinders. The technician positioned the propeller and shouted 'Contact!' I saw 'Kool' reach outside his cockpit to flick his ignition switches up and 'on' and then I did the same with the set in front of me shouting 'Switches on!' The technician swiftly pulled the blade downwards, stepping to one side as he did so, in order to keep clear of the lethal propeller as it surely must burst into life. However, the propeller did half a turn, the usual click from the ignition magneto was good, but nothing more happened. The technician stepped back into his position, placed his hand on the propeller, and threw himself into another attempt; a click but – nothing. Back for a third go with an extra, theatrical flick of the wrist as he stepped aside. The blade did its standard half turn but there was not even a hint of life. He stepped back into place keen to keep at his task, but time and time again, try as we might, we had no sign of life from the engine.

Anxiety levels rose inside the cockpit, and I could feel it emanating like rising smoke from the team outside; nobody was making eye contact.

The technician was told to pause for a few seconds. None of this was his fault as was emphasised by the dark patches of his exertions spreading across his uniform in the relentless Delhi sun. After a brief pause, I signalled him to continue again from the beginning. Sensibly, our man had a brief pause in order to compose himself. He sweated harder as he felt all eyes of the team boring into his shoulders. 'Contact'!

He arched his back slightly as he flung all his effort into the downward thrust of the propeller blade and the following side step. This time his effort was greeted with a cough and a puff of grey smoke from the exhaust. The cough from the engine kicked the propeller blade over another half-turn and then a second cylinder fired with a wheezy cough. Two more coughs in rapid succession and the coughs start to merge. The individual propeller blades accelerated into a blurred disc and the engine noise settled into a satisfying rumble. That took forever! Did we miss our takeoff slot? Were we literally late on parade?

I twisted in my seat, pushing against the shoulder straps and forcing the aching muscles into action so I could look back over my right shoulder to see how much of the flypast had gone. I had no idea what had been happening outside the bubble around me, the Tiger, and the technician. How far behind were we? Could we still catch the end of the parade? However, the flypast had only just begun! Time, which seemed to blur like lightning as the engine refused to start, had become, painfully, slow. The aircraft of the flypast seemed to dangle in the sky. There is no engine temperature gauge to look at in this old girl, just an over-active imagination of oil reaching boiling point in the tank, metal about to rub on metal, an engine about to seize...

The anti-missile flares thrown out by the display aircraft seemed to be aimed directly at us, sitting entrapped in a fabric-covered, dope-soaked, wooden tinderbox, and surrounded by dry grass for added comfort. The effect of the flares was spectacular, but surely, it was madness in this dry landscape! However, the flares seemed to flicker and die before touching the ground. With time now on my hands I found myself wondering, perhaps unfairly, if that was by luck or by design. My only other thought was, 'come on boys get a move on before my engine boils over!'

Mentally I ticked off the different fighter types as they screamed overhead, until we had the final group appear as dots on the hazy horizon. The Sukhoi Su-30 fighters split to the left and right and a second later one lone aircraft pulled up to point vertically up, rolling as he went, becoming a small dot again in seconds. That was the long-awaited signal. I waved the wooden chocks away. I pushed the little green throttle forward to accelerate the engine from its steady rhythmic throb into its own version of sheer unbridled power! Of course there was no bang and screech of metal grinding with metal from the engine; everything was perfect and so our waiting game was over. Then came the easy bit; the actual doing, no longer the waiting.

The tail of the Tiger came up to the flying attitude immediately as she moved down the taxiway, our runway for the day. From my point of view, the ground seemed to gently drop away from us until I held the aircraft down, a few centimetres off the tarmac. I wanted to stay below the level of the blue screen and out of sight from the parade ground. A big push on the rudder pedal and the Tiger slipped left over the grass, where we all stood just a few minutes ago, to fly closer to the blue backdrop. When abeam the centre of the parade ground up popped the yellow biplane into full view of the cheering crowd, with that gentle throb of the vintage engine's unbridled power sounding like a distant sewing machine after the blood and guts of the jets. As requested by the Vice Chief, I carried out some tight turns directly over the parade ground itself. The thought in my mind as I looked over my shoulder at the faceless crowd below was how did this Gora, this white face, this Welshman, end up flying in an Indian Air Force Parade?

Our final fly-by with wings waggling and 'Kool' waving furiously from the front seat signalled the re-birth of the IAF Vintage Flight, and a very visual link to October 1932.

The 93-year-old Arjan Singh told me about Harjinder Singh and his link to the Tiger. As a Group Captain, in the 1950s, he had the foresight to understand the need to educate that generation about the sacrifices of the past, and to do this through the very visible medium of flying, historic, aircraft, including this very Tiger Moth; he was the Father of the Vintage Flight.

The man who had started as a lowly Hawai Sepoy forged a life of relentless adventure, incorruptible in a time where corruption was the norm. His is a story linked through aviation but it's far more than. It is more about the prejudice of the time, about the Indian/British relationship through war, through Independence, and how these pioneers took hold of a brand new country through its very difficult birth pains.

What follows demanded to be written, after I came into possession of Harjinder's own horde of diaries, letters, speeches, notes and photographs. It is a story of intensive friendships, of massive bigotry from some quarters, but enormous understanding by others. It is about great ingenuity, generally through underhand means, and always with the humour that is ever-present in the military environment. However, it is a story that does not have a happy Hollywood, or is that Bollywood, ending for Harjinder and his family. His life is best summed up in a letter from England, to Harjinder, written in 1959 by Air Vice-Marshal Sir Cecil Bouchier KBE, CB, DFC who, as a mere Flight Lieutenant, was Harjinder's first ever Flight Commander. 'Yours must be the most romantic careers of any man in any service, anywhere in the world.'

That was in 1959 but life didn't start well for Harjinder.

One

Rebellious Beginnings

'You are not even allowed to go near those aeroplanes, leave aside fly in them. To be a pilot in the RAF you must have English blood flowing in your veins. We cannot trust Indians who follow Gandhi in their madness.'

'Here is a revolver, and here is an Englishman. Now let's see you start the revolution.'

It's your early years which form you into the person you turn out to be. Harjinder was a driven man, determined that India, and India alone, should own its own future. He could see that the best course of action was, first of all, for the country to be strong, and the best way to achieve this was through the development of technical skills, and these skills could best be achieved through experience in the military. He was driven, yes, but not blinkered to the cause, and he treated all as equal, no matter the colour of their skin, or the beliefs they held.

Harjinder's start to life was devastating, and must have helped to harden the edge of this man and produce his hallmark trait of never admitting defeat.

When Harjinder was still very young, his idyllic existence was ripped apart. His father died. A big enough event to shape your life, however old you may be, but that was not the end of it. Shortly after his father died, the plague came tip-toeing again into the Singh household and took away his

elder brother and sister. It left only the young Harjinder and his devastated
mother to pick their way through their shredded life.

Harjinder Singh Bains was born on the 4th February 1909, in the
village of Sirhala-Khurad, in the Hoshiarpur District of Northern India.
The Punjab had long been considered the food basket of India, and his
family were Jat Sikhs; agriculturists making their living from the flat plains
butting up against the Himalayas. After his father's death, he continued to
live in the village with his mother, entering the local village school with
his peers for his education. Life was settling down after this hard start, and
Harjinder had to grow up faster to take more family responsibility at this
early age: they struggled on. He had just entered his sixth year at school
when the final, thin, strand holding his life together snapped; his mother
followed his father and siblings.

Harjinder was now an orphan, the only surviving member of his
family. His father's sister took him to her home in the village of Banga,
in the District of Jullundur, where his schooling was duly completed.
The village was only about 10 miles South of his birth place and, in
geographical terms, it was the familiar flat land of the Punjab, offering the
same fantastic agricultural opportunities as his home village. The rugged
mountain backdrop to China more impressive than any line drawn on a
map. Queen Victoria viewed India as the Crown Jewel of her Empire and
the Punjab was the diamond that shone the brightest. It was the land of
sparkling rivers and golden fields of wheat, an oasis in the midst of an arid
North-West India. This region had been witness to the arrival of the
Persians, Darius and Cyrus. Alexander the Great had been through, as had
the Scythians, and the Parthians. Islam had also brought its faith to the
region before the Sikhs, with their rolled beards and multi-coloured turbans,
Harjinder's people, had taken their turn as conquerors. The Sikhs ran the
Punjab but as Harjinder grew up, the British Raj were firmly in charge.

Harjinder writes that his aunt made sure the love and affection which
she gave her brother's child was no different from that which she gave to
her own children. Despite his troubled start to life, Harjinder recalled
many happy memories of the years spent in his aunt's house. He attributed
many of his attitudes and values in life to those years of a simple and
uncomplicated village life. Uncomplicated, yes, but not entirely cut off
from the mainstream of social and political activities that began to sweep
through the country after the end of the World War I. One million Indians
had served in the Commonwealth forces; every man-jack of them was a

volunteer, and the Indian Army was the largest all-volunteer force ever assembled. Over 70,000 gave their lives on foreign soil, but those that did return had broader horizons and many believed the pay-back for their loyalty should be a greater degree of self-rule.

Harjinder's uncle influenced his life greatly during his early years, helping him to form views that were to become an integral part of his core. His uncle was the head of twenty local villages, a zaildar, in those days, a position that held a staunch sceptre of authority. The British were the masters, but they ruled India through men like his uncle, who was viewed with a mixture of respect and terror in his own area.

Some of the patriotic fervour of the time came through one of the teachers at Harjinder's primary school in the village. The seemingly exotic Khem Singh, was an ex-Havildar (*Sergeant*) from the Indian Army who gave many lectures and talks beyond the normal education. Harjinder, in particular, was spellbound by this extraordinary character. His story-telling was legend in the classroom and Harjinder took one to become a part of his inner compass. He always took delight in recounting it:

'Khem Singh joined the army sometime in the late eighteen hundreds and rose to the rank of Havildar. One day, an English Major insulted him during an inspection parade by dislodging his turban from his head with his swagger stick. This, of course, is a grievous insult to a Sikh; but in those days, not many would have dared to make a cause celebre out of it. Khem Singh was made of sterner stuff, and he refused to put the turban back on his head when so ordered to do, saying that since Major Lawson had removed it, he must put it back on for him. Khem Singh also refused to leave the parade ground when his company was marched away; he kept standing guard on his turban all day and all night. The next morning the Colonel himself came to the parade ground and ordered Khem Singh to put on his turban. Khem Singh was adamant; he wanted the Major to replace it on his head and also to apologise to him in front of the whole company.

In the end, he had his way; the whole company was fallen in, and the turban ceremoniously replaced on his head by the Major, who also offered his apology. But the "system" caught up with Khem Singh in the end; he was prematurely retired and not granted his full pension. He fought that issue also, taking his case right up to the General; and he again had his way. He was granted his full pension–no mean victory in those times.'

Harjinder not only took this story to heart, but almost re-enacted the event early in his military career!

There was another phrase, almost a plea, which Khem Singh used with Harjinder, 'If only a few of our countrymen sacrifice themselves, India could become a great nation.'

That, too, lodged itself deep within Harjinder.

When Harjinder was in his teens, Khem Singh took him to Amritsar to watch one of the batches of 500 Akali Sikhs offering non-violent resistance at Guru-ka-Bagh, day after day. The police would stop them on their way to collect firewood and slash at them with heavy brass-bound sticks and rifle-butts. This punishment continued until the whole batch lay prostrate on the ground and none could stand up any more. The Sikhs displayed unique powers of self-control and resolution, and bore the bodily torment in a spirit of complete resignation and non-violence. The onlookers stood by in silence, watching these events unfold daily before their eyes. The sight left an indelible impression on the teenaged Harjinder, and he became, 'forever determined to play my part, however humble, in the freedom movement, irrespective of the consequences to my own future'. Time and time again, Harjinder put a cause before himself, whether it was the grand plans for an independent India, or for the rights of an individual.

Harjinder was a diligent student, first in his class, hungry for information, cultivating a tremendous work ethic; and also receptive to the nationalistic feelings that had begun to swell up around him.

The young people of the day, including Harjinder, felt that a career almost inevitably meant serving the Raj. They might have to serve the British for the present, but only by staying their course, could they eventually contribute to an independent India. Engineering appealed to the young Harjinder and he clearly had a natural aptitude for it.

The turning point in came in 1926.

A letter from the Principal of the Maclaghan Engineering College in Lahore arrived, informing Harjinder that he had been successful in its open, highly competitive, examination for entrance. He was 'thrilled beyond words and shouted with joy', rushing to his uncle, a man who he looked up to with utmost respect. On translating the letter to his uncle, his response was not what the excited young man wanted to hear:

'I am very happy that you have been addressed as "Mister" by an Englishman, but you are NOT going to be an engineer, because it means spending a full five years of your youth. Have you calculated that this is a good one-twelfth part of an average life?'

This may have dampened Harjinder's enthusiasm but he thought through the reaction from his uncle, writing:

'The real issue was, of course, unstated; in those good old days, it was considered very great and honourable to be a sub-inspector of police or a tehsildar (*a tax collector, how things have changed!*). My uncle had designs of such a nature for me. Engineering or any kind of technical education was considered infra dig in the Punjab. I thought of these alternatives, but I was encouraged in my inner aspirations by my nephew. I decided to go to the engineering college.'

Thus the journey down the long, long, road had begun and, that too, against the advice of his seniors!

Harjinder left the village life and stepped into the world, the big city of Lahore, and the seat of higher education. The main building at the college was certainly built to impress the new arrivals. The double storey arches stood on bright white columns in front of every set of widows offering some shade in the stifling summer; the red brick beautifully highlighting the arches up to the roof line. Harjinder put the grandeur aside and plunged into the learning. It was not long before aviation raised its head to become part of the very fabric of Harjinder Singh.

Soon after joining the college he saw a damaged aeroplane which had force-landed in a nearby field. The fuselage was on view outside the college whilst its engine was installed in the Heat Engine Laboratory to be poked and prodded. By his own admission he remembered spending hours, standing, gazing at the wreckage, wondering, as people would continue to ponder to the present day, just how did these machines defy gravity? With Harjinder it was more than just basic curiosity. The bent structure enthralled him and appealed to his engineer's brain. He wanted to understand its inner workings, not just some scientific explanations of lift, thrust, drag and weight.

Discipline was an integral part of his college experience, it laid the very foundation of the strength of character he would go on to demonstrate, and had a large part to play in his future life. He accepted discipline as a subordinate, and expected it from his own people when he was in charge. The British Principal, Captain Whittaker, a retired officer of the Royal Engineers, and a strict disciplinarian, formed Harjinder's own outlook on the subject. A student would be suspended for a good many days if he did not polish his shoes, or did not have a proper knot in his tie.

The students were a hand-picked lot, two hundred in all. There were two classes: Class 'A' provided more theoretical than practical training, whereas Class 'B' split its time between theory and practicals. Harjinder's nephew, who was three years his senior at Maclaghan, recommended that he take the practical course, arguing that India was not yet a country of engineering designers, and therefore, more maintenance engineers were the need of the hour. Already, Harjinder was looking beyond merely becoming an engineer, but readily accepted his advice. Perhaps it is even these words that would spur him on in the 1950s to move India into the field of engineering design and manufacturing.

All Class 'B' students were paid fifty rupees per month in the first year, progressively increasing to ninety rupees by the fifth year. A rupee in those days was worth a good deal, and coupled with the knowledge that they had been successful in a very competitive environment, gave the students, in Harjinder's words, a 'very distinctive feeling of superiority' in Lahore, then the most fashionable city of Northern India. The city was growing fast, becoming known as the Paris of the East. The Nedous family had a hotel there, a popular meeting place of the British military letting their hair down. It was a destination that would soon loom large in Harjinder life, but he would have no inkling of that as he morphed from village boy into city gentleman. These were heady days, indeed, for the students, but Harjinder's view of this 'high life' experienced as a student would not find agreement with some of the 21st century population, who not only want the pleasures in life, but have come to expect them as a right. He wrote:

> 'Human nature is such that if you have enjoyed the real pleasures of life, you can settle down to austerity without regret. You can face a hard life if you have the consolation that you have had your share of the good things of life.'

In general, college students in Lahore kept clear of politics, due to the influence of their three British professors. However, during his third year of college, Harjinder was elected Secretary of the Young Engineers Association. This changed his whole career, being indirectly responsible for his joining the Indian Air Force. As Secretary, he arranged visits to big factories and engineering installations. They visited nearly all the important factories in India during 1928-29, none leaving any great impression or inspiration on Harjinder, so a career in the Railways seemed unavoidable.

Then one day, he was asked by some of the members to arrange a visit to the local Air Force Station, known as the Royal Air Force Aircraft Park.

Low buildings lay sprawled behind the wire fence half-heartedly strung around the base, a tantalising glimpse of the large structures within the heart of the compound, where the aeroplanes were probably being worked upon. The guard at the gate waved him through and on to the main road through the camp. The order and presentation of the buildings, the grounds, the freshly white-washed stones bordering the road, and the uniformed men, left you in no doubt this was a military establishment. It was 50 per cent functional and 50 per cent designed to impress.

However, it was not the location that burnt a mark into Harjinder's soul, but the words of the adjutant, an officer named Flight Lieutenant Saunders. He entertained Harjinder with tea and sweet talk, but permission for the students' visit was flatly refused. Saunders said, 'No Indian is allowed inside. What would be the point? No Indian can join the RAF.'

When Harjinder persisted, Saunders reiterated that there was no point in such a visit – Indians were an inferior race, and he didn't see any possibility of Indians flying or maintaining military aeroplanes, so why worry? Forget about even *visiting* this Unit.

Harjinder returned, utterly disappointed, especially when he saw the aeroplanes from a distance, their silver fabric skins shining beautifully in the sun, punctuated by the colourful bright blue and blood-red roundels. Surprisingly for him, Harjinder let the comments get under his skin, and the interview left him with a sense of racial inferiority. Would Indians not be able to cope with aircraft like their British masters? This would be the last time he felt that way. His views quickly hardened from acceptance to a determination to prove this officer, and all who would follow him, wrong.

It was not long before Harjinder's hardening principles clashed head-on with authority.

The city echoed with 'Long live the Revolution', motivated by the imprisonment of Bhagat Singh and Dutt, the two freedom-fighting heroes of the Punjab, in Lahore. The All-India Congress Committee held a session on the banks of the River Ravi, where a resolution proposing the celebration of the first, self-proclaimed, Indian Independence Day on the 26th January 1930, was met with little opposition.

The president of the Young Engineers Association called a meeting of the Executive Committee. It was unanimously decided to buy 250 Independence flags and distribute them among all Maclaghan Engineering College students, to be worn on what was planned as the glorious first day of Independence.

The next day the flags were worn by most of the students. These flags were miniature Congress flags with what Harjinder later described as 'the somewhat childish inscription: Up Up with the National Flag; Down Down with the Union Jack.'

At 11 am Mr Berry, the Professor of Mathematics, came to the 3rd Year Class and read the inscription on one of the flags. He was furious, and exploded, 'I do not mind your flag going up, but I expect you to have respect for mine. I refuse to teach you unless the bottom line is struck off.' Naturally, the adrenalin-fuelled students refused to do this, and so he marched out of the class and reported the matter to the Principal. Captain Whittaker gave Harjinder a direct order to remove the flags, warning him that if they were not gone in 15 minutes, he would be removed from the college. Harjinder was taken aback by the heavy-handed response, and requested the Principal to be reasonable and not too hasty, because the feelings of the students had reached fever pitch. In spite of this plea, the Principal ordered the immediate suspension of all the students wearing the flag.

And so the strike began.

A majority of the students walked out, leaving only a few remaining in the class rooms. An Indian professor, Brij Nath, came out to reason with the strikers but was shouted down and called a 'British toady'. More Indian professors came out, probably at the insistence of the Principal, but returned without results. The students' blood was up, and they moved to take over the college.

This was it; onward to the glory of an Independent India!

On the second day, there was no let-up in the passion. Harjinder and his fellow students settled in for the new beginning of the Indian State.

They moved out of their college and into the streets of Lahore, shouting the most popular slogan 'Long Live Revolution'. As they progressed into their first whole week of action, it seemed as if all weapons in their arsenal were used to gather the last few non-striking students on to their side. Looking at Harjinder's diary, it seems that the main weapon was the Student President herself.

> 'The President, Miss Manmohini Zutshi, was a charming, beautiful, tall and majestic-looking girl. Her fame had travelled ahead of her even before she arrived. We, the strikers, sent word to the few students who were still in the class rooms. The non-strikers saw her in the College premises and they also came out to join us, perhaps just to ogle at this enchanting beauty. On the opposite side of the College, the road was crowded with hundreds of students. In the middle stood Miss Zutshi, addressing us like a general would his Army, with her chappals and 'swadeshi' (home-spun) sari adding to her elegance and charm. She avoided the inquisitive and admiring glances by shyly looking down at the ground and trying to raise a piece of grass with the toe of her chappal. At the same time, she displayed considerable self-confidence. After an eloquent speech she presented us with this proposal: "Yours is a professional college; you may find it impossible to continue your studies elsewhere if expelled. Are you ready to go through with it?"
>
> All students present answered with one voice: "Yes, we are."
> She welcomed and applauded our resolve.'

The 4th February was Harjinder's 21st birthday, and eighth day of the strike. At the meeting in the Hall, the Committee felt like heroes as they were clapped and cheered. To their youthful minds, independence was almost at hand, brought about merely by chanting 'Long Live Revolution', the boycott of British goods and non-cooperation with the civil administration. Messages of support arrived from Calcutta, Bombay and Madras with students all over the country pledging to come out on strike in sympathy. The next morning, Mr Whittaker, the Principal, sent for Harjinder at his beautifully appointed bungalow, standing separate in the grounds. That afternoon, in Harjinder's own words he, 'strutted into his drawing room like a victorious general and gave him an arrogant greeting'.

Harjinder refused the tea and the chair kindly offered by Mrs Whittaker, preferring to stand tall in front of the Principal. Unexpectedly, Mr Whittaker started by asking if he knew how to shoot. Slightly thrown by this bizarre question, Harjinder blurted out that yes, he did. The Principle moved back in his chair, and opened his deskdrawer. He stood and Harjinder felt something heavy, metallic, cold and oily drop into his hands. Confused, he looked down to see Mr Whittaker's military revolver sitting heavily in his palm. When he dragged his eyes back up, Whittaker said: 'I have been hearing "Long Live Revolution" for the last seven days, yet there is no revolution. Here is a revolver, and here is an Englishman. Now let's see you start the revolution.'

Harjinder wrote in his diary:

'If ever words failed me in my life, it was then. I was non-plussed, but I collected myself quickly and muttered, "The revolution does not mean shooting the British. We want a peaceful revolution, when India shall be ruled by us, right from the Viceroy downwards." Whittaker stood up, led me to the window of his drawing room and pointed to the Lancashire boiler outside the Heat Engine Laboratory and said: "See that boiler? If we keep on shouting 'Long live the boiler' for the rest of our lives, we would still not get any steam out of it. We have to work hard, dirty our clothes and hands, fill it with water and burn coal to get it to produce steam. You Indians want freedom merely by shouting for it. You can keep doing that for a century and you still won't be any nearer it."

I stood my ground by saying: "Revolution means a complete change of Government. We want Indians to be the Viceroy and the Commander-in-Chief of our Army."

The Principal's retort: "Why not an Indian Principal?"

"No", I replied. "We would willingly pay you double salary till we find an Indian with the requisite qualifications."

The Principal smiled. "So you are trying to bribe me! You know the Viceroy is only a figure-head. The real Government of India is in Whitehall in London. The day Indians are fit to rule themselves, all the might of the British Empire will not be able to hold India. The Commander-in-Chief can be an Indian, although it is difficult to find one today. Anyway, the Indian Army is an out-of-date weapon. We, on the other hand, have the latest and most modern force; the Royal Air Force. Have you not read the Hunter Commission's Report in the newspapers?"

I had not, so I later made a point of reading it. It was an eye-opener for me; it made me think that we were missing the wood for the trees. The Hunter Commission had come to the conclusion that the British Government could put down any revolt in India just by the use of aeroplanes, like they did in Gujranwala on 13th April 1919. The people on the ground would have no choice but to submit to this aerial terror.

Although I made a vain attempt to contradict Whittaker, in my heart of hearts I knew that he was absolutely right. He convinced me of the futility of slogan-shouting.'

Harjinder realised that he and his fellows had been looking at things on a micro scale. The shouting and chanting of students made them feel good, but ideals were not enough. Whittaker was right. The sheer size and scale of India dwarfed the British and given the extremely small percentage of the population that was actually from the mother country, there was more to their hold on power than first seemed. Something more than a flag was needed if they were to rule their own destiny. They needed to be able to control, develop, educate and rule on their own.

He returned to the students knowing what had to be done. For eight days he had been at the forefront, calling for change, and for everyone to stand firm behind him. Now, he left the Principal's bungalow to walk back to his followers, who were all waiting eagerly to hear how Harjinder had driven home their demand, and cut Whittaker down from his lofty perch. But instead, he stood in front of them, head briefly held down before rising up to full height, to announce the strike was to be called off. There was uproar at this with, quite understandably, with some students even accusing Harjinder of being bought over. The words of Whittaker, and Harjinder's need to convey them successfully to the student population, was the major turning point in his adult life. Harjinder was converted and, as he admitted himself in his diary:

'Converts are always great fanatics, they say. Looking back, I often ponder over the wisdom of Principal Whittaker's advice. How right he was. It dawned on me later that we Indians are the greatest speech-makers in the world. We are builders of castles in the air, but we leave the real foundation-laying to others.'

After the strike was called off, Miss Zutshi played a leading role in parleying with the Principal. There was to be no victimisation; there would be no Union Jack flown on Foundation Day; and the Governor would not be invited. All felt greatly relieved and once the collective blood pressure had been allowed to settle, the general feeling among the students was they had won their battle after all. Of course, this was a long way off from any movement towards Indian Independence. There was another World War still to come to fuel that.

After everyone went back about their business, Bhagat Singh and his party in the Lahore jail were executed. Mahatma Gandhi, who had been parleying with the Viceroy, Lord Irwin, had failed to save their lives. There was no mistaking the fact that British rule still held India in a vice-like grip.

As a consequence of Mr Whittaker's talk, and his new-found knowledge of the Hunter Commission report, Harjinder became more determined than ever to join the Royal Air Force. If the British could stop a revolution of the vastly superior numbers in India with airpower alone, surely the way ahead was to be within that system, learn how it worked, and form a force to represent India.

The die for Harjinder's future was cast.

On 15th February Harjinder travelled to the Royal Air Force Park in Lahore Cantonment, where he was ushered into the office of Flight Lieutenant G.H. Mills, the Station Adjutant, a smart, tall and pleasant gentleman. Harjinder told him about his desire to join the RAF as a pilot. Mills smirked into his moustache and asked why he wanted to join. When Harjinder told him about his talk with the Principal and even mentioned the Hunter Commission Report, Mills' demeanour suddenly changed. Twisting his moustache he said: 'So you are a Gandhi-wala?'

Flight Lieutenant Mills ripped into Harjinder to grind these 'ideas' out of this petulant Indian. Finally, he took him outside of his office and pointed to the glittering aeroplanes lined up outside and barked at him: 'You are not even allowed to go near those aeroplanes, leave aside fly them. To be a pilot in the RAF you must have English blood flowing in your veins. We cannot trust Indians who follow Gandhi in his madness.'

Harjinder returned to the college frustrated and demoralised, but his ambitions had not been ground into dust, as Mills had intended. The RAF, and in particular, the lines of aeroplanes, had fired his imagination and his ambition.

'The wrecked piles of crashed aircraft I had seen suddenly assumed great importance in my life.'

Later that the same year, Lloyd George spoke during the Indian debate in the House of Commons: 'Gentlemen, to teach Gandhi the meaning of Home Rule, we should withdraw the RAF squadrons from the North-West Frontier of India for a period of six months. You would find not a single ashrafi (*a gold coin*), nor a single virgin left in North India.'

Long heated discussions in his college followed these remarks but it was not until 1937, as he sweated in the forts and the landing strips in that province, that Harjinder came to know how right Lloyd George had been. Even in Lahore, the population was sheltered from the realities of the lawless North-West.

Harjinder had taken to getting his hands on any aeronautical literature he could, and devouring its contents. Then one day he came across an article which caused him to take a different approach to his future plans. It was to directly affect his, and most probably, India's future.

The opening paragraph grabbed his attention:

In view of the fact that so many Indians are securing their certificates as pilots, the suggestion is timely, that it takes more than pilots to create an Air Force. The backbone of any air force really lies in the efficiency of its mechanics.

The whole article was indeed forward-looking and destined to be very close to the truth. However, if the first paragraph caught his attention, the final sentence infuriated him:

But the average Indian mechanic is very casual and untrustworthy.

The Skeene Committee's report, in which it was suggested that the Government of India should experiment with a squadron of Indians in the RAF, found more favour with Harjinder. He knew this was his golden opportunity and since this was his final year in college, he had decisions to make. The next day he requested an interview with the Principal. Naturally, Whittaker would have recalled his comments to this ringleader of the strike, but here Harjinder stood again in his office talking of military service. Was it surprise or satisfaction that Whittaker felt when he went on to complement Harjinder on his fitness, and the suitability of his aeronautical engineering training for joining such a Service? He was most sympathetic, and offered all possible help.

Things then seemed to happen suddenly for Harjinder, as a few weeks later, the scheme was to be put into force. The Government of India had decided to conduct the experiment by starting with a whole squadron of Indians. The group of six already sent for officer and pilot training at the RAF College, Cranwell, in Britain, were diverted from entering into the RAF to form the start of what would become the IAF. It was decided that the ground staff would be trained in India within the system the RAF had in place. Air Headquarters, New Delhi, saw the Railway Board as the natural pool to draw expertise from, and so a list was requested with the names of selected 'D' Class apprentices. They would be paid thirty-five rupees per month whilst under training and once in employment, it would rise to the dizzy heights of forty-five rupees. They would then be termed 'Hawai Sepoys 3rd class', no term of 'Airman' like their British cousins. These 'D' Class apprentices were mainly illiterate boys, 14-18 years of age; the sons of railway workers. These boys would have very little theoretical knowledge, and could only be trained in basic practical jobs. In the railway apprentice system they were paid less than five rupees a month. It was felt in Delhi that a large number would volunteer when offered thirty-five per month; who wouldn't? However, this starting wage was still in sharp contrast to the ninty rupees per month Harjinder was paid in his final year as an engineering student.

This financial disparity did not stop Harjinder, far from it. He used his ever-increasing skills as an orator to call upon a number of his class fellows, to form the would-be Indian Air Force. He gave them a lecture on the defence of the North-West of India, repeating Lloyd George's statement from the Commons. Destiny, rather than financial reward, was what the individual should strive for. Considering what these men were possibly giving up, he was highly successful, because four of his classmates followed his lead. Remember Harjinder's thoughts: 'If you have enjoyed the real pleasures of life you can settle down to austerity without regret.' Well, austerity was on the way if they made it into the IAF.

Harjinder spent time constructing his letter to Air HQ Delhi. He described how he had followed the debate on Indians joining the RAF as technicians; he knew he was very qualified; he was completely convinced this was the future for him, and India. However, the reply from a Squadron Leader Ardley was not what he had expected. The letter dryly stated that the RAF was not looking for qualified persons like Harjinder and his classmates, they preferred untrained apprentices. Ardley, however, had not taken Harjinder's persistence into account. Harjinder continued to pester him on a daily basis, until he finally caved in and wrote to the Railway Board who had responsibility for Harjinder and his fellow converts. It would do them no good, but he summoned them to attend an interview.

Anybody who has been interviewed by a military selection board will always remember the ordeal; fearsome officers in their finest uniform, with seemingly endless worldly knowledge. However, for Harjinder it was distinctly remembered, but not as an ordeal. He thought during the technical examination that some of the candidates knew more than the Board members! Following the interviews, their spirits were soaring, but then followed the now-familiar put-down by the RAF officers. Squadron Leader Ardley addressed ten of the educated candidates with the words: 'You must be told some home truths. You college-boys are too soft and will not be able to last the pace. You have had a misguided education. Do you know that you will now have to travel third class, eat the same food as the sepoys of the Indian Army and, what is more, wear boots and putties and the kullah turban?'

Before Harjinder could speak a word, two boys answered for all of them: 'Sir, we might die in the attempt, but we are determined to form an Air Force of our own.'

Abdul Rashid Khan Malik also remarked: 'Leave aside third class, we will even travel in a goods wagon.'

Malik was not from Harjinder's College, he had trained in Calcutta as an engineer, but never seemed to take his profession seriously. His family were well-to-do and he carried a rich man's airs. His eldest brother, Ghulam Muhammad, later became Governor General of Pakistan. Malik was very keen to join the Air Force, there was no need to coerce him, for his was an unflinching belief that the future lay in Indians serving in an Indian Air Force. These beliefs merged with Harjinder's, and this friendship formed at selection was to last over the years.

The first two to speak were Banerjee and Sanyal from Bengal: outspoken, fiery, but also cultured. This was Harjinder's first introduction to Bengalis. A popular saying in Bengal in those days was: 'What Bengal thinks today, India will think tomorrow.' In this room, with these people, that certainly seemed true.

On his return to Lahore, a number of students tauntingly started calling him a Hawai Havaldar (Sergeant). The irony was, despite his engineering degree, it would take him ten years to become one!

Considering the importance it held for Harjinder, he refers very little to the moment he was accepted by the RAF. In his diaries just a cursory: 'We were selected in November 1930 but were asked to join in January 1931, at Karachi.'

During this period of waiting, things nearly took a different turn when an offer for the post of Superintendent of the Gujranwala Power House arrived. A job which was very lucrative according to the standards of those days, carrying a starting salary of two hundred twenty-five rupees per month compared to the thirty rupees on offer from the Air Force. It is unclear whether Harjinder would have taken this post, but the decision was, quite literally, taken out of his hands when he lost the tips of three fingers of his left hand in a motorcycle accident. It seems the injury had no bearing on the Air Force because, after 3 months of no news from Air HQ in Delhi, in January 1931, he was summoned to join the Indian Air Force as the lowest possible rank, a Hawai Sepoy. The class structure was still very rigid, as a graduate engineer Harjinder would have sat high in the pecking order, with servants and a great degree of luxury. He was about to discover that as a Sepoy you were not just at the bottom of the scale; you looked up at the bottom of the scale with wonder.

A lifelong career had begun; so had the troubles.

Two

Training to be a Sepoy

Squadron Leader White:
'I have not met an Indian who had the moral courage even to admit the charges made against him.'

UK Parliament 1930: The Secretary for India:
'It takes more than pilots to form an Air Force. The Indian engineers and mechanics are casual and untrustworthy.'

Harjinder and his band of brothers were to become those 'casual and untrustworthy' engineers. It would take years of constantly proving themselves, time and time again, and the small issue of a world war, for anyone in power to admit their misjudgement.

The Secretary of State for India seemed willing to remember the exploits of the few Indians who had served as pilots with great distinction in the World War I, the most successful being Lieutenant Indra Lal Roy. Roy took his open-cockpit SE5a biplane into combat over France, scoring 9 victories in only fourteen days, proving that Indians had all the courage needed to be fighter pilots. This makes Roy the highest scoring Indian pilot to this day. His ferocious method of attack, by throwing himself at the enemy, could not last. He was shot down and killed after those fourteen days earning the Distinguished Flying Cross (DFC), having not yet turned twenty.

Then there was Lieutenant Hardit Singh Malik, the most distinguished Sikh of his time. He was a sportsman, civil servant and diplomat. Only eighteen years old when World War I broke out, he volunteered to be a French Army ambulance driver, as the RFC would not accept Indians as officers. It took a forceful plea from his tutor at Oxford, to his friend, General Henderson, for him to be accepted as an officer pilot in the Royal Flying Corps; the first sporting a turban and beard to become a fighter pilot, who scored two victories! His long hair and beard caused him to be called 'My Indian Prince' by his flight commander, the legendary Major Billy Barker, VC. During one of his dogfights in his flimsy biplane, his cockpit was riddled with hundreds of bullets, of which two pierced his legs. He crash-landed back in France. After convalescing for many months in England, he was back in the battlefield. The Secretary might remember these people and their proven flying skills, but he wasn't for having Indians doing anything technical or mechanical with the aircraft.

For a man whose ambition was now firmly fixed on joining the Air Force, Harjinder kept his successful application very, very quiet. He told no one in his family except his cousin, the district Magistrate in Sargodha. His Christmas holidays were spent constantly having to listen to his cousin trying to dissuade him to join. The cousin finally gave up his efforts, resorting to offering, the now well-known advice of, 'If God had wanted you to fly, He would have given you wings!' However, with his cousin's grudging assistance, the successful application was kept a secret. Harjinder believed that if his uncle had found out, there would have been great uproar, and the entire family would have arrived at his door to beat this ridiculous idea out of him. Would the IAF have survived the first few months of independence if that had happened? Would there have been an Indian Air Force to expand throughout World War II?

Harjinder also received a reply from his letter to Amarjit Singh and Bhupindar Singh, whilst on holiday. Before these men had joined the RAF College at Cranwell to earn their pilot's wings, Harjinder had met with them. Amarjit endorsed Harjinder's plans to join the Air Force 'in any capacity'. Encouraged by those who were well on their way to be on the 'inside', he felt vindicated in his decision.

On 21st January 1931, the bearded, turbaned, Harjinder Singh Bains arrived in Karachi to start his career in the Air Force. He was almost a local, as his military life started at the Drigh Road RAF base outside the city. There was great excitement among the new arrivals, even if the base was no heavenly vision. The aerodrome lay between the main railway and a dry, four-mile wide valley of sand-ridges, overrun with dust-coloured tamarisk, and faintly tinted green with colocynth runners. Cattle and camels wandered the site, between buildings that were erected without any apparent thought to planning. The aircraft hangars were functional boxes with low-pitched roofs, peeking out from behind slab-like doors. The newly built Officers' and Sergeants Messes reflected the splendour that has become synonymous with so many buildings of the subcontinents' colonial era – with rows of dark arches on two stories, and a flat roof of Marseilles tiles, it inspired comparison to a Roman aqueduct.

Outside the wire was no better, just a dry hole, on the edge of the Sind desert. When the winds blew through the camp, they came heavily laden with dust. They would soon learn to eat dust, and breathe dust, and think dust, and hate dust. Air craftsman T.E. Shaw was not taken in by what he saw, even though he ultimately enjoyed the relative solitude it offered. He wrote of Drigh Road: 'the Depot is dreary, to a degree, and its background makes me shiver... North of the railway is a mass of building, married quarters, officers' houses, mess, and hospital. Unattractive, since it has no plan, no raison d'être or focus, like a grown village... The camel-bells sound just like a water tap dripping, drop, drop, drop, into a deep cistern.'

It would only take a few days for the new recruits' excitement of a long-awaited dream to capsize. The contract they'd signed only gave them status as members of the Indian Followers Corps of the RAF in India, not as Engineers or Technicians. Not only was there no proper accommodation for them, they were treated like intruders. They were shown four tents, dumped on an open piece of ground. They slept 8 men to a tent, putting up with the rigours of sun and rain as well as the winter 'Quetta Breeze', that felt like it could cut a man in half if he didn't bend double in the face of its unremitting drive across the open ground. Once, when heavy rains collapsed the tents, they were given temporary refuge in an empty barrack block. However, the taste of 'luxury' soon ended, once the tents were back up. They were back under canvas even while the dry, wind-proof, barrack block remained empty.

The latrine blocks had no lighting with the excuse that lights would attract mosquitoes, which would attract insects, which would attract lizards which would then attract dangerous snakes. The long nurtured vision of stepping out in a smart uniform were dashed, for there were no Indian Air Force personnel uniforms of any kind, or any plan for there to be one. So for twelve months all wore their own mufti (*civilian dress*) to work, denied the look of a collective, military unit.

There were no cooking utensils, not even a cup to drink tea from! Coming from an environment where a cook was deemed almost as essential as the food itself, the lack of an allocated cook came as a shock. The first thing Harjinder and his colleagues did was to engage a cook, a man named Abdullah, who became almost family to them.

This group of new entrants represented almost all the technical colleges that then existed in India. In the present multicultural society, and ease of movement around the world, it is easy to forget that the norm then was for people to stay within their region of birth, and the regions of India are a massive diversity in food, culture and language. This was the first time for Bengalis and Madrasis to learn how to eat the chapattis of the North, and the Punjabis to eat rice from the South. Despite the disappointing start and abysmally low standards, Harjinder wrote 'We enjoyed every minute of our new life.'

The start to military service differs very little around the world – your introduction to the military life is marching lessons under the guidance of some fearsome, vocal veteran. Their first drill instructor was a fearsome Havildar-Major (*Sergeant Major*), an infantryman who took a dim view to this new part of 'his' military. Harjinder reports him as being only 'semi-literate', however, I think all new recruits have similar opinions of their first drill instructor, apart from also doubting their parentage! Apparently, he bore a grudge against the educated classes, or would that just be a grudge against the world? All drill sergeants offer a constant stream of discouragement and put-downs, but this particular one seemed to actually believe his own ranting and wanting to grind them into the dust. Daily, he would address his men saying: 'You biscuit-eaters will never be able to make it. I'll make you jump ditches, dig trenches and keep at the double all day. I bet I'll see you out of Karachi within a month.' Fortunately for the new recruits, he was replaced by an RAF sergeant. Their fear that a British instructor would take offence at Indians being allowed into 'his' Air Force proved unfounded. He was a fairer, more open-minded character than had been their own countryman. Harjinder had his first major surprise.

The replacement, Flight Sergeant Tilbury, turned out to be 'an excellent man'. He was a picture of physical fitness, known to be one of the best physical training instructors in the RAF. He taught physical fitness with relish but in these early days he despaired when it came to teaching drill. According to him, it would take the ten trainees six months to learn marching, he claimed to have taught complete parade ground drill to a thousand British Airmen in the same period of time. His main grouse against them was they lacked rhythm. His reasoning for this missing rhythm was because they had never had the opportunity to listen to good wholesome marching music! When you now see the elaborate dance sequence of any Bollywood movie, this reasoning seems hard to believe.

The ingrained politeness of these educated Indians did not sit well with their new military role. During early training, each trainee took it in turns to take charge of the remaining nine for the day. They couldn't click their brain out of civilian mode and frequently would say: 'Please fall in; would you please come here; if you don't mind...' On parade, these blissfully happy men would smile and laugh with each other. You can visualise the Flight Sergeants, with veins bulging out of their necks, spit flying from the twisting lips as they bellowed at the men, trying to form them into some form of military unit. Twelve push-ups was soon the punishment for every 'please' uttered.

In what seems like twisting the knife in the wound, the new recruits were taken around the RAF Airmen's barracks, which were infinitely better than the Indian tented town. If it was a deliberate attempt to dishearten the Indian recruits, it didn't produce the expected resentment their masters expected. What did surprise Harjinder and team was the RAF's eating arrangement. He remembers, 'It was quite an eye-opener for us to see how the RAF men were treated. They queued up and each airman had an enamel plate, spoon, fork and a mug in his hand. As each airman reached the counter his meals were ladled out in a lump on his plate. At the end of his lunch or dinner he had to wash his own plate. We went to our tents and held a hurried meeting. After a long discussion it was decided to part with the new crockery purchased only a week earlier and we all joined in breaking the flowered crockery ceremoniously. We decided to become full-fledged "combatants", as our instructor put it. We bought enamel mugs and plates and felt very righteous about it.'

There were the usual demonstrations and expectations of military life, including how to make the beds in the morning, sweep the floor and polish shoes. This was novel to all the recruits, since they were college graduates from good families, many of them had staff to carry out such tasks. Kit was laid out every day where it was regularly and critically inspected by the Orderly Apprentice. This set the standards for Harjinder's military life and even as a senior officer he would polish his own shoes or Brasso the buckles on his uniform. Another shocking difference from college life was that every morning, they were called upon to carry out physical training for an hour, ending with a 400-yard sprint. After breakfast, an hour's drill was compulsory. One year of this training developed them into first-class, physically fit, Airmen. Harjinder's drive to succeed always took him one step further, so much so that his P.T. Instructor wanted him to compete in the quarter-mile event at an all-India meet. His personal best was a challenge to that of Teja Singh, the record holder, meaning that he had a real chance to take the title. On the advice from the technical instructors, the idea was dropped, with the staff thinking that it would have taken up too much of Harjinder's course time.

We know of the men who influenced Harjinder's early days, but now we must introduce Warrant Officer H.E. Newing, an engineer, and his appointed technical instructor. Newing was to take this man, who had a fairly basic idea of military life, a better-than-average knowledge of theoretical engineering, but little practical skill, and shape the engineer within Harjinder. Fortunately for Newing, his student was a man who had complete dedication, determination and drive to make the Indian Air Force experiment work, and to be the best he could within it. Newing had never been to an engineering college, but after years of service, he knew his trade inside out. It was he who was responsible for giving the IAF an excellent technical start in its formative years. He was not only a conscientious instructor, but also took great pride in his Indian apprentices, something few of his countrymen would do. Although he was supposed to teach them only technical trades, he gave them all sorts of advice, and was the main force to turn them into fully-fledged servicemen. When Harjinder looks back to these first few steps, he writes that no amount of praise would be too much for this man. Needless to say, Newing was *not* the norm within the staff at Karachi.

Initially, Harjinder's gang threw themselves into their new military existence, without fuss, and they didn't question the widely-held view of those above that they were incapable of little more than eating and breathing. However, this enthusiasm could not take the continuous abuse daily showered upon them, and it soon began to fade. The honeymoon period had inexorably come to an end. Someone suggested that a letter of resignation, signed by all, should be sent Delhi, letting them know that the RAF authorities were not willing to play the game, not taking them seriously as engineers. When the letter reached Newing, it was Harjinder he called aside immediately and said: 'I know you are the ringleader. I also know that you led a strike of students in Lahore. So you must be a natural leader. You can lead these men to mutiny, or you can lead them along the right path. Staying the course here will be your chance to prove that Indians can face it, and learn to defend their own country; if you fail now, there will never be an Indian Squadron.'

There is no doubt that Harjinder held Newing in very high esteem, because he sincerely took his words in, and the truth they conveyed. He vowed there and then that he would suffer all frustration and indignity, but never quit the Air Force. He was tested time and time again, but he would keep this vow throughout his career, even as some of those around him would eventually allow themselves to be ground down in the dirt.

It was Harjinder's influence on the rest of the recruits that led them all to follow his determination at this stage, not to give up yet, to suffer for the sake of building up an Indian Air Force. The mood of the country outside the boundary of wire surrounding their camp was totally different, with the Non-Cooperation Movement at its height. Only a year before, Gandhi had walked 241 miles with his followers, newsmen following this strange caravan, to the Arabian sea at Dandi. His simple act of scooping a piece of caked salt from the beach, crumpling it and handing it out in defiance of the British salt tax, spurred the people on into non-cooperation. When arrested with thousands of others, he managed to send a last message: 'The honour of India has been symbolised by a fistful of salt in the hand of a man of non-violence. The fist which held the salt may be broken, but it will not yield up its salt.'

Released from jail, Gandhi was now requested to attend talks with the heads of the British Raj, much to Churchill's disgust. He was a staunch opponent to any Dominion Status that he felt would lead to the unthinkable Independence for India. In a speech to the West Essex Conservative Association in 1931 he said: 'It is alarming and also nauseating to see Mr Gandhi, a seditious Middle Temple lawyer, now posing as a fakir of a type well-known in the East, striding half-naked up the steps of the Viceregal palace.'

Service in the armed forces was considered unpatriotic and the Indian public looked down upon any one of their own countrymen in uniform, regarding them as tools of British Imperialism. Those who had knowingly joined the embryo Indian Air Force, were like the corn between grindstones. The British did not want them; Indians disowned them. Outcasts in both societies, even though they were trying to achieve the same end-result as Gandhi! It was under these circumstances that Newing came to their rescue, and did his very best to infuse patriotism and self-confidence in them. It is interesting to see that Newing clearly bucked the thinking of most of his countrymen around him. He did not try and anglicise the Indians, but encouraged their patriotism for a future India.

If their position in society was an issue, their technical training was, if anything, even more complicated. The authorities at Aircraft Repair Depot, Karachi, refused to believe the madness that Indians were actually to be allowed access to the Airframe and Aero-Engine Shops. Previously, no Indian had been permitted to enter, because clearly, these natives were incapable of doing a complicated job like work on aircraft engine parts. They certainly should not be allowed to learn the trade; that was preposterous! British Airmen had no problem with openly showing their hostile attitude. The Chief Technical Officer inflamed matters further, he publicly declared that he would not be responsible for the security of the equipment if Indians were allowed to work on aero-engines. Naturally, these Indians would all be thieves.

Harjinder had proved to be a natural leader, and would take most insults on the chin, but this was insulting their technical expertise. He took this blind stupidity head-on, by requesting Warrant Officer Newing to arrange a meeting with Squadron Leader F.A. Norton. During the meeting, the Squadron Leader said that he had yet to meet an Indian who could be technically trusted on aeroplanes. Harjinder laid down the challenge: 'Sir, you are a graduate of an engineering college of London University. You can pick anyone of us and test him. I also would like to show you the question papers we had in our college exams.'

The Squadron Leader was obviously convinced of his own superior training and breeding compared to these Sepoys. If not he wouldn't have agreed to the challenge, but he had faith in what he believed was an extremely difficult theoretical exam he had set. The following day they all took Norton's self-penned test and he admitted to being 'pleasantly surprised' that they did so well. Credit to Norton, he then ensured that no more doubts were cast thereafter, and they were allowed to roam the Aero-Engine Shop without escort, after having spent three months in the hangars. Nothing went missing, nothing was stolen, and every Indian threw himself into the technical tasks offered to them. After all, these men were trained engineers. That is more than could have been said for Aircraftsman T.E. Shaw who had worked in Engine Repair Section: Room No. 2 just two years before. This Aircraftman was known to millions after the World War I as Lieutenant-Colonel T.E. Lawrence, DSO, the man who had united the tribes of Arabia to fight for the British against the Turks. Aircraftman Shaw was Lawrence of Arabia, hiding from the unwanted spotlight.

Once in the shop, receiving lectures from the technical instructor, another falling-out soon followed. The instructor was essentially a practical engineer, and these recruits were mainly trained on the theoretical side. The agile hands met the agile minds on the battlefield of engineering! One day, during a lecture on Instruments, Harjinder happened to incur the instructor's wrath when he got up and mentioned the Bernoulli theorem of aerodynamics in support of his explanations. The instructor called him aside saying, 'If you know so much, you can keep clear of my lectures.' Guess what? Harjinder did!

Thereafter, Harjinder had to hunt around for knowledge at his own initiative. He wrote, 'This was a God-sent boon. I met a number of Warrant Officers and senior NCOs who were fresh out from England and consequently up-to-date in their knowledge of new developments. One such was Sergeant Wilson, a Sergeant Pilot but a Rigger by trade. During his "gen" talk to me, he mentioned the latest monoplane developments in England. When my regular instructor heard of this he was furious, because he thought Sergeant Wilson was leading us astray. In India, at that time, it was not considered feasible that monoplanes could fly with no bracings and struts to support the main-planes.'

Newing soon had another important influence over Harjinder, one that may have influenced the progression of the IAF. The recruits were to be split into those progressing to study aero-engines and those to study the aircraft structures to become 'Fitter Airframe'. Harjinder was examined on aircraft engines, and satisfied all concerned regarding his knowledge on the subject. He was stunned to learn later that he was to be given the trade of 'Fitter Airframe' (initially called Metal Rigger in those days) and protested vehemently. However, Newing's foresight again came into play. He explained that since Harjinder knew about engines, if he learnt the new trade of Airframe Fitter he would be more useful to the future Indian Air Force in repairing crashed aircraft, which needed the very best men with a good theoretical background. He added: 'A Fitter Aero-engine is

merely a spanner engineer, he simply replaces parts. Yours will be a much
more rewarding job.'

Harjinder didn't see it that way at first. 'Although I accepted the new
trade, inside my heart I still considered that a Fitter Aero-engine was a
superior trade. However, years later I felt highly grateful to Newing for
having guided me in my choice, because his advice gave us the opportunity
of a sound grounding in maintenance. I am grateful to Newing, for as a
Fitter Airframes, I helped to rebuild broken aircraft, and this, in turn, built
up my career in the IAF.' This decision may well have saved the IAF in
the early years as it was Harjinder who lead the charge, mostly through
underhand methods, to ensure that damaged IAF aircraft never came to
the attention of those in power in the ever-hawkish RAF at HQ in Delhi.

Some of the views the RAF men at ground level espoused were
understandable, considering that the men usually joining them had little
to no 'hands on' experience. On the other side of the coin, many of the
IAF's new recruits were already engineering graduates, and still thought of
themselves as white-collared supervisors: not expecting to be using their
hands The theoretical aspect was easy for them, but somehow, practical
work did not appeal to them. Harjinder in particular, it seems! The shock
came when Newing submitted his first quarterly report on Harjinder
to Air Headquarters. Obviously a good reader of men, Newing took an
unusual step in those days, and led Harjinder aside to let him read the
report, knowing the effect it would have on him. Harjinder was furious
when he saw it:

> A very smart, intelligent and daring apprentice. Very good in
> theory, but poor in practical work. He can lead the rest, but there
> is a danger of his going on the wrong path.

The effect was clear, and no doubt planned by Newing. Harjinder
pondered over the comments, 'poor in practical work' and 'going on the
wrong path'. He decided to prove that he would be the best at practical
work, and he did this in the only way he knew. Every afternoon, including
Sundays, when his other duties were complete, he was to be found on the
work bench. He then began to realise that the report was indeed true. He
could hardly use his hands, even accurate filing was beyond him.

For nine months, he worked during every spare hour available. He
worked so hard, that by the end of his self-imposed practical lessons,
the instructors showed off his prolific output to the other British

Non-Commissioned Officers (NCO's) in Lahore. Harjinder received a final endorsement of his growing skills when one day, a drawing from the Air Ministry arrived. It was brought to him for the development and making of a metal fitting as he was considered to be the best in the depot to complete the job. Whilst his colleagues enjoyed barrack life, Harjinder spurned it, instead spending long hours studying inside the big room allotted to them. They were six in one room, so in order get some privacy he hung a mosquito curtain, folded, to form a screen. This period of study may have made the engineer in Harjinder, but he reflected on these as the most unpleasant days of his career. The only time he could study in peace was in the afternoon, when the others had dozed off. One less dedicated member of the group used a taunting manner to tell the others: 'If you want to become a Junior NCO, then study behind a mosquito curtain and work in shops in the afternoons and on Sundays.' Later, Harjinder would really become a NCO, whereas the man taunting him would have to wait for years to become one.

The foundation of the man who would probably become the best engineer in the IAF had been laid. Looking back years later Harjinder wrote: 'Although I, at first, bore Newing a grudge for the adverse report he had given me, later I realised that it was this report that had showed me the light and acted as the foundation stone of my career. I have since practised this principle in life when dealing with my subordinates and it has worked wonders. I have discovered that over 99 per cent people improve themselves if you inform them of their faults and weaknesses in a constructive manner. In other words, in the long run, a kick in the pants sends you further along than a pat on the back, though a combination of the two is the best method.'

This is seen as common procedure now, but not in 1932! It was a revolutionary approach to man-management that Newing had demonstrated to Harjinder.

Newing took his responsibility for the trainees' well-being seriously, often dropping in at the barracks to help to convert them to Service life. He had some interesting, and controversial, theories on life in general, and on India in particular. One evening, he talked about the contrast between Indian and British characters. He believed that in England, a man rose in life by dint of hard work and ability. He thought the reverse was true in India. He also preached that Indians, on the whole, married young, produced hordes of children and then died young. No nation where domesticity took hold of its youth too early could achieve any greatness worthy of the name. If only India could increase the age of marriage by law, problems of child mortality and over-population would solve themselves. His advice was very immensely practical! 'One hour of football everyday keeps the thought of women away.' They practised that too!

The theme of his talks always had one moral; Service life is simple, and it builds character. An easy-going nation will always suffer defeat. He used to cite the French defeat in the World War I. Harjinder lapped up all of Newing's offerings.

> 'He became my guru in the Service. I owe more to him than to any other individual. I had become so easy-going in college, that I considered the use of my hands as beneath me. Newing cured that. There is a limit to one's requirements in a simple life, but none in a luxurious one. The demands keep on increasing until a man starts living beyond his means. A hard, tough service life saves you from such temptations, and the country benefits from the quality of each man.'

Unbeknownst to Harjinder, there was a great event occurring on 8 October 1932 in the beautiful town of Simla, where vehicles were banned from the paths that weaved through the epitome of British hill station architecture. Under the lengthening purple shadows of the Himalayas, the 'Gazette Notification' for the creation of the Indian Air Force was produced in the turreted fairytale offices of the Viceroy's summer palace. Far more relevant to these men in training, was the knowledge that the end of 1932 was to bring the next batch of apprentices. These new entrants would also be experienced having also done their three years in Indian Engineering colleges. However, as with any course, anywhere in the world, the senior course greeted the arrival of the juniors with joy, excitement, curiosity and naturally, they also took the opportunity to look down upon the new arrivals. Harjinder and team now felt worldly-wise and, best of all, there were underlings to take on the suffering they had endured. However, things didn't quite go according to plan.

During their first year, every trainee had to take turns to be in-charge of the group, giving the orders to march the team smartly from one lecture to another, from dinner hall to tented city. The sense of superiority over the new arrivals was snatched away before it could be savoured, and this produced much resentment among Harjinder's men wanting their little piece of respect. Harjinder, who had grown up with stories of his teacher, Khem Singh, standing firm on the parade ground when his rights were infringed was about to re-enact the event, in reverse, even though he later admitted 'it was somewhat petulant', and it wasn't quite with the grace of his teacher.

Apprentice Noronha was the first from the new course to take the parade. He blew the whistle outside the senior barracks and began to take the roll call. Harjinder's name was called out once, twice and three times; nothing! Then from inside the barrack block came the familiar booming voice telling him to 'pipe down', because he would not 'fall in' under a junior man. The poor trainee, in a desperate attempt to show his authority, began shouting, but Harjinder was not to be trifled with, he responded to the insult by hurling some abuses of his own. The parade marched off and quite understandably, Noronha reported Harjinder to the Administrative Officer, Squadron Leader White.

Harjinder was produced before Squadron Leader White, a regular terror, and the charge sheet was read out. Newing, always protective towards his students, in an effort to lessen the charge toned down the exchange with the phrase: 'Or words to that effect.' When asked to answer the charge Harjinder began: 'Sir, firstly the apprentice is new, he could not be my superior officer as defined by Air Force Law. Secondly, I actually used worse language than the one I am charged with. I did purposely refuse to fall in, so to assert my point. I will face any punishment I deserve.'

There was complete silence in the room. Squadron Leader White face matched his name as the blood drained. He glared for a while and then shouted: 'Case dismissed, march him out.'

This time it was the instructor's turn to be astonished. After Harjinder's having been being marched out, the Station Administrative Officer came out and said that he wanted to see Harjinder privately.

'Do you realise that you are training to be an airman?'

'Yes Sir, I do.'

'Why did you join as an airman?'

'Because I wanted to serve in the Air Force.'

'Do you know you never will make an airman?'

'I do not agree with you, Sir.'

'Will you tell me, why you dared to say that you had used worse language than you were charged with. Were you not afraid of the punishment? Frankly, I have not met an Indian who had the moral courage even to admit the charges made against him.'

'In that case, Sir, you have not met real Indians before!'

'All right! I am glad to meet one now. However, I would like to advise you not to defy authority openly. Even if you think you are right, first carry out the orders, then register your complaint. That is the proper way because then you would not get a single day's punishment.'

Harjinder admitted that he was impressed by White's attitude. The advice was sound, and he promised him never to forget it. White may have learnt about the Indians under his command, but that lesson was yet to reach all concerned. As Harjinder reached the lecture room, he found his instructor waiting for him, red in the face and quivering with barely controlled anger. He dished out his own punishment to Harjinder. He was ordered to report to the Guard Room every hour in a different form of dress every time. Furthermore, he was debarred from riding a cycle and had to cover the distance to the barracks, about a mile and half, every hour until lights out at 10 pm, on foot. Although the form of punishment was illegal, Harjinder carried out the sentence faithfully. The upshot of the affair was sore feet for Harjinder, but the new apprentices were taken off the duty apprentice roster. Harjinder had won his case after all, but in the Service you never win, really. The instructor became his enemy and never pardoned him for the rest of his time in training. Harjinder learnt a lesson from that too!

As the year 1932 came to an end, there was great excitement to receive the first Commissioned Indian Officer, Pilot Officer Tandon. Their expectations of a tall, elegant, impressive officer were dashed on meeting Pilot Officer Tandon, who was hardly five feet tall and looked like a boy scout in uniform! Anyway, they were so proud of the first Indian Officer that at times they went out of their way simply to cross his path; with enormous smiles, they would snap him their finest salute. The British Other Ranks (BOR's) were not yet psychologically ready to salute an Indian, and a number of them landed behind bars for failing to do so. It took some time before they woke up and faced reality.

The arrival of Pilot Officer Tandon led to a discussion amongst the course about the qualities which differentiated an airman from an officer. After all, before joining the military, these trainee sepoys were originally destined to have officer-like responsibilities in the engineering world. The final conclusion was that it was neither superiority in education, nor physique, that was the difference, but a matter of one's position in life, social standing and a helping of good luck. This was further confirmed when a few months later the five other Indian Officers came from Cranwell to join as Pilot Officers of the RAF. One of them had earlier competed against Harjinder for entry into Maclaghan College but had failed to make the grade. Conveniently, and to save future blushes, Harjinder doesn't state in his diary which one failed the engineering entrance test because one way or another, these pilots would book their place in IAF history. It was a chance for Harjinder to meet up again with A Singh and B Singh who had sent him the letter of encouragement to join the IAF. However, the realities of the situation came into sharp focus since they were commissioned officers and Harjinder was still a low life Hawai Sepoy. Amarjit was grieved when he realised the tremendous social difference enforced between them, and felt guilty about having somehow been responsible for Harjinder's 'plight'. Harjinder would have none of it and insisted he was very happy where he was.

The initial training for Harjinder and his colleagues was coming to an end and the Air Force proper awaited their arrival. Their engineering skills were examined and not found wanting. The officer who examined Harjinder, Flight Lieutenant GH Shaw, called him aside and confided in him about the fight he had put up for all to be classified as Leading Aircraftsmen (LAC) as would be the case for any RAF apprentices. Shaw had also pushed, unsuccessfully, for promotion to Corporal rank for Harjinder. He told Harjinder: 'Remember that nobody has ever been able to keep a good man down. You will surely go up the ladder.'

Harjinder was heartened to know that there were some sympathetic officers among the hostile RAF, but he would not even be a LAC let alone a Corporal. When the results came out, confirming they would all be just Hawai Sepoys, lower than the most junior army soldier despite their technical training, there was a wave of resentment. The RAF Warrant Officer, Nicholas, who had started off mistrusting all of the Indian technicians, was now so shocked at the injustice that he advised Harjinder to leave the Air Force immediately. The chance was to come in the next few weeks, he said, in the form of refusal to take the oath of allegiance to the King Emperor. They came into contact with all the British Airmen on the base, many of whom had been firmly against their arrival, who also expressed their shock, and advised them to return home. The skills of the IAF apprentices had won them over during their training.

Newing's influence on Harjinder had left him in no doubt that the Air Force was the only career for him, even if he was offered a salary outside the military which was ten times his present pay. His Sepoy pay would be fifty rupees per month with effect from 23rd January 1933. When looking back at his life, Harjinder considered this increment of fifteen rupees as the most welcome and hard-earned raise that he had ever worked for. The training their instructor had given them about reducing their needs had worked so well that in their two years of training had turned them into frugal and hardworking combatants.

Any training course ends with the parting warning from the instructor: 'This is only the start. The learning never ends.' Their basic apprenticeship was over, and with those parting comments still ringing in their ears they stepped out into their working life in the Air Force. Harjinder's overwhelming goal in life was to see India Independent, but he stepped up and took the oath to the Emperor ruling his country. That must have caught in the throat a little!

There was no gentle introduction. For the first 3 months, they were attached to the Test and Despatch Flight of RAF Karachi, and much to their immense excitement, each man was allotted a real-life, fully-functioning, aircraft. The very first aircraft that fell under Harjinder's protection, a Westland Wapiti, didn't fill him with pride though. The Wapiti was a huge collection of fabric, wires, struts, wheels and cables. His joy at finally getting to grips with one of the RAF aircraft he had admired from afar in his student days was tempered. He formed a very poor opinion of its maintenance because the aircraft was kept dirty with patches of red 'dope' (fabric paint), that were seldom repainted to blend in with the overall glorious silver colour scheme. This initial disappointment remained with Harjinder, and whenever possible he kept all the aircraft that would fall under his charge looking their best.

Harjinder's first Wapiti aircraft was a target towing version, flown at low level with a windsock-type sleeve pulled behind it, which soldiers then took pot shots at. The pilots given this onerous task had to repeatedly inform the troops that they were, 'pulling the bloody target, not pushing it!' How many of those patches of red dope were 'friendly' bullets whizzing through the machine?

It is easy to see this Wapiti biplane now as a dated, lumbering, museum piece, but in 1932, it was less than 30 years after man's first ever powered flight. Even so soon after the Wright brothers' historic flight, this aircraft was already starting to become an antiquated piece of machinery, in military terms, but even with technical progress charging forward so quickly, it was still not an aircraft to be dismissed. Newly arrived in the Indian foothills of the Himalayas was now a British team, financially backed by Lady Houston. The Lady, who had started life as a chorus girl in the renowned Windmill club in London, had become one of the richest women in the world though marriages to wealthy, elderly men who either seemed to die, or who she subsequently divorced, if they hung around for too long. Her sponsorship of the 1931 British entry in the Schneider Trophy seaplane race saved the project that would later develop into the iconic Spitfire. The team gathering in India was to be the first to fly over Mount Everest using two modified, and developed, versions of the Wapiti; its robust nature made it the best machine available in the world for the task. The World War I pilot aces were treated as esteemed guests by the Maharajas, with beautifully adorned elephants paraded in front of them. Without the photographs they took on this death defying, historic flight, Sir Edmund Hillary said his Everest conquering exhibition would not have been possible.

Back in the RAF, for the old hands, it was the first time they had contact with Indians who were actually trained as engineers. Until now, the Indians on a RAF Squadron were the hired help to do the dirty, hard, physical work. This previous British/Indian mix of such a unit was best illustrated by David Lee, a brand new pilot in the RAF in 1933. After training, his first posting took him from the lush green pastures of England to the rock-strewn wasteland of Northern India. His first introduction to the operations of the RAF in India was as his silver Westland Wapiti biplane emerged from the safety of *the* fort at dawn, pushed by an Indian team. At one side was a British Airmen shouting, waving his arms and cajoling uniform movement from the men. The instructions given by this seasoned RAF Corporal were:

'Puckaroo that bleeding tail gharry and push the burra sahib's hawaijahaz on to the mutti bort jeldi'

The English/Urdu instructions were understood by all: Pick up that bleeding tail trolley and wheel the Commanding Officer's aeroplane out onto the tarmac as quick as you can. The attitude towards the Indian arrivals had to change, but it would take time. This new breed of Indians were engineers, not hired hands, equal to their RAF colleagues in everything except experience. Harjinder said the first thing that they learnt in the 'real' Air Force was that although the British Airmen grumbled a lot, they did their duty conscientiously. As he rose in the ranks and dealt with the British Officers of all ranks and status, he found this to hold true with the majority of the British, even if some individuals let the side down.

However, Harjinder had not sacrificed a civilian engineering management career to be an insignificant part of the Royal Air Force. He and his band of Engineers and Technicians wanted to be in an Indian Air Force. The time for an Indian Air Force was coming after the events in British India's summer capital of Simla, and with it, would come combat, too. The seeds had been sown and not even Harjinder could dream of what they would grow into during his time serving in this brand new Air Force. His major concern was now to ensure that the Indian Air Force survived the pain and blood of these birth pangs.

Three

Eating Off the Floor

'Have these tables and benches taken out of here at once. These people from time immemorial have squatted on the sand to take their meals.'

'Not to have an adequate air force in the present state of the world is to compromise the foundations of national freedom and Independence.'

It happened on the 8th October 1932.

The Official Act was passed, and the Indian Air Force came into being, with the Gazette Notification being signed in the Viceroy's Summer Palace in Simla. In that vehicle-free town, with buildings that would have looked more at home in Sussex, rather than snuggled against the Himalayas, history was made on that crisp, cold October day.

This was the first of many events in Simla that would thread through Harjinder's life.

Earlier, in March 1932, when the Indian Air Force Bill came up for discussion on the banks of the River Thames, in the Palace of Westminster, there were not even the required members present for a debate.

One observer commented: 'It is regretted that the house was thin when they were considering one of the greatest measures ever to come before it, which might, in the course of time, prove of decisive importance in the development of India's Constitution.'

And how very astute he proved to be...

The 8th of October is now considered to be the birth of the IAF and it was 80 years later, in 2012, that I wheeled the pretty yellow Tigermoth over the heads of the surprised crowd at Hindon Air Force base. However, in India in 1932, this date was not even treated as a minor event, let alone as the major one which it was. No doubt, when the Act was passed in Parliament in London, and then signed in Simla, it was too remote to be seen as the historic event it truly was; many assumed (or at least hoped) that it would still come to nothing. Within the RAF, the Act was considered audacious, to say the least – senior officials saw this as the quickest means to syphon away their power and resources. Initially, little seemed to happen, and it was not until the 1st April 1933 that 'A' Flight of No. 1 Squadron IAF was formed at Drigh Road, in Karachi, with real people and real aircraft.

If the 8th October 1932 were to be considered the conception, then the 1st April 1933 was the birth of the Indian Air Force.

The 1st April was chosen to start operations by the British because it coincided with the birthday of the RAF, and it made accounting far simpler.

The Himalayan Eagle was selected as a mascot, and the first six officers already selected to train as pilots in the RAF, already nick-named 'The Eagles', were diverted into the new Indian Air Force when they returned from training in England.

This small beginning, with a mixture of British and Indian personnel, might have been considered a sideshow by the British, but it was seen as the seed for the future of an entire country, by the Indians serving in the IAF.

Today, the Indian Air Force is the fourth-largest Air Force in the world and has been called to arms throughout its history, in defence of the old Empire and of Independent India, along with the numerous humanitarian and UN roles in which it has given its usual sterling performance! Some sideshow, indeed!

The Westland Wapiti was to be the first aircraft of the IAF and this aeroplane has been held close to their heart ever since. Four, secondhand Wapiti IIAs were bought for a princely sum of £10 each and were transferred from the RAF Squadrons operating within India. The first Commanding Officer of the Squadron was Flight Lieutenant Cecil 'Boy' Bouchier, DFC from the RAF. They couldn't let an Indian command this unit! For a change this wasn't an example of racism – it's just that the

Indian pilots and Airmen still had much to learn, and looking back from this millennium, it seems a herculean task to be given to someone with the lowly rank of Flight Lieutenant. However, the choice of Bouchier was an inspired one. He first flew in 1917 in the Royal Flying Corps as a pilot earning a Distinguished Flying Cross in the process, in whose citation he is described as:

'A very skilful pilot, of marked initiative and courage. Has been brought to notice on many occasions for the determination shown in his attacks. His methods are somewhat original. By flying low, parallel with and behind the enemy's lines, stampeding convoys and destroying wagons, he has caused the greatest confusion amongst the enemy, to the great advantage of our own forces. Flying Officer Bouchier is a highly competent reconnaissance officer.'

By 1920, he was flying in India and in the North-West frontier, becoming a test pilot and a flying instructor. Much to his disgust, he found himself working behind a desk in Delhi on a ground job at HQ; he desperately wanted to fly again. Without an eye on history, but just an overwhelming desire to be in the cockpit again, he volunteered, and was accepted to be the first Commanding Officer of the new Air Force.

The quality of Harjinder's work was noticed by his highly competent commander from the very first day, and before long, Flight Lieutenant Bouchier gave him charge of his own Westland Wapiti aircraft. It was an honour for Harjinder, and a bold statement by Bouchier, since several British servicemen would also be in the Flight.

However, one thing was clear to all ranks, British or Indian. This new Air Force was not to be a wholly Indian affair; that was still unthinkable in the RAF of 1933.

Their first aircraft, the Westland Wapiti, was a big, robust, ungainly, fabric-covered biplane with a single Bristol Jupiter 450 horsepower engine. The pilot sat in the front open cockpit and an air gunner/wireless operator in the rear; the opposite seating arrangements to the Tigermoth. Don't think of the Wapiti in terms of that dainty two-seat Tigermoth biplane which flew 80 years later in celebration over Delhi. The name Wapiti is another term for the North American Elk. It may have been more aptly named after the immensely strong, but perhaps not particularly good-looking, buffalo. This Wapiti was no flighty deer. It was festooned like

a Christmas tree with the equipment for a wide variety of tasks, and the
pilot was a good ten feet from the ground perched atop this flying garden
shed, a master of all he surveyed.

The term multi-role combat aircraft is widely used today, but the
Wapiti can be considered one of the first. In total, 517 were built to serve
with the RAF and other associated air forces, largely as 'The Empire's
Police Force'. There was no operational duty beyond its capability, and
no part of the Empire untouched by this aircraft. It covered the sands of
Arabia, the outback of Australia, the bush of South Africa, China, as well
as all the regions in and around India. Harjinder's first Wapiti was a RAF
target-towing aircraft, but there was a seaplane version with floats, an
Arctic Wapiti with skis, and a long-range version for desert operations.

The new IAF had their Wapitis designated as an 'Army-cooperation'
Flight equipped with a long message pickup hook travelling the length
of the belly. The rear gunner had to lie on the floor of the rear cockpit
and lower the message pickup hook by revolving a reel. The pilot then
flew about ten feet above the ground. The poor 'volunteers' from the
Army would place their note in the message bag, which was tied to a long
string that hung between two rifles stabbed vertically into the ground.
No doubt there was enough incentive to keep their heads down, as the
massive propeller on the Wapiti would come scything through the air just
centimetres above them with hook dangling from the belly. It was a sort
of extreme fishing!

So no longer would Harjinder merely stand transfixed looking at
aircraft from an untouchable distance, as he had done just three years
earlier. He was now involved with their well-being, their operation, and
their repair.

He had his own view of the Wapiti:

'Its airframe was partly covered with fabric and the front fuselage
was clothed in cowlings of aluminium. The 488 square feet of
main-plane fabric needed much washing and scrubbing. The
streamlined inter-strut wires acted like a flying net for catching
birds. There were no wheel brakes. The engine starting was done
by a hand-turning gear, which took a lot of guts and an appreciable
amount of patience on the part of two Airmen (*as they had to stand
only a few centimetres away from the rotating propeller*). The alternative
was a bag-and-rope system. (*This was a bag placed over one of the*

propeller blade tips with a long dangling rope attached. A team of Airmen would line up to take a firm hold of the rope. On the word of command they set off like some demented tug-of-war team. The propeller would rotate, hopefully sparking the engine into life. The sudden disappearance of the engine resistance as it fired up would normally result in an almost cartoon-like, pile of Airmen in the dust.) The wireless also was of a very primitive type. I remember changing valves in the rear cockpit while in flight whenever the pilot touched his earphones and shook his head at me. The communication between the pilot and the passenger was through speaking tubes, open at both ends. The tubes conveyed all the noises produced by the singing wires and struts, but for human speech it was the most inappropriate machine ever invented.' It was not unknown for the rear air gunner, when the pilot was annoying him, to 'inadvertently' put his mouthpiece out into the full force of the air flow and nearly blow his pilot's head off. Obviously the pilot could retaliate, when the air gunner was distracted and not watching him, so a mutual stand-off was usually called after a time.

In the rear cockpit that Harjinder inhabited, there was no comfortable airline seat with the type of seat belt we have all become accustomed to. There was a wooden flap that flipped down to enable the occupier to half perch a buttock cheek thereon (fifteen minutes on that hard bench, and you had change to the other buttock cheek to try and cope with the horrid numbness which would necessitate this constant shift!) in an attempt to rest one's legs on long trips, but standing was the norm. The rear gunner was tied down to the floor of the plane, with what was referred to as 'the monkey chain'. The gunner wore a leather belt with a substantial chain running through a metal loop then attached to the floor. Popular street entertainment at the time was a musician grinding a musical organ whilst a monkey danced on top with a cup in its hand to collect money. The monkey was chained to the organ with a similar arrangement, and that is precisely how the men in the rear seat of the Wapiti felt: the organ grinder's monkey!

The wings had a V-shaped wing-tip skid attached underneath, so that in gusty weather the wing tip would not touch the ground. While taxying, with no brakes, the pilot had to depend upon two Airmen holding onto the outer wing struts to help steer the great machine. Harjinder swallowed his whole life's quota of billowing dust during those earlier Wapiti days.

In aircraft maintenance terms, Harjinder found the Wapiti more complex than later, more advanced aircraft. Since this was the first attempt at constructing an all-metal aircraft; new lightweight metals like duralumin were used in the structure. He found that some daily inspections on the Wapiti took a good part of the day, leaving little time to do the actual flying! However, when the aircraft flew, they proved to be ultra-reliable, and the pilots loved them.

There may have been over 500 Wapitis in circulation during Harjinder's time, but the one still being displayed in Delhi, parts of it fashioned from scrap tubing and truck wheels, is the last surviving Wapiti in the world. Its engine is a block of wood modelled like the Jupiter engine but the fuselage is surprisingly complete. The 2 cockpits, still with some controls and fittings, would have no doubt seen Harjinder's boots at some time. The Tiger was the start of the Vintage Flight, but the plans are already underway to bring this sole survivor back into the sky. However, there will be no rolling or looping in this last piece of aviation history and I think the monkey chain may have to be updated.

The crowd at the parade in October 2012 were a good representative cross-section of India. The different regions, languages and religions of this massively tolerant nation were represented, both in the crowd, as also within those serving in the IAF. Back in 1933, things were different, ably illustrated by Pilot Officer Tandon one evening when he joined the Hawai Sepoys in their barracks, as he often did. He openly criticised a certain religion in front of all Airmen. He said, 'To my way of thinking this religion is nothing but barbarism.'

The effect of his words was volcanic and the Airmen professing that religion (*Harjinder does not specify which religion it was in his diaries*) were close to taking matters into their own hands. Harjinder took up the cudgels on behalf of those boys and then channelled the argument into less drastic lines. The following morning the incident was mentioned to Warrant Officer Newing who unfortunately reported the case to the Station Commander. He, in turn, put the Sepoys' barracks out-of-bounds to Tandon. This, of course, drove a wedge between officers and the Sepoys, but Harjinder learnt a lesson from that, too. 'Never have I criticised a religion in front of my subordinates. It can lead to mutiny.'

The first batch of five Indian pilots had started their military lives as part of the RAF, were now transferred into the embryonic IAF. In terms of seniority there was Pilot Officer Sircar, next was Pilot Officer Subroto Mukerjee, then came Bhupinder Singh and Amarjeet Singh, and, lastly, Pilot Officer A.D. Awan. Pilot Officer Sircar, a very intelligent, cultured and athletic sort of man, impressed everyone immediately. Pilot Officer Mukerjee gave the impression of being a middle-of-the-road man, but one who was most humane and understanding, a person in whom you could confide all your worries. Pilot Officers Amarjeet and Bhupinder Singh were of a reserved nature, and they carried an air of snobbery about themselves. Awan was friendly and was extremely supportive of the Indian men serving under him. All the Sepoys viewed these new arrivals as first-rate officers and gentlemen.

Harjinder wrote, 'The training at Cranwell had given them a quality of leadership which could be imbibed only in that Sandhurst (*the British Army Officer training academy*) of the Air Force. There were times when their elevated status made us wistful and we suffered feelings of injured pride because of the injustice of our being kept down as ordinary Airmen; but these five young men played a commendable role in this respect and made us feel important and wanted. Although they were commissioned officers, a very high status for an Indian in those days, they proved to us that they were Indians first. Their attitude to us from the very beginning was "all for one and one for all." I remember the day when they went to see our Commanding Officer and offered to buy sports gear for their Indian Airmen. They were rebuffed by being told: "You are fraternising too much with Airmen." We felt the insult at once, but the efforts of the Indian Officers on our behalf made us feel content and proud.'

Without the understanding, sympathy, and patriotism of these young officers, Harjinder believes, many, himself included, would have abandoned the uniform of the IAF Hawai Sepoys.

Their generosity made him feel like he and the other Hawai Sepoys were the real captains of the team that would form the future IAF.

All the hardships among the ranks were forgotten, and then men lent these young officers their full support. This close knit team was the foundation of the IAF, and an incredible amount of teamwork was needed if they were to survive the first few years.

Harjinder had started off by staring at aircraft, then he had learnt how to work on aircraft, and now the time came to fly in one. We have got this far in Harjinder's life knowing about his burning desire to see India with an air force of its own, to further the cause for independence. However, it now comes to light in Harjinder's diaries that he was afraid of heights!

Came the day when he was treated to his first flight. He was strapped (he would have preferred the word 'entombed!') into the harness by Corporal Sherman, who then proceeded to frighten Harjinder out of his skin, as he trotted through the drill about bailing out with a parachute. By the time he entered the rear cockpit he was shaking. The bumping of the Wapiti stopped as the wheels lifted off and the ground seemed to drop away. All was fine until the aircraft started rolling to make a turn. Harjinder put his head inside the cockpit like a pigeon which, after seeing the cat, closes its eyes to feel secure. All of a sudden he felt a great rolling movement. His heart nearly stopped beating. He opened his eyes and risked a look forward, only to see the big grin on Flight Lieutenant Bouchier's face. He was pointing down at the hangars below. To get Harjinder's attention he had yanked the stick from right to left causing the aircraft to lurch through the air. Harjinder forced out a feeble smile but cursed him under his breath. However, when he did pluck up the courage to peek over the cockpit side, he looked down and saw the beautiful sight of fields below laid out like a map. His fear evaporated, and was replaced with the joy of being up in the air. So, was this the start of the flying love affair? Well, not quite, thanks to Flying Officer Broad who, a few days later, looped the loop without warning. It was a terrifying experience as the G force first squashed him into the rear cockpit and his restricted view turned from blue sky to green fields and back again. Also, don't forget that Harjinder was not strapped into a seat by the several harnesses you now get even on a small roller coaster ride in any amusement park in the world. He was standing in the back only attached to the floor with a 'monkey chain', whilst Broad had his fun doing loops. Perhaps this was one of those times to put the voice tube in the airflow and blow his head off? Harjinder discovered that if a passenger is not taken into confidence before any out-of-the-ordinary manoeuvre, it can destroy forever what should be a fantastic, life affirming experience. He never forgot this when, as a pilot, he carried passengers himself twenty years later.

1st April 1933 was a big day for those serving and they were all taken up in the air by Flight Lieutenant Bouchier, one by one. While the rest of India was, by and large, unaware, one of the most important events in the country's military history was taking place; and all the Sepoys waited with excitement to shake the surly bonds of earth for a short time. The British Government misjudged the Indians. They had thought that giving them only the impression of forming an Air Force would suffice. They thought that the young educated people of India of those days were too soft and easy-going and that they would quit once they found military life difficult. They hadn't factored in people like Harjinder and his colleagues who understood the importance of this, not just for the Air Force, but for the future of an independent India.

An incident took place in the first few days of 'A' Flight, No. 1 Squadron IAF, which brought that initial euphoria crashing down. On 5th April 1933, Flying Officer Broad was sitting in the cockpit of Wapiti K-1297. The normal method of starting a large, 9 cylinder Jupiter engine was by manually winding the 2 large starting handles placed in the slot that were on either side of the fuselage, behind the engine, and connected to the engine flywheel. The flywheel was spun up to speed by the airman on each handle, until the pilot engaged the flywheel to the engine, hopefully bringing it to life. Harjinder was asked to help with winding-up the starter handle on one side, with a British airman named Gillhooly on the other. It was Harjinder's first attempt at this task and, with his nose only centimetres away from the propeller, he was more than a little nervous. A combination of the exertion and fear made his hands sweat; the handle slipped. Gillhooly leant over the fuselage to face Harjinder and said: 'You bloody fool, don't you know how to keep the handle in?'

This was the first time Harjinder had been called a fool by a colleague.

He was furious and, when no pithy reply came to his mind, he responded by calling him a bloody fool in return. It would have been fine if it had stopped there, but unfortunately, Harjinder saw the red mist of anger cloud over his eyes. He pulled out the long starting handle and took a swipe directly at Gillhooly's head. Luckily, he saw it coming and ducked as the handle swept harmlessly above the fast moving airman. The pilot, who was witness to all this unfolding shouted 'Switches off' as he shut the engine down. He made no attempt to address Harjinder directly, but strode directly towards the Commanding Officer's office. Airman Gillhooly also left the arena.

Soon afterwards the Indians were asked to fall in before the Commanding Officer's office and were given a stern lecture by him. The Commanding Officer had an interesting approach to this matter, and

Harjinder not only remembered the lecture for the rest of his days, but he said it changed his outlook on life. Bouchier began:

'I have been informed of an unfortunate incident just now. It has happened because you are all new in the Service and very sensitive by nature. Although Indians are known to be very emotional, it is something which we have to guard against in the Service. In the RAF when we call a man a Bloody Fool he takes it. He knows it as a rebuke only and he does not take it to heart.'

Of course, there is plenty of truth in this. The banter of the British military is legendary and their light-hearted insulting of each other is part of the day-to-day life. Bouchier's solution to this difference in culture was arguably somewhat obtuse.

'I have now instructed the BOR's (British Other Ranks, *in this case the 12 British servicemen who were Sergeant, Corporals or basic Airmen*) posted to "A" Flight to season all of you. From now on any time you are called by name by any BOR, even if he is only an airman, you are to double up to him; halt three paces in front of him; and say "Yes, LAC". You are to carry out his orders as if he is your superior officer. And I have instructed the BORs to use the choicest RAF slang on you as often as possible.'

The official invite to abuse the Indians was taken up with great enthusiasm. The BORs probably couldn't believe that their boss had invited them to use the Indians as their own servants, and sling abuse at them at every opportunity. Harjinder took the guilt on his shoulders because he had opened the door to 'this hell' that was let loose. From then on, they became the pawns on the chess board and the BORs the players. They were pushed around mercilessly, called all the names imaginable, and the sly chuckles behind their backs were all the more galling. One day, Flight Sergeant Hills, a very kind-hearted and gentle-souled man, gave a talk which finally made sense to Harjinder. He said: 'You must not misunderstand the CO's action. He is training you to fit in with the worst situation you are likely to meet in your future career. A man who cannot take a rocket or stand Service slang is not fit for our Service. Sooner or later he will come to grief.'

Harjinder, in his later years in the Service, found these words of wisdom to be very true and, what is more, he practised the same principle with his subordinates. Later, as Harjinder rose in the ranks he was known to be a fair, but fearsome character. Were Harjinder's legendary tongue-lashings in later years fuelled by these months of his 'hell'?

The treatment of the Indians was not limited to the Sepoys. The Indian pilots were faring little better. A slightly heavy landing and the pilot had to carry the considerable weight of his parachute on his shoulder for a forced stroll around the outside perimeter of the aerodrome in the baking Indian heat. Many of the pilots used to avoid their British colleagues by resting in their cockpits after their labours, under the pretext of polishing the brass magneto switches. It was the responsibility of the Indian ground crew to alert them, when the need arose, by shaking the wing or tail control surfaces. One Saturday, Harjinder saw the Commanding Officer appear unexpectedly and panicked at the sight, thrashing the elevator on the tail up and down a little too forcefully. The poor officer came out of the cockpit, hand pressing hard on his rapidly reddening cheek, as if he had just been butchered in the dentist's chair. The joystick had nearly knocked him out in the cockpit.

Needless to say, Flight Lieutenant Bouchier, the Commanding Officer, was not a popular man with the Indians at first.

Another event which didn't help relations in those early days happened when he was flying a mission that involved cooperating with local Indian army units in the Karachi area. He found that he was unable to use his wireless, missing all the calls intended for him. After his landing it was discovered that he had not plugged in to the wireless, but he refused to admit to his mistake. Instead, he ordered all Airmen be confined to the camp for a week to pay for the 'wireless failure'. However, this view of Bouchier did not last long. Later, for his early role with No. 1 Squadron, he was referred to by many as 'the father' of the Indian Air Force and Harjinder confides 'years later we were to be grateful to the very man whom we then disliked'.

Flight Lieutenant Bouchier was definitely on the side of his Indian men.

On one occasion, he overheard a conversation between Harjinder and a British Sergeant in the Orderly Room. The Sergeant was updating his records and had to ask for any qualifications the Sepoys held before their military service. When told they were all qualified engineers who had spent five years each in the leading institutions in India, he refused to believe it. He had no knowledge of India and to him engineers and India just did not go together, and so, refused to record their degrees. Flight Lieutenant Bouchier gave instructions that the engineering qualifications be recorded, and told Harjinder, 'However, I would like you to remember one thing in your Air Force career. That is, even if you possess all the engineering degrees in the world and are a gold-medallist to boot, it will not matter the least bit. What I want to see is your application to hard work and the results in the maintenance of aircraft. I do not wish to see airy-fairy engineers floating about in the hangars, but mechanics in overalls that clean and repair aeroplanes. However, if you also have theoretical knowledge, do apply it; do not store it in your brain.'

Harjinder was not afraid of hard work, as he had proved to Newing. It was now time to show his skills within a Squadron, but he knew it was always going to be a fight against the entrenched prejudices around him.

Harjinder's patience was tested further, when a few days later, Sardar Gurdial Singh, an Aerodrome Officer from the Civil Aviation, dropped in to see Harjinder. When a British sergeant was told that the Sardar Sahib had been Harjinder's old college mate, he snorted with disdain: 'Really! The Prince of Wales was my classmate.' These incidents and the superiority complex of the British attitude towards Indians caused Harjinder to re-evaluate himself. He came to realise that although he was determined and capable enough to be an airman, he was, at this stage, most unsuited mentally. Some of the Airmen around him started to quit the Air Force. A dozen of them deliberately failed their trade tests and were discharged.

Harjinder was being dragged lower and lower, and even discussed leaving the IAF with Malik. Apparently, Malik scoffed at Harjinder's sensitivity and said: 'Let us sink or swim together.'

Malik's attitude and Harjinder's recollection of his college days, using publicity, persuasion, and faith to convince his colleagues of the importance of the IAF, changed his mind. Harjinder also believed that the five Indian pilots were suffering a worse fate than they, and this also inspired him to continue. He considered the treatment of the pilots by their own Commanding Officer, to be inferior to that he afforded the sweepers. They were King's Commissioned Officers, but were not allowed to live, or even dine, in the RAF Officers' Mess. They had inferior quarters on a little hillock known contemptuously as 'Gandhi's Hill'. At the time, Harjinder was unaware that the biggest ally they had for their Air Force was Bouchier himself, fighting hard for their corner behind the scenes.

On just the second day of his new job position as Commanding Officer of the entire Indian Air Force, Bouchier was summoned by Wing Commander Whitelock, the Karachi Depot Commander. Without introductions or pleasantries he began; 'Bouchier, I am not going to have your Indian Officers in the Mess.'

Bouchier replied: 'Sir, with respect you cannot bar my Indian Officers from the Mess. They hold the same King's Commission you and I hold, and they are entitled to live in our officers' mess anywhere else, as, indeed, they were at Cranwell. If you bar them from our Mess here, Sir, you automatically exclude me out of the Mess as well, for I am their Commanding Officer, and where they live and take their meals, there I will also live and take my meals.'

The Officer's Mess Committee had decided even before these Indian pilots arrived that they wouldn't actually mix with these men! 'Bouchier, I don't want to hear any more about it. Your Indian Officers are not going to be accommodated in the Mess. You will find some alternative accommodation.'

Bouchier continued to argue for the inclusion of the Indian Officers into the RAF Officers' Mess. His reasoning, beyond outright fairness, was that these first few Indian Officers were to become the bearers of a standard for a completely new fighting service. The RAF officers had the opportunity, perhaps even the responsibility, to teach them the high standards kept in an officers' mess, otherwise how else were they to learn? He insisted they were officers and gentlemen and that he would act as guarantor for their impeccable good manners and behaviour.

Eventually, it was Flight Lieutenant Bouchier's threat to write a petition to the RAF Headquarters for a ruling by the Air Officer Commanding on this 'vitally important matter' that won him a probationary period for his Indian Officers. He gathered them together to emphasise that they were the standard bearers in everything they did; the responsibility lay with them. He briefed them on the etiquette of the time but also had to warn them they may be on the receiving end from some 'misguided' Mess members who might have 'reservations' about the influx of Indian Officers. Within two weeks, every officer in the Mess made it a point to approach Flight Lieutenant Bouchier and say how much they admired the appearance, bearing and courtesy of his Indian Officers. The hearts and minds campaign had worked its magic.

Meanwhile Harjinder and his fellow Hawai Sepoys were to have their own small eating facilities. Bouchier was concerned about the overcrowding of British Airmen in their canteen area and therefore considered separate facilities for his Indians to be the best option. What followed was an ongoing battle to provide them with their basic needs, and overcome the prejudice ingrained in the less-enlightened senior officers. Bouchier went back to the Base Commander, Wing Commander Whitelock, to ask for some basic tables and trestles for their mess. His reply speaks volumes of the man. 'Bouchier, what on earth do you want trestle tables and benches for? Indians are used to squatting on the ground to eat their meals.'

'Sir. They are not coolies. They come from good families. Almost all of them are University educated; they speak English, and all their lives they have been used to sitting at a table to take their meals as we do.'

He got the small hut for their use but no tables or benches. His trusty Warrant Officer and Flight Sergeant were given the task to rectify this and from somewhere (*always best not to ask the professional scroungers where from!*) things appeared in place until a spotless, fully-equipped mess was in use within 4 days.

That was not the end of the matter. When the Air Commander-in-Chief India, Sir John Steel, visited and glanced into this small, inoffensive facility, he ordered Wing Commander Whitelock to 'Have these tables and benches taken out of here at once. These people from time immemorial have squatted on the sand to take their meals. They don't need these things.'

Whitelock had a smug smile, but Bouchier was shocked. During his time in Delhi he and his wife had socialised with Sir John and Lady Steel. It was then that Bouchier realised that neither Sir John nor Wing Commander Whitelock wanted his small Indian Air Force to succeed. The furniture was removed in full sight of Sir John, but Flight Sergeant Hill was on the case. By the end of the night all the furniture reappeared.

A few months later Sir John dropped in again, this time unannounced. 'Whitelock, I thought I told you to get those tables and benches out of here.' The chess game continued with, Flight Sergeant Hill supervising the removal, and, within a few hours, the replacement of the offensive furniture! It was a dangerous game Bouchier was playing, disobeying the Commander-in-Chief's orders. To justify this in his military mind, he reasoned that the order had never been given directly to him. Whitelock was ordering the removal, whilst Bouchier was replacing the furniture, shocked at the discovery that somebody was moving it from its correct location! There is no mention of this event in Harjinder's extensive diaries, so I think we can assume the Indian Sepoys were not even aware of this game of furniture chess.

The Indian Air Force had only just been formed, but there was just not time enough to rest on laurels. New personnel were joining to expand the Flight. The reality was, as a flight of four aircraft, they were just an insignificant speck within the RAF, and so expansion was vital. In 1933, that expansion included Pilot Officer Aspy Engineer, a pilot who had made a name for himself by being the first Indian to fly solo from England to India, thereby winning the Aga Khan Prize in 1930, all at the age of 17. He was the closest thing to an Indian aviation celebrity.

All the Indian pilots going through Cranwell had received honours in all forms of sport including captaining the tennis and hockey teams. Aspy added another trophy to the 'Indian cabinet'. He was awarded the caterpillar pin, given to those who have been saved by 'hitting the silk'. As a student pilot doing aerobatics his aircraft has caught fire and over the side went Aspy Engineer using his parachute to save his life and gain the caterpillar pin. On leaving Cranwell he beat all the RAF cadets to win the Grove prize for best pilot in his term. He was a truly gifted pilot and his celebrity status was a gift for the IAF.

In Harjinder's opinion Aspy was a steady, thorough and conscientious officer. He followed the King's Regulations to the letter, but had ideas of his own for the future. The first day he was on duty as the Orderly Officer, he went and saw the Commanding Officer with the suggestion that Sepoys should be allowed to employ servants in the barracks, as the British Airmen did, to clean up and lay out their daily kit on the beds. Harjinder was in-charge of the barracks and surprised Engineer when he vehemently opposed this new suggestion. Although British Airmen were allowed this facility Harjinder felt that because the Sepoys were not used to Service life as yet, they had to learn everything from the bottom up. The British men had been through three years' training at Halton as teenagers, and they had senior Airmen in the barracks to teach them the military way. The Indians were college boys who were in their twenties, less amenable to the rigorous discipline of a military life. Harjinder wanted them to be taught to do things for themselves, and Bouchier agreed with him. Pilot Officer Aspy Engineer, naturally, was very upset at his idea falling on stony ground especially as it was derailed by the very people he was trying to help. In a stunning misjudgement of character, Harjinder told Bouchier that this new officer was very methodical and perhaps idealistic but, wait six months and he will come down with a bump! Harjinder was spectacularly wrong, because Pilot Officer Aspy Engineer's career went up and up, and later, these two men would regularly spar verbally; Aspy Engineer as the Chief of the Indian Air Force, and Harjinder, one rank below him as his Head of Maintenance in an independent India. That would happen in the 1950s. Back in the 1930's, the IAF had to learn beyond just flying their Wapiti aircraft. The reality of the job was they had to learn how to use them as tools for warfare.

Four

Death Comes to Visit,
Death Comes to Stay

'I wish I had also died...'

Thus it was that 'A' Flight IAF existed, but now they had to prove they could do the job as well as, if not better than, the RAF could. The only way to achieve this was through training, training, and more training.

That training had a high price.

It was to cost the lives of 16 people...

During the spring of 1933, exercises were carried out with Sindh Independent Brigade near Hyderabad. They operated in active service conditions from open dusty strips over the browns and greens of the surrounding countryside. They flew over the pock-marked firing ranges, blasted by years of explosions on the dusty brown earth. From their back seats, Harjinder and his colleagues watch the arcing shells, fired by the distant artillery, reach the peak of their flight, seeming to hover with in touching distance, before plummeting back to earth with a shower of dirt spraying upwards from the explosion. They would scribble down the coordinates of the hits as the pilots took their Wapitis down to zoom over the heads of the artillerymen. The rear gunner placed his message in a bag, with a colourful streamer attached, and dropped it at the feet of the gun crews. With this information, the artillerymen could adjust their aim on the fictitious enemy and the IAF Wapitis would be back in place to report on the results. True, they had radios in the Wapiti, but they saw the primitive wireless sets in their aeroplanes as useless extra weight to balance the aircraft rather than as an instrument to help the pilot. They were not unique in their mistrust of this new technology. Even at the start of World War II, the senior Spanish Civil War veterans of the Luftwaffe, in their ultra-modern Messerschmitt 109 fighters, thumbed their noses at radios and at the young bucks who suggested their use. The RAF fighters had an edge during the Battle of Britain in 1940, as they were guided onto their foe by ground controllers, whereas the German pilots wandered the skies trying to pick out the tiny specks of would-be targets. Aviation can be cutting-edge in technological terms, but often, it is the minds behind the operation which can be the resistive to any change.

When their week-long exercise was at an end and the dust-streaked Wapitis of the Indian Air Force took off for home, the Indian pilots brought their aircraft in close formation with their boss. The big biplanes bounced around in the warm thermal currents bubbling up from the ground, but the whole Flight held a tight formation. Flight Lieutenant Bouchier looked left and right at these bobbing machines and suddenly felt the upsurge of pride burst forth for his little command. He now knew they were matching anything which the RAF could do.

In September of that year, Flight Lieutenant Bouchier, Flying Officers Sircar, Mukerjee, and Awan, together with Sepoy Ram Singh and Harjinder, were posted to Quetta in order to gain experience on the North-West Frontier. The base was situated in high mountainous country, 6,000 feet above sea level, in a small saucer-shaped airstrip near the Afghan border, the gateway to the North-West Frontier proper. Command, back in Delhi, felt that it was necessary to have two complete squadrons based there to patrol over the local tribes. Whilst flying into their new airfield, they had to climb to 12,000 feet and over the Bolan Pass, the drop in temperature at that height a blessed relief. Summer temperatures in Quetta were high, but not unpleasant, due to the lack of humidity. In winter, however, the flight through the Pass would be an exercise in survival, with temperatures on the ground plunging well below freezing. Quetta was very much a military town, with the Army Staff College dominating, and the aerodrome only 3 miles from the town centre. One RAF technician described the town as having only 2 sleazy cinemas, but an official brothel in Chip Street. The airman in question seemed to view the brothel as more acceptable than the cinemas! The golf course was open to Airmen and officers, but the climate was not conducive for a good course. The fairways were sand and the greens were rolled mud, cow dung and straw: best described as 'browns'. However, golf was not on minds of the new arrivals.

Attached to No. 31 Squadron RAF, the Indians saw the Royal Air Force in its true operational colours for the first time. Harjinder thought there was a casual air about them. For example, it was quite normal to see a British pilot crash an aircraft and walk away with a grin on his face, as if he had just fallen off a bicycle. The IAF didn't have the luxury to throw aircraft away. Harjinder knew, as the rest did too, that plenty of people further up the chain of command were looking for an excuse to squash them flat.

One day during their stay at Quetta, Flying Officer Mukerjee landed with Harjinder after a routine flight. Harjinder jumped down from his rear cockpit, a place where he now felt completely at home. He organised the men to start refuelling the Wapitis. This was a lengthy process – the fuel was poured slowly from heavy tins, through chamois leather-topped funnels to keep the dust, grit, water, sweat and insects out. As he sweated away, he saw an old Muslim approaching them sheepishly. When the old gent had the courage to complete his final few steps up to the working men, he asked whether the two persons who had come out of the silver machine were in fact Indians as they had the faces of Indians. When he was assured that they were, he spread out his prayer mat on the tarmac, dropped to his knees and began praying. Later, he came up to Harjinder and said; 'I am an old man. I have always seen white men fly. Today I feel very proud and happy because I have seen two of my own countrymen fly. So I prayed to Allah for your long life and may He be with you wherever you ride in this Wheel of Satan.'

Harjinder was gaining quite a reputation as a mechanic and technician to keep these 'Wheels of Satan' flying. This was mainly due to the fact that he saw it as more than just his duty to examine every nut and bolt of his aircraft in detail; he saw it as the whole purpose of his life. One day he was carrying out a check on an aircraft with Ram Singh, each checking and re-checking each other's work. Head first, Harjinder disappeared deep into the cavernous bowels of the aircraft under the pilot's seat, examining all the linkages in its belly. The sweat ran down his face and stung his eyes, but a visual check was the only sure way to stay safe. What he saw chilled the sweat on him. The main link from the bottom of the pilot's control column to the rear elevator tail control surfaces was cracked. The crack had passed through the whole of the eye fitting of the bell crank. Surely, the slightest bump on the next flight would finish the job, leaving the pilot with an interesting headache, as he pulled and pushed a control column that was no longer connected! When this was brought to the notice of Bouchier, Harjinder was rightfully praised for his thoroughness and the incident duly noted in his personal folder. However, the glow from this story so nearly turned sour shortly after. It was only saved by Divine Intervention, or was it his subconscious that was now fully tuned into aeronautical engineering?

A couple of nights later, Harjinder dreamt that a split-pin was missing in the control column universal joint bolt in a particular aircraft. For Harjinder, this was more a nightmare than a dream, and he woke up in a cold sweat. He did as we all do with nightmares, and pushed it aside, telling himself not to be so stupid; but sleep would not come...

The visions of the missing pin were lodged firmly in his mind, gnawing away, no matter what other thoughts he tried to replace them with. Finally, he could take no more, and so gave up; he slipped out of bed before anyone else stirred, and gently padded into the hangar.

A hangar at night takes on a nightmarish quality, as shadows dance, and the quietest of footfalls echo off the corrugated iron walls. He climbed up the side of the fuselage and once again wriggled in, head first, to get a look under the control column in the pilot's cockpit. In the light of his torch there was the joint with the empty hole where the pin should be, staring at him.

'I broke out in a sweat thinking of the accident that could have resulted from such negligence, and I thanked my lucky stars that some power from above had drawn my attention to it. Perhaps there was no clairvoyance involved; the explanation could be simple. For the first time in my service career I had been given a chance to look after an aeroplane; no Indian had ever had this opportunity before. Added to this was our love and affection for our Indian pilots, who were fighting against odds to establish one fact; that Indians could fly. To accomplish this, they had developed great initiative and character. They had become good pilots and first-rate officers. It was a matter of pride and pleasure for us to be with them on the ground and to fly with pilots like Mukerjee and Awan. We felt it our sacred duty to concentrate fully on our part of the job, i.e. maintenance. What must have happened in this case was that when I had changed the bushes in the universal joint I must have inadvertently forgotten to replace the split-pin. It was a complicated joint and very awkward to work upon. But after leaving the work, my subconscious mind must have been still working on me in my sleep and thus it pointed out the mistake.'

This single unit of four Wapitis, with their own Indian Engineers, was still viewed as a bit of an oddity by the RAF and one that could be ignored; after all it was bound to fail. The Indians had to win over the RAF, one person at a time.

One day, Flight Sergeant Wilson from the RAF happened to see Harjinder's two tool boxes; one, a standard Metal Rigger's tool box, and the other, full of all manner of gadgets fashioned by Harjinder himself. The Flight Sergeant was so intrigued that he called his own Flight Commander who, in turn, called Flight Lieutenant Bouchier to have a look. In front of these officers and men of the RAF, the Flight Commander complimented Harjinder, then added to Bouchier; 'If I had him in my Flight, I would have promoted him to a Corporal on the spot.'

Flight Lieutenant Bouchier, eyeing Harjinder with approval, smiled and said: 'I am not lowering the standard of NCOs in the IAF.'

Unknown to Harjinder, Bouchier was already pushing for the stripes of a Corporal to be awarded to Harjinder, but as everyone knew in HQ, Indians just weren't good enough, were they?! The reality was that Newing's adverse report on Harjinder had turned from a theoretical college engineer into a practical engineer, who stood out from among the crowd. He was now attracting the attention of the RAF's own hardened engineers; men not known for giving easy praise to anyone.

The IAF pilots were also sweeping aside prejudices as they came into contact with the RAF personnel. Those more broadminded among the RAF personnel were beginning to mutter in respectful terms regarding the standard of flying of the Indian pilots. They were quiet mutterings, but they were audible enough to create a glow for the Indian Sepoys who regarded their own pilots as heroes. The Sepoys were mortified when their pilots were ordered to scrub and clean the aircraft during one 'Servicing Day' in October 1933. You would think it normal for the Airmen to see this as giving assistance to them, but the Sepoys saw it as their pilots being made to do an airman's work, which was neither proper nor correct. They had earned a good reputation with both Indian and British Airmen, and they gave the Indian men a feeling of delight and pride in all their professionalism to the Service. They all felt that to build an Air Force was the greatest service they could perform for their country. They had jelled as a team, albeit very small, but one where respect ran up and down the power gradient.

This was the embodiment of the Squadron motto, 'Ittehad Men Shakti Hai', or 'In Unity lies Strength'.

The time at Quetta with the RAF was soon over. It was with heavy heart that they left the excitement of this operation station, but, whilst they were waiting to pack up, Pilot Officer Mukerjee solemnly approached the group. Harjinder instinctively knew this was not regrets at leaving – something was wrong.

Mukerjee was the harbinger of news about Pilot Officers Amarjit and Bhupinder Singh.

The early days in aviation were a fraught with risk. Personnel numbers always fluctuated in the Flight with people like the young star Aspy Engineer posted in.

This, however, was their introduction to the brutal reality of how their numbers would reduce.

Bhupinder Singh was considered a very able and good officer, but Harjinder always thought him a risk taker. He was fond of spinning the lumbering Wapiti. He would bring the engine back to idle but lift the nose of the aircraft to maintain the height, even as the airspeed washed away, making the wings work harder to keep the aircraft in the air. Finally, the airflow over the wings would approach the point where they could no longer sustain flight.

With his right foot, Bhupinder would push full rudder, causing the machine to yaw. The left wing would move forward slightly, as the right wing slid back. The extra speed was enough to keep the left wing flying, but the loss of lift on the right wing would tip it into a stall condition, where suddenly, all the lift holding it up collapsed. Even this cumbersome aircraft would roll quickly on to its back as it entered into an ever-tightening spin. The aircraft's nose would then swing downwards until nearly vertical, as the aircraft continued in this whirling rotation, rapidly gobbling up the height, until the pilot made the correct, positive, and full control inputs. In this early age of aviation, some aircraft would not come out of a spin, and many a pioneer died trying to discover this. Bhupinder knew of Harjinder's dislike of the spinning of his aircraft, and many times he had tried to insist that they fly together. Harjinder steadfastly refused, but Bhupinder upped the pressure by telling Harjinder that he would brand him as a coward to all his relatives. Harjinder welcomed him to do so – but he certainly wouldn't want Bhupinder to try any of his fancy aerobatics whilst he was monkey-chained in the rear cockpit.

On the 4th September 1933, at Padidan airfield, about 200 miles from Karachi, Bhupinder was again up to his tricks with his cousin, Amarjit, along for the ride in the back. There is little doubt that Bhupinder was showing off, by using a spin, to lose height rapidly from his cruise altitude, only to recover a few hundred feet off the ground and in a position to make a landing. Certainly a spectacular way to arrive but it proved spectacular in a way he didn't plan. Spinning was not fully understood then (*and some would say still, today!*) and the recovery is not completely predictable, changing with weight distribution and aircraft rigging, among many other parameters. With the Wapiti settled into the spin, Bhupinder pushed the control column fully forward and pushed the rudder pedal fully forward in the opposite direction to the spin. The rate an aircraft spins around its nose often increases initially when the controls are moved to start the recovery. The spin rate increased but the spin did not stop. Perhaps some equipment had moved in the aircraft, perhaps the rigging was different, perhaps Bhupinder hesitated when the spin rate increased and with the ground so close. At that height, there were only a few seconds left, and no time to re-try the recovery procedure. The Wapiti is a big and incredibly strong machine, but there was nothing this aircraft could do to save its passengers as it rotated into the ground, crumpling up into a tangled mass covering only a very small area. Bhupinder killed his cousin Amarjit, standing in the back with only the monkey chain on, as well as himself.

One third of the first batch of IAF pilots was now dead...

When Pilot Officer Mukerjee passed on the news, he added; 'This is the last straw, we are determined to see that no more accidents occur amongst our pilots.'

It was very reassuring to hear him make such a bold statement, but it was a wish that was not to be.

The most gruesome of incidents was just around the corner...

On the 15th October 1933, the team arrived back at Drigh Road in Karachi from Quetta. Everybody in the Flight was at low ebb after the loss of the two pilots, and this reunion with their home airfield only seemed to reignite that grief. For the next few months, they worked harder, as their allocated flying tasks were increased. It was seen as an indication that higher up the chain of command, someone had realised that this new unit could actually achieve something of worth, despite the loss of one Wapiti, and, more importantly, two pilots. The fear of all was summed up by Harjinder; 'lest some amongst us boob technically and become the cause of the loss of another pilot. The reader will find it difficult to imagine the feelings of the Airmen of those days. We had become real blood relations of these young heroes of the skies.'

On the morning of 29th October, 1933, a turbaned Sikh gentleman, with his white beard flowing behind him, came rushing up to the engineers as they waited for their machine to return. He threw his arms around Sukha Singh, jabbering unintelligibly. Harjinder realised it was Sukha's father. The old man had tears in his eyes, and in front of the astonished group he said; 'My dear son, it would be better for you to beg in the streets than to be an airman in the IAF. Your mother is crying her heart out and has not eaten food for many days. Your would-be father-in-law has threatened to break off your engagement with his daughter. Since we heard of the flying accident a few days ago, I have been longing to see you. You must come with me to see your Commanding Officer. I will not go from here unless you accompany me home.'

Harjinder and a colleague tried to convince the old man that in this world, danger was everywhere, even in your own bed if your luck ran out, so why worry about the dangers of flying? But the old man would not listen. Despite his begging, he was not allowed to see the Commanding Officer because the Adjutant repeatedly told him it was of no use. Perhaps Sukha was more afraid of his would-be father-in-law than the Air Force, he left the Service by refusing to take the Oath of Allegiance; the one sure way to get out. Another man was gone.

One week later, Harjinder was idly chatting with a RAF Sergeant fitter, an unthinkable thing even a year ago. That conversation took an unexpected turn, and left Harjinder doubting his own future in the IAF. Whilst waiting for his aeroplane L-1297 to land, he casually mentioned to the Sergeant about Quetta and the fact he was commended by the Flight Commander of No. 31 Squadron who had talked about immediate promotion to Corporal. The Sergeant's reply, said without malice, but as a matter-of-fact, was like a thunderbolt; 'Even the Prince of Wales cannot promote you because a man cannot become a NCO until he has served at least 9 to 10 years. So forget about promotion for the time being. In fact, you can safely add 50 per cent to the ten years in the case of Indians.'

A promotion appeared to be farther away than the moon. Was there any point in continuing?

The Annual Sports Meet on the 9th December 1933, distracted Harjinder from his depressing mood. Harjinder couldn't just attend these events. He had to win, and win he did. Five events in total. The 100 yards, 440 yards, 880 yards, long jump and the high jump, even though he had never even tried the high jump before. Also, the team won the one mile medley.

There is some doubt in Harjinder's mind about the 100 yards, and fairness is something that is at the core of this man. He wrote; 'I am not sure if I was really the first in 100 yards. When this event was being run, Flight Lieutenant Bouchier was one of the judges. At the finishing tape he caught hold of my arm, pushed me at the judges and insisted that his man was first. The judges were dubious but Bouchier was a man of strong personality and he would not be denied. I have always felt guilty and whenever I look at this prize medal, my conscience pricks me.'

The death of the Singh cousins had risked the existence of the IAF even before it had firmly taken root. Bhupinder's recklessness had taken 2 lives and opened the IAF to criticism. The team were clawing themselves back when another accident took place during the team involvement in an Army Cooperation Exercise. The mists of time clouds the exact date and place, but the outcome is in no doubt. The survival of the IAF suddenly seemed hopeless.

The local Army unit conceived a plan to practice their skills under a simulated attack from the air.

When the Army spotted the 'enemy' aircraft, the troops scattered to find cover; something their present location lacked. The exception was the twenty-man team, trained as the battalion's anti-aircraft platoon, who stood upright, shoulder to shoulder, point their rifles at the oncoming threat.

Flight Lieutenant Bouchier led the formation of 3 Wapitis, with Sircar as number 2 and Mukerjee as number 3. They dove down from 1500 feet, one behind the other, pulling out from the dive at 500 feet before dropping down for a second pass. Bouchier knew that this was the tried and tested attack routine, and so, added a twist. When they had completed their two attacks, they headed towards their base. Then, after five minutes, he changed course, stalked their prey and approached from a different direction.

Harjinder wrote that Bouchier criticised the pilots for not coming in low enough. Perhaps feeling that his courage was being called into question, Flying Officer Sircar, the senior-most Indian pilot, was determined to remedy this for his next pass.

Bouchier's decoy had worked and the troops were settling back in to their columns, but the anti-aircraft platoon was still bunched tightly together, so he picked them as his target.

The first Wapiti swooped away but, just behind him, the second biplane grew in size with the blur of the propeller leading the way. The Wapiti's nose came up to level flight but there was no sign of it climbing. Imagine the carnage as the propeller, started churning through the rank and file of the men like a circular saw, handled by the devil himself.

The impact of the propeller cutting into this mass of flesh and bone tipped the Wapiti's nose slightly downwards again; the propeller made contact with the desert floor. The disintegrating propeller threw wooden splinters out, like medieval arrows, felling more men. Fourteen soldiers were killed outright by the propeller, or by the aircraft wings slashing through the ranks. A large number had the most appalling injuries from splinters and flying wreckage. On landing, Bouchier and his pilots jumped onto the nearest truck and rushed to the site, passing 8 army ambulances going in the opposite direction. The IAF men arrived in a flurry of dust, to find that the army had departed leaving just 2 to stand guard. Standing next to the wreckage, which still had a whole arm dangling from the wing, were two figures. It was Sircar and his rear gunner. By some unfathomable twist of fate, both men were almost untouched. As the Army pulled Sircar from the wreckage and saw the massacre around him, it is not surprising that his first words were; 'I wish I had also died.'

The IAF men immediately whisked Sircar away from the site of the butchery and back to base. Bouchier issued strict instructions that the incident was not to be discussed, mindful of the terrible sights Sircar had seen, and the terrible guilt he must feel. No matter what was held up in his defence at Karachi, Sircar was found guilty and discharged from the Service.

Bouchier slept very little that night, fighting with his own conscious. Before dawn he decided to see Sircar to express his deep sorrow and huge admiration for him as the leader of this founding group of Indians. Despite the early hour, Sircar had already been spirited away and to Bouchier's deep regret, he never heard about him again. It is interesting that Harjinder obviously wrote in detail about the Sircar incident but there is no mention of his midnight departure. It seems unlikely he would have known nothing, or not thought it worth mentioning unless of course, it was carried out on his instructions or by his own hand.

When it seemed that the gloom hanging over the IAF Airmen could get no worse, they received another blow. They were gathered together and read a signal from Air Headquarters. No Indian Airman was to be allowed to appear for an examination for promotion from Hawai Sepoy 2 (*Airman*) to Hawai Sepoy 1 (*Leading Aircraftman in the RAF*) until after two years of their apprenticeship. Their technical colleagues in the RAF passed out one rank higher again.

Immediately after reading this signal, the Flight Sergeant, flanked by Corporal Bennett and Corporal Sherman, took Harjinder and Ram Singh to one side. Corporal Bennett concluded; 'I know how you must feel about it, but your greatest reward is that you have formed a habit of working hard.'

Harjinder's reaction?

'Our reward, my eye! Who cares about our hard work?'

However, as the years rolled by, he often recollected the consolation offered that day.

'There is something in it; because I have felt rewarded. I have met people of all types and temperaments who were my superior officers; they have all yielded to one common treatment; hard work. So I have always passed on this panacea of all Service ills to my subordinates, and in fact, I have never failed to see the fruits thereof in those who practise it.'

The future of the IAF was in the balance. However, Bouchier had other ideas, and he decided to go on the offensive to move things along in his little command. He knew that the future of the IAF depended on progression, and so it would only be a few weeks later, on 7th February 1934, when he called Ram Singh, Malik, and Harjinder into his office. Harjinder could not believe his ears. He was resigned to the idea that the Indians would be held down to satisfy the blinkered senior officers in Delhi and in the UK, but Bouchier had just announced their appointment as Hawai Naiks (*Corporals*). OK, it was as acting Hawai Naiks, meaning, there was no additional pay, but Bouchier was publicly fighting the system. He also offered some advice as he handed the stripes out to the two new Naiks; 'From this moment on, you are no longer privates, but officers, albeit non-commissioned. Your responsibilities are greater; that is, the handling

of men. An equivalent of this rank is a Corporal in the RAF, which is a
high rank. Your loyalty to the Service should be unquestionable. In case
of mutiny, or the disobedience of orders, you have to do your utmost to
put an end to it before anything serious happens. If you do not take steps
to inform your superiors as soon as you hear about it, you will be punished
more severely than the mutineers. I have to give you this additional
advice also: In India, religion is practised in commercialised form, you
use it whenever it is to your advantage. For you, it must henceforward be
different. You should set such a good example to the men that they should
never feel that you are partial to your co-religionists. As a matter of fact,
in case you have to choose between two men, one of whom happens to be
your co-practitioner favour the other man. This may sound odd, but you
would be more likely to see that justice is being done.'

Harjinder saw this as sound advice from Bouchier, reasoning; 'Too
many Indians are prone to place religious fanaticism high in their order
of values.'

A few days later Corporal Harjinder Singh and team were in Hyderabad
for further Army Cooperation exercises when just those very religious
matters raised their heads. The IAF personnel were ridiculed by both the
Hindus and Muslims serving in the Army, because in the IAF messes,
they observed no religious rites, and drank water from a common source.
According to the Muslims that made them Kafirs, and the Hindus thought
they were Christians. Harjinder could find no way around this hostility,
and elected not to fight this battle against his own countrymen; one battle
at a time.

The trip to Hyderabad was also to prove humiliating for Harjinder as
he tried to exert his authority as Corporal for the first time. One afternoon,
when catching the transport returning from the aerodrome, he noticed a
British Leading Aircraftsman (*and so junior to him in rank*) sitting in the
front seat of a truck, next to the driver. Harjinder told him to get down
and sit in the back of the truck. This he did after much grumbling under
his breath. When they had driven about half a mile he saw a Jamadar (*an
Indian Army Officer of the most junior rank*) from the Jat Regiment walking
towards his Regimental Lines, having just posted guards on the IAF
aircraft. The vehicle was stopped and a lift kindly offered. He accepted,
and silently climbed in with Harjinder. The completely ingrained belief
that no Indian could hold rank in the Air Force was evident when this
Jamadar arrived at his destination. He said not a word to Harjinder but

walked to the rear of the wagon to salute the British airman saying; 'Sahib, thank you very much.'

The British airman was all smiles, glancing at Harjinder to ensure that the humiliation was driven home.

By March 1934, all had returned to Karachi after a successful exercise in Hyderabad, restoring their pride in some small part. On the 8th, once again, the Commander-in-Chief of India, Air, Air Marshal Sir John Steele, inspected the Karachi Aircraft Depot. This time it was not to continue the chess game over the furniture. He was to make it absolutely clear what he felt about this IAF project. He came over to 'A' Flight's hangar at 11 am and, at a time when the embryonic IAF needed motivation and encouragement, delivered what must stand as the most ill-conceived speech. True, the failures of two individuals caused two terrible incidents, but let us not forget that aviation at this time, especially in the military, was a dangerous place, and crashes were quite the norm. The gory nature of Sircar's crash made it stand out, but in terms of their aircraft losses the IAF were no worse than their brothers in the RAF. With morale at an all-time low, they looked to those in power to guide the ship through stormy times, but Sir John's speech to all the Indian Air Force Officers and Airmen only demonstrated his desire to see an end to what he considered an abomination.

'I am going to give you a straight talk.

We knew fully well that Indians will not be able to fly and maintain military aeroplanes. It is a man's job; and all you have done is to bring the greatest disgrace on yourselves. You are incapable of paying attention to details, a most essential feature of military aviation. I, therefore, intend to disband the so-called Indian Air Force. So be prepared for the shock.'

Long after the Chief had stopped talking, and taken his leave, the Officers and Airmen continued to stand, stunned, looking straight ahead. It was the young Pilot Officer Mukerjee who moved first and signalled for Harjinder to join him in one corner of the hangar. In whispered tones he said; 'We have been expecting this. No one wants to part with his bread and butter. The RAF in India would not like us to progress, because then, they would have to lose their jobs and go back. You know that we, the pilots, are not risking our necks just for the pay we get. We, for our part, know that the Airmen are not out here for the meagre forty-five rupees per month, which is the equivalent of a bearer's pay. We must continue to fight for our cause. Otherwise, there will never be an Indian Air Force. It is sad that we have had this accident and brought disgrace upon ourselves because of one pilot's error. But we will fight on to retrieve our good name.'

Mukerjee seemed to have hit the nail on the head. For Harjinder, it was inspiring words from this youngster, because he knew that as far as the Airmen were concerned, they were determined to suffer, if required, but never give in. To have one of the pilots openly state that they all felt the same way, renewed their faith and determination. Sir John would not bring them down. His speech had the opposite from the desired effect. They all vowed to double their efforts to make sure the IAF would be known for only the right reasons.

With morale at an all-time low, and the powers that be looking down carefully, watching the progress of this tiny Flight of 200 personnel, you would think that the men would put themselves beyond criticism; however, not all seemed to understand as Mukerjee and Harjinder did. One day, when Flying Officer Mukerjee was on duty as Orderly Officer, and Harjinder the Orderly NCO, they went to the dining hall and saw Apprentice Misra sitting at the dining table dressed in a dhoti. Mukerjee asked him why he was not dressed properly for dinner. Misra looked up and casually replied that he was. Harjinder stepped in and told Misra to shut up, stand to attention, and behave, or he would be put under arrest. Misra, who had been studying the law before joining the IAF as Wireless Operator Mechanic, replied again, that he was dressed properly and pointed towards the notice board where instructions for dress were written down. Mukerjee and Harjinder were stunned. The instructions were very clear and they had always seen Airmen and apprentices wear slacks and shirts with long sleeves, no other dress being permissible. Groaning inwardly, Harjinder advised the Orderly Officer to place him under open arrest.

The next day Apprentice Misra was produced before Flight Lieutenant Bouchier, escorted in by Harjinder. As they stood to attention outside the Bouchier's office, Harjinder noticed that Misra was carrying a big book under his arm. He told Misra nothing could be carried when on a charge, but in reply, he said it was his defence document. Now of all times Misra was looking for a fight.

When Misra was marched in before the Commanding Officer by Flight Sergeant Hill, Mukerjee gave his evidence. When Misra was asked by Bouchier whether he had anything to say in his defence, he replied; 'Sir, I was properly dressed according to Standing Orders. The order states that Airmen will be dressed in pants and shirts.'

Brandishing the book he announced, 'According to the Oxford Dictionary, a pant is a loose garment worn round the body and I was wearing a dhoti, which is a loose garment and it was round my body at the time of dinner. I am not guilty.'

Flight Lieutenant Bouchier looked as though he would burst a blood vessel. Pressure was mounting on the IAF Flight from above, and here was an airman deliberately causing a conflict. He banged the table with his fist with such force that ink spilt over from the bottle, the books fell down from the book stand, and his own solar hat jumped up on his head. He roared; 'Shut up! You Indians are undisciplined by nature. That is why people like me are here and that is why British troops have to be here. You are great theoreticians, great philosophers, but that is all. You are no good for anything else. I am determined to teach you discipline. You are remanded to the Station Commander.'

Harjinder felt like murdering Misra, feeling that this trainee lawyer had brought great disgrace on them all, just as Sir John had said. He felt that all their work towards garnering the respect of their superiors was all for naught.

The uphill struggle was being made harder by Misra deciding to take a stand on something that Harjinder thought went with the territory once you sign up to be in a military unit.

Harjinder felt no sympathy two days later, when Misra was tried by Wing Commander Whitelock, awarded 56 days detention, and handed over to the Baluch Regiment for the carrying out of the sentence. The Baluchis were a hardy and tough lot of soldiers, and brooked no nonsense from anyone. Whether or not it was because so many of their Regiment had died at the hands of Sircar, or it was their standard treatment, they certainly gave it to Misra. Misra was a new man when he came out of dock, jumping up at every order given. However, those around him continued to see him as a hopeless case and he was discharged at the end of May, as an 'undesirable'. His IAF career was at an end.

Another apprentice, a Pathan, was also awarded detention for 28 days with the Baluchis, although Harjinder does not specify his misdemeanour. On his return, he was so terrified, that he would not even pass by the side of the Guard Room. There must have been something special laid out for him by the Baluchis, because shortly thereafter, he committed suicide by jumping into the river.

On 11th May 1934, it was Harjinder's colleague and friend, Ram Singh, who was called to appear before the Commanding Officer on the charges of entering the Station Canteen and ordering a bottle of beer. Again, Harjinder was the escort.

Bouchier, after hearing the charge, desperately tried to be sympathetic to Ram Singh, an engineer for whom he had great respect. He asked the RAF Corporal accompanying him; 'Do you realise that the man you have placed on charge is a NCO as well? If your charge is proved false, I shall see to it that you lose your stripes. What proof have you that the rupee which Acting Hawai Naik Ram Singh gave to the man at the canteen counter was not meant for purchase of a bar of chocolate?'

The British Corporal saw which way the wind was blowing now and tried to assist with matters by replying; 'Sir, I am not sure. It could be. I am sorry I have done this, and I shall never touch any Indian NCO again.'

Bouchier roared and said; 'I will excuse nobody.'

He then turned to Ram Singh, and asked; 'What have you to say?', expecting he would take the hint and fall in line. On the contrary, Ram Singh said, 'To tell you the truth, Sir, the rupee was in fact meant for a bottle of beer.'

Ram Singh believed in telling the truth!

Bouchier slumped in his chair, exasperated; partly because of Ram Singh's folly, but mostly because his efforts to support his own man had been cast to the winds. His verdict; 'Then you shall lose your stripes.'

31st May 1934 was written into Harjinder's diary as the most important day in his life. He was married. Who would arrange for their daughter to marry a man who is one of the lowest of the low in military? A man serving in a military unit that might not survive the next year. A man, who in this job, seems to have everything placed in his way to stop him progressing any further. The parents of Beant Kaur had clearly seen that there was something special about this man. They saw somebody who was going to achieve, no matter what obstacles were to overcome. It was certainly controversial, and Beant Kaur's brother, who was a respected Surgeon, was never told she was marrying a Hawai Corporal in this experimental Air Force. The future Mrs Harjinder Singh was every bit the match for the determined and driven Harjinder; 'My wife who played an important role in my career is not one of the types who can be termed as modern, but has proved to be more than a match for the ultra-modern. She shared my Service Life as if she was a member of the IAF. She helped me in my service life, first of all by non-participation in other women's gossip. Secondly, she never showed snobbery to the wives of the even junior-most servicemen in any of the units where we were posted. However, her greatest contribution was the way she changed her standard of living to suit that of mine. She came from a very well-to-do family.'

In those early days the truth was kept from her family. Harjinder also reveals in his diaries that he kept his status from his own family until 1938. Such was the lack of respect for the position he held.

12th June 1934 and the newlyweds were away on leave. In the middle of this blissful existence, a telegram arrived from Bouchier recalling him to duty. In a beautiful piece of understatement Harjinder writes in his diary that he 'was quite put out'.

The Commanding Officer's Flight Sergeant knew that the leave was because of the marriage, and since no war was on, Harjinder puzzled over Boucher's reasons for summoning him...

On arrival back at Karachi, he was rushed in to see Flight Lieutenant Bouchier. The long, sad, face told a story. Bouchier began by warning Harjinder that this could be the last leave under his command, because a serious breach of discipline had occurred. It so happened that on the evening of 9th June two new apprentices named Lorin Chand, an Electrician under training, and Iqbal Muhammad, a Wireless Operator, had decided to go to the pictures in Karachi and therefore had ordered early dinner in Mess. The dinner was served only fifteen minutes earlier than the usual time, at 6.30 pm. However, when the British NCO of the week came on his rounds and saw the two eating their dinner outside the allocated time, he took their plates away from them and threw them on the floor. The two trainees walked away from the table in utter fury. They waited till the following afternoon and saw this NCO taking a shower. They tiptoed up to the hook where his clothes were hanging and whisked them away to the nearest bushes. If they had stopped here, it would have made a statement, and in a humorous way, but the insult from the previous day was felt more deeply than that. When he appeared dripping from the shower and bemused by his missing clothes, he was set upon and beaten until he became unconscious and had to be taken to the hospital.

For beating this naked man half to death, Iqbal and Lorin Chand each received 56 days detention and were dismissed from the Service. The damage to the IAF reputation was obvious, and it played ever more into Sir John's hands.

Bouchier was very generous in his praise of Harjinder's leadership and the example he set for the men. No doubt, he wanted to boost Harjinder's morale before he faced his men. Bouchier had picked up on the mood, and sure enough, as Harjinder went back to his bunk, there were many jubilant visitors who were frank enough to describe Lorin and Iqbal as the heroes of the episode and glorify their deeds. Harjinder strode through the men's living area. He made sure his big frame and booming voice were perceived by all. Harjinder naturally commanded attention when he walked into a room so he didn't need to resort to threats, but they all heeded the unuttered words that they were to fall back into line and move forward. They were fighting for their very existence, and Harjinder expected each and every man to do his part.

After the constant attack on their position, and the ever-hostile reception from above, and sometimes even from within, there was a ray of hope on 20th September. Unexpectedly, the first publicity for the IAF appeared in the form of an article in the Daily Gazette. Albeit very factual, there were cheers and claps from the Airmen when Harjinder read it out. It said:

'Indian Air Force: A Year's Encouraging Progress
    A summary of important matters connected with the Defence Services in India during the year 1933-34 published by the Army Department states that the first unit of the Indian Air Force, which was formed at Karachi on the 1st April 1933, consisted of a nucleus of Squadron Headquarters and one complete Flight of four aircraft. The necessary minimum number of British Officers and Airmen has been attached to the unit from its formation, and during the year under review, the Flight was trained in Army cooperation duties and took part in the Sind Independent Brigade exercises.
    During the year, four cadets were gazetted into the General Duties Branch after completing a two year course at the RAF College, Cranwell. One of these was posted to the Indian Air Force for duty after a period of attachment to a RAF unit in England, and the remaining three were still in England. Owing to an unfortunate flying accident in September 1933, two officers out of the five previously commissioned were killed.

The position on the 31st March 1934, was that four Indian Officers of the General Duties Branch and one of the Stores Branch were serving with the Force, and three officers were attached to the Royal Air Force units in England.

The training of apprentice mechanics and other classes of Airmen proceeded, and nearly 60 Airmen were on the strength of the First Squadron at the close of the period under review.'

It seemed as if someone knew that they existed, something they themselves had often doubted.

The article buoyed everyone's spirits, and their morale was raised even further in November, when they took part in further exercises with the Army. They were back to practicing proper operational duties. They went back to the 'extreme fishing' of plucking the messages from the Army, placed inside the leather bag with streamers of coloured ribbons. The pilots loved the thrill of bringing their imposing machines down to 5 feet, skimming across the ground. The Army couldn't help but be impressed to see these aircraft in such close quarters, and to see the Air Force at work. During these joint exercises, another big event in Harjinder's life, and the future of the IAF, happened on the 10th November. There was a new addition to the Flight who stepped straight into this low-level training with ease. It was Pilot Officer K.K. 'Jumbo' Majumdar. When Harjinder met him for the first time, he refused to believe Majumdar was Bengali by birth, because he certainly didn't look one. Firstly, he was as fair-skinned as a European; he was tall and well-built, with classical Greek features. He was a very engaging personality, and all took an instant liking to him. He looked every inch a leader of men, and was to prove a massive influence in the coming years, making history at every turn. Harjinder had just met his soul-mate.

Things may have been taking an upward turn, but the constant fight finally proved too much for Ranjit on 17th December. He was the senior-most Wireless Operator Mechanic who had trained in Mechanical and Electrical Engineering for five years in college with Harjinder. It would be a very, very, long time before they could train another such man, and it would be difficult to find another technician of his calibre. However, he had never really been inclined to the Service, and since the day he first put on the uniform, he had been cursing Harjinder for 'conning him' into the IAF. Some used the excuse of failing their trade test to get out of the military, but Ranjit was too proud to do that. He had proved that he was more than capable, but this life in the IAF was not for him. His exit was manufactured by replacing the sputum of a TB patient with his own during his medical, and by bribing the medical orderly. After his discharge, Harjinder was left with only two former class fellows.

Ranjit was gone, and the pin-prick attacks from the RAF personnel continued. In mid-December 1934, Harjinder went into the Orderly Room to get the Christmas application form for the leave due to commence from the next day onwards. After knocking on the door he entered, to be faced with a very angry Corporal Reed, red in the face, demanding to know why he had entered the Corporal's Room. Harjinder pointed at his sleeve and said; 'Please do not forget that I have the same number of stripes as you have.'

Spittle flew from his mouth as he replied, 'I do not care about these Japanese stripes; Get out.'

Harjinder left the Orderly Room with 'fire raging in my heart' and when he saw Flight Sergeant Hill, he told him of the incident, adding that he would not like to keep these 'Japanese stripes'. Corporal Reed was summoned by Flight Sergeant Hill and ticked off, but the Corporal still had his revenge. On leaving the hangar he met Harjinder again and said; 'Sorry you will have no leave for the holidays. You have been detailed as Orderly NCO during Christmas.'

Flight Sergeant Hill called Harjinder to the Senior NCOs' Mess. He had learnt of Harjinder's fate too late, but tried to pacify him by saying that he would deal with Corporal Reed after the holidays. In the meantime, Harjinder was stuck on the base, unable to leave whilst all others departed on leave, or to seek other interests in Karachi.

The new year of 1935 began, but with the departure of an old friend and mentor. Warrant Officer H.E. Newing, was promoted to officer rank and was to take over a Wing at the Engineering Training School in Halton, UK. When he was due to sail for England, the Airmen who were trained by him took the long road trip to see him off on board the ship – such was the warmth they felt for this man. Finally, the time came for the Airmen to leave the ship, but Newing called Harjinder aside and said; 'You know about the report which I showed you. You have improved yourself because I told you about your weakness. Please remember two things in life: Firstly, never back up anyone excepting on his merits; and secondly, never leave off using your hands, even if you get a Commission. Remember how I have been at it, even though I was a Warrant Officer.'

Harjinder thanked him and promised him to remember his advice always. Looking back many years later, he thought; 'Luckily for me, I kept my promise.'

A few days later, on 22nd January 1935, the first group of Indian Engineers were called to carry out the trade test of a Leading Aircraftman (LAC). Harjinder was an acting Naik (Corporal), with Ram Singh climbing to the dizzy heights of acting Naik, before he lost it over his 'Beer Folly'. All were still Sepoys, basic Airmen until they passed the LAC test. They had been told different things by different people. Some had doubted that they would ever be allowed to take the exams, but suddenly, here they were. They had waited for this day with great expectation, on edge from the moment they knew the chance was theirs to take. Harjinder confesses in his diary that he had never been so worried before an examination, not even at his college exams. Harjinder was still a Metal Rigger, so the practical test required from him involved a very intricate drawing of a metal fitting, which had to be developed, and then manufactured in under eight hours. Newling had turned Harjinder from a theoretical engineer into a practical one, and after the hours and hours of additional work, he was fully confident. Knowing that he was more than capable of this task, he took his time in the calculations, and then carried out trial bendings on a piece of 16-gauge metal to make sure.

In the meantime, Warrant Officer Nicholas, the invigilator, came prowling, and on seeing what he viewed as lack of progress from Harjinder, he sneered sarcastically; 'Naik, at this rate you will take a full week to finish your job. Look at the others. They are far ahead of you.'

Harjinder politely informed him that his instructor had warned him never to hurry a job on an aircraft. Harjinder viewed it better to hand over a 100 per cent correct, if unfinished job, rather than a complete, but sub-standard, finished article. Nicholas chuckled and left, looking forward to his gloating for later.

The job was finished an hour ahead of time because after the trial bend, and the use of Harjinder's own magic box of self-made tools, it was a piece of cake. He was proud of his final product and took pleasure in seeing Nicholas's disappointed face.

The next day, the results were in. Naturally, the examiners could find no fault, and were more than satisfied. As a result Malik, Ram Singh and

Harjinder became the first IAF LAC's. Hearts soared and the seeds of hope for a future, for themselves and for the IAF, finally started to germinate.

The start of 1935 seemed to provide a new outlook, brushing away the gloom of the previous year. In February 1935 training was picking up pace, with something definite in the offing. Following the damning speech by Sir John Steele, Bouchier had been almost begging the 'powers that be' to let the IAF go operational over the lawless North-West Frontier. It now seemed those 'powers that be' did, indeed, have plans for 'A' Flight IAF. Harjinder was flying more frequently with his pilots, who were focusing increasingly on target practice, by using the front gun at ground targets. These were targets on the ground, made by Harjinder out of boards painted in black circles against a white background. Harjinder was responsible for Wapiti K-1297, and it was in this aircraft that he flew his gunnery practice. Standing in the back with his monkey chain attached, he held on firmly to the cockpit edge, until his knuckles were white, as the Wapiti dived down with an ever-increasing hum from the wires and blast of airflow into his cockpit. When the pilot thumbed the gun button, the aircraft shuddered and shook with excitement as it spat fire from the front. Tiny fountains of dirt followed the progress of the bullets as they walked along the scrub floor and onto the painted target. Then the control column was wrenched back to send the plane climbing with a force that seemed to be trying to push Harjinder through the floor. The Wapiti seemed to resent this manoeuvring, the fabric on the wings looked as though it was going to warp, twist, and wrinkle, while the wires between the wings shrieked and sang out. The speed dropped so quickly that the slats on the front of the wing popped out, indicating to Harjinder they were close to stalling and spinning. A total assault on the senses with joy, fear and pride all tumbling together.

The news just got better and better, when the master of motivational speaking, and clearly the main dissenter of the IAF, Sir John Steel, moved out of his position. On 8th March 1935, his replacement, the new Air Commander-in-Chief, India, Air Vice-Marshal Sir Edgar Ludlow-Hewitt (*possibly the officer with the longest calling card in India!*) inspected the Aircraft Repair Depot, Karachi. Before his arrival, Flight Lieutenant Bouchier carried out a rehearsal in the hangar. When he came to Harjinder standing proudly to attention alongside Bouchier's own aircraft he said; 'I have been writing to Air HQ for the last year and a half about your promotion to substantive Hawai Naik (*from acting Corporal to actual Corporal*), but they have turned a deaf ear. Today is our chance. When the Commander-in-Chief comes to you, he will ask you a number of questions. Speak freely to him and look him in the eye when answering.'

Bouchier knew the injustices which were being meted out to the Indian members of 'A' Flight, and had been campaigning to for some sort of parity with their colleagues in the RAF. Now the boss was going to hear it direct from the horse's mouth, and Harjinder wrote about the meeting in his diary; 'Sir Edgar Ludlow-Hewitt arrived at 11.30 am. When he approached my aircraft, Bouchier whispered something in his ear. Among other questions, the Air Vice-Marshal asked me what my age was, to which I replied that I was twenty-eight. He then asked what I had done before joining the Service. I replied that I had been at College for five years. He then asked: "What were you doing there?" I said, "Studying Engineering, Sir." This must have bewildered him, because he was used to the RAF Halton School and the uneducated Airmen of the RAF. Anyway, he seemed to have been pleased, and I relaxed.'

In the past, it had seemed that very few beyond the Flight were aware of the calibre of this small unit that made up the entire IAF. Only through direct contact was the information filtering up the chain of command. However, Sir Edgar's visit was for a reason, and what he saw must have impressed him. He spoke with Flight Lieutenant Bouchier at length. For his part, Bouchier, the committed driving force behind the IAF, suggested an expansion of the IAF. His 'A' Flight was a well-trained army cooperation unit and should be moved to one of the Frontier stations under Bouchier's Second-in-Command, Flight Lieutenant Philip Haynes, to start operations. Furthermore, he had enough personnel, if the aircraft could be found, to form a 'B' Flight to take over 'A' Flight's accommodation at Karachi. Bouchier's earlier request on this theme had been deemed 'too quick' by Sir John Steel – unsurprisingly. Now, Sir Edgar's plans for the fledgling Air Force were inspirational to the IAF CO; 'Bouchier, I want you to know that I have been told all about your efforts to make a success of the Indian Air Force, in spite of the difficulties and lack of support you have been up against. I want to thank you, and to assure you that from now on, you will receive, from me, 100 per cent support.'

These words could not have been more different from those of Sir John Steel a year earlier. When in retirement, Bouchier was to meet with Sir John Steel and Wing Commander Whitelock at the Farnbourgh air show and at the RAF club in Piccadilly, London, he was more than surprised, and most irked, with the use of the pronoun 'we', when both remarked; 'Bouchier, what a fine job we made of the Indian Air Force.' There had been no 'we', just him and his musketeers, as he subsequently referred to Mukererjee, Aspy Engineer, Awan and Harjinder.

However, Sir Edgar was from a different mould and his words were transformed into actions. 'A' Flight, No. 1 Squadron, Indian Air Force was going operational over Afghanistan, and in the infamous North-West Frontier Province, and Harjinder couldn't be happier. In their early days, death had come to visit the IAF.

In military aviation, and especially when flying combat missions, death is a constant companion as they were to discover.

Five

The North-West Frontier Province

'This achievement is all due to the efforts of the Airmen.'

Afghanistan, Peshawar, the Khyber Pass; geographical names that have a long history of conflict, linked to the warring tribes like the Wazirs, the Mahsuds, the Mohmands, the Yusufzais, the Afridis, and so many, many tribes and sub-tribes. As the Tiger Moth appears live on TV in 2012, troops from many nations have their soldiers in the area, fighting to try and attain some stability in the region, but it seems nobody ever wants to learn from history. It is sobering to look back to April 1936 and seeing that, except differences in technology, very little has changed. The brown, rugged, inhospitable terrain, slashed with canyons, valleys and gullies, is no different today than it was then. In both 2012 and 1936, the soldiers have boots on the ground, but don't actually control the fields, the tracks, and the villages around them. They use small fortresses as bases, for their own protection, venturing out on missions to "show their face" or track down reports of the enemy. For much of the time, it is chasing shadows. Aviation is their biggest advantage over the tribesmen who fight these invaders in their land, as they have done before, and will continue to do so, caring not for the nationality facing them. Aviation in 2012 is using unmanned aircraft alongside the high tech jets to take on the AK47 rifles. In 1936, it was with the fabric covered biplanes, with two sets of eyeballs taking on the ancient matchlock guns called 'jezails,' deadly accurate even over long ranges.

As the newly-formed IAF arrived to take their part in the history of the North-West Frontier, they stepped straight into an organised uprising against the British Empire. In the autumn of 1936, a serious rebellion broke out in North Waziristan calling for large-scale operations by the Army and the Air Force. At its height, as many as 50,000 troops were required in an attempt to swamp this remote border area and quell the uprising, started by a charismatic tribal leader called the Fakir of Ipi.

Any military unit that has spent years preparing to fight has an air of excitement and anticipation when they are finally given the green light. It is not the desire to fight and to kill, but a desire to put into practice the months, and years, of hard training; to test one's self, and one's team. Here with the IAF, we had an interesting situation, possibly not seen ever before or since. Briefly, an entire Air Force was being sent into operations; all 4 aircraft of it! If this whole Air Force was going into operations, then perhaps it was be time to enlarge this force. True, due to two isolated examples of pilot error, there had been 2 Wapitis lost, and a disproportionate death toll linked to it. However, the three years of training had produced a good military unit, and Flight Lieutenant Bouchier's proposal had found somebody, in Sir Edgar Ludlow-Hewitt, to drive it forward. Now was the time to double the size of the IAF. Not as grand as it first sounds, when it only means taking four more Wapitis from the RAF to form another Flight, but the significance was not lost on the IAF. They were now being viewed as a success; they had survived Sir John Steel, they had survived the Sircar crash. As 'A' Flight, Indian Air Force, left Karachi, 'B' Flight was being formed in its place soon after their departure.

The growth of the IAF and the move of 'A' Flight into the operation saw the departure of Flight Lieutenant Bouchier, the 'Father of the IAF'. Sir Edgar had asked him to stay for a further two years, but Bouchier wanted to be reunited with his family. His wife and son had been with him for his first year in India as he flew a desk around the corridors of Delhi, but sickness had forced them to return to Britain, and he wanted to end the three and a half years of loneliness. For his historic role in India he was promoted to Squadron Leader, and awarded the OBE. He wrote 'I knew it would always have a special significance for me, and as the ship chugged along, taking me further away from the India I loved, I realised I was leaving behind a part of my heart there forever.'

He had performed a seemingly impossible job under difficult circumstances, fighting his own Headquarters every step of the way, until Sir Edgar arrived. The IAF's loss was the RAF's gain. He was to command a fighter station in the Battle of Britain, plan and supervise the entire fighter cover operation for the D-Day landings, accept the initial surrender of the Japanese in Burma, and to finish his military career as Air Vice-Marshal Sir Cecil Bouchier.

He was to meet Harjinder again in 1959, after which he wrote him a very emotional letter including his thoughts on those early days, 'The Indian Air Force is what it is today because of one thing only; the imagination, the courage, and the great loyalty of the first little pioneer band of Indian Officers and men, for they were the salt of the earth; they have built up a great fighting Service, and I am proud to have been associated with this wonderful achievement, if only for a little while.'

At last the day came, in the first week of April 1936, when 'A' Flight was placed on a combat footing and moved from Drigh Road, Karachi, to Peshawar, capital of the North-West Frontier Province. Harjinder was busied in getting his personal Wapiti into perfect condition. He checked on how the other three aircraft were coming along in their preparations, and finally, that the mountain of ground equipment was all present and correct. This was the IAF's big chance, they had to perform well to prove to the wider authorities that all the earlier incidents were behind them. The four Wapitis rolled down Karachi's aerodrome and took to the hazy sky, immediately moving into close formation with each other. It was done more for a suitable farewell than any operational need. However, Harjinder was not in the rear cockpit of his aircraft. He was the Corporal in-charge of moving the ground party and getting all his men through the big bad world out there. It was the first time they had all moved as a unit into the outside world, in uniform, and the train was the main method of transport. Don't think of the Airmen entering their train carriage in the perfect blue uniforms of the 2012 IAF, with striking white belts and putties. After three years, there were still no proper dress regulations, so, when not in their work overalls, they had to put on army-type dress; closed-collar khaki tunics, boots and khaki putties, and a kulla with a turban. They resented this imitation of the army dress, because they used to look upon themselves as being a cut above the 'uneducated Army soldiers'. They felt thoroughly ashamed, and to add to their humiliation, they were made to travel Third Class, whereas the British Airmen of the same rank in the RAF, travelled Second. They were left in no doubt that they were seen as 3rd class citizens by the majority.

With the boys from Madras and Bengal, unable to speak Hindi, they started the tradition of speaking English among themselves, something which has continued to the present day. Despite the use of English, to the public eye, they were Sepoys of the Army. The uniform was a motley collection, making them look like a ragtag bunch, and not the educated section of the newest military unit in India. Harjinder's team locked themselves into the 3rd class compartment at Karachi, and didn't venture out until after dark. They especially shunned Lahore Railway Station in case any of their acquaintances were on the platform! Regulations forbade changing into civilian clothes and so Harjinder never forgot the dismal feeling he experienced on this first journey, a stark reminder of how far they had still to travel in the minds of the military, the politicians, and the Indian public. However, this move to Peshawar from Karachi gave them the feeling of bidding farewell to their nursery.

At Peshawar, they jumped aboard the sand coloured, camouflaged Crossley trucks, with the red, white and blue RAF roundels on the side standing out from the camouflage. They bumped into base only to receive a slap in the face. They were instantly rechristened 'D' Flight of No. 20 Squadron, RAF. Even though on paper they continued to retain their identity as 'A' Flight of No. 1 Squadron, IAF, it seemed an insult to the new Air Force to be temporarily swallowed up, just when they intended to make a statement. Perhaps this was somewhat inevitable, given that this fledgling Air Force only had four aircraft. This only temporarily dented the technicians' excitement. With the journey out of the way, they were now going to prove themselves in the largest, swirling cauldron of tension in the region.

Peshawar was the capital of the North-West Frontier Province, a teeming city, with large, tree-lined areas and roads with many European style buildings. A few miles North, the plain was splintered by the enormous mountains thrust upwards into the cloudless sky, forming the border between this Province and Afghanistan. The Peshawar plain narrowed until it ended at the entrance to the most famous of mountain passes; The Khyber Pass. These Himalayan foothills were inhabited by the Mohmand tribes. Beyond the peaks, was Chinese Turkestan and the 'roof of the world'. Flying was restricted to two routes, both followed the gorge of the River Indus among the 20,000 feet peaks. A desolate and awe-inspiring place, but in terms of the Frontier, it was relatively friendly.

To the South-West, the central area was less striking but still mountainous, crisscrossed with deep valleys and dried up river beds. This region was the Tirah, peopled by the Afridis, the most lawless in the area, with a reputation for cruelty. An unplanned landing here was a fearsome prospect, not least because their speciality was removing a man's most treasured body parts and stuffing them into his mouth, after, usually, he had been flayed alive. This led to all crews carrying a 'Goolie Chit' offering a five thousand rupee reward to the Afridis if the aircrew were returned intact!

It certainly worked.

When Flight Lieutenant Anderson crashed a RAF Wapiti here, he was dragged from the wreck by the Afridis. The Goolie Chit was read and a string charpoy constructed. With a broken leg the pilot endured the terrible 70 mile journey to Peshawar without any medical treatment. The men received their reward, but so impressed were they by the pilot's strength of character, that they sent a deputation to the hospital every week to enquire about his progress; the element of chivalry in warfare still existed then!

To the South, was the base of Kohat, and beyond, to Waziristan, home to the infamous Faqir of Ipi. For 40 years he was the scourge of the British, constantly hunted and hounded. He knew his land, and he knew how to use it. The British never caught him. He died peacefully of old age in his cave long after the British had left India, and this area became Pakistan.

The first job for rear gunners like Harjinder was to accompany their pilots on flying visits to the outlying emergency landing grounds. These were no more than strips of ground, cleared of rocks and boulders. They were to familiarise themselves with the landing grounds, to check the supplies that were held there, to show their presence to the tribes of the area, and to give a morale boost to the poor policemen stationed in these remote areas. There were no two landing strips the same; varying in size, shape, gradient and surface. Some were perched on hill sides, some on the floor of a deep, steep-sided valley, and the occasional one out on the wide open plain. They were normally guarded by a chowkidar (*watchman*), small, fierce-looking men with black beards, white robes, yellow turbans, an ancient rifle slung over the shoulder and a bandolier of bullets across their chest; Kipling's vision of an Indian tribesman. Their enormous wooden staff was used to drive his goats away before the landing aircraft touched down!

Sometimes, the landing grounds were viewed from the air as the Wapiti droned overhead, but often, the personal touch was required. A flare was fired from the Verey flare pistol to signal their intent. The chowkidar would get to work with his staff. If there was a police post nearby, then they too, would come flooding out for the spectacle of the big silver bird, raising a cloud of dust as it dropped to the ground. Often, they had to remove the goalposts that were used to put the open area to better use in the absence of aircraft. More often than not, the pilot would keep the engine running when he landed. The Jupiter engine in the Wapiti had the utmost reliability when it rumbled away in the air but it was a monster to start when it was hot. After landing, the pilot would take his Wapiti for a little trundle around the landing site perimeter whilst Harjinder would chat with the chowkidar, checking his supplies of fuel and flares. The first time Harjinder dropped into each of these tiny outposts, he was met with the same reaction. The chowkidar's jaw would bounce off the ground when he saw a fellow Indian climb down from his machinegun-toting cockpit. When the Wapiti completed its little sightseeing tour, Harjinder would offer his best wishes to the chowkidar, climb back aboard and reconnect to the monkey chain. The Wapiti would then position into the wind and the pilot would open the throttle. The dust plume would rise around the aircraft, but as the machine accelerated, it would slowly nose out of the dirt cloud, leaving it behind as it steadily climbed heavenwards.

The main task for the Air Force was tribal reconnaissance.

It was rare for the Frontier to be entirely free from trouble for more than a few days at a time. Occasionally, large scale operations were called for, in North Waziristan, for example, where several Army brigades were involved, and as many aircraft as the RAF could muster were called in. However, it was mostly localised trouble from intertribal blood feuds, so the mission for the RAF, and now IAF, was not only to see what the tribes were up to, but to be *seen* by the tribes. The flights would last over three hours in the often turbulent air, causing the rear gunner to bounce of the cockpit floor tugging the monkey chain tight. As they crossed seemingly deserted villages, the inhabitants would come pouring out from their huts to see this projection of British Imperial power. Harjinder would take the Lewis machine gun out of the stowage and fit it onto the ring around the rear cockpit in its firing position. They would fly at 500 feet, low enough so their armoury could be seen, and the unspoken message given out.

Flying low enough to be seen also meant low enough to be shot at. It was not unusual to see a puff of gun smoke from behind a random boulder. One of the rear gunners from RAF's No. 60 Squadron tried to reassure the new IAF gunners by saying, 'Well it's quite common in this area, but they haven't a hope of hitting us. Occasionally a bullet hole is found after these flights, but the old Wapiti can take plenty of those without much damage.'

It would take some time, but an IAF Wapiti crew had the misfortune to prove him wrong...

Remember, even though Harjinder, and the other Airmen spent long hours in the rear cockpit of the Wapiti, this was not their official job. Air Chief Marshal Sir David Lee was a very junior Pilot Officer in North-West Frontier Province at the time, flying the Wapiti. His view of the men in the back seat; 'It was an arduous job for these splendid Airmen as, no sooner were they on the ground after a long and perhaps rough flight, they had to resume their normal tradesmen's duties working on the Wapitis. It was also a great comfort to the pilot to have a skilled technician in the back as an air gunner. They could be invaluable in the event of some technical trouble arising on a remote landing ground; an engine that refused to start, a flat tyre or a tear in the fabric.'

Here, on the Frontier, the RAF Corporals were only too happy to recognise Harjinder and Ram Singh as Corporals when it meant that they could share out their additional duties as Guard Commanders. During these duties, checking that all was well in the various buildings, they both noticed how the RAF personnel wore khaki slacks and tunics in the evenings, whereas the IAF Airmen had to wear the same old boots, putties and shorts they worked in. No clean, smart, clothes to relax in when their work was done. So, on their own initiative, they bought khaki slacks with their own money, and carried out an experiment in dressing like Airmen should dress. In this new evening attire, they felt a greater feeling of belonging, part of a team to be proud of. There was still no thought from HQ of producing an identity for those in the IAF, so again it lay with the men. Later, when they confided their actions to their new Flight Commander, Flight Lieutenant Haynes, he readily agreed to this innovation and the Indian Officers lent them their support. At the end of the summer, when Squadron Leader Hancock, from Drigh Road inspected the Flight, he gave the new dress the thumbs up. That is how slacks come to stay in the IAF as the official dress.

When winter approached, Harjinder persuaded the Airmen to buy
their own warm khaki slacks. At first, they were doubtful whether the
Flight Commander would agree to this, but they took the risk. The day of
reckoning was chosen, and on that fine evening, they all wore the warmer
version of the uniform on guard duty. Nervously, they appeared in what
was effectively a uniform they were making up themselves; something you
just don't do as a military unit.

How was this bold step received by the senior Officers?

Nobody noticed! The worry and careful planning had been
unnecessary. Nothing untoward came to pass, so Harjinder had added
the official winter dress to that of the summer dress. It may seem a minor
point but; 'Our joy knew no bounds because our attempt to shed army
boots and putties had been successful after four years.'

Having shed the image of Indian Army soldiers, they took to the spit
and polish of buttons and boots with an enthusiasm that knew no bounds,
because they wanted to be superior to the RAF in all respects. This motive
to outdo the RAF was the ever-present mainspring of their lives.

The engineers now looked the part, and the Indian pilots were playing
their part. Praise poured in from all directions – from the Army and the
Political Agents. So impressed were they with the IAF Flight (*or is that
D Flight RAF?*), that whenever there was a senior Army Officer to be
conveyed to the Waziristan area, or a Political Agent tasked with a difficult
job, it was the IAF they requested rather than the RAF machines. However,
their choice may also have been influenced by the widely reported incident
of an Army Captain flying in the back of an RAF Wapiti with Flying
Officer Mavor. It was quite normal at the time to take on a few beers
and pink gins in the morning before flying; in the 21st century a criminal
offence! They were flying late in the afternoon up through the mountains
when the RAF pilot felt the call of nature. After fumbling around for
several frantic minutes he gave up trying to find a suitable receptacle and
so had to just do it on the cockpit floor. The relief spread on the pilots face
as the liquid spread through to the rear cockpit. There was a call on the
Gosport voice tube from the Army Captain to report the seeping of liquid
into his cockpit but reassured the pilot by telling him, 'It's all right, it's not
petrol. I've just tasted it!'

Harjinder, master of the understatement writes; 'flying in the
North-West Frontier was not an easy job.'

He soon discovered the treacherous summer weather. Gigantic castles of cumulus cloud would billow upwards, far beyond the height the intrepid aviators reached in their modified Wapiti over the Everest. At the base of these beautiful billowing giants, a black, sinister heart would be mixing up a maelstrom of winds, rain, hail and lightning. They brought in their wake clouds of red dust making it difficult to discern the outlines of the mountains; or tell the ground from the sky. The brownish colour acted like camouflage paint doused on the vista, to deceive the pilots' powers of observation. Furthermore, the weather forecast was at best unreliable, often bordering on the comical. Normal procedure was for the weather to be telephoned from one aerodrome to another by an Airman of the Watch in a disastrous game of Chinese whispers. One day Harjinder received the following weather report that seemed to cover all eventualities except a plague of frogs:

Dust and/or thunderstorm with, or without, precipitations likely; occasionally, temporarily and locally in your area.

Weather was extreme. Flying under the cloud would be turbulent too and carry another hidden danger; the hail. This was not your common and garden pea-sized hailstones. One Wapiti strayed into a hailstorm with the stones the size of pigeons' eggs. They crashed off the metal cowlings around the nose, producing a noise louder than the aircraft's own engine. The windscreen cracked and some of the larger hailstones passed through the fabric on the wings as effectively as any bullet. This was a more effective assault than any tribesman's rifle. 2 minutes amid this absolute chaos left the wings and the fuselage looking like the centrepiece at a blunderbuss convention, the paint had been stripped off the propeller and the wings had 164 holes to be patched up. The engine never missed a beat but the airframe, and the rear gunner now sporting a black eye, looked much the worse for wear. On landing, the sight produced the obvious question; 'Christ Sir, what have you been doing?'

Three months after the IAFs arrival in Peshawar, they carried out a bold social experiment. Flying Officers Mukerjee and Engineer called Harjinder to the pilots' room and said: 'Supposing we were to introduce an inter-community mess. What would be the reaction of the Airmen?'

Harjinder replied; 'If we introduce this new scheme both at "A" Flight here and "B" Flight in Karachi simultaneously, it will work.'

Flying Officer Mukerjee wrote to Pilot Officer 'Jumbo' Majumdar at Karachi and they came to an understanding. The stage was set for what in those days was a daring experiment for the Indian Armed Forces. The officers were warned by the RAF that in case the scheme misfired, the official wrath would come down on their heads like a ton of bricks. They took the responsibility with a smile, and their men never gave them cause to regret it.

It was announced in the barracks that 'B' Flight at Drigh Road had already started a common mess. The only food which was cooked separately was the meat, jhatka and halal for Hindus and Muslims respectively. On the same day, a similar announcement was made at Karachi. Only two men rejected the idea. They were told they could draw their dry rations and cook for themselves. Thereafter, there was no resistance; the scheme worked in both Flights.

Little does the present generation realise the significance of the remarkable foresight shown by the two young IAF Officers. It would take the Indian Army another decade to get anywhere close to this pioneering idea. It gave the RAF a good impression about the IAF, and belied the propaganda spread against the Indian people, at least in the RAF circles. Unfortunately, it gave them a few headaches when they had to actually lodge and board with the change-resistant Army Units. The shock and horror from the Army Ranks when they saw them all not only dining together on the same table, but actually eating the same food cooked by the same cook! The IAF would often be shunned like plague victims. At one station, the Army Sepoys broke the water chatties because Hindus and Muslims had drunk out of the same vessel!

On 10th August, the Flight had their first 'heavy landing', in which slight damage was done to Wapiti K-1290. Pilot Officer Narendra, came in to land and bounced. Not uncommon when flying an aircraft with a tail-wheel, but he failed to open up the engine in time to recover the situation and offer the aircraft gently to the ground again. Instead, the aircraft hung a few feet in the air with the speed decaying away. The wings could hold the lift no more and stalled, dropping the Wapiti from a moderate height. The damage was minor; the skid tube was bent and the frame was slightly dented. Harjinder knew they could have repaired the aircraft within a few hours but RAF procedure had to be followed. It was dismantled and despatched all the way to Aircraft Repair Depot, Karachi, in a railway wagon. He was quite dismayed at the lack of trust in the technical skill of the RAF technicians in the Squadron. This distrust and lack of flexibility was to stay with him; gnaw away at him. It was the catalyst for Harjinder to start taking matters into his own hands.

It was the start of the legend that grew around Harjinder...

The humdrum part of military life had to continue alongside the excitement of being operational. One day, Harjinder was carrying out the tedious task of Guard Commander. In the early hours of the morning, there was nothing much to occupy the men but chat with those from other units. He had an interesting insight from the Corporal in-charge of the Highland Light Infantry Guard into British life in India. Harjinder touched on the subject of their unpopularity in Indian circles, but the Corporal, a Highlander from Scotland, said: 'I know we Tommies, especially Highland Light Infantry, are hated wherever we go. However, look at our side of the picture. We are sent overseas to do a seven year stretch. In the British Isles, we lead a healthy social life irrespective of our ranks. Out in India, unless you are a Commissioned Officer, no girl, leave aside a European girl, even talks to us. So much so that when my Regiment was stationed at Razmak for three years, we did not see a white girl closer than a mile away. Our officers have a good time, but we are treated worse than animals. Do you blame us for our misbehaviour? The British Empire is for the few in the top class. As far as we in the ranks are concerned, you can keep your country, but give us back our own.'

The nature of operations for the IAF over the next few years was to rotate the Flights through the North-West Frontier and then back into bases further in the heart of India. On the 15th November 1936, Harjinder and 'A' Flight were sent to Chaklala near Rawalpindi for Army Cooperation Training. The aeroplanes were picketed in the open, and they lived in tents. One day, they flew in a formation of three Wapitis over the Murree Hills, while a fourth plane took photographs. This was the IAF's Christmas Card for 1936! A week after their arrival at Chaklala, some civilians from Rawalpindi came over to visit the Flight. Harjinder asked permission from the Flight Commander to show them around, to which he agreed. Harjinder passed the word round to the flight boys, and in a few minutes, there were a number of them taking groups of locals to see the aircraft. This was their first chance to show civilians round their Flight. There was a noticeable change in how the public viewed the IAF. No longer just an oddity, monkeys to the British tugging on their chain. They were very proud, because Indians were now flying and maintaining Air Force planes. However, some of the hosts got a little carried away. Harjinder overheard a girl asking the photographer whether he also flew one of the Wapitis. 'Of course, every morning' was his reply, followed by a description of the Wapiti's handling characteristics that bore no resemblance to reality at all.

A few days later, the Flight was even invited to tea by the Indian personnel of No. 5 Squadron RAF. They were entertained at the residence of the Head Clerk, Mr Labh Chand. There was Indian music and good Indian eats. The most gratifying element was to see the obvious pride with which their hosts regarded them. They were happy to welcome them because they were the Indian Air Force. The Flight's personnel returned, determined to justify all the pride and hope their compatriots placed in them. Things were changing. After years of being looked down on, their countrymen were now looking up to them. The IAF still only consisted of 8 aircraft, but it was a focus for this national pride. This is what had driven Harjinder since that day in the Principal's office.

By the beginning of 1937, the pilots and ground crew had won the admiration of No. 20 Squadron RAF. The IAF pilots, who had only really been employed as chauffeurs of the air so far, had tried their best to prove their worth in operations over the tribal area. Their first attempt to be allowed to take part in actual bombing and live firing operations did not succeed. Group Captain R.N. Bottomley, Air Officer Commanding No. 1 Indian Group, refused to allow 'A' Flight to proceed to the Operations area in Waziristan. He was always very sceptical about Indian pilots. Luckily for the future of the Flight, he was sent to UK on leave in the summer of 1937. Wing Commander McKenna, who became acting Air Officer Commanding, was more appreciative of their abilities, and he was the one who wrote the order to send the Flight on offensive duties. Progress for the IAF still depended on individuals kicking against the machine.

They moved into the sharp end of operations in the Waziristan area, towards the end of August, 1937. The advanced landing ground in Miranshah was located about 200 miles South-West of Peshawar, in the middle of the North-West Frontier Province hills. It was a large mud fort with very high walls, containing the headquarters of the tough, highly respected, Tochi scouts. The L-shaped landing strip lay outside the building, running along two sides of the fort. The fort housed the hangars, the Officers' Mess, and tented accommodation for the Airmen. The Tochi sentries guarded the fort from towers equipped with powerful

searchlights. It was unsafe to walk outside the walls in daytime, for fear
of sharp-shooting Pathans, and even the aircraft were kept within the
fort walls whenever possible. When a flight took place, the doors of the
Fort were opened, and the aircraft wheeled out on to the aerodrome. The
aircraft took off, carried out their missions, landed, and taxied into the
protective walls of the outpost. At night, it was not uncommon for bullets
from Waziri snipers to ping against the roofs of the barracks.

Harjinder and crew, received the usual reaction when they arrived
at Miranshah. The RAF personnel of No. 5 Squadron eyed the Indian
arrivals with ridicule and suspicion. However, it was not long before they
realised that they were made of sterner stuff than they had first imagined.
The IAF pilots started flying as many sorties as were humanly possible
between sunrise and sunset. The results of these operational sorties proved
outstanding. The IAF Flight had a shortage of air gunners in their flight,
partly because they had only a limited number of Airmen, and partly
because the RAF had not expected the IAF to go into operations quite
so soon. With no official training programme for air gunners, Harjinder
and the others found themselves standing within the gun ring in the
back cockpit more and more. As soon as it became known to RAF units
that the IAF needed air gunners, there were numerous applications from
among the British Other Ranks. This was really a glowing tribute to the
reputation of the IAF pilots and the technicians who serviced the planes.
News of their competence was now travelling far and wide, boosting the
pride of the Indian pioneers.

At that time, the four Indian pilots were Flying Officers Subroto
Mukerjee, Awan, Aspy Engineer and Narendra. September 1937 was their
luckiest month. These pilots carried out the maximum number of flying
hours in operational sorties that had ever been attempted by any RAF unit
in India: 337. The maintenance personnel had to carry out all inspections
in the dark after sunset. This unparalleled enthusiasm was shared by all.
Even the cooks willingly worked odd hours, giving out tea and other
meals to keep the wheels oiled. Every Indian felt that the hour of trial had
come and that this was their golden opportunity. This was the IAF in all its
glory, working hard, working well, and working together. For Harjinder
and his band of men, there was no other life but work, from sunset to
sunrise. It was 'like imprisonment'. However, the benefits were beyond
putting the IAF on the map. With nothing to buy and nowhere to go to
spend money, they were part of an enforced saving scheme! The reality

was the IAF had now been placed at the front-line, no more training, this was for real. It is slightly disappointing that Harjinder saw this period as 'imprisonment' because this was the proving ground for them all. The IAF were being watched by all, their audience continually expecting them to fail, but they were more than proving themselves.

The news of the record of their flying achievement travelled beyond the mud walls of the Fort. Squadron Leader Hancock, who was now the Commanding Officer of No. 1 IAF Squadron stationed at Karachi, flew all the way over to say, 'Well done' to his men. However, as he was nearing Miranshah, one of the aircraft in the Flight broke its undercarriage in a heavy landing. Nobody wanted the Squadron Leader to see them in this awkward situation, so they galvanised into action. Harjinder had never seen all hands gathered on one aeroplane before, but here they all were, suddenly, helping to lift it up. All officers and men tugged, toiled and heaved, until the aircraft was jacked up, and from a distance it looked fine, a bit grubby, but *fine*! The Squadron Leader was hosted and gently steered away from the lame aircraft. None guessed their plight, not even No. 5 Squadron RAF next door. When the coast was clear, Harjinder could work to bring the aircraft back to flying condition. This time he wasn't sending the plane away. He did all the work within the Fort.

During the three months that they operated from Miranshah, they continued to maintain their lead in operational flying hours. They totalled 1,400 hours in that time, and the serviceability of the aircraft was a record. Every morning the Wapitis from the IAF were wheeled out, fully serviceable, into the new dawn light, having been worked on throughout the night.

No. 5 Squadron RAF, on the other hand, had very bad luck. Of their 12 aircraft, there was hardly one they could fly daily. They lost three aeroplanes in one day, in one of those initial events that snowballs out of control. The day first started to unravel when one of their aircraft had been forced to land about 50 miles South of Miranshah. One aircraft was sent to recover the Wapiti, but somehow lost its way. When fuel was exhausted, and the rough, inhospitable terrain below offered no obvious areas to set the aircraft down, the pilot bailed-out, but Leading Aircraftman Joyce, the air gunner, refused. Who can tell what was going on in the young man's mind, but he carried on standing there, only his monkey chain to secure him, with no pilot in front of him. The aircraft came down in the moon-like landscape, killing him in the crash. The third Wapiti found the first stranded aircraft and tried to land near him. He misjudged the condition of the rocky ground and the toll of the day ran up to three aircraft. Three planes out of 12 down.

As soon as the news reached Miranshah, the only other serviceable aeroplane from No. 5 Squadron's original twelve, was hurriedly prepared. It was then that the day went from unfortunate to farcical. In a rush, the RAF ground crew hurriedly pushed the required machine out of the low-doored hangar. As the nose poked out into the sunlight there was an all mighty crack, the propeller, which had been left in a vertical position, hit the girder over the door of the hangar leaving a very sad looking Wapiti with a droopy propeller, and several red faces. The Officer Commanding No. 5 Squadron, RAF, had to go, cap in hand, to the IAF Flight and request a rescue team. It was a task they were more than happy to perform. Flying Officers Mukerjee and Engineer flew their Wapitis to the site and landed without incident next to the stranded RAF machine. They dropped off the necessary plugs and tools; no fuss, no gloating, just inward satisfaction. Thereafter, No. 5 Squadron looked upon them as their equals, if not superiors. They had proved their mettle subtly, but suitably.

The whole team were so happy with their progress, that they requested to carry on with operations, but Air Headquarters felt that they had done their bit, and ordered their return to base at Peshawar. To cushion the blow, they received the welcome news that the Airmen's scales of pay were now to be doubled!

Upon their return to Peshawar, they found that attitudes had changed. The personnel around the station regarded them as a first-rate Flight. The pilots who had previously worn that hangdog look, now walked about with a swagger and with smiles on their faces. They were no longer just air chauffeurs. The news even reached the Press, but still, India as a whole had not woken up to the importance of what was happening.

A few months later, they were on the move again, this time to Ambala, North of Delhi. On reaching there, the second Flight became operational, and flew down from Drigh Road to join them. During the year 1938, a bit of independence broke out! They had their own barracks, and they started their own internal training to show the RAF what they could do. In the barracks, the Airmen started tending to the grass with their own hands, planting flower beds on the sides of the roads, and generally taking an interest in how they were viewed by the RAF, and those beyond. The ever-present 'Tich' Tandon even set up a poultry farm. In the Airmen's married quarters, a maternity and child welfare section was organised. The

morning parade to hoist the colours up the flag pole became a competition
of smartness against No. 28 Squadron, RAF. They showed such a spirit
of healthy competition, that the local RAF Station Commander, Wing
Commander Horsley, eventually championed their cause, lending his
approval and assistance to help form an identity for the IAF.

At work, 'A' Flight competed with 'B' Flight for good maintenance.
'A' Flight, whose colour was red, had its aircraft chocks painted red, and all
the boxes and desks were marked with red bands. The Wapiti wheel covers
were red, and the aircraft also had a one-inch red band running from nose
to tail. 'B' Flight cowlings were rubbed and polished until they could be
used as mirrors. There was not a speck of dust on any aeroplane. Even the
hangar floor was polished until it shone.

During this year, 1938, they had an interesting aircraft display at
Safdarjung Aerodrome, in Central Delhi, where RAF Audaxes and the
IAF Wapitis took part. Not only did Flying Officer Henry Runganadhan
participate with his IAF Wapiti, but he won the air race. To put the
icing on the cake, he was then declared to be in possession of the best-
maintained aircraft. Ram Singh and Harjinder were presented to the Air
Officer Commanding, India, as the maintenance crew of the winning
aircraft. Harjinder never felt prouder.

Back to base, back to the mundane, and to mounting guard once
in every three weeks. This led to an introduction for Harjinder to the
corruption that operated as the norm in India. One night, when he was
the Guard Commander, he could not help but notice a sack full of broken
cement pieces, sealed and deposited in the Guard Room. Late at night, a
contractor sent word from the gate that he wanted to speak to the Guard
Commander. The visitor was escorted to the Guard Room, but asked to
speak to Harjinder alone, so the others were dismissed. He took out a wad
of notes from his pocket and thrust them into Harjinder's hand. Taken
aback, he counted them; there were two thousand rupees in the bundle.
Harjinder was astonished and not a little confused.

The man explained his story. He was the contractor who had built
the airstrip, but recently, a rival contractor had complained to Air HQ
that there was more sand in the cement than authorised. The sack in the
Guard Room was a sample dug out of a portion of the runway. If this
sample reached Delhi for analysis he would be ruined, as indeed, he had
used sub-standard materials; a fact he clearly thought needed no apology.
Thinking it would strengthen his case he continued to explain that he

would not only be sued in Court, but would be struck off the list of authorised contractors. He pleaded with Harjinder to exchange the sack for another he had with him. When he was told that Harjinder would not dare do such a thing, he asked to speak with the Orderly Officer, and could he please have the money back! Before leaving he said, 'I wish there had been a British NCO in-charge of this guard. I could have settled this business with a dozen bottles of beer.'

A month later, 'B' Flight, under Flying Officer Jumbo Majumdar, took their turn flying operational duties in the North-West Frontier Province. They moved to Miranshah, and immediately set about keeping up the good work that had begun with Harjinder's 'A' Flight, and Majumdar, who had a restless and daring spirit, continually strove to keep the IAF colours flying high. He chose the best pilots, and Flying Officer Mehr 'Baba' Singh was one of them. 'Mehr Baba', as he was known to his colleagues, had come to the attention of the senior staff as an outstanding pilot.

The day Jumbo left for Miranshah, he took Harjinder to one side and told him that there was one major goal at the back of his mind: 'We must better our own flying record and show the RAF what stuff we are made of.' He more than succeeded in his task.

It was not all about achieving high serviceability and flying hours, though. There was an operational job to do, and the dangers that come with it. On one of the sorties during this tour, Mehr Baba and his Air Gunner, Ghulam Ali, had a narrow escape. When they were strafing a hostile column, they encountered the normal puffs of smoke indicating some rifle fire coming at them. The RAF rear gunner had previously said that having bullets pass through the fabric on the wings was not uncommon, but the laws of average had to catch up with someone, and it was to be Mehr Baba. A single bullet passed between the fuel tank above Mehr Baba's knees and the engine in front of him. It sliced clean through the fuel pipe leading from the fuel tank. The Wapiti climbed away from the tribal men on the ground, as it used the small amount of fuel left in the carburettor. Then, after a brief splutter, the engine, now starved of fuel, stopped, leaving the propeller wind-milling in the breeze. The rugged nature of those mountains can't be overstated. You had to fly miles to find even a few square meters of flat ground, let alone a stretch of pastureland. The good news was that Mehr Baba found the only flat area for miles around. The bad news was that it sat perched on top of a spur on the side of a mountain. With characteristic skill, he brought the aircraft around to line up on this small area. There was no room for error, as either side fell immediately away to death in the valley below. The wheels of his Wapiti touched down at the very start of this small clearing. However, this was not a clearing prepared for wheeled vehicles, and one of the many scattered boulders ripped the wheels from the aircraft. The Wapiti may not be known for its looks, but it is a strong beast, and it remained intact, protecting its crew as it slid to a halt on its belly, shedding parts as it went, as a snake would its skin. It was late in the afternoon, and the tribesmen they had just been shooting at were not far away, and clearly not in a good mood. They both sprang out of the crumpled machine but, taking time to collect the guns from the Wapiti, before striding out for Miranshah. They walked the whole night, a hazardous undertaking in the North-West Frontier. Luckily, both were well-built men, and were mistaken for tribesmen, the Sikh and the Musalman, as they stole through the night, guns over their shoulders.

The two grimy, shadowy figures reached the outskirts of the Miranshah Fort as the sun broke the horizon. Their fortuitous resemblance to tribesmen now turned against them. The flat, open, ground around the fort had been cleared by the Tochi scouts to stop the tribesmen from creeping up on them. As Baba and Ghulam entered the clearing, the Tochi sentries in the watchtower opened fire as soon as they saw them approaching. Luckily, on this occasion, and unusually for the Tochis, their aim was poor, only resulting in dust being kicked up around Mehr Baba and Ghulam Ali's feet. It encouraged them to sprint back to the small trench encircling the airstrip, diving in head first. They felt distinctly put out to be under fire twice in 12 hours, and this time, by so-called friends. They remained hidden until it was broad daylight. Even so, they had a job persuading the trigger-happy infantry that they were friends and not foes! The incident brought Mehr Baba fame within the military, and the successful crash landing, with the walk back through bandit country, added one more laurel to the IAF crown.

Jumbo returned from the Frontier with increased confidence in his own leadership, and a blossoming reputation. It boosted him into the forefront of the IAF. However, they had to wait for another twelve months before they saw the IAF shatter all previous records in operational flying. This time the credit went to the newly-promoted Flight Lieutenant Aspy Merwan Engineer. The natural leaders were coming to the top, and, as they gained experience, they continued to break records.

Meanwhile, Harjinder's 'A' Flight were on the move again, and this time to Lucknow, the heart of British pride in India. The flag of the Empire flew day and night at the Residency in Lucknow, to remind the Indians that they had failed to storm it during the Rebellion of 1857. It was hard to tell if the British troops, with whom they operated, were shocked or surprised to see that not only were the Indians flying, but also maintaining, military aircraft. Harjinder repeatedly had Officers, Sergeants and Corporals calling on his Flight at their base. Their interest was welcome, and it was good to build cooperation between the two military services, but it soon became apparent that they were visiting mainly to satisfy themselves that it was not some joke strung together by a rival RAF unit. Indians flying and maintaining planes? Who would have ever believed it?

Towards the end of 1937 the Flight was invited by the Maharaja of Jaipur to partake in an Air Rally he was holding, to inaugurate the opening of his new airfield. At the time, Air Rallies were huge events around the world, with thousands flocking to witness the excitement of man taking to the air. Several of the Indian Maharajas fell in love with flying, and were responsible for the initial interest in aviation throughout the country. The IAF Flight moved to Sawai Madhopur, a few miles South-East of the mayhem and majestic splendour of Rajasthan's pink city: Jaipur.

On reaching Jaipur, Harjinder found that the local authorities had lodged the British Airmen in the State Hotel, costing sixteen rupees per room, whereas the Indian Airmen were booked to stay in an Indian hotel in the city, costing three rupees per day. It was the Indian authorities that now treated their own as third class citizens, but it was the British who came to their rescue. Flight Sergeant Jimmie Hickey refused to allow this disparity, insisting that all would be treated as equals. He refused to send them to the accommodation inferior to his British men, saying; 'They will all stay in one place, as always. They work on the same aeroplanes, and so, they will receive the same treatment.'

The men responded by pulling out all stops to provide serviceable aircraft to the pilots at all times. For three days, the pilots, determined to put on a good show, only left their cockpits for the briefest of moments between sunrise and sunset. On one of those days, Harjinder recorded seven hours, monkey-chained to the rear cockpit of his Wapiti. From that time onwards the Maharaja of Jaipur not only concentrated on his own flying, but also took a great interest in Air Force matters.

January 1938 saw 'A' Flight detached back to tents pitched in the barren, sandy outskirts of Hyderabad, on the Deccan plateau. Once again, they were cooperating with the Jat Regiment in helping the Artillery in target-spotting and fire-control, using Airborne Observation Officers in the rear cockpit. After a month, the buzz circulated that 'B' Flight was planning to visit too. It was rumoured that Officers were flying down and their wives were following by road.

The men were all agog with excitement, as though waiting to meet members of their own family. They worked day and night, and rigged up an Officers' Mess by joining two of the heavy tents together. When the officers and Airmen of 'B' Flight landed, they were given a welcome to surpass that of a Maharaja. The mess had prepared a veritable feast, and they had a gala night to celebrate the occasion, with officers and Airmen mixing together. The hockey match was the outstanding event, and its importance was evident as the loss suffered by the 'A' Flight team couldn't even dent the very competitive Harjinder's enjoyment of the occasion. Inspired by the hockey match, they decided to go in for a distinctive Squadron blazer. Harjinder discussed with the officers the type of crest they should have. Since it was unofficial, they agreed unanimously that an eagle, combined with the Star of India, with the motto 'Heaven's Light our Guide', should be the crest. All Airmen in 'A' Flight were fitted out with a pair of grey flannels and a navy blue blazer. An unexpected outcome was that every time they passed an Indian Army Infantry guard, the Army Sepoys used to salute them mistaking them for officers! It was very embarrassing for most, though some of the Airmen took malicious delight in keeping the footsloggers on the alert, passing them every half hour. Being unofficial, once they left Hyderabad, they couldn't be seen wearing the blazers in any official capacity. However, over the years, despite other sports kit, Harjinder treasured this blazer as a most valued possession.

Life in 1938 was good for Harjinder and his band of brothers. Not only were they were allowed to function as a real unit, but those surrounding their little India enclave treated them with respect, and saw them as equals. Those on high still seemed to look down on the IAF, however, the excellent performance by both the Flights in the North-West Frontier, heralded signs of change even from that quarter. On their return from Hyderabad, the Flights received a message from the Headquarters of No. 1 Squadron in Ambala, congratulating them on their achievements. It was a glowing tribute, as welcome as it was unexpected. The Flight Commander called Harjinder to his office to pass on the praise, leaving him in no doubt that the Flight's achievements was all due to the efforts of the Airmen. He asked Harjinder to read this message to all of them and suggested they keep the telegram as a souvenir. Harjinder did, indeed, keep the telegram, he reasoned; 'For later generations of officers, this might seem a trivial matter, but to the pioneers of the IAF, used to kicks in the pants rather than pats on the back, these incidents were the stones which built up the Air Force morale, the foundation of our esprit de corps. Like an architect who selects every stone he uses for his mansion, we carried out our daily duties always. Keeping in mind the contribution, each single act of commission or omission would make to our good name or otherwise.'

The return to the North-West Frontier for operations at Miranshah was marred when they learned of the imminent loss of their greatest supporters – Warrant Officer I.A. Hickey, was to be repatriated to England. He had served with them since the formation of the first Flight in 1933 and he was indirectly responsible for taking them into operations in 1937. In later years, after Independence, the IAF was lucky to have him back in the rank of Group Captain as Director of Technical Services.

As so often in life, the replacement was the opposite in all respects. Physically, Flight Sergeant Cooper was poles apart, his bulk being so large that he could hardly move, his colleagues wondering at the last time he had seen his own feet. The differences were just as marked in temperament too. It was difficult to reason with him, and his main job appeared to be to teach junior NCOs how to contradict their superior officers. He set a very bad example. He constantly hammered out anti-officer propaganda. He even demonstrated it by shouting: 'No, No, No' at his own Flight Commander, before the poor man had even completed a sentence or given an order. It was both a pathetic and an amusing sight to see Corporal Nair starting to pull out aircraft from the hangars. The Flight Sergeant would shout from the office: 'Push it back' and the Flight Commander from his office would yell: 'Wheel it out.'

You could hear the suppressed giggling of Airmen and open laughter from the pilots' room.

Back in Operations, time flew by. 1938 was soon at an end, and 1939 dawned with Hitler beating war drums in Europe. In Britain, the RAF embarked on an expansion programme. Their total strength until then, had been about 30,000 personnel with around 100 squadrons. The new programme aimed at expansion at the rate of 90 squadrons per year. The training machine went into overdrive and the dilution of experience could even be felt in the IAF. In the factories of Britain, new aircraft poured off the production line. The evocative names of the Spitfire and the Hurricane would all-too-soon become household names. Despite the newspapers being full of the growing tension in Europe, in 1939, the war seemed very distant in India, so it was business as usual. The usual business for 'A' Flight IAF was North-West Frontier operations in their antiquated Wapitis biplanes.

So, May 1939, saw them back in action at Miranshah, with Indians taking more control. The Flight was commanded by Flight Lieutenant Aspy Engineer and the pilots were Henry Runganadhan, of air racing success, and Mehr Baba, who hoped he could avoid being shot down, and shot at, this time. This was to be the first time that Ram Singh and Harjinder acted as NCOs in-charge of their respective Engine and Airframe trades. From the outset, determination was writ over the faces of the Airmen and officers. Indians were in charge. They worked day and night, often changing engines by ropes hung from the girders of the hangars, working by torchlight. The pilots flew from sunrise to sunset, breaking all previous records. They logged 410 hours and 10 minutes in the month of May. All, achieved by four pilots, and four Wapiti aircraft, serviced by Indian technicians.

All this was impressive, but, of course, a mere sideshow compared to events in Europe that would spread throughout the world. The second Sino/Japanese war had begun in 1937 but Japanese expansion policies had always seemed even more distant than events in Europe. However, their days in Miranshah during 1939, were to prove instrumental in the growth of this band of brothers, who learned and matured together in the arid desert wasteland. There was a World War brewing on the horizon, the Japanese would soon be coming, and the IAF was about to come of age.

Six

The World is at War; Not that the Warring Tribes Care

'We must move heaven and earth, and we will repair the aircraft here. Please try out your magic wand once more.'

On the 3rd September 1939, the Imperial Master of India declared war against the Axis powers. Could it be possible that the Great War of 1914–1918 was not the war to end all wars as they had been told? It should have been an unforgettable date in India, especially their military, but the truth was, that for the majority in the IAF, the European war appeared too remote to have any immediate effect upon them. It would be many more months before they could be considered to be operational as a fully developed Air Force, rather than a subunit of the RAF. There was also the small matter of the job to be done in Afghanistan and the North-West Frontier Province.

The date on which the war was declared became memorable in the IAF for quite a different reason. The news that began to circulate on the 3rd September was not of politicians postulating, but of the promotion for the first Indian Air Force officer to the rank of Squadron Leader. It was a real milestone, an indication that their hard work and professionalism was working. The figurehead was to be the nephew of the World War I ace, Lieutenant Indra Lal 'Laddie' Roy, DFC, the youngest child of an outspoken civil servant; Subroto Mukerjee was now a Squadron Leader.

Far more important than the rank, was the reins of power he was given to hold. He assumed command of No. 1 Squadron, IAF, at Ambala, so now the IAF had their first fully-Indian Squadron. Harjinder sent a congratulatory signal to the new Squadron Leader in Ambala. On the technical side, Harjinder led the charge to keep up their standard of aircraft maintenance, because now they had one of their own in charge, and therefore, so much more to prove.

The declaration of war was responsible for another feather in the IAF's cap. The Aircraft Depot at Karachi was the RAF's most vital airpower possession in India, so steps were taken to defend it. Who did the Senior Officers in Delhi choose to achieve this? The Indian Squadron! It was quite an accolade, when barely four years ago the same pilots were assumed to be a hazard in the air, and ordered to fly coloured streamers on the struts of their Wapitis as a warning to anybody else in the air. Now they were selected to defend Drigh Road, the important Karachi base. The perceived danger of attacks was by bombers from Abyssinia (Ethiopia). 'A' Flight, under Flight Lieutenant Awan, was chosen for this task, but the RAF couldn't stop from meddling. Instead of leaving the name as 'A' Flight, they were to be referred to them as 'Q' Flight, as if they were still some RAF unit. Somebody in HQ was still having trouble letting go.

Germany may have seemed a world away, but still the order to blackout came, and all German nationals were rounded up, to be interned until the end of hostilities. That applied to all Germans except for one particular technician. When the telephone system broke down, the only person who knew how to fix it was a German. He was cautiously taken to the base to carry out his work, but, as his time working for the British extended from days to weeks, he was given his freedom to roam, which he enjoyed throughout a major part of the war. If ever there was an incentive to never complete your task, this was it! A RAF Reserve Officer on a two week climbing holiday from the UK, had a nasty shock when he received a telegram ordering him to report to the nearest RAF unit for duties His two weeks' Indian holiday turned into five years of war in India.

It was time for the Indian Air Force to expand like their RAF brothers. The success, and perceived glamour, of the IAF was attracting a number of young Army Officers, who volunteered to transfer into the Indian Air Force (not dissimilar to the sentiments of their fathers in the previous war, to get away from the filth of the trenches, and away into the ethereal incandescence of the sky). From the outside, they had seen how this new section of the military was progressing as an Indian unit like no other, and they wanted to be a part of it. Harjinder's Flight had its quota of these transferees including Flying Officer Janjua and the blue-blooded Flying Officer Burhanuddin, the Afghan prince from Chitral State. The Flight benefited from the experience and talent of Mehr 'Baba' Singh, but new blood was arriving too – a certain Flying Officer Arjan Singh, a tall, slight, fresh-faced youth, was posted in from the last group of Indians to graduate from the RAF College, Cranwell, to join the elite group that now totalled 23. In 2012, as I stood at the party at the Chief's house, still glowing from having flown in the 80th anniversary parade, it was not at all difficult to see that young man in the face of the 93 year-old Marshal of the IAF, his eyes twinkling above his white beard, as we compared handling characteristics of Tiger Moths and Wapitis!

During their stay in Karachi, some of the pilots had the opportunity to fly the Audax aircraft. New to the IAF, these were still open-cockpit biplanes, not even close to the Spitfire and Hurricane that equipped the RAF, as they engaged in the 'phoney war' with Germany during those first few months of conflict. The Audax looked more streamlined and war-like, with their pointed noses and slender lines, as compared to the shed-like Wapiti. The fact that they always carried live bombs for anti-submarine purposes, and that their guns were always loaded, brought the war a little closer.

The IAF technical staff consisted of Flight Sergeant Cooper in-charge, Harjinder, as the second-most senior, with all the others Airmen, now Indian. The exception was Corporal Hall, an air gunner by choice, and Wireless Operator Mechanic by trade. The IAF still faced shortages in man-power, especially in the field of radios. The IAF Airmen had come a long way from those early days of being the lowest of the low, but pay and conditions were still relatively poor. Having learnt their trade in the Air Force, men were still leaving for more lucrative jobs in the open market, so retaining wireless technicians was proving well-nigh impossible.

The kindhearted Flight Lieutenant Awan was the man chosen as Flight Commander for this war role in Karachi. As the man in charge, his weakness, at times, was that kind heart. The result was that officers often paid little or no attention to his orders. One night, when Harjinder was Orderly Sergeant, he went round the Flight barracks and saw a man sleeping under a blanket using his shoes as a pillow. He woke him up and found, to his utter surprise, that it was none other than their Flight

Commander. When asked what he was up to, Awan began by cursing the royal name of Flying Officer Burhanuddin. He explained that this prince 'fellow' was the one detailed to be the Duty Pilot for the day. He kept quiet until the evening, before ringing Awan up to inform him of an invitation to the cinema by the Station Commander. Awan felt it unfair to detail another pilot on such short notice; besides, they had all done their bit. So he had borrowed a blanket from Sewa Singh, the Flight Store Keeper, and took the duties himself. When Harjinder said that he should allocate the next pilot on the list, Awan replied; 'If it was only one day in a month, I would do it, but Burhanuddin has made it a practice to be invited by the Station Commander virtually every duty day.'

Guard duty was obviously not to the liking of royalty!

On 10ᵗʰ September 1939, a one-legged pilot came to visit. It was Group Captain Henderson, the Commander of the entire Aircraft Depot, Karachi. He saw Harjinder directing the Airmen in the erection of a canvas aircraft hangar. If you have ever had trouble with a small family tent, imagine wrestling with the heavy canvas of one big enough to put aircraft in. Apparently, Henderson was very impressed with Harjinder's management skills. Later in the morning, Flight Sergeant Cooper called Harjinder in to his office to relate his chat with the Group Captain. Having seen the standard of his work, Henderson had requested Harjinder's transfer to the Aircraft Depot where he would Commission him as an Officer. Henderson had 500 Indian non-combatant section personnel working in the RAF, and it was his plan to put them under an Indian Technical Officer.

Naturally, Harjinder was flattered by this offer. It would be an enormous step up in pay and status, but he felt strongly on the subject, and told Flight Sergeant Cooper that he would never leave the IAF. He had dedicated his life, since college, to make a success of the new IAF, and he told the Flight Sergeant that he did not mind remaining a NCO for the rest of his life. Once again, Harjinder had an RAF man call him a 'bloody fool', but the circumstances now were very different. Cooper was being very sincere and he liked Harjinder, so continued to persuade him to accept the offer of a Commission and stop being so 'bloody-minded'. It was true that Harjinder was an NCO, but he was an Indian NCO. He had inferior status to a British NCO, with no jurisdiction over British Airmen, although, of course, the British NCOs had jurisdiction over him. The IAF technicians were openly told that there would never be promoted to Warrant Officer, the most senior rank an airman could attain, and therefore they would all remain NCOs for their complete careers. Despite the doom merchants, the men didn't change their views. The esprit de corps of the fledgling service was too strong to break, and Harjinder was not going to desert them for the sake of becoming an officer.

A few days later, Flying Officer Jumbo Majumdar summoned Harjinder for a long talk. Someone from No. 1 Squadron had suggested that he talk with Harjinder to persuade him not to accept the commission he had been offered in the RAF. They felt that he was irreplaceable at this point in the IAF's early life. Jumbo began by showing Harjinder a copy of the letter Henderson had written to Air Headquarters requesting him to be sent to the RAF. Jumbo told him that without his influence the future of technical personnel in the IAF, would be in jeopardy. He also said that sooner or later the IAF was going to expand, and then, he believed they would commission him as a Flying Officer directly.

Harjinder let Jumbo have his say before stepping in to assure him he had not joined the IAF just to get a thirty-five rupee job and to desert to the RAF at the first opportunity. He had as big a stake in building up an Indian Air Force as anybody else. He told him that he had already turned down the RAF offer. Jumbo was on his feet and all smiles. He shook hands with Harjinder saying; 'I am proud to be your friend.'

It is probably at this point the two men changed from being colleagues, with mutual respect, to become the closest of friends, both with the unwavering resolve to see a strong IAF serving an independent India. It was the start of a very interesting partnership, now about to be hardened in combat.

Despite the pessimists there was movement on the promotion front. On 1st November 1939, Harjinder was promoted to the rank of Sergeant (Hawai Havildar), finally reaching the rank that was used as a joke by his course mates in training. He discovered that for the past three years, the officers had been recommending him for this promotion, but the British staff in Air Force Headquarters held out with the excuse that they had wanted at least three different Flight Commanders' recommendations. The promotion created quite a stir in the Aircraft Depot, with several British NCOs paying a visit to 'Q' Flight to see what this enigma, this Indian with Sergeant Stripes, looked like! They had never expected to see this in their service life and several of them could be seen peering around corners and door frames to see this oddity in their world. As Flight Sergeant Cooper put it, the Sergeant is the real boss of a Flight. Well,

being a Sergeant, he would say that, wouldn't he?! The reality is that the
Sergeant is the lynchpin that keeps the Squadron running smoothly. All of
the officers were so delighted, that a party was arranged at Clifton Beach
the next day.

Harjinder was allotted a special office containing all the aircraft log
books. These books were now his responsibility. Additional responsibilities
were to keep the Flight Inventory up to date on behalf of the Flight
Sergeant. This promotion wasn't just a stunt to have an Indian Sergeant;
in fact, he took on more duties than a RAF Sergeant would. However,
nobody was willing to take a decision regarding the issue of Harjinder's
uniform. A RAF Sergeant wore an open collar tunic with a black tie, like
their officers, but the word came from upon high that Harjinder was not
permitted to mirror his RAF colleagues. It meant that there would be a
very visible difference between the RAF and the IAF. Naturally, then, the
RAF Airmen would view the IAF differently from their RAF equivalent.
Harjinder was proud of his new rank, but felt that it was devalued by being
made to appear different and inferior to RAF Senior NCOs.

Once out of training, Harjinder's military career involved serving
with a majority of Indian Officers. Based upon mutual respect, he
had built up very good relationships with them, and those who joined
subsequently. Away from the day-to-day formalities, a bond of friendship
existed between him, the founding Officers and the new arrivals. For
instance, even Flying Officer Burhanuddin, the Prince from Chitral, came
to Harjinder for assistance, not to his fellow officers. He caught Harjinder
at his desk and said, 'Harjinder Bhai, I saw your wife driving about in your
Talbot car. This put me to shame because I have never learned to drive,
and me a pilot! You must teach me.'

It seems his shame was less about his abilities as a pilot not stretching to
driving, than about the fact that a woman was commanding an automobile,
whilst he could not!

So Harjinder began giving Burhanuddin driving lessons in a small,
secondhand Morris which the Prince had purchased for this very task.
However, this pilot seemed to be hopeless. He was entirely without
mechanical sense, according to Harjinder. The grinding and shuddering
of the gearbox could be heard echoing off the hangar walls. He just could
not get the hang of changing gear, and could not understand why the
damned gears were necessary, when in an aircraft just one throttle lever
was all that was necessary to pick up speed. It took some persuasion to

prevent him from running in first gear, engine screaming at full revs, as he tore around the airfield.

The Prince had not completely mastered the idea of changing gears, forcing it through the gearbox as he picked up speed. With this dubious level of skill, he viewed his problems to be at an end, saying; 'Driving is pretty easy, after all. Even a child can do it. Now I must take my car out on the road.'

In spite of Harjinder's warning, he headed out without his teacher, who took cover because he could see carnage approaching. Somehow, Burhanuddin persuaded Flying Officer Khan to agree to take a ride with him. Khan was probably unaware that all the others had scattered with fear, knowing Burhanuddin's lack of promise as a driver. Who knows what would have happened if he got as far as the main road, but luck was with Khan. The Prince jumped into the car which was garaged in the aircraft hangar. He smashed the clutch to the floor, started the engine, and with a knowing wink at Khan, revved the engine up to the maximum. He let the clutch out in the hope to impress his friend with a flying start. Khan was thrown against the windscreen and His Royal Highness was flung over the steering wheel as the car shot off backwards at speed. The IAF's Wapitis were spared destruction, as Burhanuddin missed them by inches. The racing engine noise was cut short by a tremendous crash as the car reversed straight into the far hangar wall. The wall shook, with dust and debris falling on the car and the Wapitis alike, but, fortunately, it held firm. Unbeknownst to the blue-blooded pilot, the car had been left in reverse gear. Their first job after calming the shaken prince was to explain to him the existence of a reverse gear! He exploded, saying; 'I always told you this was a useless gadget. NOW you tell me the damn thing also moves in reverse. I am through with cars!'

The latter part of this outburst was unnecessary, because actually the *car* was through with *him,* now decorating the rear hangar wall like a modern-day sculpture of twisted metal. That was the last of his driving, much to the relief of all.

Flying Officer Janjua was another Army officer seconded to the Flight, an excellent officer and a good man. As is to be expected from an Infantry officer, he was an excellent manager of men. The men simply loved him, and it was also useful that he turned out to be a daring pilot.

It was Flying Officer Mehr 'Baba' Singh that Harjinder held in the highest regard, second only to Jumbo Majumdar. He referred to Mehr

'Baba' Singh as a first-rate pilot, a good hockey player, physically tough, and a good friend. When Baba bought an Austin car, they would often race each other up and down the runway. To boost up his engine, Baba fitted a little helical screw between the carburettor intake and the engine, proving that he was no mean engineer. No matter how much Harjinder tweaked his car, he could not keep up with him. Baba's engineering empathy combined with his natural flying ability, was to serve him well in the years to come.

Burhan was the eccentric among the officers. He explained that he was the sixteenth son of his father, and there were more sons after him! He was always speaking against his brother, the Mehtar of Chitral. Before he went on leave to Chitral, he willed that his belongings be sent to his wife, in case he was imprisoned and then done away with by his brother. That is brotherly love for you! Harjinder wasn't surprised by this request. He knew that frontier families were always fighting among themselves.

It was clear to Harjinder that these were the men he would be serving under when the war finally came. Meanwhile, some of the tasks of war, albeit tedious ones, were already filtering through. The Flight was given the task of patrolling the seas off the coast of Karachi, searching for German or Italian submarines. Day after day, the pilots would search the waters for miles around, carrying 250-lb bombs, looking deep into the heart of the sea when the weather was in their favour. They became experts in nature watching, plenty of whales to spot but no sinister metal tubes under the surface.

With his promotion to the rank of Sergeant, the paperwork increased. Had he moved into engineering management for the British Raj on completing his degree, he may have been happy with this side of his profession; but Harjinder had become a man who wanted to work with his hands, thanks to Newing. There was a small number of Sergeants who continued with their initial trades as they progressed to the highest level. In Harjinder's case, this would be as a Fitter Grade 1. The smouldering desire deep inside grew into a burning necessity to qualifying as a Fitter 1, and to have an Indian at the peak of that trade. Unfortunately, there were no courses run in India for this at that time, and the notion of sending an Indian Sergeant to the UK had not entered the consciousness of any British Officer. There was only one thing to do, he would return to his old tricks, and spend his free afternoons in the Depot's Engine Repair

Shop. With the eager assistance of Warrant Officer Herbert, who was in-charge of the Repair Depot, Harjinder manufactured his own course. In time, Herbert was so impressed with his enthusiasm, that he ensured that Harjinder was made to feel welcome by all the British technicians, be the Warrant Officer at the top, or the junior Airmen at the bottom.

In the UK, Rolls Royce Merlin engines were pouring off the production lines and into the Spitfires, Hurricanes and soon into Lancasters. The earlier Rolls Royce Kestrel, considered to be the mother of what became the Spitfire's Merlin engine, was the new thing on the block in India. It may have been superseded in UK, but it was regarded as a piece of cutting edge machinery in Warrant Officer Herbert's engine shop. After the antiquated engines from the Wapiti, the tolerances on this Kestrel engine seemed very fine, and to keep things 'tight', components were liberally rejected by technicians in the viewing bay. Harjinder learnt a lot of mechanical knowledge during these self-structured lessons. The views of the British Sergeants and Corporals changed towards him as he became one of the team. The man who flew into a rage after being called a bloody fool for the first time was now fully part of the RAF banter and tea break chats. The main topic of discussion among the British, was the inexperience of the new British Airmen who came straight from the engineering schools during this massive expansion. They even started to believe that India Command was being used as a sort of unofficial Training Command by the British Air Ministry. As the war was now becoming real in Europe, it could well have been the case that the top trainees were pressed straight into action in UK, and those who struggled, were sent to the 'quiet backwaters'.

Harjinder found some of those new British Airmen were naive in the extreme, 'with hardly any general knowledge'.

At that time, the war in Europe was taking a very critical downward turn, and the British Other Ranks in the Depot were very perturbed. A new, and frightened, airman asked Harjinder in all seriousness; 'What will happen to us in India now? We are losing the war. Will Gandhi ask you to finish us all off? We are at your mercy!'

Harjinder did his best to educate them on the contemporary political environment including giving them a long talk on Gandhi, the man whose peaceful protest lay at the core of Harjinder's own beliefs. He wrote in his diary 'I gave them a background of Indian political and social history, and I must say, they soon got rid of some of their ignorant pre-conceptions.'

There is little doubt that the attitude of the British personnel towards the Indian Air Force began to change as the British felt the tide of war was turning against them. The German invention, Blitzkrieg, or Lightning War, swept through Belgium and Holland. The Brits began to regard the IAF more as direct allies and not just a hindrance. The news spread of a volunteer reserve of pilots and Airmen being formed within the IAF. Before the outbreak of war, many UK businessmen already holding pilot's licences, or those with an interest in flying, had formed a unit of 'weekend warriors' whilst keeping their weekday jobs. Having joined these Auxiliary Squadrons mainly for a 'jolly good time' these well to-do businessmen found themselves in the thick of it. The same blueprint was used for the Indian chapter, and was established using aircraft pressed into the military from a previous civilian role. Throughout the IAF, the rank system, and designations were being changed to the RAF pattern, and even the uniform would be changed to the RAF style. For Harjinder, this was great news, because, with the new uniform regulations, he could wear the open collar tunic and tie he had been longing to for so long!

On 26th May 1940, the invincibility of the British seems to have finally ebbed away. News of the evacuation of all forces from Dunkirk came through. France was lost, and British forces had limped back to the relative safety of their island. The next day, Harjinder went to the Officers' Mess to pick up Flying Officer Mehr 'Baba' Singh and Pilot Officer Arjan Singh, as they were to travel together to Clifton. When he reached their room, he found them hunched on chairs around a third man. He was an astrologer telling these two bold aviators their future. With the way things had gone during the last few years for the IAF, and now the British failing in Europe, you can imagine why these young men were so eager for a glimpse into the gun-smoked future. When they finished having their palms read, Mehr 'Baba' Singh told Harjinder to have his fortune told by the astrologer while they dressed for the journey; 'I am not a superstitious man and demurred, but which astrologer would pass up an opportunity to find a victim? He soon had me in his net.' He opened up by saying; '*Sahib, you will be promoted within a month.*'

I told him: 'You can have your four annas, but spare me the embarrassment. I was promoted only seven months ago and it will take years before I get the next rank.'

However, he was quite definite; '*Sahib, you will not only be promoted next month, but will meet a man who will take you overseas. You will become a very big Sahib when you return from overseas.*'

I did not want to argue but handed him some money. To my surprise he refused to take it. His parting words were: '*If you are promoted within a month, then you will believe me. You will search for me, but you will not find me.*'

I laughed, but I half believed him too.

On 10th June 1940, Harjinder was called into the Flight Commander's Office. He'd thought that this would be to discuss the news that Italy had declared war against Britain. He could not believe his ears when the Flight Commander congratulated him, and told him that he had been promoted to Flight Sergeant. As he digested the news, his mind went back to the astrologer. Now he wished he asked him more about his future! That afternoon, as predicted, he searched in vain for the astrologer, to thank him more than anything else. He had not even accepted the few annas which he had offered. Furthermore, Jumbo Majumdar was promoted to Flight Lieutenant, and had been appointed Station Commander of Fort Sandeman in the North-West Frontier. His first action was to specially request for Harjinder as the Station Engineer. The Wapitis were to be in his charge again. The very next day, Harjinder was detailed to go with him, but little did he know that it would be Jumbo who would be taking him even further from home, just as the astrologer had predicted.

Finally allowed a chance to put a uniform identical to that of the RAF, Harjinder decided it was time to make some personal changes too. He decided to get rid of his beard. Harjinder was already deviating from the Sikh customs by trimming his beard and cutting his hair so that it would not show under his turban. On the train between Karachi and Fort Sandeman, he decided to make the full change. As the train clattered and puffed slowly along the track stretching away from Karachi, he entered the bathroom in one form and came out in another, clean shaven and hair cut to RAF regulation length. Harjinder's full name had been Harjinder Bains Singh, which identified him as a Sikh. He decided to drop the Bains and become just Harjinder Singh. An old Sikh gentleman, a co-passenger, began vehemently chastising Harjinder for being so faithless. They entered into a long argument. Harjinder wrote; 'It was impossible to convince the old timers in matters of religion in our country. Finally, I consoled myself in the famous saying of Thomas Hardy; "*Your religion begins where your reasoning ends.*" This is very appropriate in India, where we worship everything that we cannot understand.'

On 17ᵗʰ June 1940, the locomotive slowed to a halt, and the carriages clanked together, until the bucking, shaking and squealing finally subsided, as they pulled into the Chamanbagh Railway Station. Stepping out through the hissing steam Harjinder met Flight Sergeant Allan, the RAF Senior NCO whom he was to replace. Allan had not come to the station to give Harjinder a grand welcome, but to catch that same train as it returned to Karachi. Harjinder was surprised that his predecessor was leaving Fort Sandeman before he had set foot in it. He had expected a handover and some detailed explanation of the operation he was expected to run. However, Allan explained that Jumbo Majumdar had advised him that he need not wait for his replacement, since he looked ill, and obviously needed rest. To Harjinder, Allan looked fit as a fiddle; he even told Harjinder that he had never felt better. On reaching Fort Sandeman, Harjinder learnt the truth from Jumbo Majumdar; he had wanted Allan out of the Station so the two of them could begin their endeavour with a clean slate. It was a bold move, but he was more than convinced that Harjinder was up to the job.

Harjinder was one of those few people who walked into a room, and automatically commanded the attention of all present. He was certainly not going to slip quietly into Fort Sandeman. All the Officers and Airmen had reserved a welcome good enough for royalty. Excitement buzzed through the men, gathered to receive their Flight Sergeant. They all felt the last piece of the puzzle had dropped into place; to have a complete Indian unit at last. Sleep escaped Harjinder that night; 'I felt that this was the day for which I had been training myself for the last seven years. We would make history in Sandeman, Majumdar and I. We would ensure that our little effort in nationalising Fort Sandeman would become one of the landmarks in the annals of the IAF.'

He was not wrong, but any thoughts of being secure would be fleeting.

The time was right for the Jumbo-Harjinder team to flourish. Both men were natural leaders. Jumbo had been promoted ahead of his fellow pilots, but all were happy to follow this young man. Some saw him as a reckless flyer, but in combat, 'reckless' changes its form to 'fearless,' and becomes a virtue. With the war in Europe not going well for the British, the powers-that-be knew that expanding the IAF was essential, and Jumbo's future as the head of the IAF was already being discussed.

Jumbo and Harjinder were now running the newly formed 'C' Flight of No. 1 Squadron Indian Air Force. On 18th June 1940, Harjinder had all the Airmen on parade. His booming voice suited his new role as Flight Sergeant, inspiring both confidence and fear in his men. He gave them a 'pep' talk, to reinforce their *esprit de corps,* and also to introduce himself as their Flight Sergeant. He emphasised the need for technical excellence, and good maintenance, so that the pilots could always rely on their machines. This was the basis of Squadron efficiency, he told them. He ended his address with; 'You can rest assured that by the time I leave here, I shall train every one of you for two ranks higher. Our pilots have proved their worth in the air. We on our part must not let them down. I am going to demand that all of you follow a rigid discipline in this Flight, because I believe that a disciplined technician is the most reliable and safe, technically. Also, I would like you to keep physically fit, always. In your personal bearing, I would like you to walk as if you are always on parade; and your dress should always be smart. I do not expect it to be kept clean while at work, but it must start clean and be well pressed, because your dress is an index to your ability and character. I expect every man to go at the double when his superior officer calls him up. Saluting the officers will be done with the intention of real saluting and not just making a gesture. As for discipline, I do not believe in putting Airmen on charge, but if I do, he will be punished most severely.'

A routine check through the various sections of Harjinder's hard won Indian Flight, revealed that there was a single British Corporal lurking in the system; a wireless mechanic. When this was mentioned in passing to Jumbo, he hit the roof, this man spoilt his Indian unit. He instructed Harjinder to inform this interloper to get his luggage ready. Jumbo was so incensed he arranged to send him out by air to Miranshah. However, Harjinder was not as blinkered in his unending drive for a strong Indian Air Force. Reality had a part to play. He said; 'Sir, I am not a Wireless Mechanic. All I have here is a bunch of Airmen: Bhatt, Mukerjee, Jaykant and Singh. I am not sure if they can run the Wireless Station as well as maintain our aircraft.'

Jumbo's reply was typical; 'Harjinder, if I can be the Station Commander, and you the Station Engineer, then why can't they rise to the occasion and become Station Wireless men?'

So for once, Harjinder did not get his way, and the man was told to prepare to leave. Jumbo gave the man a few weeks, not to just pack his bags, but to pass on as much of his technical expertise as possible. The newly arrived Pilot Officer Prithipal Singh, was detailed to airlift the British Corporal Wireless Mechanic off the base in Wapiti J 9735. As the dust on the strip settled, and the slivery wings diminished to a speck, it signalled the first fully Indian IAF unit. Or did it?

Thirty minutes later, they heard the rumble of the aircraft returning. Unless an individual is totally engrossed in an important job it is instinctive to pause and watch an aircraft come in to land. When Harjinder realised that it was Prithipal Singh returning, he assumed that he had some minor snag, so he took extra interest as the aircraft approached. It soon became clear that Prithipal was coming in too low. They all watched with increasing horror, as the aircraft dipped lower than the wire fence on the Southern boundary. Pilot Officer Singh needed to give the Wapiti a big burst of power. The big heavy Wapiti was named after a deer but was not known for its sparkling, athletic performance. The slight increase in engine note didn't change the aircraft's path enough as it continued towards the boundary, still descending. The fence seemed to grasp at the wheels and pluck the Wapiti from the air. They saw the aircraft rip the fence to shreds before it was consumed in a cloud of dust with only a brief view of a tail pointing skywards. Harjinder jumped into the nearest vehicle and was first to the site of the accident. The dust billowed skywards as he dived into it, but he could just make out the outline of a broken aircraft. Harjinder made straight for the cockpit; 'I saw a sight which I have never seen before and never hope to see again.'

The pilot was sitting in the cockpit, staring forward; hand on the engine throttle as if still waiting to complete his landing. Somehow, the engine was still running, kicking more dust over the wreck. The front fuselage had snapped, leaving a nine inch gap between the struts holding the wings in place, and the end fuselage plate holding the engine in place. One wing tip was resting on the ground because one of the undercarriage legs had completely given way.

Without thinking, Harjinder bellowed with his signature booming voice over the sound of the engine; 'You idiot, don't you know what you are doing?'

Pilot Officer Prithipal Singh was too stunned to react, his mind still waiting to land his plane. So Harjinder climbed up through the swirl of wind from the still rotating, shattered propeller stubs, to switch off the engine. In the meantime Jumbo Majumdar and Mehr 'Baba' Singh had

driven up. Harjinder never saw Jumbo so furious. The poor pilot and RAF
Corporal were taken away, still in a complete daze.

Harjinder studied the crash site. He sent his men off to gather
equipment whilst he poked his head in, out, and around, the dirt-covered
machine. He managed to get a jack under the wing to lift the Wapiti out of
the dirt, high enough to remove the collapsed leg. He then used a flexible
cable to tie the semi-detached engine to the struts that held the wings in
place. It took them three hours to wheel the sad looking Wapiti to the
hangar, a mile away.

The next day, a meeting took place in the Commanding Officer's
office. All the pilots were present; Mehr 'Baba' Singh, Nanda, Surjit Singh
Majithia, Das, and the hangdog Prithipal Singh. That meeting was to form
part of the legend that stayed with Harjinder throughout his career. Jumbo
posed the question that started the ball rolling; 'Harjinder; is it humanly
possible to repair this aircraft?'

'Sir, the damage is extensive, even the top longeron (*the length of metal
running from front to back of the fuselage*) is broken in two. Although we will
try, it appears doubtful.'

'Even if there is one-in-a-million chance, you must try it. Our prestige
is at stake. We cannot let the IAF down. If you do repair it, I promise
not to let Air Headquarters at Delhi know about it. Thereafter, you will
preside over a Subaltern's Court Martial and I can assure you that Pilot
Officer Prithipal Singh will have no choice in the matter but to yield to
your decision.'

This was the boss of the IAF's 'C' Flight, in front of all his pilots and
his Chief Engineer, discussing the court martial offense of not reporting
an accident. It was not just to save the career of poor Pilot Officer Singh.
The war was on, and eyes were looking to the IAF to assist the Empire's
war effort, but the traditionalists still wanted them to fail, to know their
place.

Harjinder knew that the stakes were high, he knew what he had to
do; 'If ever in my life I was determined to complete a job it was that day
after hearing the Commanding Officer. I promised to repair the aircraft
in three days.'

Harjinder rushed back to his office and sent a signal to Aircraft Depot,
Karachi, requesting immediate despatch of a top front longeron for a
Wapiti. He had a good look at the damage and found that the bottom
beam underneath the main auxiliary tank had buckled too. Sergeant

Pritam Singh was instructed to finish the job initiated by the pilot: the removal of the engine. Corporal Sharma, with Leading Aircraftsman (LAC) Mahboob, was to strip off all the cowlings. It was midnight before all the damage had been logged, because every single tubular rivet had to be checked for bending. Being the first all-metal aircraft, not much was known about the various components' strengths. If it hadn't before, it now became startlingly clear Harjinder that he was going to be extremely busy during the next two days. He arranged for the Flight to work round the clock in four shifts, with each getting only four hours sleep at night. The tea stall (*you can't perform miracles without tea!*) was shifted to the hangar and cakes and pastries were in abundance; the tea on the boil all night.

Not surprisingly, the Aircraft Depot, Karachi, sent a signal in reply to Harjinder's request, querying the IAF demand for the Wapiti spare part. It read; 'No Unit has ever demanded a top longeron. It cannot be changed anywhere except in Aircraft Repair Depot, with the aircraft completely dismantled. Confirm your demand.'

Harjinder replied; 'Demand confirmed; requirement top longeron. It is possible to change the longeron. Aircraft cannot be transhipped to Depot due to metre-gauge railway line connection between Fort Sandeman and Quetta.' This last comment was a quick, if not entirely accurate, afterthought.

The die was cast. They had now officially notified the Aircraft depot of damage, but not of the crash. There was no going back, and no way out, other than this Wapiti, with the front snapped in half, taking to the air again. If the Depot refused to send the longeron, all the grafting in the hanger would have be in vain, and the whole unit would have been caught out by Air Headquarters. The very next day, their collective prayers were answered. Imagine the relief as they peered into the cargo wagon of the next passenger train to see the unmistakeable, long wooden boxes of the longeron and beam. As the parts trundled through the barren, brown, rocky landscape, every other damaged area on the aircraft had been repaired with the assistance of endless cups of tea.The fuselage was laid open, top and bottom, waiting for the new parts to arrive. The man whose engineering practical skills had been found lacking by Warrant Officer Newings stepped up to the plate. 'During the fitting of the two parts I worked with my own hands and all the metal riggers watched. Leading Aircraftman Siddique, Aircraftman Daulat Ram and Corporal Sharma were surprised to see how fast I could work (*so this Flight Sergeant wasn't just a booming voice they thought!*). All my practical training and my own-time Sunday courses were paying dividends.'

They were not only paying dividends, they were coming to the rescue of the IAF's reputation.

Exactly seventy two hours after the crash, the haggard technicians stood back from a completed Wapiti, sitting back on its own undercarriage. One of the pilots climbed into the cockpit and started the engine on a test run. After the engine roar died away leaving the ticking and clicking of a cooling engine, Mehr 'Baba' Singh proclaimed Harjinder the 'Technical Wizard'. As Harjinder looked upon the aircraft, he felt very proud of himself. All his college education and training in the Air Force had led up to this moment. He knew in his own mind, however, that this was just the beginning, that there were greater disasters to come.

The next day, Mehr 'Baba' Singh stepped forward, keen to test fly the repaired aircraft. As he was taxying out, Pilot Officer Das playfully joked with Harjinder; 'I hope it will stand the taxying loads.'

However, Harjinder stood in silence, praying inwardly. Everyone around him seemed confident.

Then, all of a sudden, the aircraft's engine opened up to full power for takeoff. It surged forward, but just when the tail lifted, the engine was suddenly throttled back. Mehr 'Baba' Singh turned the aircraft around and taxied back towards them. Harjinder groaned and all around him the shoulders of the technicians dropped. However, instead of bringing the Wapiti up to the group and shutting the engine down, Baba swung the aircraft back into wind and, without a pause, opened up to full power. This time the aircraft wheels left the ground in a cloud of dust. He banked the Wapiti into a turn and flew directly over their heads 'like a white dove'. There, in the dust blown by the departing aircraft, the oily, tired, drawn faces were split with smiles, as relief and pride glowed on every face. The pilots standing near Harjinder also began to laugh. They had known what Mehr 'Baba' Singh had been up to; he had wanted to test the aircraft to see if it would stand the strain of a takeoff and whether the rigging was accurate before leaving the safety of terra firma. There had been nothing wrong with J 9735. It was back on the inventory and nobody outside this small group knew any different. As soon as Baba landed he climbed out of the cockpit with a face splitting smile, and congratulated each and every one of them on the excellent job done on J 9735. 'C' Flight, IAF, had all of the aircraft it had originally been issued with. There was no record of a crash and therefore, no crash had ever taken place. What doesn't appear in Harjinder's diary is what the RAF Corporal, who was in the crash, thought of the whole incident and what he was instructed to say! Would anybody have believed him on his return if he told stories of a crash that never happened, and an aircraft that was snapped in half, but flew him back to base three days later?

So, true to his word, Jumbo Majumdar asked Harjinder to convene the 'Subaltern's Court Martial', an unofficial form of discipline adopted from the Army. Harjinder headed the Court Martial the next morning and an hour later the verdict was conveyed to Jumbo: The pilot is fined 200 beer bottles and recommended to be posted away. The sentence was promptly carried out, and Pilot Officer Prithipal Singh was posted to Karachi. You would think the pilot would have been grateful for the act that saved his career, but Harjinder wrote; 'I don't think he ever forgave me, either for his punishment, or for calling him an idiot to his face.'

Prithipal Singh's career was saved, and not only did it progress, but their paths we set to cross again soon.

In the RAF, things were heating up. A few tribes causing trouble on a remote border of the Empire, now seemed insignificant, and certainly not newsworthy. The headlines were full of the aerial battles in the fight that would become legend, the Battle of Britain. The pilots of the RAF Spitfires and Hurricanes were hurling themselves at the German fighters and bombers. Bombs were falling on Great Britain, and the possibility of a German invasion was at its highest. In British homes, pounded with bombs, and under the threat of invasion, the radio was the primary way in which the public could hear their news, and the Government used this as a mouthpiece to try and boost morale. The same was true in India. On the evening of 25th July 1940, Squadron leader Subroto Mukerjee broadcast a talk on the radio from Delhi, regaling his fellow countrymen about life in their fledgling Air Force. It was an unabashed recruiting drive. Subroto's talk gave a brief history of the IAF Squadron, its achievements, its organisation and its movements. It was voted a very good talk by the whole Flight who listened, huddled in one room in utter silence. Then, as it drew to an end, the room exploded in wild cheering. This was the first time an IAF officer had spoken to his countrymen over the airwaves. The men listened, bursting with great pride.

Soon after the radio speech, the Flight received a signal from Air Headquarters authorising them to join in with the Royal Air Force with the issue of a new blue uniform. Their joy knew no bounds, but no directive from the RAF could be without a catch. The signal did state that old RAF uniforms held in store in India may be first used by being issued to the lower ranks of the IAF. Where the stock of the old uniform was nil, only then would the new versions be made under unit contracts. Jumbo took the word 'may' in the signal to heart and authorised the men to use new material. Leading Aircraftsman Suri, the Equipment Assistant, was instructed to issue the brand new RAF blue material from the Stores Section, employ a whole fleet of local darzis, and get a set of new uniforms made before anyone could stop them.

The uniformed numbers of personnel were soon swelling as the IAF Flight welcomed their first batch of Volunteer Reserve Airmen. They were met at the Railway Station, a group photograph taken, and much fuss made of them to boost their morale. They received a conducted tour of the Flight, where Harjinder told them about this being a nationalised unit, stressing that this was the first nationalised unit of the IAF, the sapling which would grow into a full-fledged tree one day if they nursed it diligently. Harjinder reported; 'Among them Deb and Arunachalam were outstanding. Little Roy was a very smart and pleasant airman, Jaykant a little shabby!'

The air war in Europe was brutal. The RAF was reaching its 'Finest Hour'. The 'Few' were inflicting more and more casualties on the German Luftwaffe. The civilians would suffer for the RAF Fighter Command to survive. As Churchill planned, Hitler was so enraged after a small, audacious, bombing raid on Berlin that he released his strangle hold on the RAF Fighter Command stations and turned his bombers loose on British cities. Few people realise that during this time, at the height of the Battle of Britain, twenty-four Indian pilots were sent to the UK to undergo conversion training and participate in Operations. Even though they could take part only after the Battle of Britain, many of them distinguished themselves flying operations with the Fighter, Bomber and Coastal commands soon after. Of the twenty four, eight were destined never to return. In Britain too, Indians fought to prove that they could fly and fight with aircraft.

However, back at 'C' Flight, IAF, bombing operations out of Fort Sandeman were being held in a more gentlemanly fashion. The tribesmen were still very hostile, and the IAF had no problem with machine gun attacks against the riflemen who took pot shots at them, but attacks on villages were viewed differently. When the IAF were tasked with an attack on a wayward village, messages were dropped beforehand, informing them that a lesson was about to be dished out with a little bombing. When the raids began, the crews would often see the villagers gathered in the surrounding hills like spectators in a football match; they seemed more confident of the pilots' aim than some of the pilots themselves. Apparently, one village chief was so impressed by the accuracy of the bombing, that he sent a telegram of congratulations to Air Headquarters in Delhi. How very civilised!

As 1940 ended, and a new year began, the RAF had stopped the Germans in the air, and shattered their plans to invade. However, the halting of the German invasion plans was the only encouraging news to be had. Elsewhere, the Italians had invaded North Africa and marched into Egypt; the Japanese were doing their own expansion through China. The war seemed to be edging closer to Harjinder and his band of brothers.

In March 1941, the possibility of direct involvement in the wider war seemed a real possibility, so Squadron Leader Mukerjee visited the Flight to raise morale. His trip to metaphorically pat his men on the back very nearly became his last. It was normal procedure for visiting pilots to take an aircraft into the tribal territory to update themselves with the present location and movement of the tribes. Time ticked on past Mukerjee's expected return estimate. The occasional glance at a watch turned into faces scanning the horizon for a sign of his Wapiti. No amount of staring, and wishing, would bring his plane into view, so when he was several hours overdue, the order went out to prepare all available aircraft for flight. Harjinder ordered the maintenance checks to be doubled whilst all crews gathered for briefing. The fort became swamped with noise as all the engines flashed into life. The search aircraft bumped along to point into wind and without delay they launched off in all directions, up to a radius of 100 miles. In hindsight they realised that letting their senior officer fly off over the horizon without leaving a copy of his intended route was foolish. The rear gunners hung over the rim of their cockpits, pulling against their monkey chains, in the hope of spotting the missing biplane. As eyes became exhausted, so did the aircrafts' fuel supplies, so all homed back in to the airfield at the same time. The hope among the men gathered on the ground was soon dashed, as the aircraft drew up and shaking heads descended from them. By the time evening came the levels of concern had crept higher and higher. All personnel congregated at the airstrip, anxiety etched on their countenance. The uniform look on the faces was one of tension for their first Squadron Leader and a much-loved man.

As the sun dipped below the horizon, the Airmen laid out the gooseneck flares on the airstrip. These petrol-filled pots were lit, adding to the shimmering heat haze. All the hangar lights remained on, a beacon for their returning leader. Then, Mother Nature stepped in to deliver the final blow. There rose one of those Frontier dust storms, the red-dust disturbance, in which even birds prefer to walk, and visibility drops to less than a hundred yards. The shoulders of the men dropped and even the small part of the faces left exposed after scarves were wound around for protection, illustrated the strain. They all felt that they were staring disaster in the face. Some prayed for his safety and some were actually heard sobbing. Flight Lieutenant Majumdar tried to console all who would listen; 'I know him; he is an excellent pilot; he must have landed safely somewhere.'

However, the weather was atrocious, visibility was almost zero, and it seemed he was speaking out of nothing but blind optimism.

To keep the men focused, and keep them from spiralling into a dark place, Jumbo Majumdar gathered them together, outlining his plans to start the search in the morning again. Once Harjinder was satisfied with the mechanical readiness of all the machines, he wanted him to occupy the rear seat of his own Wapiti as Jumbo's observer. The briefing over, the men reluctantly turned in for the night, though not many were able to sleep. Most were up after a few hours, preparing, and double-checking all the equipment, time and time again. Now it seemed that the sun would never rise.

Jumbo could wait no longer, so, at 4.30 am, still in total darkness, he and Harjinder took off in a Wapiti. Other aircraft were detailed to takeoff at intervals of one hour and to search in different directions. Harjinder reasoned that by having gaps between the returning aircraft his technicians had time to prepare the aircraft to go straight out again. Jumbo and Harjinder headed in a South-Easterly direction, but as soon as they reached their cruising altitude, the ground below disappeared in a mass of red dust. The storm had subsided since the previous evening, but the red dust still hung suspended in the air and they knew from experience that this would continue for days. Searching in these conditions was almost impossible. They flew for an hour with blue sky around them but nothing

below, just the soupy swirl of red dust hanging in the air. Harjinder was
beginning to believe that the search was hopeless, but Jumbo kept on
peering to port and starboard alternately. All Harjinder could see was dust
and more dust, the despair was rising in his throat.

All of a sudden, without warning, Harjinder was smacked into the
right-hand side of the cockpit as the aircraft violently rolled left. He
regained his balance, gripping on to the gun ring encircling the cockpit,
to prepare for the roll to the right. Jumbo was signalling to Harjinder; he
must have spotted something. Harjinder pulled half his body out from
his rear cockpit moving as close to the front cockpit as his monkey chain
would allow. He followed the pointing hand of Jumbo towards a gap in
the dust haze which in turn revealed a narrow lane formed between two
ranges of high hills. The visibility was not ideal, but it was slightly better.
Jumbo eased the Wapiti down into the gap, but once in among the dusts,
the visibility became poor on both sides. The dust gloom had looked
sinister as it bubbled below them but now there were hills in that darkness;
ready to kill them at any moment.

Looking down at the small sector of ground below them, Harjinder
could see what Jumbo was following. There, in this pathetically small
gap, was a railway track stretching out as if to remind them that life could
exist in this seemingly desolate place. Then, to prove the point, life came
into view in the form of a labouring train, puffing through the flying grit,
adding smoke to the swirling dust. The black locomotive engine merged
with the background but the painted red bar behind the front buffers
and the little orange water tender behind the engine, provided a splash
of colour. The cream-coloured carriages behind did, indeed, contain life
which, however irrelevant, seemed to add hope to their mission. The
movement of the rattling train was what probably attracted Jumbo's eye
in the first place. Harjinder watched a hand appear from the cockpit and
move rapidly up and down, finger pointing to the ground. They were
going lower, so that Jumbo wouldn't lose sight of the train. Knowing
what was coming Harjinder tightened his grip on to the gun-mounting
ring as Jumbo put the Wapiti into what felt like an almost vertical dive.
The inter-plane wires and struts screamed in protest, and the fabric on the
wings looked as though it would part company from the ribs. Harjinder's
stomach nearly heaved up into his mouth. The G force squashed Harjinder
down into the rear cockpit as Jumbo heaved back the stick, the Wapiti's
nose protesting as it came back towards level flight at around 500 feet,

pointing along the railway line. Harjinder wondered what he was up to, because the railway line could lead them almost anywhere. As the dust seemed to close in on them, he told himself that Jumbo must know what he was doing. Jumbo must have sensed the concern oozing from behind him, so, after looking at the map, he made a pencil mark and passed it back behind his seat to the rear cockpit. Harjinder returned it, nodding. It was however, a mechanical nod, meaning; your guess is as good as mine, or God only knows where we are.

After flying for another fifteen minutes, hanging on to the sight of the railway line in the red haze, they finally saw the shapes of houses, huts and fences emerge from the blur. It was a big town, that is, big for that part of the world. As they circled the town, their eyes were drawn to a large field on the southernmost boundary. Two small sheds sat on the edge of the field but it was the peculiar markings that grabbed their attention, markings that would only be visible from the air. Had the local farmer finally succumbed to the harsh conditions of his surroundings and gone completely mad? Any ploughing of land traditionally, throughout the world, was carried out in straight lines but this field seemed to be ploughed in circles. There were hundreds of these circles overlapping with each other. Then at last, at the furthest boundary they saw an aircraft, lying with its nose down in a nullah, or ditch, with its tail sticking up vertically like an elaborate telegraph pole. They zoomed low over the field and saw crowds of people waving at them. Was this good or bad news? The circular plough marks were an indication of strange happenings, and clearly, Jumbo didn't fancy landing there. There seemed very few options for landing sites, but Jumbo seemed to be concentrating on a nearby ploughed field. They flew low over the area to have a better look, but both knowing, without the need for conversation, that they would be taking a huge risk if they used this field to land. Jumbo brought the aircraft down parallel to the furrows. He gently placed each wheel in the straightest groves he could find and eased the nose up as the speed bled away. As soon as the wheels made contact with the first-hint of soil the aircraft bucked and bounced but the tail dug into the earth to bring things to a rapid stop; they were still in one piece. The people came running up gabbling about an aircraft that had crashed the day before. All they heard was the two most important words – pilot and safe They calmed one young man enough to be told that the pilot in question had been housed with the Militia guards. Half an hour later their eyes encountered the sight they'd been hoping to see all night. Mukerjee, looking distinctly worse for wear, was still a sight for sore eyes. They congratulated him on his narrow escape before giving him a moment to relate his misadventure.

After he had taken off from Miranshah the storm had overtaken him. He had carried on flying blindly in the sand storm for over three hours, his life reliant in the accuracy of his instruments and his instrument flying skills. He was desperately lost, looking for landmarks in the gloom. Soon it was nearing 8pm, and almost too dark to see when, all of a sudden, he came across a town glowing through the dust haze, and immediately he started circling. Luckily for him, and the IAF, a Jamadar of the Militia heard the drone of the Wapiti, saw his plight and had the sense to jump into action. He raced to the little airstrip and started firing flares one after another in the direction of the open runway.

With the help of the Jamadar, Mukerjee made a perfect landing. However, perhaps out of sheer relief, he made a massive error. He taxied the aircraft up to the shed on the landing strip as the storm threatened to pound even this ox of a biplane to pieces. All knew that the Jupiter engine was a complete pig to start when hot, and knowing he could not push the aircraft into the shed, he decided to leave the engine running. With the engine at idle, he swung his legs over the side of his cockpit and dropped the considerable distance to the ground to look into the shed. As he made his way over, head bent into the wind, the throttle slowly vibrated itself open. When Mukerjee next looked back he saw the silver plane starting to pick up speed across the field. If it had been a screening of the latest comedy film back in Karachi's cinema, the IAF personnel in the crowd would have roared their disapproval at the impossible scenario, but here it was. Squadron Leader Mukerjee, the boss of the IAF ran across the airfield after the rogue aircraft managing only to get one hand gripped to a wing tip. Mukerjee was not one to give up easily and finally managed, whilst running at full speed, to work his hands along to catch hold of the outer strut between the top and bottom wings. The open space of the airfield was fast running out, with the perimeter ditch fast approaching. Digging his heels in he swung the Wapiti around on the wing tip to keep it from leaping into that ditch. Now held firm, but only on one side, the aircraft kept circling round and round, with him at the centre of the circle. His feet could not dig in sufficiently to the hard surface, so he found himself being dragged around the airfield. Unable to see much in the dark, and unable to work his way closer to the cockpit, he had no option but to continue this absurd waltz; man and Wapiti spinning across their dance floor. The marks seen by Jumbo and Harjinder covering a large area of the airfield showed how long he must have been in this situation. Blinded by the dust of the storm, and the wind from the propeller, disoriented by the twirling of man and machine he didn't see the ditch that finally stopped the show. The aircraft pirouetted its way to one side of the airfield and the wheels crept over the edge of a deep ditch. Down the Wapiti crashed to the bottom. The sorry episode was at an end.

Harjinder made his way into the town of Tonk and phoned Miranshah, passing on the welcome news that Mukerjee was alive. Flight Lieutenant Narendra was dispatched in another aircraft to fly down to them as the dust cleared. Harjinder managed to collect a few willing Pathans to assist and a few lengths of rope were located. They all gathered around the sad looking Wapiti, and under Harjinder's guidance, they physically lifted it off the ground and out of the ditch. They then manhandled it back to the lowly shed, re-designated as a hangar. Now came the problem of how to despatch the shattered aircraft from Tonk back to Fort Sandeman. Harjinder's white lie to main base at Karachi was true here. The metre gauge railway would not be able to cope with it.

When Jumbo looked at Harjinder, he could almost hear the cogs whirling around in his head. Harjinder had an idea what was coming; 'Harjinder, why not repair it here?'

'Sir, do you realise where you are? There is not even a screw-driver or a hammer here. The ground equipment and spares required will take a full ten days to get here. There will have to be a new propeller, aileron and undercarriage required. It is quite impracticable, if I may say so.'

Harjinder had formed a reputation for being Mr Fix-It and with this reputation, miracles were now expected! Jumbo left to discuss the matter with Mukerjee and Narendra before approaching Harjinder again. 'You yourself say the pilot deserves commendation. He has been brave and daring. He is our first Squadron Leader, first Squadron Commander, on his first base inspection. Through no fault of his (*although his judgement must be questioned*), he has had his first and only crash. We must move heaven and earth, and we will repair the aircraft here. Please try out your magic wand once more.'

Harjinder thought about it hard. He believed the accident was his fault, reasoning that the fitters who worked for him, rightly or wrongly were at fault for not having adjusted the throttle so that it would not open by itself. He believed the pilot indeed, had, displayed great strength of character in staying alive in the storm and fighting with the aircraft on the ground for over half an hour trying to salvage the situation. Harjinder's brain kicked into overdrive as he tried to think of ways in which he could carry out the repairs. After half an hour of sitting in the corner of the shed, looking at the damaged beast, deep in thought, he approached Jumbo Majumdar. Jumbo knew Harjinder's answer before he knew it himself; he knew Harjinder would not be able resist a challenge.

Harjinder asked for two aircraft to be put at his disposal and for them to begin a shuttle service between Tonk and Fort Sandeman carrying spares.

Naturally, Jumbo agreed, and then laughing, added Mukerjee had already agreed to face Harjinder's 'Subaltern's Court Martial' if he repaired the aircraft on site. It was Harjinder's turn to laugh. He thought Mukerjee deserved a medal, not a fine of beers. Once again, the reputation of the fledgling IAF was on the forefront of everyone's mind, and again, they decided that this accident should be reported as a precautionary landing, and not as a crash. A Court Martial would be flying around if their subterfuge was discovered. Time for the Harjinder's magic, and the extensive consumption of tea.

Mukerjee was flown back to Fort Sandeman by Jumbo, and two hours later, two aeroplanes appeared in formation as they closed in rapidly to the new 'Harjinder Singh's Tonk Aircraft Repair Station'. Flying Officers Surjit Singh Majithia and Mehr 'Baba' Singh brought repair tools, as well as two of Harjinder's best men, Aircraftsman Mohd Siddique and Aircraftsman Daulat Ram Bhatia. They meant business.

They had commandeered twenty locals and an interpreter from the Militia Commandant, with whose assistance, they started stripping the damaged Wapiti back to a basic structure. The undercarriage was shattered so most of the hired help was placed under the wings, their backs ready to take the load. As soon as the cross-bracings of the undercarriage were loosened the aircraft started to quiver with all the weight suddenly coming down on the Pathans. They were so scared many wailed, threatening to abandon the load and flee. Harjinder admitted later, that at one time he thought casualties were inevitable. Mohd Siddique had been detailed to keep the hired help in place. He took no chances and, brandishing a wooden stick, he whacked at the leg of any man who tried to move out of his position. The shouts and curses from Siddique left each man in no doubts of their fate if Siddique caught the individual alone after deserting his post. With fear of the IAF airman more than the fear of being crushed to death, the conscripted help held. Harjinder demonstrated his faith in the men when he dived under the fuselage and began rigging up the new undercarriage.

The Wapitis continued the shuttle runs back and forth, in what was still appalling weather. One pilot Harjinder singled out for praise was Flying Officer Majithia. This daring pilot never took a break from his duties, shuttling between Tonk and Fort Sandeman throughout the stormy weather. He brought all the necessary spare parts, some of them lashed under the fuselage, and some tied on the top of the rear of the fuselage. Majithia's father, Sir Surinder Singh Majithia, came from a ruling family of the Punjab and was one of the richest men in the area, yet his son was in the Air Force as a Flying Officer. Despite his wealthy and privileged background he was the most disciplined and popular officer Harjinder had ever come across.

In just two days, the aircraft that had looked like a telegraph pole, was ready to go. The engine was tested and this time Harjinder knew the routine for the test flight, not being fooled by the initial fast taxi test run. The report on the first flight? It flew beautifully. Then there was the small matter of ferrying the phoenix aircraft to Fort Sandeman. The tussle between Squadron Leader Mukerjee and Flight Lieutenant Jumbo Majumdar was interesting. Jumbo wanted to prove that the repairs done by his men were fool proof, and he wanted to show his confidence in them by flying the aircraft. Squadron Leader Mukerjee felt responsible for the whole sorry affair and would not allow it. Being of higher rank, naturally he had his way. Harjinder volunteered to go in the back of the newly restored plane in a joint show of faith. It seemed as though Mother Nature was not pleased to have missed Mukerjee the first time, and as the two aircraft took off, another dust storm sprung up. Within minutes, it was not possible to climb over the hills that lay across their course. Mukerjee kept the newly repaired Wapiti low, making detours to find the valleys clear of the ever present dust. The walls of brown rock and boulders zoomed past the wing tips, and the dust blowing above them. Harjinder though what a great experience the last two days had been. He just had to survive the breath taking return flight!

True to his word, Jumbo arranged a Subaltern's Court Martial and Harjinder once again presided over it. He sentenced Squadron Leader

Mukerjee to a fine of two hundred and fifty rupees which went to the Flight Entertainment Fund. He paid up willingly and remarked that he was surprised that labour was so cheap in their Flight! The IAF was up to full aircraft strength, and the RAF had not found out about the incident. That is, they didn't find out until a strange decision taken by Mukerjee.

This recovery of an aircraft in a remote corner was a remarkable feat for the newly nationalised Flight, and clearly, Squadron Leader Mukerjee felt he should spread the news, clearly forgetting the minor fact that it was a secret. After his return to Ambala he assembled all British Senior NCOs that were attached to the IAF at Ambala and gave them an account of the wonderful performance of the Indian technicians! Later, a British Airman revealed that the chat amongst the British after their talk with Mukerjee was to "fix" Harjinder at the first opportunity because, at the rate at which he was going, he would very soon be promoted as a Warrant Officer and therefore put a British Warrant Officer out of a job! With that in their mind, it seems incredible that not one passed the information up the chain of command about the crash that never was. Perhaps, with Mukerjee's complete openness on the subject, they all assumed that it was carried out with Headquarters' blessings. Maybe they were relying on one of their officers to do the needful.

Those British Airmen would have done well to discuss Harjinder with a few of those Warrant Officers they thought they were protecting. One such Warrant Officer was Simms, the Station Engineering Officer at Peshawar, with whom Harjinder had a good relationship. Simm's status was further raised after a visit by Wing Commander Carpenter DFC, the India Command Engineer. Harjinder rang up Simms to warn him of the VIP's imminent visit. His response was very casual and matter of fact. 'Bring him along to the workshops', was all he said as he put the phone down.

Harjinder accompanied the Command Engineering Officer throughout his tour of their facilities. On reaching Simms's office, he rushed ahead to announce the visitor. To his horror the Warrant Officer made no attempt move but just said; 'Okay. Bring him in.'

Harjinder stopped in his tracks and looked around the workshop. He noticed that there was only a stool beside the chair on which Simms was sitting and the place hadn't even been tidied up. Harjinder quickly suggested that he rush out and tell the chaprasi to fetch another chair, but Simms told him not to fuss. The Warrant Officer on seeing Wing

Commander Carpenter enter said; 'Come in, Sir, and sit down,' pointing to the stool. Harjinder shrank back in the shadows and left the office.

As soon as the Command Engineering Officer left the Station, Harjinder hurried back to speak to Simms. He made no bones about his very casual behaviour towards a senior officer. With a mischievous look in his eye Simms beckoned Harjinder to sit down and listen. 'Wing Commander Carpenter was an air gunner in my Squadron', he said. 'In fact, it was I who recommended him for a commission after I turned down the offer myself. Besides, I am an MBE. Don't you know that an MBE outranks a DFC?'

Harjinder took Simms's comments at face value, and thought a Member of the order of the British Empire, the MBE, was like a passport to heaven. In the future he would change his mind twice about that.

The World War II was rattling around them now with the ebb and flow of the Italian and German troops in North Africa being the main focus of attention. Understandably, little attention outside India was turned on the North-West Frontier Province, and the exploits of 'C' Flight IAF. However, for the first time, a completely Indian unit had completed a year-long operational tour of duty, leaving with the same aircraft they arrived with, although several aircraft had many shiny, new parts included in them! When the time came for Harjinder's Flight to take their leave from Fort Sandeman, the IAF 'B' Flight, under Flight Lieutenant Narendra, came from Ambala to take over. As Harjinder gratefully returned to his loving wife, and the long awaited family life, he knew a new chapter in IAF history had been written. Every man who had been stationed there took immense pride in their achievement, as they left the rugged outpost behind them. Their performance was the forerunner of things to come, and the perfect rehearsal for a full-fledged Air Force about to enter the wider arena of war on a global scale.

That global war was one step too far for the long serving Wapiti; the flying shed, the lumbering ox, the festooned Christmas tree, the ultra-reliable collection of wire, fabric, oil and grease which had served them far beyond the wildest dreams of the original designers. However, a new ferocious enemy would surely call for a modern, state-of-the art aircraft wouldn't it?

Seven

A New Aircraft but Old Prejudices

> 'You people think you are superior to the RAF, but you are not. We come from a country which is the pivot of civilisation. Every man there is a born engineer.'

> 'I have been in the RAF over 25 years, but I have never before met such a madcap like you, Flight Sergeant Harjinder Singh.'

> 'Harjinder; to doubt your technical ability is to doubt one's own existence. What they have tried to do to you is what I call the last kick of a dying mule.'

After the excitement of their year-long operational duty, it was back to Ambala. But for Harjinder the drudgery of training was partly offset by the chance to finally sample married life. It was unclear what role his IAF Squadron would play in the World War that was closing in around them, since Britain was under the cosh there was no doubt that the IAF would soon be in the thick of it. Their training was taking on a new edge; further heightened by the exciting news that No. 1 Squadron's aging Wapiti would indeed finally be replaced. One of their Flights had already been equipped before they headed to the North-West Frontier to take over from Harjinder's Wapitis; the Hawker Audax was a sprightlier biplane with sleek lines that showed the way to future designs. This was a temporary measure with plans to replace those machines on their return from the front. However, not all the Audax aircraft would return from that lawless Province. A certain Flying Officer Arjan Singh left his crumpled aircraft amongst the grey, boulders on that desolate landscape. Like Mehr 'Baba' Singh before him, Arjan took a rogue bullet through the forward fuselage that sliced through his fuel pipe as it exited. The rear gunner owed his life to Arjan Singh not once, but twice. Arjan kept death at arm's length, using his unparalleled flying skills and carefully positioning the fuselage of their Audax between the scattered boulders. He accepted the loss of wings and wheels in the impact to keep him, and his gunner alive within the crumpling framework. The gunner's second escape from death, came when he correctly fled from the wreckage, away from the chance of fire, and away from what was now a beacon to the tribal fighters. The problem was that he ran directly towards the fearsome, uncompromising, warriors. Arjan chased after him, with blood flowing down his face, throwing him onto the ground before pointing him in the correct direction and setting him off again like a racing greyhound. The scars from that crash are still visible today on Marshal Arjan Singh's nose, and provide a very tangible link to the IAF biplane days over Afghanistan.

The eagerly awaited, new aircraft would be coming in the second half of 1941, so the men had to prepare for their new mount. The new aeroplane signalled the end of the biplane era, because the new Westland aircraft that they would take to war were monoplanes. The slab-like wings sat on top of the large barrel shaped fuselage. The large, round, radial engine, bolted on the front, was still only a development of the Wapiti's engine, but it gave more power. This was no slick machine like the Spitfire or Hurricane. The long, gangly undercarriage was fixed, not retractable, with 2 machine-guns in the wheel covers and little stub winglets that could only carry tiny practice bombs. The long glasshouse that extended rearwards from the pilot's cockpit, under the slab wing to the observer/ air gunner in the back, had a sliding rear section to uncover Harjinder's only, doubtful, offensive capability; the rear facing machine gun. Perched high atop the fuselage, with the wings extending out at his head level, the pilot's visibility was excellent to carry out the aircraft's designed role as an Army cooperation machine. This was not a new aircraft in the RAF inventory by any stretch of the imagination, with its poor top speed and complete vulnerability to fighters.

1st April 1941 was another big day for the IAF. Having proved themselves in operations over the past years, and equipped with a training system that was producing sufficient numbers, No. 2 Squadron, IAF, was raised at Peshawar. The command was initially given to Flight Lieutenant

AB Awan. You would expect a new Squadron, especially in time of war, to be raised with cutting edge equipment. Not so for the IAF's second squadron. They had the cast-off, hand me down aircraft from their sister unit, No. 1 Squadron – the now utterly obsolete, Westland Wapiti. It had a unit establishment of 20 officers and 164 men and they took their Wapitis to war as coastal reconnaissance machines. Harjinder had to say goodbye to six officers from No. 1 Squadron who were sent to the new squadron, and hello to another seven arriving from training to replace them. Flight Lieutenant Aspy Engineer, the teenage pilot who flew from London to India to win the Aga Khan trophy, became the commander of this new IAF Squadron in June 1941. The band of brothers, the Musketeers, were being whittled down, but Harjinder found solace in the fact that ultimately, this was what he, and the other founders, had been yearning for; expansion! They had a credible air force, and now it was doubling in size.

In Ambala, Harjinder stepped straight back into a towering wave of resentment from the British personnel. They resented the fact that British personnel had been shunted off the base at Fort Sandeman during the IAF's stay, even though it was a location which they had previously complained about to anyone who had the misfortune to enquire about the conditions at that outpost. The British Sergeants and Warrant Officers began to shun him as the instigator of the 'Indianisation' plan. In Headquarters, Harjinder's desire to officially continue working with his hands, developing his role, was recognised and a month later, he was detailed to undergo the Fitter 1 Conversion Course he had wanted so badly to enrol in.

Harjinder's Indian colleagues hinted that he ought to watch his back during the course, but he laughed it off. He assumed that a college education, years of practical experience, the extra work in the Engine Repair Shops, all reinforced by knowledge gained at Aircraft Depot at Karachi, would be all that was required to sail through the course. Why should he 'watch out'? Harjinder wrote: 'I was not worried at all. I thought I will teach the Chief Technical Officer (*who happened to be the old ex-Warrant Officer Herbert from Karachi, now commissioned as a Squadron Leader*) quite a few things, leave aside others below him. My Commanding Officer (*Jumbo Majumdar had taken over as the Commanding Officer*) also warned that I would be the target of the whole RAF, being the first, and the only, Indian Flight Sergeant. They would do their best to pull me down.'

Harjinder assured his boss that he could take care of himself.

Harjinder reported to the now Squadron Leader Herbert, at the School of Technical Training, who was far from welcoming, 'I do not think you will pass out as Fitter 1. I advise you to return to the Squadron under some pretext or the other.'

Harjinder recovered from his shock and, not one to take an insult lying down, retorted that he had joined the IAF only for one purpose; to prove that Indians could do anything which RAF technicians' could, in fact, they could do even better.

Herbert was enraged. How dare this Indian Flight Sergeant talk back to him like that! His blinkered sensibilities couldn't conceive of an intelligent Indian airman, he assumed they were all useless and trying to teach them would be a waste of his time. He was about to be proven very wrong. Before Harjinder could even join the class, Herbert wanted to check his basic knowledge, proving that he really didn't know Harjinder at all! He started by asking him what a Eutectic alloy was. Harjinder smiled and answered correctly. Herbert tried to ask him other complicated questions to catch him out, but naturally, failed. Harjinder had been a theoretical engineer long before being a 'hands on' engineer. Herbert became more and more infuriated, and as Harjinder admitted, he became cockier with his replies. Squadron Leader Herbert ended the interview, furious.

Harjinder joined Abdul Salaam, U.K. Nair, Rabbani and Harchand Singh, the other Indian classmates on the course. Part of the course was elementary mathematics, which Harjinder felt was inferior to his High School standards. However, the despair of going back to basics, and the return of the blinkered RAF personnel around him, was offset by joy in another direction. The Lysander aircraft would soon be arriving into the IAF, so the training programme was in full swing for the technicians. It might not be a fighter aircraft, a Spitfire or Hurricane, or even a light bomber, but the Lysander was a step up from the old Wapiti.

Finally, it was time for the final examination for the fitter's course. The Indians had worked far beyond the course's requirements, any doubts they might have had about their performance were banished. On the morning of the exams, Squadron Leader Herbert put in an appearance and asked to see Harjinder. He was taking no chances, and had decided to examine Harjinder himself. Herbert's excuse, 'Because you are the senior-most Indian and about to become a Warrant Officer, we must not leave anything to chance.'

Whether Herbert was insulting, or complimenting, Harjinder, remains unclear, but he was predicting that Harjinder would become the first Indian Warrant Officer, so Harjinder played his part in this charade. Besides, he wanted to show off his knowledge to the man who had doubted his abilities right from the beginning. After Herbert had finished the examination, there was little doubt he had been won over by Harjinder.

But he also gave a grave warning. 'There are higher politics over which I have no control.'

What had he meant by this? Once again Harjinder shrugged off this ominous warning, not taking note of those who knew the system and how the system worked. It certainly seemed as if all was in order because the following week, when the results were published, Harjinder had passed with a 'credit'.

On the day prior to their departure from the Station, Herbert called Harjinder once again. The Commanding Officer had ordered Harjinder to take the original Sergeants' Confirmation-in-Rank Test. Harjinder pointed out that he passed all that in 1937, with honours no less, and consequently was appointed an Instructor at RAF Station Peshawar. There were no more examinations for him to take. Herbert seemed happy with Harjinder's response, so told him just to appear in the Lysander Conversion Course, and impress all the staff with all the new 'gen' he had picked up. That would be an end to it all.

Naturally it wasn't. Harjinder and the others, who were Acting Sergeants, were asked to sit an examination at the end of the course. They assumed it was a Lysander Conversion exam but as they took their places in the examination room, it became clear that the test had nothing to do with the subject at hand. All questions were ridiculously simple and pertaining to Wapiti repairs. We know Harjinder had become the world's expert in putting shattered Wapitis together even if HQ had little knowledge of it! Harjinder's first instinct was to walk out of the examination hall. On second thoughts, however, he felt sure of sweeping all the questions before him. He dived into the exam, actually taking some delight in it. He raced through the questions in about half the allotted time. Once he had finished he walked over to the Squadron Leader Herbert's office, informed him about the 'mistake' with the exam, all before the allocated time was over.

However, Herbert had a bigger surprise for Harjinder. He gave him a copy of the daily duty orders, which, unusually, had not been made available to Harjinder's team that morning. Harjinder read the duty orders, motionless, seething with rage. 'The following Senior NCOs of the IAF are to appear in the Acting Sgts Confirmation Test today' was the title with a list of names topped with Harjinder's. He had been conned into the exam room to sit the Sergeants' Confirmation Test.

After their previous conversation, Harjinder was furious. He asked Herbert how this could have been allowed to go unchecked, but Herbert, very matter-of-factly reminded him of their previous conversation, *this* was the higher politics he had warned Harjinder about.

So Harjinder and the others waited, checking the notice board for the results of the completely irrelevant exam. They had sat two papers, each with an expected pass mark of 70 per cent. For two days, their results were held back, and declared only one hour before their departure for Peshawar. Harjinder had scored 96 per cent in Paper 'A' and 69.5 per cent in Paper 'B'. So that was it; a fail – Harjinder would to be prevented from being promoted to Warrant Officer. One can only assume that they didn't want him repeating the same experiment as he had done with the Flight at Fort Sandeman, with the Indians taking over!

Trembling with rage, Harjinder walked into Squadron Leader Herbert's Office and demanded to see his answer sheet. The very act of Herbert showing Harjinder, in confidence, the offending examination sheet demonstrated had had been won over by Harjinder's knowledge and performance. Harjinder scanned through his answer sheet twice. Everything was correct except where the examiner had written in the margin, 'What is this?' in red ink, next to a well-known, and widely used abbreviation. Harjinder knew his fight was no longer with Herbert. He politely thanked the Squadron Leader and asked his permission to copy his exam paper. Herbert readily agreed, but asked him to keep it to himself.

Storming out of the base, Harjinder, picked up his belongings and without a word to the other IAF Engineers, all who were awarded passes in the exam, left for the train station. Harjinder with a temper was a fearsome prospect, and so on that train to Peshawar, all the others kept their distance from the volcano that was threatening to blow. At Peshawar, Harjinder burst into Jumbo Majumdar's office, only to be informed that the Commanding Officer was away on an inspectional visit to Miranshah. He knew that Jumbo was the only one who would feel the depth of rage as he had, and who would take up the cudgels on his behalf, fight the RAF brass, if need be, and see that justice was done. Harjinder was not one to

sit and brood, he was a man of action. He requested an immediate flight
to Miranshah to see him.

As the Wapiti finished the landing run, and taxied towards the parking
area at Miranshah, Harjinder was already released from his monkey
chain and swinging his legs over the side. He jumped down onto the
hard packed ground before striding out to track Jumbo down. From the
moment Jumbo saw Harjinder, he knew something was about to need
his undivided attention. Trying to keep his anger in check, and his voice
level, Harjinder laid the story out in front of him. Any doubt Harjinder
may have had on Jumbo's stance was immediately dispelled, 'Harjinder,
to doubt your technical ability is to doubt one's own existence. What
they have tried to do to you is what I call the last kick of a dying mule. I
promise to fight your case until we win. I shall appeal to the Air Ministry,
if required. You leave it to me.'

So Harjinder left it to him, knowing that Jumbo Majumdar was a man
of his word. He let the rage slowly drain from his body. Jumbo arranged
for Harjinder to fly in the rear cockpit of his Wapiti on the return flight
home, the next day. Strapped into the rear cockpit, Harjinder brooded
over the events. It seemed that the enemy they were heading towards was
no longer the tribes squatting in the ravines and behind the boulders, but
the British in Delhi Headquarters. The following day Jumbo, true to his
word, had written the letter to Air HQ. It read:

> 'Flight Sergeant Harjinder Singh is not an ordinary airman.
> Before he joined the IAF he had a political trend of mind, but it
> is fortunate for the IAF that he eventually has followed the right
> ideas. He is the mainstay of my Squadron, an inspiration to his
> juniors, and an excellent guide to my junior officers. He has proved
> his technical abilities time and again. He studied Engineering for
> five years before he joined the IAF. If the Air Headquarters have
> any doubts, he is prepared to compete with any technical officer
> of the RAF in India or abroad in a written or practical test. If he
> fails to beat him, he is prepared to revert back to LAC rank. I, who
> know him more than anyone else, guarantee that if he fails, I am
> prepared to revert back to my substantive rank of Flying Officer.'

It was more than Harjinder could have hoped for. He was fully
reassured and left the matter in Jumbo's hands, throwing himself into his
work with renewed determination.

That letter set in motion a series of events that unfolded at breakneck speed. It appeared that the Commanding Officer of the Training School had also written a letter to Air Headquarters, but to complain about Harjinder's behaviour. The Group Captain flew to Peshawar and addressed the Indian Squadron's Officers and men. It seems he may have taken inspiration from Sir John Steel in his methods of man management. He began; 'You people think you are superior to the RAF, but you are not. We come from a country which is the pivot of civilisation. Every man there is a born engineer. Some of your Senior NCOs have criticised our instructors at school. I am warning you all that we shall not spare any undisciplined man.'

Jumbo, who was standing to this RAF Officer's right, winked at Harjinder and smiled as the Group Captain unleashed his antiquated ideals.

The Group Captain then asked Commanding Officers of both No. 1 Squadron and No. 2 Squadron to fly to Ambala immediately to see the disputed papers. On reaching, they were on the receiving end of a technical lecture from Flight Lieutenant Harper as he tried to prove that his marking scheme was fool proof. Jumbo could see no logic to what he was being told and so fired back at Harper, 'Of course, my challenge on Harjinder still stands. I am not going to withdraw that letter. He wishes to send these papers to Air Ministry for marking.'

Having seen the exam with his own eyes Jumbo returned with even greater confidence in Harjinder than before.

Air Headquarters realised they were walking into a minefield, and so suggested that Harjinder reappear in the examination. He dismissed that request immediately, saying it was an insult to his abilities and his moral compass. Air Headquarters took a different line and wrote to Jumbo to inform him that the Technical School had been instructed to send Harjinder's answer books to the Air Ministry, for marking. However, on receipt of the request, the Training School replied that they were sorry to inform all concerned, that the papers were lost. A very convenient, if desperately unoriginal, excuse! So it was decreed that there was no alternative and Harjinder would have to reappear in the test. No one in the IAF took this retest seriously. A smug Harper unabashedly approached Harjinder, when he was leaving Ambala, to drive home that all their efforts were in vain. 'If the School of Technical Training does not want to pass a man, he fails. No one in India can do a thing about it, least of all a Squadron Leader of the IAF' (*meaning the outspoken Jumbo Majumdar, of course*).

The exams were taken, the papers were marked, and the marks were declared. There were no prizes handed out for predicting the results; once again the School had failed Harjinder, this time with one mark less than before. Air Headquarters were taking a closer interest now, and once again requested for the answer books to review the examination themselves. Perhaps it was the same careless clerk who was put in-charge of the answer books, because, once again, Harjinder's books, and only Harjinder's books, were lost. Who would have thought?

Consequently, Air Headquarters asked the School for an explanation, but the rather terse response from the school Commanding Officer was; 'If Air Headquarters are so favourably inclined towards a Senior NCO of the IAF, and do not trust me and my staff, I am prepared to be relieved of my Command.'

Just imagine the huffing and puffing at the head offices in the School, as the key players discussed this outrage – they would decide who, and how, the IAF technical department progressed, how impertinent for these Indian upstarts to think they could actually progress without their approval.

Imagine also these faces when the orders arrived one morning informing Wing Commander Simpson, Squadron Leader Herbert, and Flight Lieutenant Harper, that they were all relieved of their positions as per the letter. Air Headquarters went even further, declaring Harjinder successful in the examination, and all results from his record of the two previous 'failures' were expunged. The whole experience did nothing for Harjinder's opinion of the RAF. He claimed it was the first time in his service career that he learnt that not all RAF people were like Flight Lieutenant Bouchier, or Flight Lieutenant Hickey, or Flight Sergeant Hill, who had given him the impression of extreme fairness. After that experience, he became almost hostile to the British. However, the whole unfortunate episode did show that the blinkered, self-superior, self-serving people were only in clusters.

The whole battle with the RAF had taken nine months to come to a satisfactory conclusion, but the world never stands still, especially with a World War to take into account. The Germans had stormed through Greece, Yugoslavia, also taking the island of Crete in a daring parachute raid. On their Eastern border, the seemingly unstoppable Germans had rolled into the Soviet Union, reaching the outskirts of Moscow and taking parts of a city very few people had heard of; Stalingrad. That name was about to become a famous symbol of resistance, never accepting defeat whatever the human cost. War in the streets of Stalingrad was stripped of technology and reduced to basic survival on both sides. In the meantime, Harjinder had the new Lysander aircraft to 'play' with. He had soon put the troubles of the last few months behind him and was up to his old tricks – rebuilding aircraft 'written off' by the RAF, bringing them back to life with his team of Indian technicians.

In the August of 1941, between his 2 'attempts' to pass his Fitter 1 course, Harjinder and his team were ordered to proceed to the Aircraft Depot, Karachi, for re-equipment to 'modern aircraft'; their Lysanders. Harjinder believed Jumbo singlehandedly persuaded Air Headquarters to reequip the squadron with the Lysander. This does seem unlikely because their new aircraft were financed as a gift from the citizens of Bombay. It fell to the Indian population to raise funds to bring a more modern aircraft to their men. This display of benevolence from the inhabitants of that great city, led to the squadron's rechristening – they came to be known as the Bombay Squadron.

The IAF's No. 1 (Bombay) Squadron, proceeded to Karachi with their Squadron pilots and a hand-picked maintenance crew. The RAF's No. 28 Squadron were also detailed in Karachi for conversion training at the same time. This kept the strong rivalry, but friendship, between the Squadrons bubbling away, as they prepared for combat together. As the pressure increased, so did the banter between these two units.

At Karachi, while the pilots crawled all over the new aircraft there came news of a setback for the IAF. Jumbo silently handed Harjinder a signal from Aircraft Park, Lahore, which coldly stated that Flying Officer Nanda had crashed an Audax the previous evening at Lahore, and Flying Officer Jagdev Chandra had crashed in a cemetery near Jammu. Both of them had left for Lahore, following different routes from the Chenab River. Chandra went North and Nanda went East. One reportedly crashed because he could not find a landing ground near Jammu, possibly because there was none! Chandra learned the hard way that from the air, a cemetery can look very much like an open field, but, in reality, when close up on your final approach, it makes a poor landing site, unless your plan is to achieve cremation and burial all in one step! However, on this day, fate smiled on the IAF and both pilots survived their separate incidents. The

only 'fatalities' were the aircraft, without Harjinder on hand there was no
one to rebuild them. Jumbo's face was turning red, with a combination of
rage and concern. He said; 'Harjinder I feel ashamed. At this rate, if we do
go to war, we would be written off in a week. Look at these senior pilots.
One of them has done civil flying over a number of years, the other one is
senior enough to be a Flight Commander and look what they have done.
The RAF must be laughing at us.'

It was Harjinder's turn now to show his confidence in Jumbo and the
pilots under his care. His bold statement was; 'Sir, it is just a piece of bad
luck. It could happen to any pilot. We must make sure that we take new
and young pilots in our Squadron and train them according to your ideas.
If they crash, I promise you I will rebuild the aircraft, even if it breaks into
a thousand pieces.'

Jumbo brightened at this; he shook Harjinder by the hand, and holding
his gaze, said: 'Between the two of us, we will build a completely new
set. When I lack inspiration, you supply it, and I will do the same for you.
We will be successful. Come what may, we will go into action and prove
our mettle.'

A few days later, the Squadron assembled. They could barely contain
their excitement, but all the crews prepared their new mounts with extra
care and meticulous attention to detail. With this lumbering giant, the
IAF found themselves in the age of the monoplane. They started their
engines together, taxied out, and one after the other, they bumped
along the runway at Karachi to head out on the first leg to Peshawar.
The Jumbo-Harjinder partnership was well-established now, so it is no
surprise that Harjinder flew in Jumbo's rear cockpit, taking off last, and
aiming to land first, as an example to the rest. Jumbo eased the control
column back and the slab wings lifted their aircraft off the ground. With
the glass of the cockpit sides coming down to his waist level, Jumbo felt
less like he was sitting *in* an aeroplane, and more like he was viewing it
from above. Looking down, the only thing to interrupt his panoramic
view was the wheels, and undercarriage, dangling uselessly in the air, and
the reassuringly robust 'Vee' strut attaching the mid-point of the wings
to the fuselage. The ground dropped away as the Lysander climbed into
the cloudless sky. Jumbo turned his head, scanning the horizon. The front
edge of the wings extended out along his line of sight, and by ducking
down, or stretching up, he could look below and above the wings. The
ample glass above his head gave him an excellent view to scan for an

enemy that would be the threat in the not-too-distant future. Harjinder faced backwards, enjoying the relative tranquillity of his rear seat, when compared to the open Wapiti cockpit. He surveyed his new brood, his new charges, bobbing in the air currents around him. These were not modern aircraft, but it felt as if the IAF had just leapt forward a quantum leap in technology.

As they circled the skies above Padidan, the Lysanders with their fixed undercarriage, and high wings, looked like vultures on the prowl with talons poised. One by one, they peeled off to make their approaches. Each pilot knew the weight of expectation was on their shoulders, and despite their best efforts, shoulders and arms stiffened as they manipulated the controls to bring their new, precious, machines into the landing attitude. Jumbo had briefed each of their young pilots, and consequently, the first arrival for the squadron was uneventful. The new pilots were Pilot Officers Moolgavkar, Satyanarayana, Malse, Namgyal, Deuskar, Henry Runganadhan, Nanda, Homi Ratnagar and 'Andy' Ananthanarayanan.

Their perfect start didn't last when they reached Multan at 2 pm. Each aircraft rolled to a halt after landing except the last but one in the line. Andy was the pilot, with Daulat Ram in the rear seat. Lysander P9180 seemed to touch down normally, but suddenly they violently slewed left, kicking up the dust as they went. The swing left seemed consistent with a burst port tyre. It happened with enough speed for the aircraft to teeter up on one wheel bringing the wingtip crunching onto the ground. The tail returned to ground with a thud, and the violent screech of metal tearing. The skin around the tail-plane was ripped open, breaking the main tail spar as it went. The mini version of the wing 'Vee' strut, which held the tail on, was ripped clean off. Jumbo, who was watching, put his face in his hands in agony refusing to believe what his eyes were telling him. One of his new aircraft, only days old, had been ripped to shreds in front of him. The two crew members climbed down the steps in the fuselage, and down the leg strut, to the ground below. Looking shocked and bewildered they walked, heads bowed and shoulders dropped, to where the Squadron mates stood.

Harjinder looked around him and the despair on the faces was evident. He took Jumbo by the shoulders and gathered the other main players around them. In that hurriedly convened conference he tried to cheer up the Squadron by telling them not to worry, they would not be seen by No. 28 Squadron here, and he would fix everything. However, Harjinder admitted; 'In my heart of hearts I knew it would be almost impossible. I asked myself: But how? There isn't even a welding plant here.'

Jumbo knew nothing would come of hanging around looking at the wreck. He set his crew to work preparing their other Lysanders, giving instructions that the rest of the Squadron should takeoff immediately after refuelling. Jumbo knew that as the Squadron boss he needed to lead the rest of the unit on to their destination, but there was only one man to complete the task discussed in the conference, his own rear seat observer. He arranged a swap, leaving Harjinder behind to work his magic. Believing when you fall off a horse, you must get straight back onto it, he assigned Andy to take Flying Officer Nanda's aircraft. So Nanda was detailed to stay behind with the two Aircraftsmen requested by Harjinder. Daulat Ram may just have been in an accident but Harjinder rated him as a 'hands on' engineer, so he remained along with Ghulam Rabbani. It was 3.30 pm when the last aircraft took off from Multan airfield, including the slightly pale Andy. The dust plumes kicked up by the departing Lysanders were still in the air as the one pilot and 3 technicians kneeled next to the damaged aircraft. The vulture-like Lysanders did a turn over the airfield as a final farewell, waggle of the wings as a sign of good luck, before they faded into the horizon. Harjinder was already too busy to pay much attention, but he appreciated the kind thought.

Flying Officer Nanda was not a new boy, and despite seeing how, and why, the legend that now shimmered around Harjinder had formed, he was doubtful of their success. It was not surprising when you consider that the aircraft type was brand new to the IAF, and even though Harjinder had done theoretical work on the Lysander, he had only had very limited practical experience with the machine. The training he had received was to keep a serviceable aircraft flying, not rebuilding one from broken remains. As they stood next to the damaged aircraft, Nanda called Harjinder aside and aired his misgivings; 'Look here old boy, you are a married man and so am I. We have to safeguard our careers. Why take this unnecessary risk? I can see that it will be impossible to do any major repairs here. Let us call it a day and catch the train.'

Harjinder told him to cast his mind back to the aircraft he had repaired at Fort Sandeman, which had been much worse than this. He firmly told Nanda that they had no alternative but to repair the Lysander. The RAF would laugh at them if they saw them minus one Lysander on the very first day of the re-equipment with 'modern' aircraft. Nanda looked doubtful;

'In that case, you are going to fly with me when I take up the aircraft. I won't let you go off by train.'

Harjinder had no problem with that. Nanda clearly didn't think Harjinder could do it this time. Not only did he not get involved with helping Harjinder, he went to stay at the Multan railway station ready to complete his journey through steam power.

Harjinder went around Multan City looking for a welding plant, but to no avail. There was no organised workshop, no facilities that could be of any use. They were running out of time, No. 28 Squadron would be landing at Multan the following morning. The mantra was; 'They must not see our crashed aircraft.'

Yet again, a crash was to be kept from the higher echelons.

Harjinder carefully assessed the damage, looking at every affected part very carefully. It was late at night when he decided that the only way ahead was to take a very bold step. He would repair the fuselage structure, where the tail-wheel assembly was fitted, by sleeving. This meant that he would straighten the buckled fuselage tubes running along its length, and fit a tube of metal, the sleeve, around the damaged area. All he needed was the material to make the sleeves. When the aircraft were kept outside in windy conditions, the men would drive large stakes, or pickets, into the ground and then attach ropes from the pickets to the wings. Harjinder took the pickets from the rear compartment and sliced them up. The mild steel wasn't the best to use, but to its credit it was a very thick gauge. The problem now was the tail-plane, where the rivets had sheared.

Harjinder looked, examined, and pondered, until he ran out of ideas. He kept reminding himself that the RAF Squadron were hot on their trail, and the parting words from Jumbo; 'I am not reporting this accident now. You must bring it flying by tomorrow, not later than 1 pm. Failing that, I shall have no alternative but to report the accident to Air Headquarters.'

Filing a report almost 24 hours on would instantly expose their attempted cover up. Indeed, this was a desperate situation, and pacing up and down the hanger, he did something quite uncharacteristic, he began to pray for guidance; and someone must have heard his agonised appeal, because he was suddenly struck with an idea. There were hundreds of screws on this aircraft. Supposing he removed one screw in every four, it would not matter a great deal (*I wonder if the Lysander design team in Britain would have agreed with Harjinder's reasoning!*). They straightened out the skin of the tail-plane as best they could and found the screws fitted perfectly in the holes left by the sheared rivets.

In the darkness, the wounded Lysander returned to its proper shape, if not quite as good as new. When Harjinder paid a visit to the single story, white washed Railway waiting room, with the steep, blue, corrugated iron roof, he found Nanda still unconvinced. Once again, he warned Harjinder of the risk they were taking, but in return, Harjinder reassured him as best as he could. Harjinder didn't receive any encouragement on his return to the airfield either. Rabbani shuffled along as he strode to the aircraft and said; 'I am not sure that the tail-plane will hold.'

Even as he assured Rabbani that the aircraft would be fine, he began to doubt himself. As he finally turned in for a short cat nap, right before dawn, he kept dreaming about the disasters that might befall the plane as it took flight the next day.

Doubt in his own abilities was not something Harjinder often felt! It drove him out of his makeshift bed and back to the Lysander. He went to check the aircraft again, rechecking the creased, dented, but complete tail unit structure; naturally, everything was satisfactory.

Early in the morning, a rather creased and crumpled Nanda arrived from the train station waiting room, still looking concerned. This did nothing to calm Harjinder's own nerves. The two men gingerly climbed up the side of the Lysander as if their extra weight would destroy it. The two aircraftsmen followed them up to help with the seat harness, before being despatched to the train station. The engine started on the first try, disturbing the dust in the still, early morning air. They bumped along the ground, wincing with every jolt, as they taxied in to takeoff position on the airstrip. The throttle went to full power and the engine noise rose to the usual crescendo. With most tail-wheel aircraft you raised the tail off the ground as soon as possible on the takeoff roll. Not so the Lysander. The tail was kept firmly on the ground until, at 80 mph, the aircraft was flown off the runway in that tail-down climbing attitude. Could the tail take the strain of roaring along the ground until the correct speed of 80mph was reached, without shearing off? Harjinder realised how much Nanda doubted the safety of the tail-plane as he started twisting his head around to try and make sure the tail-plane was still there. Harjinder thrust his head into Nanda's field of vision and shouted at the top of his voice over the engine noise; 'I will tell you if the tail falls off! You keep your mind on the flying.'

Harjinder's concern about the tail evaporated for those brief seconds, being more concerned that Nanda would kill them both if he didn't pay attention to what the aircraft was doing.

Nanda kept facing forward, head unnaturally, rigidly, in place. The main-wheels left the ground and the shadow of the IAF Lysander shrank as it seemed to drop away from them. They circled, climbing over the relative safety of the strip, before heading away. Harjinder did glance at the shadow of the tail-plane, as if to have extra confirmation that his machine was intact. The creaks from the fuselage seemed louder than ever but he told himself that this was his heightened senses; nothing unusual. He resisted the temptation to stare at the tail, so instead made a point of scanning the horizon, as much for Nanda's benefit as his own. He felt the first glow of satisfaction; not a single RAF aircraft in sight. However, Nanda didn't relax. Up ahead of them was the range of hills between Kohat and Peshawar. 'There is going to be lot of bumpiness', Nanda said, 'Do you think we will get through in one piece?'.

Harjinder's concerns were being pushed further and further to the back of his mind. In fact, he was starting to take Nanda's negativity as a personal slight. Again he offered an observation; 'You have got a parachute, haven't you? What are you worrying about? In any case, we have to stay in the aeroplane. How the hell can we get out?' Nanda admitted later, at that point he could have murdered Harjinder. It wasn't too much later when a different IAF pilot proved you could bail out of a Lysander!

The Lysander shook, but nothing moved; nothing ripped. Soon they were approaching Peshawar, where all came out to watch the return of the wayward child, their wounded soldier. Harjinder found Jumbo waiting for him at the airfield. He came and shook hands with him, glowing. He told him; 'I have just heard that No. 28 Squadron have pranged (*crashed*) three aircraft between Karachi and Kohat. Fancy that! We had no prangs!' he added with a wink.

The next day, the Warrant Officer Engineer of No. 28 Squadron, an old timer, came to find Harjinder. He wanted to discuss the issues they were having with their own Lysanders. It was becoming very apparent that the aircraft had a weak spot; its tail-wheel. These inflatable tyres were bursting left, right and centre. The hard, dusty landing strips in India were littered with small stones that were slicing these tail-wheel tyres to pieces. The RAF Warrant Officer told Harjinder that they were already out of spares, so his plan for the next burst tyre was to stuff the carcass

with straw. Not a particular good idea. Harjinder was already forming
a plan in his mind with regards to this weak link. Something had to be
done because the conditions in India were taking a toll on these "modern"
aircraft even faster than Harjinder had feared. Within a month of their
conversion course, the heads that had been held high had dropped once
again. Their Lysander tail-wheel tyres were now all damaged, and no
spares were available. Then, the news arrived of the sinking of a cargo ship
off Gibraltar. The battle in the Mediterranean was a fearsome contest, with
the Royal Navy escorting the desperately-needed cargo ships against the
ships, submarines, and aircraft of the Germans and Italians. That particular
cargo ship was the one holding all the Lysander tail-wheels earmarked for
India; all the eggs were in one basket and that basket was at the bottom of
the sea. The excitement of the previous month evaporated. Both the IAF,
and RAF, Lysanders were grounded at Kohat.

Meanwhile, at Peshawar, another milestone was ticked off. No. 3
Squadron IAF was formed, but they knew that the issue of the Lysander
tail-wheels would not bother them. A year after the Battle of Britain had
come to an end; the modern RAF Spitfires and Hurricanes had fought the
Luftwaffe to a standstill to finally dispel the invasion threat, this newest
of IAF Squadrons was to come into existence still in the biplane era. No.
3 Squadron IAF would get the few remaining hand-me-down Hawker
Audax biplanes.

When it was confirmed that their replacement tires were lost,
Harjinder was called into Jumbo's Office in Peshawar. The order given
by Jumbo to Harjinder was very 'unmilitary'. He produced one of his
well known, disarming, smiles and instructed Harjinder to use his 'magic
wand'. Harjinder had been brooding on this problem and told Jumbo that
he was prepared to do his part, to do his 'magic', provided Jumbo was
prepared to trust him and fly an aircraft with a wooden, yes wooden, tail-
wheel. It seemed that Harjinder wanted to drag aviation back to the age
of horse and cart, so he added that he would guarantee its safety. Jumbo
didn't flinch, didn't pause; 'I would fly it even if there were only one
chance in a hundred of success. We must prove to the RAF that No. 1
Squadron can keep going while the RAF remains grounded.'

It seems that rivalry was foremost in Jumbo's mind, more than the
thought of possible combat requirements!

Harjinder asked for 24 hours to sketch a design for his 'wooden wheel'.
It was a complicated business, not just a case of a block of wood, a hammer,

chisel and some sand paper! The description of the design is best left to Harjinder; 'The wheels I designed were internally sprung with 3/8 inch shock-absorber cords sandwiched round the hub in helical grooves. There was a central disc of mulberry wood which would not crack easily and on either side were rubber discs and steel shims held by counter-sunk bolts. On the outer periphery was a steel band shrunk on to the wooden disc, like a tonga tyre (*the cart drawn by an ox, used extensively in India*). These "wooden wheels" were produced at Khair Mohd Motor Works at Peshawar.'

Although Harjinder was fairly certain of success, he confessed to gnawing doubts. If they had a mishap, what would happen then? The IAF, only recently equipped with Lysanders, would become the target of much criticism and ridicule. You can see his point. The letter of apologies to Command for destroying their new aircraft, having fitted wooden wheels, would have made for an interesting read. Jumbo knew the risk, but he was not a man to shy away from taking chances; 'Only dead men take no risks' was the phrase he used when Harjinder confided his doubts to him. After this short, perfectly weighted comment, he told Harjinder that he had full confidence in his abilities as an engineer: 'Do not even let me know how you made this wheel. I will try one out for you.'

The phrase 'make do and mend' was being widely used in the UK, as the success of the German Kreigsmarine submarines strangled the supply routes to Britain. The phrase wasn't being taken too seriously by the RAF Chief Technical Officer, Flying Officer Wood. He had been told about Jumbo and Harjinder's plans, and told them up front that they were playing with fire. He didn't stop there; 'I have never before met such a mad-cap like you, Flight Sergeant Harjinder Singh. You will face a Court Martial soon, because on takeoff, or landing, this wooden darn thing will split into two. The flattened wheel will not revolve and it will tear the tail end of the structure (*he didn't know Harjinder could put tails back together if called upon!*). Then, by friction on the tarmac, it will catch fire. The whole aircraft will then burn up. I tell you again, you are mad, and your Squadron Commander is equally mad. I tried to warn him of the danger, but he seems to have blind faith in you. Anyway, you will not find me a party to this unholy alliance.'

Harjinder did not discuss the matter further, but responded: 'Sir, I am fully aware of all the eventualities that can arise, but I have allowed for all of them.'

Wood dismissed Harjinder with a wave of his hand. With his eyes closed, he said; 'Go to hell if you want to: it is your own funeral.'

To Flying Officer Wood's credit, after his opinions had been fully aired, he made no attempt to stop Harjinder, no direct order to stop the plans, no report higher up the chain of command. He took the only path he could in order to give the IAF the space to carry out their 'madness'. He took a week's leave and left the station. Hear no evil, see no evil, speak no evil!

On 9th October 1941, K-9180, the first Lysander with a wooden-tail-wheel, flew. There could only be one choice of pilot and rear seat observer. Jumbo and Harjinder took the aircraft into the air. They carried out several 'touch and go' landings. No tail was ripped off, no aircraft bursting into flames. It was so successful, so normal, that as the engine fell quiet, except for the metallic ticking of the cooling cylinders, Jumbo turned in his seat to half face Harjinder and instructed him to equip each aircraft with one such tail-wheel, and to make some spare ones.

Jumbo gathered the IAF personnel together. He insisted that the wheel was to remain a secret, and told all the pilots and Airmen not to discuss this project with anyone. If anyone persisted in asking questions, refer him to the designer he said. He then asked Harjinder to paint the whole wheel with black paint to conceal the details of its construction. Was that a lack of brotherly conduct within comrades, or the best way to show the IAF in the best light? He did add to Harjinder; 'Let them first acknowledge our superior technical standard: then we might tell them.' Might? In his defence, there may have been a war on, but the war hadn't reached Northern India yet! Jumbo was still thinking of the IAF first; beating the Japanese was secondary!

The flurry of IAF Lysanders taking to the sky in Peshawar again meant that the news travelled to other nearby stations. Within a few days, the Warrant Officer Engineer of the RAF Kohat Squadron, came knocking and asked to see Harjinder, probing for details of his design. 'It is made of wood; that is all there is to it', was Harjinder's reply.

The Warrant Officer returned to his Unit, and went straight to work in the carpenter's shop to turn out his own version of a wooden wheel on the lathe. It was fitted to one of their aircraft and off it went. It was never going to be strong enough for the job, and on landing, it split along the grain. The Lysander swung round in a full circle, and ended up with a damaged tail unit. Harjinder doesn't write if he felt any guilt about the damaged RAF aircraft, but since no one was hurt, and IAF's standing climbing rapidly, I doubt he had. Thereafter, No. 28 Squadron gave up using wooden tail-wheels and the grounding of the whole Squadron was confirmed. The personnel must have watched with bewilderment as the IAF continued to fly a full day's flying programme, day after day after day. It may have been underhand keeping this information to themselves, but it certainly paid a handsome dividend because, when the opportunity came, it was not the RAF, but No. 1 Squadron IAF, who were chosen for the air display at the 'War Week' being held in Calcutta.

November 1941 saw IAF No. 1 Squadron depart for Calcutta. There seemed to be a constant stream of bad news from the front. The Royal Navy Cruiser named after the city, HMS Calcutta, had been sunk in June as they had prepared to leave their base. As No. 1 Squadron stopped en route to Calcutta, news broke about the aircraft carrier HMS Ark Royal, sunk trying to keep Malta alive. However, for the IAF Squadron, this job in Calcutta was to be 'a wonderful time, flying sorties every day, doing aerobatics and other star turns'. The IAF mixed in with their RAF brethren easily and soon, any initial misgivings of the Indians being amongst them, was swept away with a great friendship. General Wavell came to congratulate the IAF, and Jumbo introduced Harjinder to him as the first Indian Air Engineer. Harjinder wrote in his diary about how he burst with pride as he stood to attention, listening to the praise for him and his Air Force.

The contribution of the IAF, and the RAF, to 'War Week' was reported as the highlight of the show. It was tragic that on the 1 December, a very unfortunate incident cast a shadow on the events. One of the RAF Hawker Audax aircraft, K3686, was carrying out aerobatics over Calcutta to wow the inhabitants. The biplane dived down for speed, engine at full power and propeller at maximum revs. The pilot pulled the nose of the aircraft up from the dive and continued skywards to start a loop. As the nose reached the vertical, the engine chose that moment to let out a metal on metal screech before coming to a halt. The pilot was not much more than a passenger as the plane ran out of speed towards the top of his loop, the aircraft approached the upside down position, the airspeed rapidly decayed to nothing. One wing dropped and the nose fell through the horizon to point directly at the ground as the aircraft started to spin. The pilot obviously put in the full control inputs to bring the rotating aircraft out from the high speed rotations but in the time taken to stop the spin, there was not enough height to come out of the inevitable dive. For

the people at the War Week demonstration, the Audax disappeared behind
the buildings, But for those in Amratolla Street, who had been craning
their heads skywards towards the racing of an aero-engine and the whine
of the wind through the flying wires, they now had to flee as the silent,
silver machine accelerated towards them, and crumpled with a sickening
thump at their backs.

On 8th December 1941, Pearl Harbour was to earn its unfortunate
place in History. Hoping to catch the Americans unawares, the Japanese
planned to bomb the US Navy aircraft carriers moored on this Pacific
Island. By an incredible stroke of luck, that turned the tide of war, the
American warships were at sea and therefore saved from the carnage.
However, the immediate result was that America found itself at war,
standing alongside the British Empire. The Japanese war machine was
turned up to full speed, and spread in all directions. On the same day that
the Japanese Navy launched their attack on America, the Japanese Army
crossed the border into Siam (Thailand), Malaya, Hong Kong, and the
Philippines. If they continued marching in that direction, it would be
Burma next. The Army of Burma seemed powerless to stop the Japanese,
but surely the virtually impenetrable landscape of the country would be
the barrier to keep them at bay – at least, that was what the British High
Command believed. If Burma was overrun, it would be India, the Jewel
in the Crown, which would be next. When the news broke, Harjinder and
team were still in Calcutta. Jumbo was like a war horse scenting battle;
eager to jump into the fray. However, Harjinder was not so sure. The case
of Harjinder's recent dealings with the School of Technical Training had
brought out a strong anti-British bias in him. He didn't want to fight a
war for the British.

Jumbo knew of Harjinder's feelings and tried reasoning with him;
'Harjinder, if we do not fight in this war for the damned British, we shall
be nothing better than a flying club when the war ends. We must fight,
and we must aim to expand the IAF while the going is good. After the
war is won, India will be a Dominion, and we shall have to run our own
Air Force.'

Harjinder replied; 'The British will never give us Independence.'

'In that case, we shall fight the British; whatever it is, we must learn to
fight now. A Free India without an Air Force would be a helpless country.'

Jumbo's focus was on the best way to achieve Independence. For now,
if the Japanese came, he would fight them, if it meant that his beloved

IAF would grow. For Jumbo, it was a means to an end. They must have doubted an eventual Allied victory, when two days later, the news filtered down of another Japanese victory. The Royal Navy flagships in Asia, the battleship Prince of Wales and Battle Cruiser Repulse, were sunk entirely through the use of Japanese aircraft, off Kuantan in Malaya. The British fleet, under Admiral Tom Phillips, had been in action without air cover. The method of warfare had changed, and the British military was lagging behind.

The orders now came thick and fast; they were to return to Peshawar as soon as possible and to prepare for war. Meanwhile, Harjinder had formed a plan in his mind to score off the RAF. On the way down to Calcutta, when they had touched down at Lahore to refuel, he had seen a damaged Lysander there, N 1212, belonging to No. 28 Squadron. It had been classified as Category 'E'; that is, beyond repair. Harjinder had not been able to get the image of that aircraft out of his head. It pained him to see the way in which the RAF was quick to discard an aircraft. They didn't feel the need to cosset every single machine, as the IAF did. Harjinder's reputation, with his 'magic wand', was soaring, and he had worked on aircraft in a worse condition. He couldn't leave this one alone.

He informed Jumbo of his plan to go on ahead to Lahore, and repair the crashed Lysander. Then, when the Squadron passed through, they could place their moral claim on it and bring it into the family that was No. 1 Squadron, IAF! Harjinder's zeal was not just to see an injured bird take to the sky again, or indeed to have an additional aircraft on the squadron, it was more to make No. 28 Squadron RAF smart with humiliation!

With all their cloak and dagger rebuilding operations in the past, these two men had become thick as thieves, so it was little surprise when Jumbo fell in with Harjinder's suggestion. So off he went to Lahore, two days ahead of the others. He took the best of the technicians with him, Mohd Siddique. Operation Humiliation was underway.

Arriving at Lahore, Harjinder's first port of call was the Chief Technical Officer, a young Flight Lieutenant. When Harjinder told him about his intention, he was quite incredulous; no one had ever before suggested repairing a Category 'E' wreck. 'Try, if you dare', he sportingly challenged him, thinking Harjinder would slink away and forget the crazy idea.

Naturally, they did better than try; they succeeded, and soon resurrected the Lysander back into flying condition. When Harjinder asked the young

Flight Lieutenant to come to see the result of their efforts, he would not believe his own eyes at first, full of doubt and suspicion. Not believing this Indian Flight Sergeant could do such a thing, he made him check, recheck, test, and demonstrate for a full hour. At last he was satisfied and he played his role in the proceedings. 'It's all yours, old boy, I want no part of it. Officially, I have not even seen the repairs.'

The Indian Lysanders appeared low in the sky at Lahore, as they arrived from Calcutta. As per normal procedure, they circled the airfield before splitting off one at a time to come in for landing. Harjinder had the 'new' aircraft waiting in the open for Jumbo. The IAF Lysanders parked around the new member of the flock, almost in a protective huddle. Harjinder proudly showed his handiwork to Jumbo, who beamed with excitement over the additional Lysander that No. 1 Squadron now possessed. He agreed that it should fly with the rest of the gaggle to Peshawar, and since Flying Officer Rup Chand, the Adjutant, was a spare pilot, he was asked to fly it.

When they took off from Lahore, the superstitious number of aircraft didn't pass everyone by. Someone remarked: 'There go the unlucky thirteen.'

Jumbo, quick as a flash replied; 'Unlucky for the Royal Air Force, not for us. They are the ones who are gnashing their teeth.'

Jumbo loved every minute of Operation Humiliation.

Harjinder admitted, 'I was never happier in my life than seeing the thirteen Lysanders circle over Lahore. We broke off into three flights of four each, with one to spare. As we neared Peshawar we reformed again, and Majumdar ordered the formation tightened until it looked as if all the Lysanders were part and parcel of one huge aircraft with numerous propellers. We kept on circling over the Cantonment, actually showing off, and inviting the Officers' Mess inmates to count the number of aircraft.'

By the time they landed, all the Indian personnel, and most of the RAF on the base, were scattered around watching the new fleet. From their cockpits, the aircrew saw the sea of faces, beaming up at them. The Station Commander, who came down to receive them, was more than a little confused, 'Jumbo, where did you get the thirteenth aircraft from? You left here with twelve only.'

'Sir, we felt that since there is a war on, we can ill-afford to lose a weapon, and such a weapon as an aircraft. The RAF does not feel the same way. Harjinder and his gang have showed their skill this time to the RAF boys at Lahore. I don't know all the details, I only had to fly the aircraft. He will tell you the rest.'

Harjinder was taken aback but, blushing and stammering, he told the full story of how he came to repair the 13th Lysander. At the end of it the Station Commander shook hands with him and said; 'The IAF is lucky to have you.'

They all felt that their standing within the Royal Air Force was further raised and they walked about with their heads held high again. The pilots showed their appreciation in a special manner, breaking Air Force law to do it. As only an NCO, and not an officer, Harjinder should not have been in the Officer's mess, let alone accept the multiple beers but they all wanted to buy, to show how strongly they felt. Harjinder was not one to take praise and accept it as most people would. He thought his contribution; 'rather over-valued and so felt determined to do more and better things for them.'

The 'thank you' only spurred him to do more.

The pilots did get into trouble over the celebration, but Harjinder didn't find out until years later. He discovered that as a result of being invited to Mess, the officers involved had been hauled up before the Station Commander, because officers were only allowed to entertain NCOs in the Officers' Mess on Christmas Day. Flight Lieutenant Niranjan 'Joe' Prasad, the ex-Army Gurkha Officer, found a novel excuse. He took the blame squarely on his shoulders, then added that he had invited Harjinder because, in the Army it was common practice to invite the Sergeant Major of the Unit for a drink. Further, he was unaware that he had contravened any laws and was dreadfully sorry. How he justified the entire pilot force being there with him was not mentioned!

They knew that it would not be long before they received their orders for active service in the spiralling World War. The unbelievable speed, and scope, of the Japanese successes in Malaya made it obvious that soon, they would be spilling over the border and into Burma. By taking the capital, Rangoon, they would have an ideal port to supply their forces instead of the long overland route through China. The allied air forces available to defend Burma were woefully deficient, so it looked certain that the IAF would get their chance of combat soon.

The Squadron activity built up as preparations were made. One day, Pilot Officer Henry Runganadhan was despatched, on some long-forgotten task, in a Lysander to the RAF Station at Kohat. At first, it seemed strange to Harjinder to be told, in a telephone call from Henry, that he had missed his lunch. Why drag him away from his work on this petty subject of missed meals? Then the rambling Henry got to the point, and the reason *why* he missed lunch. He had broken his Lysander, he could not face the other pilots in the Mess, and so had hidden alone in his room with just his guilt for company. On landing, Henry pranged the Lysander, leaving it broken, astride the runway, for all to see. Unfortunately for Henry, Squadron Leader Aspy Engineer was in command of No. 2 Squadron IAF stationed there, and Aspy could not bear any embarrassment for the Indian Air Force. He had dealt severely with Henry.

As always, there was nothing more important to Harjinder than the good name of the Squadron, and in particular, the IAF pilots. Henry's report of the damage wasn't very specific, but Harjinder understood it included the undercarriage, wing and propeller. He could now fix damage like this in his sleep. He thought that with his current band of men he could handle that. He sent for eight Airmen, and the spares required. They climbed aboard two trucks and, leaving plumes of dust in their wake, made straight for Kohat. As the trucks shook over the rough roads, a plan was made, and rehearsed, time and time again. With no official sanctioning of their trip, they knew there was trouble ahead, and they needed a plan of action. When they reached the police checkpost between Peshawar and Kohat, the guards stopped them and they were not allowed to proceed unless they presented the authorisation. The plan swung into action to negotiate their way around the road block. The occupants of one of the vehicles dismounted and engaged the guards in conversation, whilst the second vehicle slipped under the barrier and raced towards Kohat at breakneck speed. The guards shouted and gestured at the runaway driver, and then turned their attention to Harjinder. As they angrily protested to him, Harjinder upped the ante and pretended to be even more furious than they were. With a booming voice, he cursed the driver of the runaway vehicle to hell and back, promising he would have him court martialled as soon as he caught him. So saying, Harjinder tore open the door of the second lorry, jumped into the driving seat, and drove away in apparent hot pursuit of the first vehicle. After all, he had a promise to keep.

And there was Henry, cutting a sorry figure, waiting just outside Kohat. He took them into the RAF Station as the sun was setting. There was little time to waste. The lorries sped over the airfield and on to the runway where the offending Lysander was forlornly abandoned. Before the dust cloud behind them could settle, the technicians were already spilling out of the cabs and straight into their various, pre-allocated repair jobs. The all-important tea was summoned from the kitchens. All through the night, broken pieces were removed, and new pieces riveted, screwed and bolted into place. As the sun rose at six o'clock the next morning, the rays of light illuminated a complete Lysander. The aircraft engine was tested it then taxied into wind and, with a very grateful Henry at the controls, it took off for Peshawar. Harjinder loaded the shattered parts into the trucks and told the equally shattered people to wait for him on the Peshawar Road, five miles from camp. It was time to head over to Aspy, and Harjinder's mischievous side was looking forward to playing with him.

Aspy and Harjinder knew each other very well from their time on Wapitis in the North-West Frontier. Harjinder strolled, perhaps a little too nonchalantly, into his office! Harjinder went to say hello to the Commanding Officer, but Aspy, still furious about the accident blurted out; 'You think No. 1 Squadron is fit to go to war? You will crash all your aircraft and walk back from Burma. Look at that aircraft Henry crashed yesterday. Your pilot has put all of us to shame.'

Impassive, he chuckled inwardly and waited for the fury to calm down before saying; 'Sir, I do not know what aircraft you are talking about. My Squadron has all its Lysanders at Peshawar and they are all serviceable.'

Aspy's voice raised a couple of octaves; 'Come on, Harjinder, don't pretend you don't know about your blasted Henry and his pranged Lysander.'

So saying, he got up and pointed with his finger towards the airfield where, naturally, he imagined the broken aircraft was still sitting astride the runway. Suddenly he retracted his hand; 'Oh! Perhaps they have finally managed to tow it into a hangar.'

And with that he instructed Harjinder to accompany him to the technical area.

A comical pantomime ensued, as the IAF personnel searched all their hangars, all of the neighbouring RAF hangars, even the Chief Technical Officer's hangar, but guess what? No broken Lysander! Finally, Aspy turned to Harjinder, puzzled, and asked if he knew anything about it. 'Have you dismantled and carted it away?' he hazarded a guess. Harjinder, with a small smirk on his face answered; 'I don't know about that, Sir, but I did see one Lysander takeoff this morning and head for Peshawar.'

Aspy checked with Flying Control and discovered that Flying Officer Henry Runganadhan had, indeed, taken off with his Lysander. He placed the phone receiver back on the cradle and looked directly at Harjinder. However, Harjinder could not keep it in any longer and so shyly confessed what they had done. Aspy was forced to concede; 'Hats off to No. 1 Squadron. If that's their tradition, they will really do well in Burma.'

They did.

December 1941 was busy. Not even Harjinder magic could rectify the event on the 20th. Pilot Officer Paljor Namgyal returned from his training flight, and from some distance away, he lined his Lysander up for landing. In all the activity nobody paid much attention to his approach. If they had they would have seen him too low to make the runway. Whether there was a down draft of air, or just an error of judgement, no one knows. What was clear seconds later was his Lysander hit the ground short of the airfield. The Lysander tumbled end over end on impact, giving the pilot no chance of survival. The Prince of Sikkim was dead, and the IAF had their first fatality on the Lysander. This time there was nothing Harjinder could have done. With the massive build-up for the move to Burma, and no doubt combat in the near future, another aircraft was allocated to the Squadron and life continued without a pause. The RAF tradition of celebrating Christmas day was still a major part of the IAF's December, but this year, there was to be no celebration. Following Palijor's death, the news of the capitulation of Hong Kong to the Japanese came through. The news of British success at Benghazi, in North Africa, seemed of little consolation. The Japanese had been lampooned in the press as small, short-sighted, bumbling soldiers, but their reputation was now becoming that of an unstoppable force here in the East.

January 1942 was off to a bad start, it seemed, with the Japanese taking Manila on the 2nd and Kuala Lumpur on the 11th. Then the Japanese Fifteenth Army, under Lieutenant General Shojiro Iida, launched an attack from Northern Thailand over jungle-clad mountain ranges into the Southern Burmese province of Tenasserim. The British had thought the jungles impassable, but the low tech approach on the ground, using beasts of burden and bicycles, worked for the Japanese. The order for deployment finally came for No. 1 Squadron of the Indian Air Force; it was time to move, time to fight!

They loaded up all their ground equipment on a special train to Calcutta, en-route to Rangoon. The non-existent, spare RAF Lysander, brought up from Lahore, threatened to become a problem until Harjinder had a brain wave. Why not split it up into its major components and take it to Burma as well? Jumbo laughed heartily; 'That means we are virtually stealing it.'

Harjinder pointed out the advantage of having such a rich reserve of spare parts, and Jumbo fell in with the plan. Jumbo Majumdar had come to have a great respect for Harjinder's judgment and advice, which was reciprocated in the high regard Harjinder held him. It was the perfect relationship to have on the eve of combat.

They loaded the aircraft, its fuselage and engine in one crate in one wagon, and the wings in the other. Everyone pitched in to help with the 'stowaway', including the driver, Corporal Tara Singh, who was only too glad to help, turning a blind eye at the same time.

It was never a good sign when an Equipment Officer came over from Air Headquarters, and this one wanted to know what happened to the 13th aircraft from Lahore. Jumbo, either off the top of his head, or with a pre-planned story, threw him a curved ball. He told him that since the aircraft in question landed at Peshawar, they had nothing but bad luck, so they decided to break it up and use it for spares. He sent for Harjinder and instructed him, with full military pomp, to show this officer where he had used the spares. Harjinder took the baffled Officer on a tour of the IAF hangar, pointing to various aircraft explaining how the complete aircraft had been distributed amongst the gathered flock – this piece of undercarriage is from the extra plane, this engine was from that plane too, on this plane we used the wing; on and on he went. He may have been a little over-zealous allocating the 13th Lysander's parts leaving the visiting officer with the impression that the Lysander had started out with 3 wings, 2 propellers and a handful of tail-wheels!

In January 1942, at the age of 10, the IAF entered the World War II. Harjinder now had the job to divide his men between those who flew to war, and those who went by train! He placed the majority in the ground party, under Flight Lieutenant Rup Chand, the Adjutant. The heavens opened up, as if to comfort the parched ground, the day they left for war.

Left behind was the air party. Harjinder remained with his brood of 12 Lysanders. There was never any doubt about whom he would fly with as the Air Gunner.

This was the IAF entering the World War, and it seems only right that the names of the participants should be recorded:

Jumbo was the Squadron Leader with Harjinder.

There was the ex-army officer, Flight Lieutenant Niranjan 'Joe' Prasad with Sergeant Ghyara.

Flight Lieutenant Prithipal Singh was back, having been sent away earlier by Harjinder's Subaltern's Court Marshal. He was with Sergeant Cabinetmaker.

The fiery Pilot Officer Moolgavkar was paired with Kartar Singh Saund.

Pilot Officer Satyanaraya was with Ghulam Ali, the gunner who had survived Mehr 'Baba' Singh's crash in the North-West Frontier, and subsequently shot at by their own Tochi Scouts.

The other Pilot Officers were Rajinder Singh, Jitendra Deuskar, Homi Ratnagar, Rustomjee, Yeshwant Malse, 'Andy' Ananthanarayanan, P.S. Gill and finally, Henry, 'I missed lunch, and by the way I crashed my plane' Runganadhan.

While waiting for the big move across India, and into Burma, they carried out full war load tests on their aircraft, carrying all the normal combat load of ammunition. The rain that was 'a good omen' continued, and there was mud everywhere, leaving only the main runway fit to land on. Jumbo, Pilot Officer Malse, and Harjinder were standing near a hangar one morning, when Jumbo turned and announced; 'Malse, you know what I dreamed last night? I woke up with the sweat pouring down my face because I dreamed that we had been debarred from going to Burma as there have been too many crashes in our Squadron.' Then, again in my dream, I heard Harjinder telling me: 'Sir, do not worry. Even if all the aircraft crash, I shall wave my magic wand and I shall repair each one within 24 hours.'

Jumbo had barely finished speaking when Malse shouted; 'Sir, look, there is a crash.'

They rushed forward from the hangar side and sure enough, Pilot Officer Andy Ananthanarayanan had touched down on the semi dry runway but had not been quick enough to catch the swing of the tail in the wind with his rudder pedals. As the back of the plane tried to overtake the front, the Lysander tipped up onto its wing-tip until coming to an abrupt halt back on its wheels.

Harjinder did a quick mental audit of the situation, deciding that the pilot would be ok, but the aircraft was definitely damaged. Jumbo

Majumdar leapt into action as they were due to fly out any time now, and they needed a full Squadron, otherwise his nightmare might come true. He began to ring up Air Headquarters for a quick replacement, and was still cranking the field telephone handle, when those still outside saw a second Lysander coming in to land; trying to squeeze in alongside Andy's abandoned aircraft. Pilot Officer Ratnagar had seen Andy's fate and tried to keep the damaged, stationary Lysander to his right. However, he had strayed into the kutcha, the mushy rain-fuelled bog, and his fate was sealed. The left wheel dug into the waterlogged ground, flicking the aircraft left, sticking the right wing straight into the runway. The Lysander tripped up on to its nose, shattering the spinning propeller. Now they were two aircraft down before their imminent deployment. However, not all the Squadron's aircraft had returned from their training flights. Hardly five minutes elapsed, before there was a third Lysander starting the approach to landing, this time with Pilot Officer Satyanaraya flying. He was greeted by two broken aircraft on the runway in front of him, so he headed to the left of his two stranded Squadron mates. All knew what was going to unfold, but stood powerless. The moment the sliver of light between wheels and ground disappeared, the kutcha grabbed at the flying machine to claim its third victim. The crashed aircraft were laid out across the runway in a perfect air display formation, frozen in place.

Harjinder describes the next few minutes; 'My thoughts were for Majumdar. I knew that this would break his heart. At that time we were standing by to move to active service at 24 hours' notice. All our tools, equipment, and ground party, including all technicians, excepting me, had gone by rail party to Burma. I rushed out and looked for Majumdar who had gone away somewhere. I tracked him down in the Station Commander's office. I was so excited that I went in without any formality, nor did I remember to salute. I caught hold of Majumdar's hands and blurted out: "Sir, don't worry, even if all of them crash, I shall repair them." By this time Jumbo was too stunned and bewildered; partly because of his dream, and partly because all his previous dreams had been about showing off the IAF flag in Burma, which now seemed to have disintegrated.'

Harjinder heard him speaking on the phone to Air Headquarters: 'I have to report another crash, Sir. Yes, yes, I know... No I am in my full senses; there are *three* aircraft crashes.'

Harjinder wrote that he had never before seen Jumbo look so dejected before.

There was nothing to be done by standing in the office, so Harjinder left him and began to plan for repairs. He knew they had to do something to get those aircraft going. His earlier exploits now seemed child's play, or at least the warm up for this, the main event.

The Squadron Commander No. 28 Squadron heard about the IAF's misfortune and came over to see his unfortunate Indian colleagues. The RAF were due to move into Burma with the Indians, and, having operated with them for so long, there was a great mutual respect. After offering his sympathy, he asked if there was anything he could do to assist No. 1 Squadron IAF to get back on their feet again. Harjinder was grateful for his offer but told Jumbo that No. 1 Squadron had always been proud of its traditions; it always did its own repairs. He asked Jumbo to put all the pilots at his disposal, he would repair all three aircraft, in three days, without any help from the RAF. This time Jumbo did not smile, cheer up, or rib Harjinder about his magic wand. He was too anxious, acutely aware that they were at 24 hours' notice. Anyway, he 'spared' Harjinder the embarrassment of refusing his request, and told Harjinder to do the best he could. There was no conviction in his voice or his body language. Jumbo could see his dreams for the IAF lay broken with the Lysanders sitting in frozen formation on the landing ground.

The majority of the technicians were chugging along on a train somewhere between Harjinder and Burma. The remaining personnel were mainly pilots and rear gunners. However, they had to start somewhere so Harjinder borrowed a wrecker vehicle from an Army Motor Transport Company and dragged the three aircraft out of the mud and into a hangar. What was next in Harjinder's arsenal of doing the impossible? As usual, he arranged a tea stall, with plenty of sandwiches and cakes. If there was magic running through Harjinder's engineering fingertips it was powered by tea.

The tools were distributed to all the air gunners and pilots Jumbo placed at his disposal. In Harjinder's opinion; 'This was the most risky technical operation which I ever undertook in my whole life in the Air Force, because three crashed aircraft were to be repaired for war service with nontechnical labour, with myself as the sole supervisor. I planned my work on paper and, subdivided my crew into teams consisting of a pilot and an air gunner, allotted each a task. We took on one of the aircraft first, and each gang was given instructions as to how to go about their allotted job. As the operation progressed, I moved from gang to gang, checking and guiding. Wherever an operation needed finer adjustments or technical touch, I took over. I found that Pilot Officer Malse showed a great technical bent of mind.'

No one slept that night. The tea-powered crews hammered, riveted and bolted all through the night and the next morning so that by the next afternoon, the first Lysander was fully serviceable. Harjinder pushed the aircraft out into the daylight, but when he rang up Jumbo with the good news, he found him, emotionally, in pieces. However, the Commanding Officer, upset as he was, said that he would come round and test it himself.

Jumbo had already earned his reputation as a fearless pilot, but even Harjinder thought he went too far whilst testing the aircraft. When he was happy that all things were normal, he dived the Lysander down, pulled it up into a perfectly vertical climb continuing until the speed was almost zero. He then kicked in full rudder control to bring the nose to swing to the left through the horizon to point vertically at the ground; he had just performed the aerobatic stall turn manoeuvre at low level; in a Lysander. He then pulled up from the ensuing dive to zoom across the parade ground at tree top height; all over the heads of No. 28 Squadron who were on parade. Not only was this a sign of relief, but it also served to attract the attention of the RAF; to show the side number on the aircraft to the RAF. After he landed, he looked like he might actually embrace his Flight Sergeant. The grin threatened to split is face in half, and then the words came tumbling out. The aircraft flew better than new. Harjinder didn't need these words of encouragement, but they found their target; his pilots and air gunners worked like they never had before.

The team all broke off for a bath, and a few hours of sleep, but then got to work again in the evening. Harjinder's theory was heavy dinners made them lethargic and sleepy so the men's diet was tea with pastries. He needed them to be sharp and alert. The pilots vied with the air gunners in their technical chores, and with the help of this friendly competition, by the next morning, the second aircraft was rolled out, serviceable, in to the sunlight.

With work going well on the last Lysander, Jumbo called Air Headquarters to let them know that no replacements were required. If the desk pilots in HQ were surprised when they first heard about the three consecutive crashes, they couldn't bring themselves to believe that all were flying again. They were probably starting to doubt Jumbo's sanity, and not for the first time.

The third aircraft had come off the worst in that mad ten minutes, so it took a little more time to repair. Again Jumbo was the one to take the Lysander up for the test flight. Less than thirty-six hours after the crash and it was an optimistic Jumbo who parked the last aircraft to make twelve once more. The Squadron was back to full strength, and ready to go to war to prove their worth. It had been an extreme, and very productive, example of team building.

When Jumbo bounded up to Harjinder, he suggested that they celebrate another of his miracles by promoting him to Warrant Officer, but Harjinder balked at this. He had made up his mind not to accept a promotion to Warrant rank. He believed there was unjustifiable discrimination between the IAF and the RAF. Indians could only be promoted to Warrant Officer Class II, while their RAF equivalents were made Class I Warrant Officers. Not for the first time, Harjinder took a stand. He preferred to remain a Flight Sergeant, where at least the ranks in the two Services were equal. He realised, of course, that his continued refusal would mean that eventually some of his juniors would be promoted to fill Warrant Officer II vacancies, and would supersede him, but he was quite prepared for that, and told Jumbo so. But Jumbo too was a man of principles. He managed to find a temporary solution to this problem by promoting Harjinder to 'Acting (Unpaid) Warrant Officer I'. He also allowed him to wear the blue RAF uniform, even though Nanda, as Stores Officer, objected to this unauthorised issue. In the end, Jumbo paid for the uniform himself.

Harjinder had to wait another nine months to win the legitimate rank of Warrant Officer Class I, after three of his juniors had accepted the rank at Class II. So it came to pass that just as Harjinder was the first Indian Corporal, Sergeant, and Flight Sergeant, he was also the instigator for the introduction of the rank of Warrant Officer I in the IAF. He was told at a later date, that if he had delayed any further, he would have stayed a Flight Sergeant for the rest of his life. With the events that would unfold after the war, that seems unlikely, but in 1942 they feared that they were going to be on the losing side of this World War.

Throughout the world, the women behind the troops were united in worry as husbands, brothers and sons fought, or prepared to enter the fight. The wives of the IAF had been used to their husbands disappearing for months on end into the North-West Frontier, there were risks but happily a fatality was rare, but this conflict was a completely different prospect. Causalities were growing alarmingly, the Japanese seemingly unstoppable, and rumours of their cruelty abounded. We know that Harjinder's wife was something special. She stood shoulder to shoulder with him from the time he was the lowly rank of Hawai Sepoy. He was now the most senior IAF airman, and clearly would be in the thick of it, when the time came, but he would travel with her full support. She had willingly taken on the role of counselling the other Airmen's wives. However, just before his departure for Burma, Harjinder's wife had a serious operation. The doctor recommended that she be confined to bed for three weeks. Under normal circumstances, Harjinder would have taken leave, and looked after her, but they were ready to move at any moment. He knew that if he didn't leave now he would be left behind for good. The IAF, and the war, would go on without him. That just wasn't an option for Harjinder. This was his Squadron, his responsibility, his family. Harjinder's wife knew all of this, and there was none with greater bravery and understanding as her. She told Harjinder that he must go with the Squadron. 'I can look after myself and there are so many friends here. Don't worry about me.'

Harjinder wrote of his admiration for his wife. However, he could not report the same of a small minority in his charge. The vast majority had embraced the endless training, and now they wanted to put these skills to the ultimate test; combat. Some, like Harjinder and Jumbo, were even looking beyond the advancing Japanese in Burma, towards an Independent India. Harjinder wrote; 'It is sad to record that one or two of our pilots seemed not so enthusiastic about going to fight in Burma; probably it was their parents who had put them off. The air was such an uncertain element for most Indians that many people assumed that going to war with the Air Force meant certain death. I remember, during our stay at Kanpur, a good number of prospective pilots had confided in me that their parents were opposing their plans for taking up flying as a career. For some of those parents, I arranged flying experience, after which they were more amenable.'

Jumbo was a man to motivate, although his bullishness made some nervous. Harjinder singled out another man to raise morale. This simple, shy, unassuming man was Flight Lieutenant Rup Chand. He had taken to flying in his youth, having flown in Germany and England. At the time the war broke out, he owned his own aeroplane, a Vega Gull. He promptly gave his aircraft to the Air Force in India for use as a communication aircraft and joined up in the Volunteer Reserve of the IAF, and was posted to Karachi to command one of the Volunteer Flights. There he met with a very serious flying accident during night flying, after which he was posted to No. 1 Squadron at Peshawar as Adjutant. However, he was so determined to go into action with his Squadron that when the order came to move to Burma, he approached Jumbo and asked him if he could go as a pilot. Jumbo knew that his medical category did not permit operational flying, and dodged the request very tactfully. Rup Chand was not so easily put off. He came to Harjinder and begged him to persuade Jumbo to change his mind. Harjinder tried, but failed. Rup Chand, however, kept on appealing to Jumbo. On the trip back from War Week in Calcutta when they dined with Rup's father at his house, he told Jumbo; 'If you do not take my son to Burma, it will break his heart. Please do not disappoint him. The IAF, and your No. 1 Squadron, means everything to him.'

Finally, Jumbo's resistance crumbled. He caught Harjinder when he was alone and explained that he had decided to let Rup Chand come with them; 'but do not let him know as yet', he added. 'We will tell him when we are about to takeoff.'

Quite why Jumbo wanted to keep it a secret is not clear but it remained a secret until they were actually in their cockpits. When Rup Chand was told, he started jumping with joy. That was what it was like, in those early days of the Indian Air Force. Each man was dedicated to his job, and desperate to do his bit. Rup Chand's excitement at the prospect of seeing action in Burma exemplified the spirit of the IAF.

It was February 1942. A big part of IAF history was about to be written:

> 'The day we left to go to war was like any other day. The sun rose from the East just the same, and the same old noisy crows ushered in the morning. To the pilots and air gunners of No. 1 Squadron, however, it was one of the most momentous days of their lives. The excitement of going into action for the first time showed on everyone's face. There was one common point I noticed in them: they were all proud to belong to this famous Squadron. On talking to these youngsters, I also felt happy and proud.'

Jumbo, who thought of everything, called Harjinder aside and said: 'Keep an eye on Henry. He lost his brother in an air crash at Miranshah recently and is emotionally upset. He has a premonition that he is also going to go the same way. He is a good lad, but needs an eye kept on him.' (*Henry's brother was not in the IAF, at least, no confirmed records tell us so. Aviation historian, Mukund Murty, suggests it might be a corruption of another, very poignant story. In a weird juxtaposition of the dates, Anandaraj Samuel Gnanamuthu, died on 11/7/41 and his younger brother Bhaskar Daniel Gnanamuthu, died 7/11/41. Anandaraj was in No. 32 Squadron RAF when he was killed. Daniel was with No.1 IAF. Could they have been related to Henry? Or even friends from Madras, where Henry had learnt to fly at the Madras Flying Club, and where he still holds the unrivalled record of going solo in an aeroplane after just one hour of flying training!)*

Their Station Commander and Air-Officer-Commanding No. 1 Group were there to see them off from the base. The pilots of No. 2 Squadron IAF also came to wish them good luck on their mission. There was of course, the disappointment of not to be in that first group to put their skills and character to the test, but also a hint of relief to be out of harm's way, but they were all filled with an overwhelming sense of pride to see the IAF going into action.

The first refuelling stop was at Lahore, where they met more Indian Airmen who crowded around them with different emotions passing over their faces. Their countrymen ushered them over to the offices of 60 Squadron RAF who had recently arrived from the front. It wasn't to be what Harjinder hoped for. The Anglo-Indian Airmen they met were all very demoralised. Being the most senior airman, Harjinder was singled out by one of the senior RAF Airmen; 'Your Squadron is committing suicide by going into Burma with Lysander aircraft. You haven't a chance against the Jap Zeros (*the nimble, Japanese, fighter aircraft*). Our Squadron had Blenheims (*a twin engine light bomber*) and even then, they were all shot down over Bangkok. Our Commanding Officer and Adjutant were the only ones to escape, because they were smart enough to stay on the ground (*so much for leading from the front!*). The RAF know all this and are sending you instead, to be sacrificed.'

It would have been understandable for Harjinder to take these comments at face value. But we know he had a low opinion of the senior RAF people in India, so he was having none of it. He told the RAF man to stop being so defeatist and also forbade them all from spreading this unhealthy defeatist talk among any of his IAF pilots.

Next, the crews flew over Delhi, looking down on the grand buildings stretching along the Kingsway, leading to the Viceregal Palace. They touched down at Palam air base on the outskirts of the capital, only for the news to break that they were one aircraft short. Somehow, Pilot Officer Padam Gill had been separated from the gaggle. Jumbo was disheartened and took on some of the responsibility himself. He said to Harjinder: 'If this happens while we are still in our own country, what will happen when we reach Burma?'

Harjinder did his best to give Jumbo confidence. 'These are our teething troubles, Sir. We will soon overcome them.'

Later, they learned that Padam had got himself lost and force-landed at Meerut, they sent Malse to escort him back. When they took off from Meerut, they were separated again. Ultimately, Padam 'pranged' his aircraft on this flight. This was not the time, or place, for Harjinder to go into action breathing life back into the damaged aircraft. The war wasn't going to wait. There was nothing more to do except to send Flying Officer Raza, and Ghulam Rabbani, to bring another aircraft from Lahore. This close to combat, and with a, 'all hands on deck' cry from the war in Burma, the RAF were too distracted to score points against the IAF.

Things continued to go downhill, when on the next hop in Kanpur where Andy Ananthanarayanan burst the inner tube in the main-wheel tyre while landing. Yes, the Lysander had a big inner-tube like an oversized bicycle tyre! The resemblance didn't stop there. The designer, having fixed the wheels dangling out in the breeze, decided to streamline the main-wheels with very thin inner tubes. This was the first, and last time, Harjinder had seen such a design on an aeroplane. Although his tubeless wooden tail-wheels had become almost accident proof, the main-wheels were now a problem. These slim line tubes used to burst when they were pinched between the tyre edge and rim as soon as slightest sideways pressure occurred. Harjinder took the bull by the horns again and decided on a bold course of action. The wooden tail-wheels were working well, so it was time to redesign the main-wheels before going into combat. He purchased a number of 32×6 inches thick, heavy, truck tubes and fitted them to all the IAF aircraft at Kanpur. Unfortunately their valve nozzles were too long and stuck out awkwardly, but that could not be helped. Thereafter, with these industrial tubes squeezed into the tyre and the nozzle flailing around in the airflow, there were no more cases of tyre-burst in any of their aircraft during the whole of the Burma Campaign. What would have been the fate of the IAF Lysanders in combat, in Burma, if he had not replaced the maker's flimsy tubes?

The next halt was Gaya where they met a stranded RAF Sergeant Pilot of No. 25 Squadron. Harjinder could not quite believe the attitude of his RAF cousins. This RAF pilot had suffered engine trouble but their Squadron technicians had been brought up in the RAF tradition to follow a rigid maintenance schedule. Even in this time of all-out war they were making no allowances to get these valuable assets to the front-line. The pilot, and his aircraft, had been abandoned. Harjinder had a quick look around the aircraft and within an hour diagnosed that there was no spark getting through to the engine; there was clearly a problem with the magneto. A quick look in the magneto showed that the contact breaker needed replacing. He changed the contact breaker points, synchronised them, measuring the required gap using cigarette tin foil to gauge the thickness required. Harjinder stood back and let one of his pilots fire the engine up and run it through the full power checks. The Sergeant Pilot was amazed to see how easily Harjinder and team blitzed the job. He told them that his Squadron engineer had spent hours looking for a lamp and battery for synchronising the two magnetos. He used a few choice descriptions of his own technicians before volunteering to accompany the IAF as the thirteenth member! Thirteen was fast becoming a lucky number for No. 1 Squadron.

They pushed on, landing next at Calcutta, but with more pressing requirements than the last time. No air-shows this time. Harjinder had already decided this was where he would carry out the servicing of his aeroplanes. With all the required routine maintenance completed, it would leave the aircraft clear to fly plenty of hours when they arrived in Burma. Harjinder was up until midnight with his technicians, doing the required servicing chores, but on their return to the billets, he discovered that the windows of their room had not been blacked out. They could do nothing at that unearthly hour, and they were staying only for one night, so they decided to turn in for the night.

They had hardly gone to bed when Harjinder heard a commotion outside. He got up and saw a drunken RAF Pilot Officer, standing with his face inches from Sergeant Ghulam Ali, asking for the senior man among the Indians. Ghulam Ali replied; 'I am the senior.'

There upon the Pilot Officer started calling him a fool for not knowing that there was a blackout in Calcutta. Ghulam Ali, who was about twice the size of this officer, caught hold of him and dragged him on to the veranda. The officer was too drunk to know what was happening, so Harjinder shouted at Ghulam Ali to control himself. Ghulam Ali reluctantly obeyed but grumbled and said: 'This is the type of Sahib we are going to fight for; cowards, and they are our rulers. They can't even stand against Japs whom we are going to face. They have run out of Burma and on top of that, he calls me a fool.'

Harjinder told Ghulam Ali to say no more and approached the Pilot Officer, realising he was the duty Orderly Officer. Harjinder said: 'Sorry Sir, you have been talking to the wrong man. I am the senior man here.'

The officer then turned to him and said: 'Then you are a bigger fool.'

On hearing this Ghulam Ali stepped forward once again, threateningly, but in the meantime, the other air gunners had come out of the rooms and held him in check. Harjinder ordered them all to go into their barracks. He took the Orderly Officer to one side and tried to reason with the drunk, saying: 'Firstly, you as the Orderly Officer should have seen to it that our billets were properly blacked out. We do not have the time to do anything about it. We have come here only for one night and we are leaving early tomorrow morning. Secondly, you as an Orderly Officer should not have behaved in the way you did.'

But he was too drunk to understand and stumbled off on his way to the next set of barracks.

Early next morning Harjinder reported the matter to Jumbo who insisted that he accompany him to the Station Commander. The latter was furious when he learned of the incident. Jumbo insisted on having their evidence recorded before their departure, the Wing Commander agreed, and a Summary of Evidence was held immediately. They discovered that this man was an Equipment Officer recently posted to India. The charge against him was: 'Misbehaving and maltreating subordinates which could have caused mutiny.' The Station Commander called Harjinder in his office and commended him for 'cool action under provocative circumstances.'

Later in the morning, all the pilots and air gunners were called into the Station Commander's office for briefing. He gave them all the information he had about the land and air situation up at the front, and then chalked out their route for them. There seemed to be no good news, even as he ended his briefing, he warned, 'In case you find fog over Toungoo, divert to Rangoon–Mingaladon. You are likely to meet Japanese Zero Fighters in the area, so look out. I wish you the best of luck.'

When they came out, all seemed to be nervous. Suddenly this all seemed very real. This was not another posting up to the North-West Frontier. The very idea of meeting Zeros was enough to give them the shakes, because the pilots were under no illusion about the fast, agile, Japanese fighters. They had spent hours digesting all the latest intelligence reports on the enemy equipment. If caught, their Lysanders would be sitting ducks. Of that, there was little doubt.

Finally, on the last day of January 1941, they took off from Calcutta and headed to their last Indian base before heading into Burma; Chittagong. The flat flood plains they flew over would be part of East Pakistan in a few years' time, and then Bangladesh after that, but to the pilots who had been flying operations on the brown, mountainous, boulder-strewn moonscape of the North-West Frontier, this was the first signal, that things would be different. The flat flood plains with the endless twists and turns of rivers and streams would soon turn into dense jungle, covering the hills and mountains that had been thought to be impenetrable, before the Japanese proved the Allied commanders wrong.

All the pilots had been briefed about how difficult it would be to re-supply spare parts in a war theatre, so they approached their task with greater resolve and thoughtfulness. The thought of facing the enemy, in an antiquated aircraft, over unfamiliar terrain, brought all their minds into focus. Harjinder wrote; 'The quality of their flying, I must say, improved thereafter. Even Padam Gill, who had crashed his Lysander P 9179 at Meerut only three days ago, seemed to have matured overnight-confident and reassured in his demeanour. He had taken over P 9197, with Sergeant Zia as his Air Gunner. I felt very happy because I knew that I was among a very brave bunch of young pilots and air gunners. We refuelled at Chittagong and drank a lot of coconut water, quite new to most of us. It was Joe Niranjan Prasad who introduced us to this delightful drink. He was a grand and gallant officer. He combined the esprit of our wonderful Army with the daring of our young Air Force.'

Harjinder watched the men as they found ways to prepare themselves for the unknown. He took time to reflect on this family, and he felt responsible as they headed into the biggest test any of them could imagine:

Pilot Officer Deuskar was a quiet and unassuming Maratha, whose courage knew no bounds; Flight Lieutenant Raza was all smiles, a brave heart hidden behind a becoming gentleness; Satyanaraya – intelligent and deliberate; Ratanagar, with bags containing tennis racquets and a blazer, seemed to indicate he wasn't entirely aware of what was facing him; Henry Runganadhan was waiting for the chance to meet a Japanese aircraft, not the slightest bit daunted by the disadvantage in speed. He was always telling anyone who would care to listen; 'I would rather get bumped off in aerial fight than be burnt on the ground like my brother.'

Pilot Officer Malse had the demeanour of a seasoned pilot. He already could see that the only way to survive was to get down to the tree tops. He talked about evading Zeros by steep turns, wing tip touching the tree, so that his air gunner could let off a 'fun' blast at the Japanese aircraft when they meet one. How many of these young men would accompany Harjinder back to India? Would there be an India to come back to if the Japanese couldn't be stopped? Harjinder could not stop the question popping into his head; would he be coming back?

The Japanese were successfully rolling through Burma. So far, they had shown no apparent weakness, but the Indians' hopes were pinned on the British stronghold at Singapore. That fortress would surely stop the Japanese and draw their forces from the Burma front. The IAF's No. 1 Squadron was entering the combat arena, and what they needed was a quiet start to prepare themselves for the fight. They needed time to get accustomed to the new surroundings, and the new style of operations.

That didn't happen.

Eight

Into Burma

> 'I have come here to fight a war and not observe formalities and ceremonies… You have won the admiration of my aircrew.'

The Squadron followed the flat lands of the coastal strip South into Burma. Further inland, the forest canopy became denser as it cloaked the hills that rose beyond their left wing tip. Delhi had been a little chilly, Calcutta and Chittagong warmer, but now the temperature was on the rise. These were the conditions they would operate in, that they would fight in. The long beaches, lined with palm trees, pointed the direction for the team to travel. Still flat along the coast, numerous rivers and inlets broke through the flooded, swampy plain to cut into the beach. Two larger rivers sliced through the land to leave a substantial peninsula. On the bottom-most corner, tucked against the beach, was the airfield for the coastal town of Akyab. It was mid-afternoon by the time the last Lysander's wheels touched down in this foreign country. Harjinder was first out to start the refuelling and dispersal of the aircraft. The tension hung heavy in the humid air. The Japanese seemed to have demoralised the RAF, because the talk from everyone they met was of abandoning Burma 'any day now'. One Senior RAF Sergeant approached Harjinder and said: 'You people are going the wrong way. You ought to be heading West. Everybody else is.'

Harjinder firmly told him to shut up and not to demoralise his air gunners. The RAF man had the grace to apologise and leave them to their work.

The arrival of the IAF meant they had already done better than the
'bloody shambles' of the RAF reinforcements leaving India at the same
time as they. The eighteen, desperately-needed, Hawker Hurricanes had
left Calcutta, led by a twin engine Blenheim bomber, whose job it was to
do the navigation. Somehow, the Blenheim crew got horribly lost as night
fell over the Shan mountains. All the precious aircraft and pilots were lost,
dropping through the forest canopy when their fuel tanks ran dry, some
never to be found. The RAF were trying to fight the Japanese with the
outdated, obsolete fighters in their inventory. This, compounded with the
use of wrong tactics against them, trying unsuccessfully to out-turn the
nimble Japanese fighters, led to horrific losses. The Americans quickly
realised the 'dive and zoom' tactics were the only way forward.

In Akyab, there was a full moon that night, so all of the air team
decided to walk around the airfield and drink in the sights and sounds of
Burma. Sergeant 'Cabby' Cabinetmaker put his mouth organ to good use,
and the beautiful music had the effect of a soothing blanket being laid over
the men. Some of the young ones sang songs, some clapped to the rhythm.
Everyone's morale soared. They felt part of the team, and they felt ready.
A glow of satisfaction spread through Harjinder, mainly because he could
see that his men were brushing aside the negativity of the RAF personnel
returning from the front.

The next morning, white wisps of condensation whipped off the
Lysanders' wing tips as they took off in to the moist air at 0900. They
left the coast, and the protection of the sea behind them. Not only did
the coastline make navigation easy, but it also offered the crews a chance
to land a sick aircraft on a beach, or to put it down in the surf if the
engine stopped. Soon, this option disappeared when they turned inland
and the vast areas of lush green jungle canopy stretched out for miles on all
sides, with only the occasional stream carving through the green. The all-
important capital city, Rangoon, was in the Southern part of the country.
Beyond that was only a narrow strip of the country continuing on South,
butting against Siam (*now Thailand*). The Japanese were successfully
fighting through the jungles to the North and East of Rangoon, putting
the city in mortal danger of being cut off. Away from the coastal strip,
Burma consisted of high, North-South mountain ridges that were split
by the four great river valleys flowing through them. The jungles that
covered the ridges had been thought impassable, but the Japanese, with
their low-tech approach, were proving the Allied Commanders wrong,

yet again. The rivers Chindwin, Irrawaddy, Sittang and Salween would be impassable when swollen by monsoon rains, even to the ingenious Japanese, but in January, they were at a more manageable level. The Japanese were working on a time table to reach the coastline, take the capital, and have a port to stage their push towards India.

The IAF gaggle of aircraft looked more and more like vultures searching for a nesting site as they climbed up, and over the hills. They had turned East to pick up the central Burma lowland around the mysteriously gorgeous city of Mandalay. Their final destination was Toungoo, 175 miles North of Rangoon, sitting on the main, broad, flat Sittang river valley floor, which runs down the spine of Burma. Jumbo told Harjinder, quite unnecessarily, to keep a lookout for Japanese aircraft as they floated above the sea of green jungle below them. Both heads scanned back and forth constantly. The rear guns were fully loaded, and Harjinder admitted that he was itching to press the trigger. However, nothing more sinister than some curious birds were sighted and, with eyes tired and itchy after the constant scanning, they approached their new home. The airfield was on the flat valley floor, but just a few miles further East was the sawtooth mountain wall, shimmering in the blue haze, guarding the Burma-Thailand border beyond. Jumbo lead the Lysanders in a circle overhead the airfield, before dropping down onto the approach for the single North-South runway. The whole squadron was on the ground by 11 am.

The Lysanders came to a stop and, after one final burst of power, all the propellers came to a click-clicking halt. The pilots and air gunners, streaked in sweat, climbed down the steps in the fuselage, on to the step atop the large main-wheel cover, before dropping to the ground. Waiting for them, seeking out Jumbo, was the Station Commander, a Wing Commander, whom they had known in Peshawar in 1937. It was heartening to see old friends in this new and exciting land. He wasn't the only old friend because, as expected, No. 28 Squadron RAF had already taken up residence there. Harjinder did a quick scan of his surroundings. The asphalt runway meant that operations could continue during heavy rains, if any. There was a small control tower, some office-type buildings and several hangars. Harjinder discounted the hangars immediately; they would offer a juicy target to any attacking Japanese aircraft. Harjinder gathered his men together and ordered the twelve aircraft to be scattered around the airfield, tucking them under any tree cover where possible, to make them a difficult target for any enemy air attack. Some of the RAF's

No. 28 Squadron pilots had a good laugh. A cheeky young man said
to Harjinder: 'What are you scared of? Toungoo has never been raided
so far.'

However, Harjinder was not to be put out by these taunts and set his
men to work.

The refuelling was nearly complete when the whine of the air raid
warning was sounded. Nobody at Toungoo had bothered to dig slit
trenches for cover in the event of bombing raids. So, with no organised
destination in mind, the aim of the individuals seemed to be to run, and
take cover, as far away from the aircraft as they could go. Some showed
some hereto unknown athletic skills as they seemed to go mighty fast,
and mighty far, before diving to the ground! This was their first air raid,
and Harjinder admitted that they were all scared out of their wits. Any
thought of this being an exercise was quickly dashed as the roar of Japanese
engines, at full power, filled the air. The mind–numbing din of the first
aircraft engine screamed overhead in an angry statement of intent, but that
suddenly seemed tame, when the scream was joined by the crump, crump,
crump, of the first bombs going off. The shockwaves reverberated over
the airfield and through the chests of the men, who were now trying to
be at one with the earth beneath them; all trying to make themselves as
small and thin as possible. Large dirt fountains showed the progress of the
bombs over the ground. In reality, it was all over in seconds, but for every
man lying prostrate on the ground, with hands over heads, it seemed an
eternity before it took all the aircraft to drop their loads and scoot over
the horizon at tree top level. When Harjinder felt it was all clear, he stood
up and looked around at the other men slowly getting to their feet and
wiping the dust from their working uniforms. Harjinder blew a whistle
to get some order and get all the heads back to thinking about the job in
hand. He collected all the Squadron Airmen together, wondering who
would have 'copped it' in the raid. One by one the men, some of whom
had shown Olympian qualities in both speed and distance, reappeared,
and it became apparent to Harjinder that all were present and correct. The
men had scattered to all corners of the airstrip, so each brought news of the
damage done. Excitement rippled through the men as they realised that all
their precious Lysanders were intact.

The welcome from the Japanese had woken the IAF up, but left them
intact. However, the same couldn't be said of No. 28 Squadron, RAF. Every
single one of their Lysanders had received some degree of damage, lined

up as they were, providing perfect target practice for the Japanese. There was one casualty from the raid, within the Indian community. Harjinder had been allotted a personal assistant by Jumbo, Leading Aircraftsman Chatterjee, a carpenter by trade. He was supposed to carry a machine gun and accompany Harjinder on the move around the airfield. It was not the Japanese bombs that did the damage but the poor, unfortunate Chatterjee broke his leg whilst diving for cover! From that point onwards, Harjinder had to be Chatterjee's personal assistant, looking after *his* daily needs!

It is doubtful whether the bombers were on the hunt for the IAF's, or even for No. 28 Squadron's Lysanders. They were almost definitely looking for the American Volunteer Group (AVG) pilots and aircraft, who had been causing them disproportionate trouble, especially on their recent Christmas day raid. The Japanese sent two waves, totalling 80 bombers and 48 fighters, to hit Rangoon. The AVG knocked down 23 of them, the biggest victory of the war so far, with reportedly six more shot down over the Gulf of Martaban, to the South. The AVG did not lose a single plane. The Chinese national leader Chiang Kai-shek had agreed to pay for the formation of the AVG, which consisted of men from the US Army, Navy and Marines Reserves, led by Claire Lee Chennault. Either thrill seekers, or desperate for the impressive wage, they all had a story to tell. Their mounts were the lend-lease P-40 Tomahawk fighters, shipped in from the USA. The men had copied the shark's teeth mouths painted on the noses of the RAF P-40's in Libya. Somehow, the shark had been lost in translation and the nickname 'Flying Tigers' had stuck. Back in America, these laid-back, veteran pilots, hired at a daily rate of $600, and paid a $500 bonus for every aircraft shot down, were becoming legends. Hollywood couldn't let this opportunity slip by, and so, even Disney became involved, drawing up what became their emblem of a Tiger jumping through the 'V for Victory'. After being formed in China, Chiang Kai-shek had sent the AVG into Burma to bolster the poorly-equipped RAF forces. The AVG had originally used Toungoo as a training airfield, during which they had had been at the end of some minor Japanese bombing; 'practice bombing', as one of the technicians had called it! At some point in the last 48 hours, the Japanese had figured out that the AVG training base was now an offensive platform. Having sent the bombers screaming in, they now realised this AVG fighting base was shared with the IAF and the RAF; Toungoo, in the Sittang river valley, was in for a rough ride.

And how rough it was to be...

The airfield took its name (pronounced 'Taangoo' in Burmese) from the town to the South. The small track from the airstrip emerged onto the main Lashio Road next to a pagoda guarded with statues of ferocious lions, or Sinthe's, from which Major General Wingate's Special Forces group got its name, the Chindits. This road was the main artery from Rangoon to Kunming, in China, via the seven hundred mile, winding, Burma Road. Six miles down this road, past the hulks of abandoned trucks, was the Main Street of Toungoo, constantly vibrating with the lorries carrying vital supplies day and night to China. The road was flanked with shops on one side, and market stalls on the other. Further into the town, the narrow, twisting, streets were lined with bamboo shops and huts. The so-called hotel was nothing more than a brothel for the lorry drivers. Away from the squalor of the packed humanity, the countryside had a truly tropical beauty, with flowers climbing the gnarled trees. However, even though the exact position wasn't known, beautiful as the jungle looked, it was clear that it contained Japanese soldiers pushing towards the airfield and towards Rangoon in the South.

What do you do in a jungle clearing, with a collection of slow, obsolete reconnaissance aircraft?

If you are Jumbo Majumdar, and it is the 2nd February 1942, you get Harjinder and his team together, and put forth an outrageous proposal...

Jumbo hadn't come all this way to float around the heads of the Japanese, offering them some additional target practice. He had decided that the IAF would become an offensive unit; a bomber squadron! He gave the order, or perhaps more of a firm request, to see if these lumbering beasts could be converted into bombers. He was keen to go into action, but not merely on a reconnaissance flight. It was more than just his desire to attack the Japanese, it was because he felt the IAF's reputation would not grow if they tiptoed along the periphery, if they didn't attack. The Lysanders were designed to carry six, tiny, 20 pound Cooper practice bombs, but he knew that Harjinder's technicians could do better than this; he wanted a 250 pound bomb under each wing. Back at the Westland Aircraft Company, in Yeovil, Somerset, pencils would have been snapping on design tables had they heard this jungle conversation. Harjinder and his men went about their task and hung 250 pound bombs in place. They rigged a basic rope system to tug on, thereby releasing the bombs down on the Japanese, but hopefully not before, since as one AVG pilot wrote, they were 'posing a serious risk of self-destruction as they clattered along the runway!'

Jumbo decided not to ease into combat, not to settle into their bombing war role by carrying out some testing. No, he wanted to test out his obsolete reconnaissance Lysanders on a bombing mission against the most heavily-defended Japanese position; why waste precious bombs, was his stock answer to those who questioned him. He was determined to do his bit in the actual fighting, no matter the restrictions they faced with their slow, reconnaissance aircraft. Being of the same mind, Harjinder was thrilled to hear that the first mission in Burma would be a bombing one, and naturally, being the premier crew, with Jumbo, he would lead from the front.

Harjinder had trained eagerly for this role, for this moment in time, for this, his moment in history.

He had stepped away from the life of a civilian engineer, to further India's struggle for Independence through the IAF, and this was the focus of all that effort. Jumbo could see the excitement in Harjinder's demeanour, and so took him aside and asked him to listen carefully to what he had to say. He delivered the earth-shattering shock in a carefully-measured tone; Harjinder was to be replaced as Jumbo's rear gunner.

It took a few moments for Harjinder to register what he was being told; once he did, he sprang to attack – they had trained as team, they should stay together as a team. A fair point, but Jumbo soon dissuaded him. His argument was that the Squadron could not afford to lose both of them at one go in case his aircraft was shot down. It was the problem faced by squadron commanders before him, and squadron commanders right up to the present day. Do you pair up your best people, forming the best crews, to give them the best chance of success? Or do you dilute the experience over the squadron, reducing the chance of loss, but reducing the chance of a successful mission too? Jumbo had other concerns that influenced his decision as well; 'You are as important to the Squadron as I am, perhaps more so, because you maintain the morale of the Airmen as well as the technical part of the Squadron. In my absence, a new Commanding Officer would need your guidance and advice.' It also showed that Jumbo was under no illusion about the task ahead, there was a very reasonable chance he would not return.

Harjinder was frustrated, of course. He viewed being Jumbo's air gunner as a great privilege, but he had to yield to him because he knew that he was right; Harjinder could not help looking at Rustomjee with envy, as he took his place.

Whether you were British, American, German or Japanese, the lessons from early aerial warfare was that you sent your bomber raids with a fighter escort. Jumbo was willing to, and planned to, go it alone. Also stationed in Toungoo was a group of New Zealand pilots flying in the RAF with 67 Squadron. One of these pilots, learning of Jumbo's aggressive plan, insisted on flying as his escort into enemy territory. It seemed the New Zealanders were as mad as the Indians! As the bomb-loaded Lysander waddled out to take up its takeoff position, all the IAF, RAF and AVG pilots turned out to wave him off. How many did not expect to see him again? The Lysander accelerated slower than normal despite the engine giving the full throaty roar as usual. It was much further down the runway than normal when the wheels left the ground and Jumbo struggled to make height to clear the trees. The New Zealand pilot raced off after him looking deceptively agile. He was in a Brewster Buffalo fighter that looked like a barrel with wings stuck on as an afterthought. These fighters offered little real challenge in a proper dog fight against a Japanese fighter. However, the New Zealanders, and the AVG operating with them, had used their skill, more than better equipment, to give the Japanese a real bloody nose throughout January. Harjinder watched the two aircraft fade to dots and wrote; 'The aircraft headed East and our hearts went with him. We prayed for him and kept a watch on the sky for his return.'

Harjinder admitted that he had never known such a long and anxious wait. You can imagine the men trying to find something to do now that the boss, their talisman, had left.

Jumbo settled the Lysander down into the now super-slow cruise speed lowering his aircraft towards the top of the jungle canopy. He skimmed the tops as close as he dared, flicking the occasional top most branches, both sets of eyes sweeping from horizon to horizon. About a mile away, slightly back and slightly higher was the barrel-like Buffalo zig-zagging above, and behind, to keep station at this unbearably slow speed. Low and slow being the worst conditions for a fighter. His presence probably made detection more likely and his usefulness in doubt against anything except a lone attacker, but it was still a comforting sight; they weren't completely alone. Nobody likes the unknown, and this was the height of unknown.

Waiting is harder than doing, and the two hours on the ground seemed to stretch into days. The hands of the clock seem to be playing games;

the negative thoughts started to push themselves to the front. Distraction was no longer an option and, along with the others, Harjinder started to scan the Eastern horizon until suddenly the long-awaited shout went up. It was just a speck but surely it was an aircraft heading their way. When the speck in the sky soon became two specks they all jumped with joy. Briefly all military bearing evaporated. The Lysander landed; the wings were clean; the bombs had been dropped. It seemed to take an age until the propeller came to rest. The crowd stood back to let Jumbo step down. Jumbo Majumdar jumped down letting the details spill out to Harjinder and the gathered pilots. He had located the nearest Japanese airfield, Mae Haungsaun, climbing to gain some height, putting himself in full view. He pointed the nose down to dive at a higher speed (you couldn't call any speed in a Lysander high!), through the expected machine gun fire. As he dragged the nose back onto the horizon, he pulled on the rope, and the aircraft leapt into the air like a scalded cat, as the weight of the bombs left the racks. One crashed through the roof of an aircraft hangar, the other into a wireless station before exploding, demolishing both. Jumbo held the Lysander down low, pleading for the aircraft to give him any possible additional speed as he expected the world to explode in machinegun fire around him.

The pilot who escorted the Lysander was full of praise for Jumbo, he saw the hangar burning, and in his opinion Jumbo had struck a significant blow against the Japanese war effort. If perhaps a slight exaggeration, it was the first offensive strike against the Japanese for some time in that region. All the young IAF pilots now wanted to emulate Jumbo, and begged Harjinder to modify their aircraft. The news of Jumbo's attack was flashed all over Burma, and his name became known overnight. The first day of operations was a resounding success, and a surprise to friend and foe alike.

Night fell on their first day of combat. It had been only one aircraft and one bombing raid, but the IAF had *achieved*! In fact, they had achieved so well that the Japanese were not going to let it go without a fitting reply. At three o'clock in the morning, the Japanese engines could be heard in the area, and within seconds, the air raid warning started its wailing. The men ran and dived into the newly-prepared slit trenches. The Japanese gave them a real working over. The whistling of the bombs and the blast of their explosions were terrifying. Cabby took his mouth organ into the trenches and even while bombs were bursting around him, he kept on with his morale-raising music. Harjinder was annoyed with the troublesome Japanese. He thought when a man has been disturbed in his sleep it was bad enough, but when the cause is an air raid, he really had something to curse at! The silence after the bombers left was short lived. The drone of the second wave was close behind and soon the whistles and explosions created more havoc, and, one would assume, more cursing from Harjinder! Sleep was off the menu for that night. Harjinder wrote; 'In the morning we were dead tired, partly due to lost sleep, but mostly due to the fear we had felt.'

It was only the second day in the combat, only the 3rd February 1942, but the IAF were now part of fighting the Japanese, and they wanted to make more of a statement. Later in the day, another bombing attack was planned, this time with the majority of the aircraft, because after Jumbo's exploit, no one would agree to be left out! Harjinder and team prepared all the Lysanders, and he supervised the loading of the bombs on the home-made bomb racks. One of the Indian armourers helping to load the bombs was Saigal. He had joined as a Sepoy just as Harjinder had, and it was clear that he had the same sort of drive like Harjinder; he was one to watch for the future.

One of the Lysanders was going to miss the big show. The IAF were tasked to fly a Chinese General named Yun to Lashio. Ratnagar heaved a sigh of relief when Satyanarayana was selected to be the General's personal chauffer. Ratnager wouldn't miss the squadron attack.

Before starting, Satyanarayana reluctantly went about his job, as the others were being briefed for the mission they all wanted to be on. With the General in the rear seat of Lysander P9131, he helped him with the web of straps. Having made sure his passenger was secured, Satyanarayana took the quick way down and jumped from the side of the rear cockpit to the ground. As he jumped, the ring on his right hand caught on the ammunition box stowage for the rear gun.

Satyanarayana fell to the ground in pain, the ring having very nearly severed his finger completely. 'It was hanging by just the flesh', recalled Ratnagar. Satyanarayana briefly shouted in pain before passing out. It was pretty obvious that he was not going to do any flying. It was an awkward situation, Gen Yun was sitting in the rear seat of the Lysander, all strapped in and ready to go, and there was no pilot to fly him! Ratnagar's blood turned cold as Joe Prasad approached him. He knew he was going to miss the chance of being a part of history!

The early days at Karachi Air Force Base

Harjinder (standing centre) on one of those early training exercises

The bag and rope method to start a reluctant engine

The IAF Army Cooperation Wapitis with the long hook underneath

Sepoys arming a Wapiti

Harjinder as a rear gunner in the leading Wapiti

Bouchier sitting front and centre with 1 Sqn IAF

Harjinder, in cap and webbing belt, looking at the camera, travels 3ʳᵈ class by train

Preparation for operations in the North-West Frontier

Sergeant Harjinder Singh, with medal, stands in front of his Wapiti

Harjinder and team working on a Wapiti propeller

OFFICERS OF No. 1 SQUADRON. I.A.F.
MIRANSHAH· 1940-41.

A signed picture of Harjinder, with his back to the camera, choosing a gramophone record

Harjinder, wearing the tie, with his team and the 'new' Lysander

Practicing for war

Amit Saigal, pictured in Burma, would become Harjinder's closest friends

A brief moment of calm in Burma for Saigal and the men

This is.. PRING

The Flight Sergeant who shoots them down quickly. A cool nerve, a clear brain, and unlimited 'guts', that's what it takes to make an ace-pilot like Pring. But that's not all. Shooting down Jap raiders takes more than courage. It takes the best we can give in good aircraft, serviced to the minute,..one hundred per cent effective in every detail..reliable,..positively unfailing. It takes good men to service good aircraft And our aircraft ARE good, and so are our MEN.

and this is.. SINGH

He is a Technical Officer in the Indian Air Force. He hasn't always been an officer. Ten years ago he was an "unknown",.. a student in an Engineering College in Northern India. He gave up a good stipend to join the Indian Air Force. But he had foresight, had Harjender Singh, foresight plus ability. That's why he's now a Technical Officer drawing Rs. 590 a month. He was the first technical trainee to join the Indian Air Force. And he was with the first I.A.F. Squadron to go on active operations in this war. Did he do well? Well, he's an officer now, isn't he? And he wasn't then.

The propaganda poster confused many people into believing Harjinder was the pilot!

*Jumbo, front row second on the left, was a last minute addition to
No. 263 Squadron RAF before D-Day*

The raw materials Harjinder had to work with to form IAF bomber squadrons

Happier times ahead for Harjinder

The Harvard aircraft unofficially flown by Harjinder

The Tempest aircraft used by Moolgavkar in Kashmir, and kept flying by Harjinder

Harjinder flies the Spitfire

Harjinder stepping out of Asia's first jet: The Vampire

Another challenge for Harjinder. A sad looking Aero 45

Harjinder shows Menon the Kanpur-I aircraft he designed and built

Harjinder prepares to start production of the Avro 748.
Is the Haig Whiskey crate by chance or design?

Harjinder left with Subroto Mukerjee

Nehru inaugurates the Avro 748 named "Subroto" by Harjinder

Harjinder leaves the IAF in his Bonanza

Air Vice-Marshal Harjinder Singh MBE

Harjinder sporting his IAF pilot wings

Harjinder's coffin

Found in a Hangar still showing the holes after the Mirage crash;
The HT2 in front, a Vampire and Harjinder's Spitfire

As the secondhands on every pilot's watch ticked away to the allocated time, all propellers started turning in unison, to be joined by the sound of the engines arriving from different corners of the airfield. The aircraft rattled, shook, and lurched from their individual jungle hideaways to the assembly point at the end of the runway. The desire to take the fight to the Japanese was infectious and two aircraft from No. 28 Squadron, RAF, also joined the party! Harjinder watched his pilot, Jumbo, once again taking to the air without him. This time he was like the mother goose, leading the unsteady fledglings into the air. Jumbo's aircraft circled once overhead before turning East when the other aircraft formed up close enough around him to keep him in sight, but giving each other enough room to weave whilst scanning the horizon. Jumbo then took the formation down to tree-hopping height, introducing the others to the sudden snap of a random extra-long branch getting in the way. As they crawled up the side of a hill, approaching the crest, each one would skim over the shoulders of the hill trying to keep their silhouetted aircraft visible for as little time as possible. The many months of flying over the rough country of the North-West Frontier had taught them much, but now they closed in on a different enemy. They were relying on their camouflage to keep them out of sight of the fighters. All the information they had, was that the Japanese liked to stay high, therefore low, low, low, was how they would fly. Zig-zagging behind them were two of the New Zealand Buffalo fighters, and protecting their base was some of the American AVG pilots; a real multi-national attack.

Each cockpit was its own little world of a pilot and his tail gunner. Some exchanged a few words but all had their total concentration focused outside the cockpit, scanning for fighters. Fighters meant death; it was that simple. Jumbo led them over the ragged, green, carpet of jungle towards Mae Haungsaun, the Japanese airfield. Staying a few feet, sometimes a few inches, above the trees, offered them some protection. Any engine malfunction now and that protection would only offer them death.

The Lysanders closed in together. Then as one, the Squadron climbed into position, and prepared to unleash their loads. They faithfully followed Jumbo's lead as he pushed the nose down to dive over the perimeter of the airfield. Each pilot picking out his target, checking left and right to ensure no comrades were drifting into the same bubble of space, before concentrating on exactly where his bombs would end up. The painful wait was at an end when the Lysanders accelerated into their dive, then

one by one, after the sharp tug on the rope in the cockpit, they jumped
heavenwards as the weight of the bombs was shed. They played merry
hell with enemy installations causing the last few Lysander pilots to fling
their mounts around in an attempt to avoid the plumes of smoke, dirt,
rubble and shrapnel. Every pilot knew the routine – the second the bombs
dropped from the aircraft; drag the aeroplane's nose up until it rested on
the horizon; keep the aircraft as close to the ground as you dare until at
the tree line, then pop up no more than absolutely necessary. They all
headed for Jumbo's machine, now able to coax more speed out of their
machines with the bombs gone, and fuel used, but this was still a painfully
slow return in this obsolete, reconnaissance-turned-bomber aircraft.
There was no time for rejoicing, shouts of joy, or slaps on the back. All
felt the thrill of completing their first raid, but they had to get home
first, and with the fires burning behind them, it felt as if every Japanese
fighter in Burma must be after them. Facing backwards, the rear gunners
expected the hornets' nest they had just kicked to explode, with swarms
chasing them. All eyes were once again, endlessly, rotating in sockets,
looking for fighters as the pilots pushed the aircraft even lower. The jungle
canopy was their saviour, but a slight misjudgement, and it could also be
their killer.

On the ground, the technicians managed to occupy their minds in
the waiting game a little better than the day before, but all stopped when
the first aircraft engine was heard. In the head of each man, the Lysanders
were ticked off one by one until all were accounted for. They touched
down perfectly, and relieved faces looked out from their high perches
in the cockpit. As engines stopped, the grins on the ground were finally
joined by the grins in the cockpits.

The whole Squadron was now to become famous. How did they know
they were famous? The Japanese told them so. A Japanese radio broadcast
announced: 'We know that the Indian Air Force Squadron has come to
Toungoo. They are brave, unlike the RAF, but they should be ashamed to
serve British masters. The British are using them as cannon fodder. Why
are they sending only the Indians on these raids? Where is the RAF? We
warn the Indians that we will hit back harder next time, though we are
friends and we want India to be free. They should remember this when
they are ordered next time to fly.'

Harjinder wrote; 'We were jubilant. We are superior to the RAF;
even the Japanese say so!'

The Japanese held their promise and subjected the IAF to more raids, but by now these attacks held less fear. In fact, it was already becoming a problem for Harjinder to order the nonchalant men into the trenches. It sounds amazing that bombs and bombing can become routine only three days after their entry into the World War II, but Harjinder reported; 'We had two more raids today. The Airmen have become fearless. The messing staff reported a raid on the stocks of cigarettes from the mess during the air raid. I warned them against the dangers of splinters from bombs, but apparently they love their cigarettes more than their lives.'

Along with Singha, Harjinder saw a sight during one of the raids that snapped him back to reality. A Burmese guard, on duty, was marching up and down near the aircraft. It seemed that they were also getting blasé about the bombings. However, the deadly intent was brought home when a bomb splinter completely cut through this guard's neck. Harjinder said that the headless body, with the rifle on his shoulder, walked two more steps without the head before it collapsed and fell. Robert Keaton, the AVG test pilot, was also caught in the raid and saw the Burmese guard fall. Keaton had jumped into a car with two technicians when the sirens sounded. He jammed his foot hard down on the accelerator pedal and promptly careered into a ditch! Trapped by a jammed door he had a ringside seat to the bombing, counting thirty direct hits on the runway, causing dirt to fill his car. The deadly shrapnel whizzed around him like machinegun fire but unlike the poor Burmese guard, the car's occupants escaped injury.

The next day they were metaphorically, and for one poor airman, literally, caught with their trousers down by the Japanese bombers. They relied on observers, using heliographs, to flash warning signals to the control tower but with the Thai border so close there was never much more than a few minutes' notice. This day they had no notice. Did it perhaps mean that the observation team were also getting a little complacent? Saigal, and the rest of the armourers, had just finished hanging the large bombs under the wings of the aircraft when the Japanese came. The humming noise of these aircraft had become familiar to their ears. As Harjinder took cover he had time to ponder, and find it very curious, that the raiders always followed a Burmese Tiger Moth which carried mail for the Station. Were they following him; was he leading them in, or was it just coincidence?

As the jungle erupted with the noise of the attack, for some, the distance to nip into the trenches was too great, so they threw themselves flat on the ground. The natural instinct is to seek shelter and some of them dived under the outstretched Lysander wings. Not a wise choice as the aircraft would naturally be the main target for the attackers, if spotted through their camouflaged dens. 'Corie' Singha was one of those under an aeroplane and he had a narrow escape. His Lysander, P-9120, had been loaded up with bombs and he had just finished writing 'A Present from India' on the fins of the bombs with chalk. He laid himself flat under the wings of P-9120 as the bombs detonated around him. Not normally one to pray, Singha made up for lost time by getting a lifetime of praying into those few seconds. One bomb explode dangerous close to him with the shockwave moving through him as the super-heated air moved around him. The bomb splinter flew inches over his head and body. The clanging of dirt hitting the machine was complimented by a 'ping' noise letting Singha know that shrapnel had struck the aircraft above him. Then came the sickening thud, and pain, in his leg. He had been hit! After the raid was over he was the last one to be seen gingerly trying to stand. Once successfully sitting up he bent over to pick up his own bomb fin from his legs. The fin, still with 'A present from India' written on it, had been sheared clean off and dropped on to him. It had stunned him so much that he sat there for some time thinking one of his legs must have been sliced off. When he confirmed he was not only fully intact, but unharmed, he showed the 'Present from India' trophy to everyone, grinning from ear to ear. The Indians' luck was still holding out.

Once the last of the Japanese had set course back for their base, no time was lost. The team sprang from the trenches and ran to the Lysanders. The final preparations were completed as the pilots and air gunners strapped in. Engines were started and without waiting to form up for an organised takeoff the individual aircraft blasted off the ground, and went after the Japanese. Despite their slow speed, they appeared over the Japanese air base just as the last Japanese aircraft had landed at their home airstrip. In went the IAF, and once again their approach was undetected. They went about their task with gusto, bombing and strafing, with the air gunners enjoy this 'game', spraying gunfire over the aircraft that still taxied around. When they had finished with their bombs they resorted to an old World War I trick. Empty beer bottles were thrown out. Not an attempt to take out an enemy soldier, or even to register disgust that the Japanese were restricting their supply of beer, but when the bottles fell they also made a whistling noise similar to a dropping bomb keeping the Japanese gunners' heads down!

The next day, another IAF raid went ahead. This time, on landing, Pilot Officer Gill put one wheel into one of the many bomb craters. The aircraft was fine except that the undercarriage was spread out by nearly 2 inches on one side. Harjinder told Gill everything was fine but the pilot was dubious. Jumbo came to know about the incident and Gill's apparent lack of conviction. His answer was straight forward. Jumbo offered his Lysander P-9120 to Gill and he took over the 'damaged' one. True to his word, Jumbo flew the aircraft on the next mission, shaming Gill into asking for his own aircraft back.

Despite the daily raids, the precious IAF Lysanders remained serviceable and the men untouched; except for one of Harjinder's men performing an overzealous dive towards the ground, and Singha's bruise from his own bomb fin. On the 5th February, the Japanese attacked with 17 bombers and 13 fighters. One of the RAF Sergeant pilots was injured very badly in the raid, and he was found by Harjinder's Sergeant Sud, who bandaged him up by tearing strips off his own shirt. The IAF Equipment Assistant, Sohan Singh, had a narrow escape after finding himself alone in a trench. Photographer Gurmukh Singh called him over to his trench; a bit of mutual support perhaps. Sohan Singh had taken a few steps when he was blown forward, arriving face first, into Gurmukh's trench. Sohan picked his face out of the dirt to look behind him. His recently vacated trench smoked from a direct hit. The two looked wordlessly at each other knowing how close Sohan had come to be scattered across the airfield. In the distance four RAF aircraft were burning, pouring smoke over the airfield as a beacon to the enemy. Later, in the debris, 5 more RAF planes were found to be badly damaged.

6th February, under a week into combat, and the Japanese knew that the IAF had arrived. Jumbo led another raid, this time on the Moulmein railway stations and dockyards. Three fires were seen burning brightly as they left. Just as importantly, the action was seen by the allied army on the West bank of the river. Seeing the Japanese have some of their own medicine was heartening for the down-cast troops. The Air Officer Commanding, Burma also announced that the AVG had shot down their 100th aircraft in the defence of Rangoon. Some good news was getting through.

Meanwhile, the Japanese had also made it clear that they wanted to dispose of the Indians. Things were getting too hot on the ground at Toungoo, so the Squadron was split into three Flights at different landing grounds. After all, they could rendezvous in the air for bombing missions. It also meant they could assist local forces in their own areas. There was plenty to organise. Harjinder decided to split the repair and salvage section, placing the two halves under Flight Sergeant Bhaskaran and Flight Sergeant Mohd Siddique. Their training on the North-West Frontier, and the experience gained in repairing the crashed IAF aircraft, had given them valuble experience, which Harjinder now intended to make full use of, in order to maintain 100 per cent serviceability. Harjinder's men had worked non-stop whenever the need arose – carrying out repairs in torchlight, in the dead of the night – Harjinder wanted to maintain this ethos, even when they were split up.

Harjinder had three other Acting Unpaid Flight Sergeants: Atma Singh, Waryam Singh and Sharma. They were given charge of the daily servicing of each Flight. Harjinder would be in overall charge, but his Flight Sergeants would all be running their own small shows. Maintaining the 100 per cent record was his aim. Losses seemed likely, so all the ground equipment and spares were split into two, and the location of these sections were arranged such that in case of any damage to one by enemy bombing, the other would still be operational.

As always in war, rumours spread like wildfire. The current rumour was that enemy agents in Burma were lighting fires around their airfields to guide the Japanese bombers to their targets easily. There were even unconfirmed reports that a Magistrate in Toungoo was an enemy spy and had been arrested. The stories about the bombing havoc at Rangoon were clearly not just rumour. The IAF team felt they were dealing out some opposition to the Japanese, but they were just twelve aircraft in a small sector of Burma. The Japanese may be slowed down slightly, but they were still pushing forward, and it seemed that a retreat was inevitable.

The 7th February was one whole week in Burma for the IAF. They say a week is a long time in politics, but when those politics involve bombing and being bombed, a week can feel like a lifetime. The men felt like veterans; whether it was their general keenness, their professional training, or the smoke of the battle in their nostrils, the pilots took their missions in their stride like men with months of operations under their belts. However, if this Japanese bombing continued, they would soon cause casualties in both men and machines so the main party moved North to Lashio. Jumbo headed even further up the flat valley floor. The tree-covered head of the valley was visible to the North of their new airstrip. A natural pass turned right into the next river valley which led directly into China. Harjinder organised his ground party, collecting men and material at the train station in Toungoo. He loaded them all into the train, already bursting at the seams with refugees moving away from the advancing enemy. The train chuffed and rattled its way North, first towards Mandalay, where it would turn East and continue to Lashio. Harjinder settled into the slow rocking rhythm and the clanking noises from the track. The soporific sounds of the train suddenly slipped into insignificance as aircraft engines, at full power, roared overhead. The trees that had been pressing in at both sides of the track were torn apart by gun fire. The initial chaotic swirl of noise, torn vegetation, and train steam, only briefly subsided as the planes returned to strafe the train again. This time the driver, and fireman, were having no more. With the brakes wound fully on, the train screeching to a halt with carriage smashing against carriage, the two of them jumped from their still moving cab. They were last seen disappearing at full speed into the outskirts of the town they were just approaching. Whether the Japanese thought the clouds of steam indicated a direct hit, or they were spooked by allied aircraft was unclear to Harjinder, but when he jumped down and ran to the front he found the Japanese seemed to have missed the engine completely. After walking up the track he discovered they had been abandoned near the railway station at Meiktila, about halfway to Mandalay. He found the Station Master, but any conversation with him seemed hopeless. With plenty of threats directed at him, he did, finally, ring up the Area Superintendent, who proved to be equally helpless; no spare drivers were available. Harjinder now found himself separated from his aircraft, with all his men gathered together on a train which offered a perfect target for any passing Japanese aircraft. He sent a party of Airmen to search the vicinity for the driver, but they returned without success Harjinder was desperate. The aircraft would be useless without the technicians and their tools, and they had all the ground equipment on the train. No plan involving spanners and hammers, invigorated by tea or otherwise, would work this time, so another plan was required, something a little cheeky perhaps. Harjinder had officially been an apprentice on the railways during his college time. He had learnt all about locomotives in those college days, when he used to go to the Loco Shops of North Western Railway at Moghalpura for technical experience. The driving part was simple, wasn't it? He knew the theory of how the brakes worked, didn't he? So Harjinder approached the Station Master of Meiktila asking if he could drive. If a man in uniform, in fact, a fearsome man in uniform, asked to borrow your train, what would you say? Not surprisingly, he refused point-blank. Harjinder then told him that he was a qualified driver and in a blatant show of faux confidence, suggested that the Station Master test him. He still refused! So Harjinder went a level up, and asked him if he could speak to the Area Superintendent direct. He managed to get the Superintendent on the line, but he, too was adamant in refusing him permission. No great surprise there, then.

There was a war on, they were stranded, the IAF pilots also would be stranded with the Squadron immobilized if Harjinder didn't take the law into his own hands. His reasoning was, better to risk a train rather than a Squadron, so he told the Station Master: 'In the name of the Government of Burma, I take over this train and ask you to inform the next station of our arrival.'

The Station Master wanted it in writing, so paper was produced and in his neatly formed writing, Harjinder formally took over all responsibility for the train, not knowing if he could legally do such a thing, but signing pieces of paper seemed to make everything alright! With a sweep of the pen, he was now Warrant Officer Harjinder Singh: train driver. Things seemed to come full circle to those early apprentice days, apart from the fact that he had never actually driven a train!

Even though the fireman was missing, the mouth organ playing Sergeant Cabinetmaker rose to the occasion and volunteered for the job. He shovelled more coal in to get the pressure up as Harjinder studied the controls. As soon as he moved the brake handle forward, the brakes went off and the vacuum gauge registered; a good start. Once underway Harjinder celebrated by letting out a long blast on the train's whistle. Well you would, wouldn't you! Then he moved the throttle handle to the right to see if anything would happen. There was such a jolt forward that Harjinder hit his head against the pressure gauge. The poor passengers must have had a very uneasy time, possibly thinking of abandoning ship, but the train continued to move forward and so, by accident, they were underway. Going was one thing, but stopping seemed far more important, so Harjinder thought he had better put in some practice whilst they were

still near a station. He travelled about a mile and then shut off steam to
stop the speed building up. After about two minutes he gingerly turned
the brake handle about a quarter of the movement before letting it go.
The next time he moved it to one third and let go. Another minute and he
pulled it fully back. There was another big jolt, although he was ready for
it this time, and more importantly, the train hissed to a stop. He reversed
the gear lever, released the brakes and, ever so gently this time, he opened
the throttle. It was pure delight to feel the train reverse very gracefully.
He repeated the operation for stopping, again with a more delicate touch,
and the train came to a stand-still like a well-trained horse under control.
That was enough practice, time to do or die. 'I was confident and felt sure
that we could drive the train as far as it would go, but only on the plains.
What would happen when we came to a hilly section? I left that in the lap
of the Gods.'

They steamed off at what they estimated was about 20 mph. This must
be every schoolboy's dream, your own steam train to drive, just so long as
you can forget you are firstly, in the jungle, secondly, in a war, and thirdly,
a nice, big, juicy target for fighters that have already appeared once this
day! After they had gone about 50 miles, Cabinetmaker took over. Two
train drivers fully checked out! Things settled down, and they relaxed
into their new role. The miles clattered by but it couldn't last forever. The
Station Master at one of the more major towns must have been warned,
because he had both incoming and outgoing signals down, possibly as a
safety measure in case they overran the station. Experts were watching so
the pressure was on to show that they knew what they were doing – after
all Harjinder had told the previous Station Master that he was a driver!
They started shutting-off the steam but unfortunately a little too early.
The train nearly stopped so Harjinder gave it another burst on the throttle.
Too much! The wheels spun on the track initially but then they picked
up speed too quickly and watched the station, and various faces, chug past
them as they struggled to shut off the steam and get full brakes on without
taking the train off the track. Finally, they overshot the station by a whole
mile. The reversing Harjinder practiced earlier came in useful, and very
slowly, he drew them up, backwards, to the platform. The Station Master
came rushing up to the cab. Seeing them in uniform he spoke to Harjinder
very politely but certainly very firmly. 'I have received a telephone from
the Area Superintendent. He has despatched a driver by car, so please
do not move any further. It is very dangerous. There is a bridge ahead;

a long and twisting one. There are also hills ahead, so you need another locomotive in the rear from the next station onwards.'

Cabby Cabinetmaker was all for going on anyway; his blood was up and he was clearly having the time of his life! Tempting as it was, Harjinder saw the sense of it and gave in, much to Cabby's disappointment. The driver came two and a half hours later and Harjinder admitted; 'nobody was more relieved than me. The poor refugees were equally relieved, I suppose, because they had had a good taste of our driving.' How many passengers' heads needed bandaging, I wonder?

Harjinder went on to describe the final part of their journey; 'We passed through some beautiful countryside, especially in the hill section. Mamyo was an enchanting town up in the highlands, the climate cool and invigorating. Then we descended into forests of teak, for which Burma is justly famous. I must admit that after the engine driving episode was over, we enjoyed every moment of our journey *(perhaps taking notes on how it should be done?)*. Late in the evening we reached Lashio near the Burma-China border, all in one piece, and rejoined the Squadron's airborne component. As usual, there was a warm welcome from Jumbo Majumdar.'

On 8th February, Harjinder and the team, got a proper look at their surroundings at Lashio. It was the railhead of the Burma-China Road, a flourishing cosmopolitan township with the airstrip to the North of the town, but all the troops housed to the West. From this place, long convoys of trucks carried war supplies to Chiang Kai-shek's China. The whole thrust of the IAF, the RAF, and the AVG in the area, was to keep this supply route open. If the Southern areas of China crumbled to the Japanese, all would be lost. Once this land route was cut, which now seemed most likely, the only supply route would be by air, over the Himalayas; over the hump as it was to be known! Every additional day with an open land route, gave China more time to prepare their resistance against the Japanese assault. The IAF's role, on top of their new-found bombing skills, would be to carry out reconnaissance for the Chinese Army.

All knew that it was only a matter of time before the bombers would attack this strategically important town. As they made their preparations this time, it was as seasoned campaigners. Bombing seemed to have lost its terror by now, after the previous week. They dispersed the aircraft and ground equipment at different points, again to make things harder for the enemy. Harjinder also divided the technical Airmen into three parts – in case of a direct hit on a group of men, they would only lose only 33 per cent of a particular trade.

The next day, Jumbo sent for Harjinder in his room in the Officers Mess, a huge room at the end of a long barrack. He wanted Harjinder to shift his personal luggage there and move in with him. Harjinder was 'surprised beyond words'. Jumbo's explained, 'After all, I need your advice on every action. It is difficult to contact you every time because your present quarters are four miles away.' (*Apparently his concern about flying together didn't stretch to being in the same place during bombing raids.*)

Harjinder was still taken aback, he told him: 'Sir, I am proud of the personal regard you have for me, but ranks mean a lot in the Service. I am a Warrant Officer and there are Flight Lieutenants in our camp down there. They will resent it. Also, imagine if an RAF officer sees me living in the Officers Mess and that too in the Squadron Commander's room!'

But Jumbo was not to be put off so easily. He said: 'I have come here to fight a war and not observe formalities and ceremonies. Besides, you are a guide and adviser to all of us. You have won the admiration of my aircrew and they admire your qualities.'

Harjinder thought and replied. 'Sir, do you realise that in case of an air raid the men would need me more than the officers would? Besides, I have to brief and de-brief the air gunners every time they leave for, or return from, a sortie (*Harjinder always made it a point to talk to the air gunners and the pilots before they left for an operational sortie, firstly to keep morale up and, secondly, to discuss mechanical details of each individual aircraft*). My presence among the Airmen is a dire necessity. I'll tell you what is really needed. If I am allotted a transport you can always expect me here within a few minutes of your call.'

Harjinder's argument worked! A car was found for his use and military protocol upheld.

'In my heart of hearts, of course, I felt very elated that Majumdar had such high regard for me. I felt I should do much more to prove that I really deserve the esteem in which he held me. It is not the rank, but the man Jumbo had implied. Who could ask for greater recognition?'

The Japanese cared not an iota for rank, reputation, or the individual. If the Indian Air Force had briefly given them a bloody nose after the unexpected offensive, it only spurred them on to snuff out the annoyance, like a tick on the skin. The Japanese had their own job to do and taking Rangoon, and thereafter Burma, was a priority. The attacks stepped up a gear; the pressure became untenable.

Nine

The Fighting Retreat

'I have come to Lashio to personally congratulate No. 1 Squadron of the Indian Air Force. You have made history within this short time.'

'Harjinder, you can make him see sense. If you don't, none of us will ever return to India alive.'

Combat can be a very lonely place. The IAF had always operated as a complete, close-knit team, but now they were scattered throughout Burma with communications difficult, at best, and at other times, non-existent. Harjinder's team were the largest and remained in control, albeit loosely, over the other scattered Lysanders. The pilots Hrushikesh Moolgavkar and Homi Ratnagar, both Bombay boys, had become friends in the days of their training at Ambala. If these young men were intrigued to be sent to Johnny Walker and John Haig, the mystery behind these mouth-watering names soon evaporated when they discovered that these were the names of the satellite airfields on the outskirts of Rangoon. However, for Moolgavkar, it was better than whisky; it was the chance for more combat. Alone, or with his friends, he just wanted to be in the thick of it.

Some of the individual Lysanders would take part in their original, lonely, role of loitering above the enemy's heads to guide troops, or artillery fire, to the correct location, whilst offering up their aircraft as excellent target practice for the Japanese troops on the ground. The IAF were flying several times a day, and this would normally involve one mission where the Squadron would meet at a predetermined spot to form up for a full-strength bombing raid. After every raid, all the IAF pilots brought their gangly vultures back home. The grins on landing were now gone but there was still determination etched on their faces. As the sweaty bodies climbed down from their exposed, glassy, perches, the grins often returned to the Lashio crews as they gathered together having parked their Lysanders under trees at different parts of the airfield. The individual views of the raid came pouring out, of the bombs hitting targets and tracer rounds whirring around them. The aircraft were proof that the Japanese were no longer caught unawares, since every day, plenty of additional holes would appear in the aircraft structures, and Harjinder would be kept busy patching, repairing, and replacing parts and panels.

Despite Harjinder's overflowing schedule, he could not help but notice the goings on with one of the RAF Lysanders in the adjacent hangar. Every day, the Sergeant in-charge, ordered it pushed out and the engine run. He would ponder a while, stroking his chin, before having it pushed back into the hangar. They had discovered that the engine was not delivering full power, but when the IAF Flight Sergeant offered his help to find a solution, his assistance was curtly refused. Either the RAF considered it beneath their dignity to get help from the IAF, or they were in no rush to fix it. Harjinder wasn't any better disposed towards the RAF officers who were stationed there to operate this aircraft. The RAF pilots in the Mess went out for a partridge shoot every day, which was sometimes hours away from base. In comparison, the IAF pilots and air gunners, in general, were clamouring to go on more and more missions; to avoid being the ones left behind. Some of the RAF, it seemed, hadn't changed even when things were looking grim.

However, in mid-February, Harjinder had to deal with one of his own men. Sergeant Loyal (*an unfortunate name in this case*) refused to fly as an air gunner; he looked pale and jittery. It was clear to everyone that this poor man's nerves were shot as he even refused to take a step towards any aircraft. Flight Lieutenant Niranjan 'Joe' Prasad showed his caring side, suggesting that Loyal be shot for cowardice! Jumbo thought this would, 'give us a bad name throughout Burma'. He came up with another plan which seems harsh in the clarity of peace time, but it has to be remembered this was war, with no room for unproductive personnel and the risk of fear spreading. The news from lower Burma was very discouraging. The Japanese had taken most of the Southern Burma peninsular and Rangoon was under constant bombing. One of the IAF's flights was based at Mingaladon, the main airfield for Rangoon, and clearly the main target for the Japanese aircraft. So what did Jumbo do? He sent Sergeant Loyal to Mingaladon and made him act as a bearer for the other Senior Sergeants, polishing their shoes and running errands. Under constant bombing raids, he soon came to the conclusion that it was safer in the air, and requested his transfer back to Jumbo's Flight of Lysanders as a tail gunner; he was refused, and later reduced in rank to airman. Now, of course, the unfortunate airman would have been diagnosed with post-traumatic stress disorder and pulled out of the combat zone, but this was 1942.

The 12th February was an important day for the Squadron. News of their successful bombing missions was now known at all levels. Prasad and Moyers, his British, temporary tail gunner, had shown how well the IAF and RAF could combine so some of the RAF Lysanders were assigned to operate with the IAF. The combined unit was to come under Jumbo's command, officially, for the first time. Harjinder knew this was an incredible, almost unimaginable milestone, and so promised the pilots that no aircraft would let them down. He felt the time was right for this reassurance to boost their morale, especially because it was clear to all that the jungles of Burma would devour any pilot and aircraft that had the misfortune to force-land in those forests. Surviving the crash would be unlikely and it would be very difficult to find any trace of them once they disappeared through the foliage. These weren't empty promises – instead of doing the required checks and spark plug changes every 25 flying hours, he brought it forward to every 10 hours, not an easy prospect with the limited resources they had.

Jumbo took 'A' and 'C' Flights of the IAF into the air, with the Lysanders of the Royal Air Force joining in formation under his command. Together, they headed towards Chieng Mai and Chiang Rai in occupied Thailand, dropping down to ultra-low level; an environment that now felt like home to the IAF. The area they operated through stretched over the Chinese, Burmese, and Thai borders and despite combat being on the minds of everyone it was impossible not to admire the terrain. Jumbo led his combined force down into these gorges and valleys whenever possible, to get them out of sight of the Japanese fighters in the air above. The jungle gave no indication of the border as they entered Thailand, not that the eyes were looking earthwards – they were too busy scanning the sky for the

enemy, or keeping the nearest Lysander in sight to follow Jumbo's lead . A
Flying Tigers pilot later wrote that the low and slow-flying Lysanders were
almost impossible to spot from above, against the jungle background. This
was a good thing, as the area above them seemed to contain every Japanese
fighter in the region. The American Flying Tigers were only too happy
to escort these mad Indians on their bombing mission, but there were so
few of them in Burma that even a handful of Japanese aircraft would rip
through the Americans, to cause carnage to the Lysanders beyond.

As the treeline/foliage thinned, Jumbo knew that the target was
approaching. He waggled his wings and the pilots dutifully nestled closer,
ready for the attack. Jumbo took them up and away from the relative safety
of low level, before giving the nod and peeling off to lead them down on
to the target. As Jumbo's aircraft lumbered into an area which the Japanese
had thought was safe, he stirred up a hornets' nest. They had only one pass,
with bombs exploding and tail-gunners shooting at anything that was not
burning, as the smoking airfield retreated, behind them. Jumbo then led
his vultures back home over the jungle canopy, seeking twisting valleys to
drop into. Harjinder's work was evident as all the aircraft appeared back
over the airfield with not a single engine missing a beat. However, his work
was to begin immediately as most of the aircraft carried a few reminders
of the troops guarding the airfields, or splinters from the explosions they
had caused.

The next day, unlucky 13th, Pilot Officer Henry was taxying out,
loaded with bombs, when Harjinder noticed the number of his Lysander;
R-2033. This seemed strange to Harjinder as he recalled this aircraft had
been on a major inspection and he had not personally given it a thorough
check on completion. Harjinder ran over to the taxiing Lysander, waving
his arms as he went. All must have thought he had gone mad in the heat,
but he succeeded in getting Henry's attention, stopping him and getting
him to go back to the dispersal area. Harjinder bounced off the steps on the
wheel cover, lodged his foot in the steps built into the side of the fuselage,
then stuck his head through the now open canopy window. Not knowing
exactly why, he asked Henry to move the control column forward. As he
did so Harjinder's heart nearly jumped up to his mouth. The elevators on
the tail that should move down had moved up; they were connected the
wrong way! Once the tail had risen during takeoff, and he acquired flying
speed, Henry would have pulled back the stick, expecting the nose to
come up and for them to take to the sky – but they would have remained

pinned firmly to the ground with even greater force. The airstrip at Lashio sat perched precariously at the edge of a ravine nearly 200 feet deep – had Henry been allowed to begin takeoff, he would have run off the cliff, gone on his back, and into the deep ravine below. Since he was loaded with bombs, Henry would have been blown to smithereens even if he had survived the crash. Very shaken, Harjinder asked him to climb out of the cockpit. Henry was obviously unaware of his narrow flirtation with death since he began to argue with Harjinder because the time of his sortie was 0630 and he was getting late! That was how focused the boys were on their job. Harjinder had to calm him down by saying that he would be responsible to the Squadron Commander for this particular delay and they bundled him into the cockpit of another aircraft. When Henry asked if there anything wrong with his R-2033, Harjinder casually said: 'Oh, nothing, nothing, just an additional check.' Henry didn't know that by now he would have been in another world, wearing a pair of his own white wings and flying a pretty, fluffy, cloud.

Harjinder sent for the Senior NCO who was responsible for the cross-check and placed him under close arrest. However, after turning the issue over and over in his mind, he decided not to pursue the matter further. The charge was too serious; he would have to be tried by court martial in the field, and he would be reduced to the ranks. The aircrew would not only come to know about this incident, but would also be demoralised in the bargain. So he decided not even to tell Jumbo as Squadron Commander, reasoning that he had enough worries of his own. He released the Flight Sergeant from close arrest but removed him from the Flight, and placed him on Ground Equipment.

There was no time to dwell on this lapse in discipline. The next day, the 14th February, required Harjinder to step up a gear and apply another dose of his inventiveness. He received a message from one of his flights asking for a specialist tool; a propeller spanner. This particular Lysander was operating from a strip about 200 miles from Lashio. Harjinder had the one and only spanner in Burma so he decided to make a copy. Their interpreter knew about a Chinese shop and from his description it sounded like it might provide what was required. However, when they arrived late at night they found it, unsurprisingly, locked. They did search for the owner but with war swirling around them, nobody wanted to be conspicuous. There was no other option Harjinder went to work breaking the lock. Concerned that his team may be viewed as thieves,

Harjinder wrote another of his official sounding notes and pinned it to the door.

'In the name of the King Emperor, I have taken over the contents of this shop because they were most urgently required for the efficient prosecution of the war. The owner is entitled to a fair compensation, if he presents this note, with the cost of the materials taken, certified by any Commissioned Officer of His Majesty, to any treasury in His Majesty's Realm.'

He was getting good at these made-up-on-the-spot notes. He didn't know if there was a procedure, but felt he owed it to the owner. They took enough steel to make three spanners but now they needed a blacksmith. That search turned out to be straight forward, and this time, the owner was on hand, sleeping near his forge. The interpreter asked the man to light up the hearth, but the man said: 'Nothing doing, I have been working the whole day and I am dead tired and need some sleep.'

Harjinder tried his best to persuade him until Flight Sergeant Muhammad Siddique took over and tried threatening him with the police. Just when they were thinking of giving up, Harjinder thought of an idea. He drew up close to the man and told him, if he wouldn't get up, Harjinder's aeroplanes would not be able to fly and the Japanese would bomb Lashio like they were doing in Rangoon. This seemed to have an electric effect on him. He got up babbling: 'Please do not let those devils come near Lashio. I shall work as hard as you want.'

He fired up the furnace and forged the three spanners as per Harjinder's orders, with the various slots and grooves which this specialist tool required. He was ably assisted by Mohammad Siddique and worked for the remainder of the night without a wink of sleep. By 7 am the next morning there was a Lysander, with 'Sathi' Satyanarayana at the controls, hopping along at low-level on spanner delivery duties.

The Indians' baptism of fire was in full force, with flying operations every day, and crews exposed to ground fire on every mission. There was the ever-present threat of being caught by Japanese fighters. A camouflaged soldier, lying still, can have an enemy almost step on him, because it is movement that the human eye detects. The Lysanders may have been slow, but move they did, and with more aircraft taking part in the raids, they were dramatically increasing their chances of being caught. Pilots reported Japanese 'Zero' (although the Nakajima 'Oscar'

fighter was the main fighter in Burma) fighters flying directly over them
as both pairs of eyes, in each cockpit, remained glued to the swarming
white or green-coloured shapes in the sky, expecting them to peel off
and come thundering down; bringing death with them. However, time
and time again, the enemy just continued on their way. The Japanese had
superiority in the Burmese sky, but not complete control, thanks to the
endless courage of the American Flying Tigers, and the Commonwealth
pilots in their outdated fighters. Their presence distracted the Japanese,
who would have been scanning for the allied fighters trying to sneak up
on their tails, and therefore not looking for lumbering Lysanders snapping
the top-most branches of the jungle canopy. The strain on the IAF pilots
and gunners was immense, but most strapped in day after day to get the
job done. However, on the 16th February, the first crack appeared. Jumbo,
the steadying figurehead, had been away every day for the previous
three days, taking various numbers of aircraft on bombing raids, but this
morning, one pilot was left behind to carry out a solo mission in the
Northern sector. It is true, as a lone aircraft you have a better chance of
remaining unseen by fighters, but the pressure on the individual grows
exponentially. You have no one in the formation scanning the horizon
for fighters, no one to confirm your navigation, no mutual support when
attacked, and, the fear that lurked in every crew member's brain, no one
to report where you came down if the engine stopped. The final splash
of petrol on the burning embers of tension was the rumours of increased
activity of the Zero fighters that day. The lone pilot strapped in without a
word and took off at about 10 am in the usual way, but returned after half
an hour. He landed and switched off the engine. He reported excessive
magneto drop (a fault in one of the 2 ignition systems) and promptly left
for the Mess. The engine fitter clambered up the side of the Lysander and
swung himself into the pilot's seat. He fired up the engine, running it
at different power settings, turning off each ignition system alternately,
expecting one of them to result in a big loss of power, but nothing was out
of the ordinary. Harjinder was told of the situation, so within minutes, he
was in that cockpit carrying out the checks for his own benefit: nothing
unusual! He drove up to the Mess, found the young pilot and reported that
the engine was now serviceable and that he may proceed with his mission.
The reply was rather casual; 'I couldn't care less for this damned war',
he said.

Harjinder tried to give him a way out by suggesting a late night, and that flying fatigue was setting in, but he refuted this and said, defiantly; 'I have had seven hours sleep, and am perfectly fit.'

Harjinder knew this was not the time to push this person any further, but firmly insisted the pilot accompany him to the airstrip.

The pilot wearily took to the steps on the side of the aircraft and back into the cockpit to run up the engine with Harjinder watching. The pilot gave Harjinder a lethargic thumbs-up signal, so the chocks were pulled away, and Harjinder watched as the aircraft rumbled into the air. The Lysander had hardly disappeared over the trees before it was back, touching down on the strip and taxiing back in. Harjinder signalled for him to keep the engine running but that was ignored and the propeller came to a stop. The pilot just climbed down, refused to wait for Harjinder to try the engine, and quietly slipped away to the Mess again. Of course the engine was once again faultless so back Harjinder went to the Mess. Once again, Harjinder asked him if he was feeling fit and he replied: 'Absolutely fit.'

There are very few people who have no fear, as it lurks in most of us; different people cope in different ways. The fear had got hold of this young man but it wasn't hysterics, it wasn't tears, it wasn't shouting and bawling. He was very matter of fact about not flying that day. Harjinder knew the pressure they were all under, and knew the effect on this individual, and possibly others, if this went unchecked. Harjinder faced him quietly, but firmly, spoke to him, taking time with the speed and clarity of his voice to ensure each word was understood; 'Sir, I give you one more chance to takeoff and carry out your sortie. If you do this, I promise to say nothing to anybody about this incident. But if you refuse I will report the matter to the Squadron Commander, and I shall recommend that you be put under arrest and summarily tried for being a coward.'

The man's face went pale. He got up slowly, paused, and said; 'I am extremely sorry that I have given you this impression. I am not a coward. I will prove to you that I would rather die in the air than on the ground.'

Harjinder, still with very slow deliberate words, replied: 'The proof of the pudding is in the eating. You have to prove what you have just said.'

'I will', he said, picked up his flying helmet and led the way to Harjinder's car. They drove at breakneck speed to the airfield. No one said a word as they drove back to the aircraft. Who can know what went through the pilot's mind as he struggled with his demons.

He climbed into his cockpit, strapped in, and quickly went about his checks to bring the engine to life. The tail gunner must have known what was going on, and understood the importance of the next few minutes. Did he say anything, did he offer words of encouragement, did he want to get out and leave the pilot to prove himself alone? The pilot smiled at Harjinder as he waved the wheels' chocks away once again. The pilot's signals seemed far more positive so Harjinder smiled back and, on the spur of the moment, rushed up the steps in the side of the fuselage to lean into his cockpit. Above the rumble of the idling engine, and the propeller wash tugging at him, Harjinder shouted into his ear: 'I am very sorry, Sir, for what I said just now. You are indeed a brave man. I wish you good luck.' He watched him takeoff and carry out a climbing turn to set course for his mission. There seemed a purpose in the way he flew off and, when 30 minutes had gone with no sign of a returning aircraft, Harjinder knew that what passed for normality in this crazy world of combat had been restored.

When the Lysander finally returned, it was the rear gunner who first bounded down, relating the pilot's daredevil low attacks over the enemy. The fuselage bore scars from the vicious anti-aircraft gunfire they had run into that morning. The pilot had ignored the thick flak, zoomed over the target, and strafed the Japanese defences to press home his attack. Later, when Harjinder went to the Mess he congratulated the pilot on his excellent work for the day. The pilot was in the finest mood anyone had ever seen him in and a little later, he caught Harjinder alone, saying; 'Thank you. If you had not done what you did this morning, I could not have done my bit. You called me a coward. I wanted to prove that I am not.'

Harjinder wrote in his diary; 'I apologised again and returned pondering over the peculiarities of human nature, which is a composite of bravery and cowardice in all of us, with a thin razor-edge dividing the two.'

On the 15th February, Churchill gave one of his legendary speeches, but there was no good news. 'Tonight I speak to you at home; I speak to you in Australia and New Zealand, for whose safety we will strain every nerve; to our loyal friends in India and Burma: to our gallant Allies, the Dutch and Chinese; and our kith and kin in the USA. I speak to you all under the shadow of a heavy and far-reaching military defeat. It is a British and Imperial defeat. Singapore has fallen. All the Malay Peninsula has been overrun.'

The Japanese were now expected to step up their war against Burma and it was later discovered that the 150 Japanese aircraft in Burma had jumped to 400 almost immediately, with Singapore out of the equation. Morale in the RAF and the Army slumped – after all, if Fortress Singapore could not stop the Japanese, was India also lost? However, in the IAF Squadron, morale remained high under Jumbo's influence. He still saw everything as an opportunity, and, if the Japanese were coming in increasing numbers, they would be ready to face them. He talked to Harjinder about getting the Squadron ready for guerrilla warfare. They would keep on fighting in the air as long as they had supplies and then they would fight their way back to India over land, fighting the Japanese all along the way. Under Jumbo's leadership, the IAF had no intention to turn and run.

Harjinder spoke to all the Airmen in the afternoon. You would have expected trepidation and fear, but they all took the news with enthusiasm. If they could find a strip of land to operate from, then they were happy to continue the fight against the Japanese; the Airmen would follow Harjinder anywhere. Harjinder showed it was not to be an idle threat, or a thrown-together, tin-pot idea. He made out a training programme for every evening, to prepare them for long route-marches, carrying their own dry rations, arms and bedding. Jumbo was serious and, so, therefore, was Harjinder.

The respect of his men, and of the pilots, especially Jumbo, was not universal for Harjinder throughout the Squadron, though. Harjinder was aware that one or two of the younger, newer pilots, resented the excessive authority he seemed to wield in this Squadron, and probably a little envy because of his close rapport with the Squadron Commander. It was true that in general, Harjinder did only take orders from Jumbo, as they were on the same track, the same mind-set, but naturally, some of the junior officers took offense at this, and Flight Lieutenant Rup Chand warned him as such, from the chatter he'd picked up. This issue came up on that evening's practice Route March with the men, led by a junior officer.

All the available men were in formation, including Harjinder. The junior officer ordered 'Warrant Officer, fall in!' even though he was already there, part of the team ready to march. It seemed as if all knew that it was a dig at him, an attempt to stamp authority. As they marched the whistles and cat calls started from the Airmen. It only increased after the officer stopped the men and threatened them with court martial if it didn't cease. Harjinder knew that both sides were testing each other, and took a dim view of it all considering that the Japanese were so close, and far more important things were afoot. He knew that indiscipline could be infectious, so he, in very few but pointed words, told the men to shut up. He caught up with the officer who heard the order to 'shut up', and asked him to halt the men which he did. Harjinder's booming voice was enough to strike fear in the hearts of these men; even the jungle responded with an unearthly silence as he told his men to stop behaving like a crowd of refugees; 'There is no chance of our surviving a forced march to India if you continue in this manner.'

He then asked if the officer wished to take over again. The young man could see that he had risked making a fool of himself, and asked Harjinder to continue. On the way back, Harjinder had the Parsees of the group lead the column with music on their mouth organs, and the whistles and cat calls stopped. It would be madness to say that they looked forward to the prospect of a route march, but they would do whatever this war, and Harjinder, required of them.

And so, route march practice in the evenings would continue, but there was the small issue of their primary day job. The next day, a very battered Lysander arrived from another bombing mission. There is no mention from Harjinder of the pilot and air gunner's thoughts as they brought their aircraft back, wings riddled with bullet holes from ground fire. Was it all getting so routine with them? His diary only mentions the need to replace the aircraft's wings, although the underwear of the two men may have required replacing too, if the battle damage was severe enough to warrant new wings! Harjinder had the benefit of parts from the 'extra' aircraft they had brought with them by train. Replacement underwear was an issue for another pilot in Burma, but we have yet to get to his laundry story.

Flight Sergeant Bhaskaran was in overall charge of the job, with Corporal Balakrishna organising the finer points of the work. There were no jacks to hold these heavy wings up, but Harjinder's mind drifted back to the Wapiti days, and the rescue mission for Subroto Mukerjee. Once again, they brought in a group of local labourers, coolies, to act as human jacks and take the weight of the wing. As the last bolt was knocked away, and the weight fully transferred to the shoulders of the men, the air raid siren chose that moment to burst into life. The siren was almost superfluous, because it was only seconds before the growl of aircraft engines gave a far greater warning of the bombs about to rain down. Some of the coolies started to edge themselves from under the wing and make a run for it. In another flash back to that Wapiti incident, Flight Sergeant Bhaskaran ran up to add his shoulder to the team effort whilst shouting at the remaining coolies to 'stand fast'. The Flight Sergeant and Corporal now had to share in shouldering the weight, which was colossal, with the small number of men at their disposal. Bhaskaran kept up the shouting, threatening and swearing at the coolies above the noise of explosions, stuttering gun fire and screaming propellers. He was constantly 'encouraging' them not to leave, or else...

For twenty minutes, the bombs exploded around them, bullets thudded off rocks, pinged through the aircraft sides, while friendly guns returned fire. It was just another day at the office in Lashio; except that they would not normally be standing next to a big target, with a wing on their bruising shoulders. If one or two more labourers had left, then the wing would have fallen and the remainder would have been crushed to death. It was only after the 'All Clear' had sounded, that some of the Airmen from another dispersal point broke cover and ran over to relieve the sweating bodies of the Sergeant, Corporal and loyal coolies.

The next day, 18th February, the repaired Lysander was back in action, but Jumbo wasn't. A meeting took place that could have had serious implications for Jumbo, Harjinder and the entire IAF. Marshal Chiang Kai-shek arrived at Lashio from China on a visit to boost morale, and Squadron Leader Jumbo Majumdar was granted an audience with him; after all, Jumbo had become famous after just weeks of fighting. The Generalissimo congratulated him on his excellent leadership and they sat down to discuss the war, and the IAF in particular. Jumbo returned from his interview with the Chinese General inspired with new ideas.

Jumbo summoned Harjinder into his room that evening to discuss the seeds of a long harboured plan that was now being nurtured from across the Chinese border. He had always been obsessed with the necessity, and urgency, to expand the IAF into ten squadrons, and he was forever cursing the British for dragging their feet in this respect. After his discussion with the Chinese Head of State, he wanted No. 1 Squadron, IAF, to head Eastward when forced out of Burma by the Japanese offensive; into China instead of India. Under Chiang Kai-shek's aegis, he proposed that an expanded IAF could be quickly raised in China, with Indian pilots and

Airmen airlifted from India. America would provide the aircraft and other necessary equipment. He was hoping that once the Chinese President gave the go ahead, Churchill would have to fall in line with the scheme. His idea was for the Squadron to disobey the RAF orders to retreat into India, and instead, make their way into China with the guerrilla tactics they had been preparing. Jumbo was highly inspired by the American Volunteer Group; even here, in the jungle he wished to establish something similar to the Flying Tigers. Would Churchill just 'fall into line'? Many senior RAF officers still regarded them as inferior, as an abomination that took away what should rightfully be theirs. They would surely consider Jumbo's actions-taking personal possession of the King's equipment, stealing across the border into a foreign country, and offering his services there – as mutiny, theft, and the actions of a mercenary.

Jumbo even proffered the idea that once they had raised and trained ten Squadrons, then fought the War from bases in China, they could return to India as a ready-made IAF, which would otherwise take twenty years to build up. This was not just an off-the-cuff scheme that he, and now Harjinder, romanticised in their minds. Jumbo was dead serious. He even began to work out a number of details: compositions of the squadrons, rank structures, pay scales, etc., so that he would have a concrete proposal ready before their arrival in China. After some pressure, he did agree to modify his plan. He submitted to the idea of a small part of the squadron returning to India so that a new No. 1 Squadron IAF could be re-raised in India from that nucleus. Harjinder drew up a list, headed by Pilot Officer Malse, together with 12 Airmen to be a part of that unit.

Jumbo's plan was to be kept secret, or was it...?

Jumbo had hardly departed into the night, when there was a knock at Harjinder's door. Flight Lieutenant Rup Chand was standing there in his dressing gown, having heard everything, blaming the paper thin walls. The cat was out the bag, and Harjinder found himself already having to justify the boss's plan; 'This is our golden chance, Sir, the only chance we shall get to expand and train our Air Force.'

Rup Chand had a practical understanding of the global situation; he was the calming influence to the exuberance of the romantic idea. He grimaced, then let loose: 'It's a mad plan. The Squadron Commander is too young and romantic. Does he ignore the fact that India needs every pilot and aircraft for its defence today? The Japanese war machine will head for India after conquering Burma. What is the use of planning to train in China where there are no facilities? Furthermore, to strike a practical note, how can we suddenly ask Indian youths to go and live in war-torn China? Listen to me. I am older than both of you. Why don't you ask Jumbo to think over these matters a little longer? I know that if he listens to anyone, it is you. Harjinder, you can make him see sense. If you don't, none of us will ever return to India alive.'

Harjinder left it at that for the moment. He thought there was something in what Rup Chand said, but he was still for Jumbo's scheme. Was the strength of a future IAF more important than defending the threatened homeland?

The following day, the global news should have reminded Harjinder and Jumbo of the need for India's defence, because it was Australia's turn to feel the force of the Japanese. The city of Darwin had been bombed, but Harjinder was still thinking of a future based in China, which sent him briefly into a reflective mood. His unit was being forced on to the back foot, by an enemy that seemed to succeed at every turn but he wrote in his diary; 'We have a set of very brave aircrew. The pilots are always clamouring to go on extra bombing sorties. This morning I overheard Pilot Officer Moolgavkar grumbling to Majumdar (*Jumbo*) that he has not been on the same number of sorties as others. Of course, he knows this to be quite untrue: he has had more than his share. So he winks at me while bluffing it out with the Squadron Commander. He is mad keen. A cool customer, this one; he is determined to top the list in operational sorties. This spirit of aggressiveness is evident in many others among the young pilots. Pilot Officer Henry led an RAF flight on a bombing raid on Moulmein, a great feather in his cap. Henry is not worried any more. If you dread what you do, the fear of death is strong. Henry has passed through that stage and, like other aircrew members, is now fearless. I think that this all goes back to Majumdar's daring raid on the first day we entered Burma. That set the pace for No. 1 Squadron in the Burma Ops. The air gunners are so keen that they are becoming a nuisance, almost. Each one is trying to cheat or out-manoeuvre the other when a call suddenly comes for an air gunner. The Parsee gang are the biggest crooks of all in this respect. Whenever I hear a loud altercation in Gujarati, I rush out of my office knowing what it's all about. I have to calm down Cabby (*our famous train driver*), who is holding Rustomjee by the neck because this is the second or third successive sortie that the latter has wangled himself on. Ghyara is grumbling, because he is being bypassed by Sud. Sometimes they agree to toss for it, the lucky one shouting and cavorting like a crazy schoolboy. This is the daily routine: it is all very un-business-like, but it is wonderful, and the morale-raising scene that I see every day.'

It wasn't just the IAF that was keen to have a go at the Japanese. One of the American Volunteer Group pilots was enjoying his brief moment of bliss, wallowing in a small tin bath as the air raid sirens started their wailing. He jumped into his newly arrived Airacobra fighter to attack the enemy. Speed is of essence in air combat, gain height on your enemy; don't be caught low and slow. He minimised the time to get airborne, and close for the attack, by cutting out time normally taken for getting dressed! Not only did he leave terra firma in his birthday suit, he shot down one of the raiders and so did a victory roll over the airfield. When he landed the IAF boys carried him to the hangar on their shoulders (*careful where you put those hands, lads!*) and presented him with a bath towel.

Just two days after Jumbo explained his plan to Harjinder, he called him back into his room showing the retreat signal from Headquarters.

It read:

'All flying units in the area are to prepare for withdrawal. For detailed instructions, Squadron Commanders are to report to Headquarters for personal briefing.'

Jumbo told Harjinder to put the Chinese plan into action. He was already referring to them as 'the Indian Volunteer Group'. He announced that he would refuse (*now that word alone could be seen as mutiny, or extreme bravery in the face of the enemy, a fine line*) to withdraw Westwards. He told Harjinder not to move from Lashio until he received a personal telephone call from him. If he used the word 'Peechey' Harjinder would stay put, but if he said 'Aagey', it would mean pack up to move Eastwards immediately. In both cases, he meant to eventually end the retreat in China.

Harjinder was going with the plan, but doubts were gnawing away. He asked him the obvious question: 'Sir, supposing the Air Officer Commanding orders you to move back to India?'

Jumbo replied: 'I will out-argue him. The RAF has shown no guts for a fight, and I will refuse to follow its example. It is we who have done all the fighting here in the last few weeks. Today, if we had ten squadrons of Indian Air Force, with modern aircraft, we could have held back the Japanese and saved our soldiers from the butchery at the

Sittang River, where hundreds have been drowned during the retreat. The British are still dreaming of the John Company days (*the early days in India when the East Indian Company policed the entire country*) when, as at the Battle of Plassey, 4,000 British troops fought 40,000 Indian troops under Siraj-ud-Daula. They felt secure in the East if they had just a few white troops and some Western equipment. The Japanese have now showed them what's what, and they are demoralised. However, I don't share in their defeatism. I am not going to let the Japs force us to retire. We will go where we can get an opportunity of fighting.'

All of what Jumbo was suggesting could be seen as fighting the enemy at all costs but, equally, and more likely, it would be seen as disobedience, disorder, or even outright mutiny. The majority of the British, be they Navy, Army or Air Force, were also delivering a supreme effort, but with insufficient numbers and obsolete equipment.

The next day, Pilot Officer Malse and twelve Airmen, were informed of their early return to India. Harjinder reflected that out of the 225 Airmen under him, he could have carried out the same duties with even half that number, a testament to their efficient and tireless attitude. 'They are a set of boys to be proud of, all from good families. They love the Air Force and they are very proud of No. 1 Squadron. What makes them volunteer to do extraordinary tasks over and above their normal duties? I feel it is their love for the Squadron Commander and faith in him (*there can be little doubt it was their complete faith in Harjinder, too*). Thus do people show their real worth under operational circumstances.'

The call from Jumbo was 'Peechey'; to hold position for the moment but Pilot Officer Malse and others were still detailed to go back. In what was to typify the attitude of the IAF, they all created merry hell about being sent away from the combat zone! They wanted to stay, but they were told they must obey orders (*unlike what their Squadron Commander was planning to do*) because the future of No. 1 Squadron IAF, might be resting upon their shoulders.

Jumbo had just returned from his visit to Headquarters, with glowing news from the RAF about them. They not only acknowledged the fighting qualities and flying skill of his pilots unreservedly, but that of the ground crew, as well. They considered them a bunch of wizards who had maintained a 100 per cent serviceability record. Everyone at HQ asked him how he kept the Lysanders flying with wooden tail-wheels. They also wanted to know what modifications they had carried out in order to be able to carry heavy bombs on the Lysanders and how the pilots carried out their bombing missions in such slow aircraft, and without fighter escort. Jumbo finished his report, the grin dropping from his face as he added; 'We are famous, but we have not finished yet. Please talk to the men and tell them that we have completed the first part of our mission. Now we want to cash in on it. Expansion of the IAF is the second part.'

The glowing praise made Harjinder a very happy man but, for both men, fighting the Japanese was all about building an Indian Air Force, and that was a stepping stone to an Independent India.

As the rumours spread about the British plans to abandon Rangoon, the men naturally became jumpy about how *they* would get out of Burma. They knew that space aboard ships was at a premium, especially for Indians, so Harjinder thought it time to tell them all about the Chinese plan. In the afternoon, he spoke to the senior Airmen, and far from the reservations he had expected, he was told; 'If we have to walk all the way into China we shall do so with the greatest of pleasure. This is our only chance (*to help expand the IAF*).'

The 12-man party, under Pilot Officer Malse, was sent on their way, with the intention that they would be flown back to India immediately.

The talk was how to get all the men they started with, safely back to India. Harjinder's thoroughness had kept several of his crews alive through the conflict but there was nothing he could do save Pilot Officer Deuskar and his gunner Sergeant Kameshwara Dhora. They were only about 40 miles from Lashio when they died. Deuskar committed the well-known sin of staying too long over his target, strafing and bombing the Japanese aerodrome. They miraculously survived the numerous passes over the target, but on the way back, Dhora detected Japanese movements on the ground. Deuskar couldn't let this go, so they circled over the target, kept watch, making notes on the composition of the enemy. It seems they ran out of fuel, probably with a leak from their tanks as a result of the earlier attacks. The assumption was that the pilot had apparently tried to crash land through the forest canopy, although most believed that it would have been wiser for them to hit the silk. When talking 70 years later with Arjan Singh, in his front room, I asked him about that very dilemma; to force-land or jump. He thought a little and, with a twinkle in his eye, said neither! After another pause, he did go on to say that there was no hope on earth of making a successful forced landing in that part of Burma, so a parachute it would have to be, to have even a minor chance to survive, and a minor chance to be found. Deuskar's aircraft was close enough to home base to be seen going down, so the wreck, and the two youngsters that perished in it, was eventually found. An officer and Harjinder, accompanied by 40 men, attended to the funeral performed according to Hindu rites. They managed to get a band from the nearest Burmese Army Unit to give these men a suitable send-off in difficult conditions. Jitaindra Kumar Deuskar and Kameshwara Dhora were the first of the Indian Air Force to be killed in action in Burma.

There was no time to grieve, and the next day, the 24th February, Lysanders departed on, what was already thought of as, the 'usual' mission. Harjinder gathered all the men and gave a speech about the plan to go to China. He explained Jumbo's reasoning and added; 'Look at the way they gave up in Singapore. So we can expect nothing from them. They will neither fight for India nor let us fight.'

He asked to see, by a show of hands from the men, how many Airmen of them felt the same way as their Squadron Commander. Inwardly Harjinder's heart soared as all hands rose heavenwards as one. There was no time for pleasantries or backslapping. He outlined a plan which included expanding the long route marches, carrying their own self-sufficiency kit. Each airman was to be independent in rations and clothing during a march that would be several days in very difficult terrain.

That evening, when the pilots returned from their sorties, Harjinder conveyed the news of the unswaying support of the men for the China Plan. Jumbo was all smiles; 'I knew it, I knew it. The Airmen are with me in this scheme as much as the officers are. We make a good team in this Squadron.'

In Magwe, the 25th February 1942 was to be an interesting day. This was the gateway into, and now more often, out of Burma. James Lansdale Hodson, a war correspondent, flew into the chaos of aircraft arriving, aircraft refuelling, troops milling around, troops waiting for orders, and refugees trying to grab a seat out. As he made his way to a bungalow for that evening, he passed a group of Indian Air Force personnel in the melee. It was Pilot Officer Malse's party, who had only succeeded in getting as far as Magwe before grinding to a halt. They ought to have flown out two day previously, but were held back because British Airmen were being evacuated first. Aircraft after aircraft took off for India, but the IAF personnel were brushed aside and told to wait. They were at their wit's end. Was this their fate to sit passively, until the Japanese arrived? Up stepped Corporal Tara Singh. He was a man known to be of initiative and guts; the same man who drove the 13ᵗʰ Lysander, with a blind eye, to the train station in India in what seemed like a lifetime ago. He took matters into his own hands when he saw a car driving up with a flag fluttering from the small flagpole jutting up from the bonnet. Protocol is to stand to attention and salute the flag as it passes by, not jump out in the middle of the road and gesticulate wildly for it to stop! It was the car of the Air Officer Commanding, Burma, and stop he did rather than run this, clearly unhinged, man over. After throwing him his best salute, Tara Singh began a haranguing in his well-known Punjabi English: 'Sir, I famous No. 1 Squadron Indian Air Force, brave, very brave. Our pilots more brave, our Airmen more brave. We bomb Japanese, fight Japanese. We not afraid. Your British men running from Burma. British no brave. I, my officer, don't go India but you order me go. Now you send British, all British first, not send Indians. We wait many days. No Justice. Please excuse.'

Another perfect salute was presented to the boss of bosses before Tara Singh stepped out of the way!

The Air Officer Commanding, Air Vice-Marshal Stevenson, at first taken aback, realised that a grievance of some dimensions was being aired and, full marks to him, he decided to have it investigated. He sent his Staff Officer to speak to Tara Singh who had the bit between his teeth and was not going to hold back on this officer either. He made more wild gestures and apparently hurled more abuses on the RAF, and praise on No. 1 Squadron IAF! However, finally, he was able to make his grievance understood with the aid of a few translators! The news was relayed to the Air Vice-Marshal, no doubt with the language cleaned up a little, and some punctuations added. He drove up at once to halt the aircraft which was even then taxying for takeoff with a full load of RAF personnel. He told the pilot to hold his position, ordered 14, presumably very annoyed, British Airmen to be taken off, and made sure that Pilot Officer Malse and his party were airborne and on their way to India before he left the scene. The first members of No. 1 Squadron were heading home.

The next day, James Lansdale Hodson travelled the road from the overnight bungalow back to the airfield and flew into the war-ravaged Rangoon. He drove past the lines of refugees shuffling North, carrying what few belongings they could. Unnoticed, he passed a mother and three sons heading through Magwe, crossing the river by boat with their sights on the nearby village of Minbu. The youngest was young Ramesh

Sakharam Benegal, 16 years old. The paths of James and Ramesh would cross again in a few days' time, but this time with Harjinder present, too.

James negotiated a flight into Rangoon and waited with anticipation for the pilot, having been told they were the splitting image of each other. James had often been mistaken for this man, so he stared in horror when the cadaverous, terribly thin, knobbly-nosed, grey-wavy-haired image arrived! The pilot told him that the situation in Rangoon was desperate, and after a half-hearted attempt to dissuade him from going, he just shrugged his shoulders. All eyes were put to work searching the sky for enemy fighters, but their attention soon became fixed on the city as they approached the column of black and yellow smoke spiralling 1,000 feet up into the air. The airfield at Mingalodon was devoid of serviceable aircraft, those that could fly were up on missions, so it was the 9 or 10 burnt-out, shot-up machines, all horridly gnarled that greeted James. After he was driven into the city he wrote in his diary describing the unfolding chaos;

'No hotel, bank, restaurant, or shop of any description is open. A good many are broken; a good many burnt out. Not much damage caused by enemy bombs; most of it is due to looters. The only people left in Rangoon are clusters of Indian servants, deserted by their masters. A company of them are encamped, sitting about, making small fires in the square, or setting out in driblets to walk towards India.'

For the majority of the IAF remaining in Lashio, it was several more days of flying mission after mission, with news of Japanese gains all around. They received a signal on the 26th which read: 'The last ship leaving shortly after which only animal transport will be available.'

So their masters expect them to go back to India riding on mules! However, Jumbo and Harjinder were still focussed on China, they had no intention of going back to India.

Whether it was nationalist verve, personal pride, or just the sheer fatalism of combat fatigue, the pilots had become more and more daring as the number, and ferocity, of the Japanese attacks mounted. The IAF were still trying to operate from Toungoo, the strip where they had started their operations. The constant bombing had reduced the military presence down to one aircraft. It was a single IAF Lysander with Flight Lieutenant Raza flying, Sergeant Dildar as his air gunner, and 'Cabby' Cabinetmaker (*Harjinder's fellow train driver*) keeping them in the air. Contact with them had been lost for several days, but when a call did finally get through, Jumbo ordered them out to regroup with him and Harjinder in Lashio. After two weeks alone, fighting a private war with no contact, what was their only complaint? It was that subject of underwear and clean uniform. According to Raza it was hard to come by! When he dropped his scarred Lysander on to the strip in Lashio to join Harjinder, the story of their private war took some telling. Their airfield was bombed, machine-gunned and photographed daily but they had set up dummy aircraft and dummy tents around the shattered strip. The dummies took all the hits day after day, as they moved them around to keep the Japanese guessing. They carried out daily flights into Siam (*Thailand*) reporting troop movements, and attacking the airfields of Messaring and Maehongson for good measure on the return flight. Their own field suffered a fierce raid on the 27th. They pulled their Lysander in nose-first under a little tree cover at the edge of the airfield, so Dildar could jump into his tail gunner's seat, open fire at, and hit one of the 15 attacking aircraft. It was two days later that they were ordered out, but in the IAF tradition, that was being written in combat, they didn't take the direct route. Instead, as a farewell, they flew via Maehongson again, this time catching the Japanese in the open. Raza dropped his bombs right on top of the wireless station and Dildar saw it crumble, achieving what multiple RAF aircraft raids had failed to do, on two earlier occasions. However, there was no room for Cabby for the trip to Lashio, he would have to make his own way. How did he do that? Well, according to one account, he used his newly acquired skills and commandeered a train! He enlisted a volunteer to stoke the fire, and made his was to Lashio to join his comrades. Cabby, himself, remained tight lipped.

The Squadron had developed very clear-cut tactics by this time, a necessity for survival. They took off from their several dispersed airfields to rendezvous at a predetermined landmark, forming up as a complete squadron for their attack. After completing their mission, the procedure was reversed but to make use of every second they were flying they broke off into individual Flights to carry out reconnaissance for the Army until their fuel ran low. The Japanese had not discovered the various locations of the IAF aircraft but Jumbo and team were building an unrivalled picture of the Japanese positions. On one occasion, an Army Liaison Officer, Captain Watson, attached to the Squadron, didn't believe the airstrip at Ywathit, Siam, was in enemy hands. Nonchalantly, Jumbo told Watson to jump in the back of his Lysander; they would go for a look. After the brief tree-skimming flight, Jumbo pointed to what looked, from the air, like a stretch of road in front of them and told Watson that it was, in reality, a Japanese airstrip. Watson refused to believe this and foolishly said so to Jumbo.

He regretted vocalising his doubts a few minutes later.

Jumbo moved away from the area and climbed the Lysander to 10,000 feet before, to Watson's horror, shutting down the engine. He then glided the silent aircraft down, back towards the airfield. Initially the trees seemed to slowly grow below them but suddenly they were just feet above the last trees surrounding the disputed clearing. Jumbo rolled the wheel down the runway, calmly pointing out enemy soldiers on both sides. He flicked the magnetos back to 'on', and the engine sparked backed into life. That certainly attracted the attention of the surprised enemy gunners who managed only a few shots in their general direction to punctuate Jumbo's point. On the way out, Jumbo shot up a few gun positions as he exited at tree top height, with a speechless Captain Watson in the back. When Watson was back on the ground, and finally finding his voice back, he said; 'I have not met another pilot of such cool courage in my life.'

In Rangoon, James Lansdale Hodson had taken up residence in a deserted house. All the owner's belongings, right down to the shaving kit in the bathroom, remained. In the street, abandoned cars were daubed up with slogans like; 'To Blighty via Tokyo' and 'To let'. An RAF Wing Commander told him; 'The Japs are good and brave pilots who make their machines do things they never intended to do.'

An Army Officer described the ground war to him. 'Most of the fighting has been at close quarters, often hand to hand. In the jungle, you can't see more than 10 yards, often less. At times, our men fought anything from 2 to 6 days with little or no food. Crossing the Sittang River was possibly worse than Dunkirk, for, as troops swam, they were subjected to gunfire and dive-bombing. The River seemed full of bobbing heads.'

Life for the IAF was tough, but life in the jungle for the Army was brutal. Another man hewn from the same Punjabi rock as Harjinder was Sam Manekshaw, a Parsee who'd grown up in Amritsar. When Sam's father refused to send him to Cambridge to study medicine, he joined the Army in a fit of rebellion. Thus, he found himself as a junior Second Lieutenant in the 4/12 Frontier Force Rifles, a Baluch unit, in Burma, with orders to counter attack the advancing Japanese in Rangoon. His objective, Pagoda

Hill, was the key position on the left of the Sittang bridgehead. Half of his company lay dead around him as he flushed the last of the Japanese from their positions. Capturing the hill would give the troops more time to cross the Sittang River and escape the noose closing in around them. The enemy knew it, too. They hosed the hill down with machine gun fire and the young Parsee Company Commander was the main target. When Sam arrived, by stretcher, at the initial CCS, or Casualty Clearing Station, Major General 'Punch' Cowan spotted this man who led the charge of Pagoda Hill. The seven bullet wounds in his stomach told the story. Fearing the worst, Major General Cowan quickly removed his own Military Cross medal ribbon and pinned it onto Manekshaw's blood-stained tunic saying: 'A dead person cannot be awarded a Military Cross.'

Back in Rangoon, reports came in about the jails in the city and Insein, the lunatic asylum in Tadegale, and a leper hospital nearby. The Indian warders had fled North in a desperate attempt to make the long trek back to the Indian border. A single, junior officer was handed the dilemma of releasing his inmates or leaving them to starve. He chose to release them, but the criticism that was heaped on him was so intense that he finally shot himself. Of the 1,500 criminals and 800 'lunatics' he had released from prison, the rational ones joined the 'human crocodile' that was crawling past the airport and heading North. The rest headed East and directly up to one of the bridges that crossed the Sittang River, just as the Japanese arrived at the other side, having finally recaptured Pagoda Hill. The Japanese began their customary demonstration of yells and war cries with hand grenades exploding to disconcert the enemy. They were completely outdone by the 'lunatics', who appeared to think that the Japanese were playing a game with them, and so responded with fanatical gesticulations, comic dancing, and complete disregard for their own safety.

However, as a British Captain told James, some of those released turned their attention on the city; 'The disorder, the looting, the attacks made by the criminals, or insurgent Burmese, on poor Indian servants, will never be a tenth part known.'

The main fire raging in Rangoon was at the docks, pushing great columns of black smoke skywards, driven by belching red flames. The dying city had smaller fires everywhere. The pavements glittered with shards of glass from shop windows and smashed bottles. Rangoon no longer functioned as a city.

The IAF knew that they would soon be leaving, but with perfect timing, General Wavell, the overall Commander of India 'dropped in' at Lashio to address them all before the inevitable withdrawal from Burma. Had he heard of Jumbo's plans? It certainly seemed so from his speech.

'I have come to Lashio to personally congratulate No. 1 Squadron of the Indian Air Force. You have made history within this short time. I need not tell you that the RAF have acknowledged your bravery and skill with respect and the Air Officer Commanding Burma, has nothing but praise for you. I am also aware of your ambition to expand your Air Force to ten squadrons.'

That caused a ripple of shock throughout those who were listening intently. He continued;

'I promise you all the help to fulfil this ambition. This is a gentleman's promise. The best place to build up an IAF is in your own country, where you can pick and choose from the young men. I would also like to tell you that we shall have to fight and ward off Japanese attacks on India; the Japanese dream of the invasion of India must be shattered. This will be your main task when you get back to India. I congratulate Squadron Leader Majumdar for his superb leadership; and also his pilots, who have performed miracles in the present crisis. The ground crews have won the admiration of all of us for keeping all aircraft flying under the most adverse conditions.'

Wavell was just disappearing when Jumbo added his bit to the assembled men: 'May I add to the Supreme Commander's words. I would like to say that it has all been made possible because of the Airmen's devotion to duty. I owe them a lot. We pilots would have spent our days sitting on the ground and perhaps in trenches if there had been no aircraft to fly.'

Then came the words that probably saved Jumbo's, and Harjinder's, careers, and the reputation of the IAF; 'Our aim is to expand to ten squadrons; where and how we raise them is immaterial. I would be quite happy to go to India after what General Wavell has promised.'

The Chinese adventure was off just like that, but when alone with Harjinder, Jumbo recognised that things were not going to be that easy. They had painted themselves into a corner. 'The last ship for India has sailed from Rangoon, there is no motor transport left anywhere here, no trains running. Animal transport is out of the question. How do we get our men back? The aircraft can hardly carry a dozen men and we have 250. In any case, the Army needs these aircraft to provide cover.'

Harjinder didn't see this as a major disaster, just another problem to overcome. He told Jumbo that if he would entrust the withdrawal to him, he would not let the Squadron down. Jumbo agreed, although you could see in his eyes that he didn't believe it. Had his Chinese dream just condemned his men to capture, and probable slaughter? Harjinder rushed off to Lashio bazaar to see what he could scrounge. On almost his first stop he came across a shop which contained five Chinese lorries undergoing repairs, two of them could only really be described as junk. He struck a deal of sorts on the spot and returned to Jumbo, telling him that they would be in Magwe within 36 hours. Harjinder only ever worked to ridiculously tight time scales.

Having commandeered the five lorries, Harjinder put his technicians to work on them. After the Lysander's battle damage, the lorry seemed a very basic machine. They succeeded getting all of them running even if one vehicle was completely devoid of any foot brakes, but beggars can't be choosers, so they decided to take that one, too! By Harjinder's magic, and no doubt some tea, a motor column was soon formed.

In Rangoon, James met with General Wavell and Air Vice-Marshal Stephenson, the former fresh from his visit to the IAF in Lashio, the latter fresh from his meeting with the babbling Corporal Tara Singh! James was full of admiration for Wavell who flew over the battlefields, through the danger zones, to carry out his meetings as if attending the races at Ascot. Also reporting to them was a Wing Commander who had been exploring the road running North of Rangoon, and what was fast becoming their only escape route. This Officer had been compelled to drive over the dead bodies of Indian refugees lying on the road. It was time to accept that Rangoon was lost. It was time to leave; but how?

The IAF ground crew prepared their collection of battered vehicles in anticipation of the push Northwest towards the coast. Flying Officer Rup Chand was detailed as Officer-in-Charge of the road party but he gave Harjinder full freedom to organise this extreme version of a road trip. Harjinder distributed 45 men per lorry and asked them to carry only light luggage because of the long journey, and the breakdowns he was expecting along the way. He wasn't wrong!

As dawn broke over 3rd March 1942, the majority of No. 1 Squadron IAF ground troops pulled out of operations in Burma, although the aircraft would continue to fly. An Anglo-Burmese family living opposite their quarters came out to wish them good luck. The head of the family came out to shake hands with Harjinder and said: 'Officer, I would like to tell you that your Airmen are perfect gentlemen. They have stayed here under war-time conditions, but we have never had any cause of anxiety. They have behaved most chivalrously. My family has nothing but praises for them. We wish you good luck and pray for your success wherever you go.'

If you can fight a war and keep the locals on your side as the bombs, meant to obliterate you, disrupt their lives, you are doing something right. But it was time to go, and these villagers would soon have Japanese masters.

The beard on the recently arrived RAF Regiment officer made him stand out; RAF officers should be clean shaven. The Australian accent added to the melting pot of national tongues in Lashio. A self-proclaimed 'Defence Officer', he fitted right in with the Indians at Lashio because he was there having arranged his own transport to the front-line. Glen McBride's only qualification as Defence Officer was a brief chat with a man who, allegedly, had once worked in that role. He started the process of handing over the defences to the Chinese troops. He was shown the sketch map of the various locations of aviation fuel supplies, piled high in cans over several sites under camouflage netting, down many winding, dirt tracks leading away from the airfield.

Glen watched the ragtag convoy of IAF 'acquired' lorries heading out of town along one of the muddy tracks. They rattled and shook over 180 miles when, while crossing a river, one of the transports got bogged down. All attempts to free it failed even with all the men pulling, pushing, sweating and swearing. It was hugely frustrating for Harjinder, there was nothing mechanically wrong with the truck but time was slipping through his fingers. There was only one thing to do; they loaded all its occupants into the other four lorries and abandoned the vehicle there. One vehicle down already, and now severely overloaded, they couldn't afford to lose another. Towards evening they reached the hills around Mandalay. This stretch of road had hairpin bend after hairpin bend. Naturally, this was a big issue for a lorry without brakes, and, of course, Harjinder had volunteered to drive it (*although we don't know if the passengers 'volunteered' to be in that lorry!*). The only way to make it around each turn was full use of the hand brakes hoping it wouldn't burn out. The tension in the swaying cab stayed at heart thumping levels as the smell of hot brakes from the rear wheels indicated total, imminent failure. The rear parking brake continued to slow the bucking vehicle until the slope eased and the life-threatening track straightened. Somehow, they got across the hill section without an accident, and parked at 6 pm on the crest of a hill for a break and a brew. As the tea came to the boil, Flight Lieutenant Rup Chand brought out his battery operated radio set and tuned in for the news from Delhi. The grins broke out all around as, totally unexpectedly, they found themselves 'mentioned in despatches' on the All India Radio broadcast news. Sitting in a convoy of bolted together, mud covered, battered, trucks in the jungle of Burma, with Japanese hot on their tail, the words from home seemed unreal:

> 'Units of the Indian Air Force operating against the Japanese in Burma have been so successful in their bombing and reconnaissance raids over enemy territory that they have been especially commended by the Commander-in-Chief, General Wavell, who has sent the pilots and crews a congratulatory message, in which he said "Well done! Your raids made all the difference.'

With rear brakes shot to pieces, but straighter roads, Harjinder could run his lorry gently into the back of the preceding vehicle, allowing it to brake for both of them. Despite little control left in his own lorry, the overloaded convoy did reach their destination, albeit late in the night. They camped out in the fields adjacent to an even more chaotic Magwe airstrip. They fondly patted the torn mudguards of their trusty steeds as they parked them for the last time; though dilapidated and old, they had stood them in good stead at a most critical time.

In the morning, the team headed into the chaos that was the brick-red dust-covered Magwe airfield. A sole RAF Blenheim aircraft droned constantly overhead to try and give the four surviving Buffalo fighters from No. 67 Squadron, the four RAF Hurricanes, and six AVG Tomahawks some warning of a Japanese air attack. It was Harjinder's opinion that Flight Lieutenant Rup Chand should go on the first available aircraft with a party of Airmen, but he had a difficult time in persuading him to accept his suggestion. Rup Chand said; 'As I am an officer it is my duty to remain here till the last of our men leaves Burma.'

However, Harjinder got his way in the end, with the oldest trick in the book; he simply lied to him! He said that the instructions from Jumbo were very clear, the Officer-in-Charge of the party was to proceed to Calcutta immediately and arrange for the reception of the whole Squadron. Rup Chand was an exceedingly well-disciplined officer, so believing Harjinder's statement to be true, he reluctantly agreed to go back by the next plane, but you could read disappointment written all over his face. When his aircraft rumbled down the runway, Harjinder stood to one side saluting; 'one of the bravest men I have met. Medically unfit, senior in age to all of us, he nevertheless shared all our hardships and would have gone on every mission if the selection of aircrews had been left in his hands.'

With the Japanese only 10 miles away from Rangoon, the order was given to abandon the city. All air transport had stopped, the airfield being too dangerous for the big transport aircraft. James Lansdale Hodson found a RAF Officer with a spare seat in his car, a lumbering old Dodge, with incredibly dodgy steering. At 2 pm, the demolition charges in Rangoon were blown. At the oil refinery, the column of smoke rose to 3000 feet, with flames reaching 500 feet. As they drove up the Burma Road, they crossed over countless bridges being prepared for demolition, and aircraft buzzed overhead, IAF Machines included, to cover the withdrawal of the final soldiers. The Governor, Sir Reginald Dorman-Smith's convoy was just behind James.

At Lashio, Glen McBride took an axe to the first 40-gallon fuel drum at the first fuel dump. The axe dented the drum but otherwise bounced off. Finally, a pickaxe was found and the pointed end did the trick. Soon fuel was glugging into the ground around him. Three attempts at firing flares from a pistol failed, proving to Glen that his aim wasn't as good as he thought. They were running out of time and ideas. He had already destroyed all the IAF paperwork in case he was captured, so it was with a long face, and slightly embarrassed look, his Corporal offered up the only piece of paper available them. A strip was torn off the Corporal's sweetheart's letter, and that provided the start to the burning of Lashio. It took all night, and careful rationing of the love-letter but more than half a million gallons of petrol went up that night. Passing through the airfield Glen saw, to his consternation, an abandoned RAF Lysander covered in netting. Presumably abandoned because there had not been time to repair it. Glen poured petrol into the cockpit and up it went. As the magnesium began to burn, it sent a white sheet of flame skywards. If any beacon was needed by the Japanese, this was it. It was time for Glen to leave, but he knew it was too late to follow Harjinder. He headed into China where the American crews of the AVG would all eventually re-group.

At Magwe, when Harjinder reported to Group Headquarters, a double-storeyed building in town, he expected the usual lukewarm reception from the RAF. What Harjinder still didn't realise was that the IAF's action in Burma was being told at desks, mess tables, and over the radio throughout the combat zone. The Wing Commander in-charge of evacuation shook hands with him as he entered the room and introduced him to all the other officers saying; 'Here is an engineer officer who has kept 100 per cent serviceability in his Squadron and even fitted wooden tail-wheels to the Lysanders. He belongs to the gallant "Jumbo Squadron".'

Harjinder's chest puffed out when he heard his Squadron being called 'The Jumbo Squadron', a most appropriate name. Less than three months since they left India, and everyone's perception of them seemed to have changed.

The praise poured in. Harjinder stayed in the Senior NCO's Mess with an astounding mix of American, British, Australian, and other nations' personnel. Every man wanted to talk with Harjinder, and not only did they know about the IAF, but they all raved about the Squadron's exploits. Harjinder delighted in pointing out that even though he had been ordered out, the pilots were still flying, helping in whatever way possible during the fighting retreat.

It was only later that Harjinder discovered just how true these words were about the continuing IAF operations. Pilot Officer Rajinder Singh had no problem finding Rangoon, because the main body of smoke billowing from the refinery was like a beacon. He was forced to fly through smoke erupting from fires all around Rangoon; landing there was going to be interesting. The Japanese were flowing through the city and had reached the city's main airfield. The defenders still had a fingernail hold on the West side of the airfield, as Singh's Lysander scraped over the fence and abandoned vehicles, to touch down. Somehow, two RAF Hurricane pilots had squashed in to the single rear gunner's seat. Two Hurricane fighters had been damaged earlier in an air raid, but some of the RAF technicians, clearly wanting to show that they were also as brave as the IAF, had managed to bring them to a flyable, if not pretty, condition. With Hurricanes at a premium, Jumbo had authorised the very risky mission. Singh kept the Lysander's engine running as the two pilots prised themselves out of the single seat, dropped to the ground, and ran to the

waiting Hurricanes as two Japanese aircraft roared overhead. The three
machines lifted off together – the last Allied aircraft out of Rangoon.

Back in the North of Burma, the melee of Magwe was enacted against
the stunning beauty of the Burmese sunset. As the sun lowered itself
behind the Arkan hills, its rosy glow cast a spotlight over the vulnerable
Indian/Burmese border. The mountains seemed to float like clouds amid
the dust and flames that signalled the collapse of the British Empire to
their South.

Most of the IAF had left Magwe over the last few days, but it was not
until the 8th March 1942 that Harjinder was down to the last few members
of his team waiting to get out of Burma. During the night, Japanese
bombers had turned up unannounced, and destroyed some of the aircraft
on the ground. The airfield was smoking, rubble and metal shards were
scattered liberally around. Another shock was when the Japanese field guns
announced they were now close enough to throw their deadly shells into
the mix. The allied fighters, including the AVG, tried to locate them and
keep them silent for as much of the day as possible. It was a hive of activity,
but somehow, through the chaos, there seemed to be some order, with
aircraft arriving and leaving through the smoke and occasional explosions.
The word was already circulating that Magwe was to be abandoned by
the end of the day. Harjinder and team assembled to await their turn for a
plane ride out.

The Governor's retreat from Rangoon, and charge to Magwe, was
slowed down by a bridge being blown up prematurely. Harjinder could see
the refugees also massing at the airfield in the hope to get a flight home. At
the front of the mass was the 16 year-old Ramesh Benegal, his mother, an
elderly relative, and his two older brothers, who James Lansdale Hodson
had passed on his arrival in Burma only days earlier. James was ahead of
the Governor into this nest of humanity, abandoning the car amongst
the refugees before finding someone in a position of authority to try and
negotiate his flight out.

Harjinder and his men were ready to depart, but even this retreat could
not dampen their spirits. The Parsee boys volunteered to go in the last aircraft
with Harjinder, and he spent the time thinking about these boys who had
done what was asked of them, and much, much, more. That day he wrote;

'Although we are happy because we are heading for home, in our
heart of hearts, we are sad because we are being made to run away
from the field of war. The only consolation we have is that we

have done our best, and our worth has received due recognition. So, when our turn comes to emplane, we walk up the ramp with smiles on our faces and our heads held high. We have been able to look at our colleagues of the RAF squarely in the face, as though to say, "We have shown our worth. Don't ever feel superior, again."'

In the Captain's seat of one of the waiting transport aircraft was Indian pilot Biju Patnaik. His orders were to wait for the delayed Governor's convoy. It was his second trip that day into Magwe and, as he watched the refugees being pushed away, he decided he couldn't wait idly by anymore. In the smoke, and confusion, he called over a group of the Indian refugees to fill his aircraft. There was only room for the women and the elderly, so Ramesh Benegal, his brothers and his uncle said good bye to his mother, one of the lucky ones to be plucked from the crowd. The pilot must have received the reprimand of his career for not waiting when the Governor eventually arrived at Magweand realised that his aircraft had left without him. He had to continue the drive for a considerable distance to another remote strip, Myitkyina, where the RAF managed to get air transport for him. Meanwhile, Biju Patnaik had saved Ramesh's mother, along with the plane full of his kinsfolk. His flying career may have been compromised, but later he went on to become the Chief Minister of the Indian state of Orissa.

Back in Magwe, Harjinder, and 13 of his team, made their way over to the silver-coloured American Flying Fortress bomber. They settled into the belly of the aircraft. The door was closed once, but then briefly flung open for another man to enter. James Lansdale Hodson wriggled his way on to the aircraft. The American pilot called back; 'All the crap in now?' He must have got a thumbs up from somewhere because with a shout of 'Ok. Let's go!' the door slammed signalling the end of Harjinder's Burma adventure.

When their Flying Fortress touched down, James and Harjinder both went their separate ways. James went to find a train to take him to Delhi, and Harjinder was met by a Flight Lieutenant Shafi, who embraced him in typical Indian fashion. He excitedly told Harjinder how proud he was of the Squadron and about all the press releases on No. 1 Squadron's exploits in Burma. Harjinder asked to see Flight Lieutenant Rup Chand, but confusingly, he was told that Rup Chand would be arriving the next day! On seeing the puzzled expression on Harjinder's face the story of Rup Chand's narrow escape was told. The aircraft made an emergency landing and had to be abandoned; Rup Chand finished his journey by sea. So much for the 'favour' Harjinder did by sending him out first!

Jumbo and team flew until the 11th, covering the retreat, but eventually, they were ordered to hand over the majority of the faithful Lysanders to the Burmese Communications Unit. Four Lysanders did make it back to India. The final aircraft, P9180, was the Lysander Harjinder first rebuilt after the landing accident a lifetime ago in India, before fitting it with his first of his wooden tail-wheels.

An IAF pilot and an air gunner had been lost but the rest of No. 1 Squadron, IAF, was back in India.

At Magwe, Ramesh Benegal's relief at his mother's safety was short lived. Magwe was not to be his gateway to freedom. Ramesh, and his brothers set off to try and walk to India, but were unsuccessful. The Japanese overtook them, but through a combination of good luck, and quick thinking, their lives were spared. They were briefly held by the Japanese soldiers before being ordered back to Rangoon.

Although much younger, Ramesh was very similar to Harjinder and their paths would cross again. Ramesh was also driven to see an Independent India and, like Harjinder in 1932, he also thought that air power was the key. Ramesh believed it would be through the Japanese that India could gain Independence. Ramesh decided to join the Indian National Army, the Azad Hind, being formed in Burma by the Japanese. He became one of only ten Indians who were selected to travel to Japan to train as pilots, and serve in the Japanese backed Air Arm of the Indian National Army. The trip to Japan became a marathon, involving being torpedoed in a troop ship, abandoned on the railway system, narrowly avoiding starvation, and by the time he arrived in Japan, he found that the war was already on the turn. He finished his basic soldier training, and started flying training, when he witnessed the firebombing of Tokyo. The next time Harjinder crossed paths with Ramesh, it was not over the battlefield, as could so easily have happened, but when they were both pilots in the Air Force of an independent India!

The last words on the retreat through Burma have to go to Harjinder:

'It has been a great experience. It was a great hour to live through.'

He had lived through the 'great hour,' but there was the small fact that the Indians, the British, the Allies, were losing the war. The Japanese had moved on to Indian soil.

Ten

To India: To England: To Jail?

'Actually, we came to arrest you.'

'In the past we have met some of your countrymen who claimed to know everything on earth, but on discussion we found their knowledge limited and shallow.'

The Squadron was reunited in India. Jumbo and Raza were the last out, almost overtaken by the Japanese; it had been a close call. The enormous emotional crash after the intensity of combat, and the jungle, was partially cushioned by the men experiencing the bliss of reunion with their families after the life-changing events in Burma. The families had little warning of their menfolk's departure, although they knew it was only a matter of time. The news that came out of Burma during their separation was infrequent, and delayed, but as the exploits splashed across front pages, it left no doubt that they were in the thick of it. As Burma crumbled to the Japanese, the anxiety must have been unbearable; constantly building and building. However, out of Burma came all of the ground crew, and all bar one of the flight crews (Deuskar and Dhora). No mean feat against the 'unstoppable' enemy in the unforgiving conditions they'd fought in. Now, for a time, the families were back ogether. Harjinder's wife was on the mend, if still not fully recovered; Jumbo was back to his wife and young daughter. It may have been a retreat, but the pride of the 'Jumbo Squadron' knew no bounds.

The achievements and accolades of the Jumbo Squadron were known far and wide; a heartening story of resistance in a sea of bad news. Jumbo was held up as the figurehead, but Harjinder was becoming a well-known figure too, not only because he was the senior-most Technical Warrant Officer in the Service, but also because Jumbo, and other well-wishers, had heaped praise on him The Public Relations department of the military went into overdrive to disseminate this positive twist on what was, in reality, a disaster.

As the rest of the Squadron were enjoying their brief period of leave, the Indian Defence Secretary sent for Harjinder and Jumbo. When the Secretary heard Harjinder's story, he was visibly stunned with the details of his early days, and immediately ordered production of a film to depict his life for use in the IAF recruitment drive.

Jumbo and Harjinder would come together to make the film, but in terms of No. 1 Squadron, IAF, it was time for the two men, to part. Their partnership was special, for a special time. In 1949, K.N. Dutt wrote about that Jumbo/Harjinder relationship as they emerged from the jungle combat:

'The intrepid Harjinder Singh served with Jumbo as an air gunner. He attached himself to Jumbo body and soul, with such affection and admiration as are quite exceptional. Karun (*Jumbo*) himself reposed great trust in Harjinder's qualities as a man and as a technician.'

In a subsequent meeting, Harjinder told Dutt; 'the inspiration of that great man is the motive power in my life.'

Jumbo was posted to Head Quarters in Delhi. He was now the most senior man in the IAF, jumping ahead of several of his IAF pilot colleagues, and it was felt that he could best serve his country at the helm of the IAF. Flying a desk was not in Jumbo's nature, but he understood that this was from where he could fulfil his dream of ten squadrons in the IAF. His thirst to be in the thick of things would not let him inhabit an office, at least not for long. His office needed to be a cockpit.

Harjinder, along with No. 1 Squadron, was stationed to Hyderabad in Central India. The Nizam of Hyderabad became increasingly jittery when the Japanese occupied the Andaman Islands, raided Calcutta, Kocanada and Madras, and with their aircraft carriers found in the Indian Ocean. The Nizam had begun to suspect that the Raj, under which he and his forefathers had flourished to amass astounding wealth, was not invincible. He wanted air cover, so re-equipping the Squadron directly under the nose of the Nizam made sense. He wanted fighters, but, for the moment, he got Lysanders. However, it was the Lysanders of the famous Jumbo Squadron and that seemed to allay his fears for the short term. He clearly didn't know that the Lysanders were now completely obsolete.

As the command of No. 1 Squadron, IAF, passed from Jumbo, a tragedy befell Flight Lieutenant Rup Chand when one of his sons died. It was a grievous blow to him, and it also seemed to him that No. 1 Squadron IAF was now apparently finished with fighting for some time, so he resigned his commission and went home.

The sudden departure of, not one but, two of their fearless leaders, left the Squadron feeling lost without their leading lights. A team that has served together in combat finds itself bound together in their deep knowledge of each other, this was going to make life very difficult for Jumbo and Rup Chand's replacements.

It was a reunion with Mukerjee for Harjinder, but as the new boss, Mukerjee was obviously going to find it hard to become part of that tight knit team. Rup Chand's replacement was, as Adjutant, a bit of a 'stick-in-the-mud' and believed in following King's Regulations to the absolute letter. Mukerjee understandably seemed to begrudge the cocky attitude of the members of the Squadron, feeling that they put on too many airs about having seen active service.

The new Adjutant made his position felt early on. It resulted in many Airmen being severely punished on minor charges, confined to camp, and carrying out marching drill in full battle dress in the Hyderabad mid-day heat. Worst of all for Harjinder, he was detailed to supervise these punishments. Harjinder took a few days' leave to spend some time with his wife, only to find on his return, the irrepressible Parsee Gang locked up in the adjacent Army camp, sent there by the Adjutant.

Next on the Adjutant's list was ordering the Airmen to dig slit trenches, allocating an area which was known to be very rocky. Harjinder appealed for a more sensible site, but to no avail. The results were obviously slow, and when the Mukerjee came to see the progress, which had amounted to only 3 inches for a morning's work, he vented his anger. He laid the blame on the senior Airmen, including Harjinder, claiming they had been slack in supervision. Harjinder knew that arguing would get him nowhere, so he requested the officers to supervise the digging. When they saw the picks bouncing off the layers of rock, the idea was finally abandoned. Life after combat can be difficult, but this pettiness justly caused Harjinder's mood to spiral down.

One event descended into comedy, but also showed how the men feared the Adjutant. Harjinder was forced to supervise four men whose punishment was marching drill, at double time, in the scorching heat. The sweating bodies were running up and down, turning on Harjinder's orders given with as much sympathy as he could muster into his voice. There was a strong wind blowing that day, and during one particularly strong gust, Harjinder's order to about turn, and head back towards him, was rendered unintelligible by the breeze. Harjinder was known to have a voice that would command whole parade grounds, so this must have been a veritable hurricane. Not hearing any order the men continued, in good military fashion, exiting the parade ground and carrying on at break neck speed through the dust. Harjinder initially shouted for his bicycle but realised he would lose them forever without immediate action, so set off after the men. By the time he reached them, they had run nearly a mile, across a ditch and over several hedges, and were bathed in perspiration, and scratched from head to foot. Harjinder felt terrible and thought this was 'punishment' enough for one day, so ordered a stop to the proceedings. However, all four told him not to do so in case he got into trouble. 'We are prepared to carry on until the time is up. If the Adjutant comes to know of our being let off, he would report you to the Commanding Officer.'

Things improved during April and May, returning to the job at hand to do some intensive training. The pilots once again had focus as they took to the air again. Most were now seasoned veterans; there were also a few new boys who had to be brought up to standard. They took the battered Lysanders with which they had been re-equipped, up into the clear sky above Hyderabad to carry out dive-bombing, flight formations, dog fight procedures, camouflage observation, army cooperation, reconnaissance and low level attacks. Harjinder could also get back to his old tricks and it wasn't long before the tea would soon be required in large quantities. He spotted a No. 20 Squadron RAF Lysander lying in one of the canvas hangars. The sorry looking aircraft had crashed on the 20th January 1942. After five months of no progress, a RAF Flight Sergeant finally came over to ask for Harjinder's help. It was literally in a thousand pieces, the parts spread out all over the hangar floor like the intestines of some grotesque beast. On inspection, however, Harjinder discovered that the actual damage was not so extensive. He further enraged the RAF Sergeant telling him that instead of 'playing about with it for four months' it was a four day job for the IAF to fix the machine.

The Flight Sergeant first thought that Harjinder was joking, but on realising that he was serious, he threw down a challenge; always a mistake with Harjinder. Harjinder asked the RAF Flight Sergeant for complete control of the hangar, to withdraw all his men, and to come back on the fifth day. He agreed, but went away shaking his head in disbelief at this obviously deluded Indian.

Harjinder called Flight Sergeant Siddique, showed him the job, and told him to get cracking. As per their usual practice, the Airmen were soon working away, busy as bees, with Harjinder ensuring that they remained fortified with the IAF Engineer's elixir of choice, tea.

With 24 hours left, the aircraft was re-assembled but the engine wasn't attached; a fairly vital part! Here was the big problem; no engine cranes or hoists were available. After much scratching of heads, and the turning down of various suggestions, Harjinder decided to dig a sloping pit into the hangar floor; clearly not put off by the earlier slit trench debacle. After pick and shovel had done as they were bid, the wheels were rolled into the trenches and the rest of the aircraft sat perfectly placed for Harjinder's team to lift the engine, and bolt it in place. In the morning the aircraft was test flown by the dauntless Flight Lieutenant Niranjan 'Joe' Prasad, who reported it in excellent condition. Not only was the RAF Flight Sergeant suitably impressed, when the Group Engineer at Bangalore heard the news, he was so amazed that the 'hangar queen' was flying, that he arranged to allot this Lysander as an additional aircraft to Harjinder's Squadron. Gaining Lysanders was becoming a bit of a hobby with Harjinder.

On 29th May the Squadron was sent to Trichinopoly, or Trichi as it was always referred to. Most of the ground staff had left for Trichi when Harjinder was told that one of the RAF's twin engine Blenheim bombers had crashed about 20 miles away. They were leaving, but technically, No. 1 Squadron was still the nearest Unit. They were asked to salvage it, which would first involve emptying all the fuel from it. Harjinder had no drums, or containers, to store the fuel, so sent all the Motor Transport drivers in to help. They managed to drain out every ounce of petrol, but later on, when Harjinder enquired how they had disposed of it without being caught by the police, a certain Abdul Majid smilingly remarked: 'Sir, that was no problem. A senior officer of the police himself helped us out by storing all the 200 gallons in his bungalow. We were even paid two hundred rupees for our cooperation!'

Harjinder left for Trichi with a clear conscience, leaving behind a very happy Police Chief; just as long as he remembered not to smoke in his bungalow until he had sold his entire windfall.

Luckily, the Squadron's role of coastal reconnaissance at Trichi was short-lived. It was officially described as an 'operational role' because the Japanese had raided Calcutta, and Trincomalee in Ceylon, but the pilots had no patience for this routine chore, droning around over the sea, after the cut and thrust of Burma. Also, there was nothing at Trichi except the landing strip and their canvas accommodation; no picnic in mid-summer. A fortnight after their arrival some news started to buzz around the tents. Not only was the Squadron moving to Risalpur, but their time with the Lysander was over. It was to be Hurricanes for the IAF. The pilots were jubilant: a fighting aircraft at last, albeit one almost withdrawn from the European theatre. This was still a big step up for the IAF.

The Hurricane had served well in the Battle of Britain. The Spitfire may have made headlines with its graceful, and thoroughbred looks, but the Hurricane was the work horse. The pilot could even place his foot in a stirrup that lowered from the fuselage, to get a leg up onto the wing. With the narrow canopy slid back, the pilot stepped onto the seat, then lowered himself into the tight fitting cockpit. If he bothered to look over the armour plating in the back of his seat, past the large radio set, and into the structure of the fuselage behind, it would not be the modern construction, like the Spitfire, he would see. No sleek monocoque structures like the aircraft today where the aircraft skin is part of the structure. The Hurricane had more akin to the biplanes like the Wapiti rather than the new generation being flowing in the wider war. It had a metal frame, with numerous complex joints, on which wooden longerons ran the length of the fuselage to take the fabric covering. Far heavier than the Spitfire, but, as many pilots could testify, it could take one hell of a pounding from enemy fire and still battle on. Because of its structure the Hurricane was easier to repair after combat damage than its sleeker cousin, a very important factor in combat flying.

Harjinder lamented his last days as a rear gunner, but was desperate to get to grips with the legendary Rolls Royce Merlin engine. As it so often happened, Harjinder's initial enthusiasm was crushed, this time when he discovered that the whole Unit in Risalpur possessed only one engine description handbook. He thought of copying out the whole volume by hand, but that was too much for one man. Instead, he divided the book into 15 parts, and asked 15 Airmen to write out 15 pages each; the job was completed in one week. Harjinder then read, and re-read, the maintenance chapters until he knew most of it by heart. However, it was the repair of the complex joints in the Hurricane's structure that would soon need his attention.

By the end of August 1942, the pilots had more or less completed their conversion to Hurricanes, flying nearly 25 hours each. The standard of their flying impressed the RAF Instructors, and it was the same in the workshops. The technical instructors soon found out about the standard of technical expertise the IAF possessed, so much so, that the RAF Station Commander wrote a letter to Air Headquarters commending their efficiency and high technical knowledge. Could it be that the RAF had finally realised that the IAF were not to be laughed at and ignored? On top of their war service, their day-to-day performance had established quite a reputation for the Squadron, and for the IAF. They now had an aircraft which they could use to attack the Japanese, and as the news came in about the first attempted landings by the Americans on the Pacific Island of Guadalcanal, they wanted to be back in the conflict.

One afternoon, Mukerjee arranged a meeting with Harjinder at the swimming pool. Mukerjee had returned from meeting with Jumbo in Delhi, with a message for Harjinder. He said that Harjinder had proved that Indians could be first-rate Senior NCOs, and Warrant Officers, but it was time for Harjinder to accept a Technical Commission, to become a full-fledged officer. Jumbo felt that if he did not accept it immediately then others, less qualified for the job, would be promoted above him.

Harjinder was caught unawares, not least because Jumbo had told him right back in 1939 that he should remain with the technicians until India had built up an Air Force of ten squadrons, with the necessary maintenance and technical base. When he tried to explain this to Mukerjee, the reply he got was:

> 'I very strongly feel that you should accept a Commission now, because we are about to get some new officers: I am not certain that they would give you the respect due to you if you remain a Warrant Officer. There will be quick promotions, and immature officers will be on top of Flights and Squadrons.'

Harjinder assured Mukerjee that this did not worry him. If they could not learn to handle him, he was convinced that he knew how to handle them, he had done so on many occasions! To this Mukerjee said:

'Let us not argue on this subject. You have confidence in me, and Jumbo, and it is our considered opinion that you should accept a Commission now in the greater interest of our Air Force. Please say "Yes".'

Harjinder had the greatest respect for these two men, and so his answer had to be; Yes! So, not one to take chances, Harjinder began to prepare for the interview board. He was getting flashbacks to a year before, and his last 'difficulties' at the School of Technical Training.

On 30th August 1942, a group of technicians was called up for the interviews by a Board of Officers presided over by a Group Captain. The Squadron Leader began by asking technical questions. This certainly played into Harjinder's strength, besides, with Jumbo sitting on the board, representing the IAF, he was further inspired to lock horns with the interviewers. He not only answered all the questions, but also added many technical details not known to the examiner. When the subject drifted onto the Merlin engine, the heart of the Spitfire and the Hurricane, Harjinder questioned the whole design of the one-piece cylinder block:

'It is amazing why this item was not discarded while still on the drawing board. It is; uneconomical to cast; uneconomical to machine; uneconomical to repair; difficult to work on in the field. Even simple engine designers now have accepted the two piece cylinder block as standard practice. However, Rolls Royce is still sticking to the conservatism typical of the British.'

The Board obviously knew who they had in front of them, Harjinder's reputation was already legend, they would have known him as an outstanding engineer, but now they knew that he was no mild mannered yes man. The President of the Board could not restrain himself from laughing out loud; he turned to Jumbo:

'Jumbo, this chap seems to be the kind of man we want. I am prepared to accept him in the RAF as a Flight Lieutenant (*missing out the officer ranks of Pilot and Flying Officer*).'

Not being sure which way the wind would blow, Jumbo had been looking worried, but now he beamed, adding:

'Sir! If I had not stopped it, he would have been commissioned in June 1939, and by now he would have been a Flight Lieutenant.'

The next day, the India Command Engineer, Group Captain Collin Weedon, interviewed Harjinder. Well aware that he was potentially authorising the first Indian Engineering Officer, he started by saying;

'I have heard from my Technical Officer, who represented me on the Selection Board, that you are a very knowledgeable man. I would like to make sure, because one day, you are going to hold a key post in the IAF. I would like you to tell me what aircraft and engines of American type you know and give me a brief description of each.'

Weedon had been expecting him to talk about one of the few types seen in India, and was pleasantly surprised when Harjinder talked at great length and in great detail about the American Airacobra fighter. There were no planes like this in India, but of course, Harjinder had seen them these arrive in Lashio when the AVG was being re-equipped. His natural curiosity had made him poke around and absorb all the technical information he could during chats with their engineers.

The next question about how many rivets were needed in a certain piece of metal, actually made Harjinder laugh, and point out that he covered that in the 1st year in college; a whole 16 years ago. He even added; 'I expected more difficult questions from the Command Engineering Officer.'

Weedon was annoyed at first, but seemed to calm down, and when he stood at the end of the interview and shook Harjinder's hand with a smile on his face, Harjinder knew he was about to make IAF history.

On 2nd September 1942, the Indian Air Force were notified of their first Indian Engineering Officer. Fittingly, it was Jumbo who broke the news when he called Harjinder into his office, pumping his hand in the warmest handshake he had ever received. He congratulated him, but added:

'You have set a problem for me. The President of the Board is bent upon commissioning you directly as a Flight Lieutenant. I feel that that would be incorrect. The RAF standard practice is to commission really good Warrant Officers to Flying Officer's rank (*one rank lower than Flight Lieutenant*). Looking at it from the IAF point of view, you would be looked upon as a very odd case. I feel that you should be a Flying Officer for, say, 12 months or so. I know you will climb the ladder pretty fast, so why worry?'

After offering his thanks, Harjinder's reply could easily be guessed:

'Sir, I never asked anyone to give me a Commission, leave aside a Flight Lieutenant's rank. I do not believe rank makes any difference to a man who loves the Service. As far as money is concerned, more rupees do not add to your health and happiness. I feel I have achieved great happiness by contributing my share in building up an Indian Air Force. You can tell the President that I would rather be a Flying Officer, as per custom.'

After being the first Corporal, the first Sergeant, the first Flight Sergeant, Harjinder was now the first IAF Engineering Officer. Jumbo was thrilled at Harjinder's reaction and pumped his hand again. Harjinder's musings on becoming an Officer were as predictable as his reply to Jumbo:

'On 3rd September 1942, I became a Commissioned Officer, a far easier job than being a non-commissioned one, in my opinion. However, I, for one, intend to prove to the RAF in India, that the IAF had better technical officers than they. Furthermore, I intend to keep my hand in, on the practical side, as I was advised by Warrant Officer Newing, my old instructor, when he left for England many years ago.'

Ram Singh and U.K. Nair were also commissioned as Pilot Officers and fittingly, the pilots of the squadron, led by Flight Lieutenant Raza, gave all three of them a dunking in the swimming pool on their return to Trichinopoly. No longer would there be an official divide between these men. They were all officers together.

Now, put yourself in the shoes of one of the newly qualified pilots commissioned in the legendary No. 1 Squadron IAF. The Station Commander seems very gentlemanly and easy-going. The veterans have an ease about them, which only comes from experiencing life in combat. You think the way you should act as a member of this legendary force is to turn up to work at a time that suits you, and when you are told to fly, you can tell the relaxed boss that you don't fancy it today, but if you happen to change your mind, you jump in and go. This was not the attitude of all, but just that of a few young bucks. Imagine how the world of these swaggering youngsters suddenly imploded when Harjinder received his commission. The Warrant Officer who struck fear into them (*as Marshal Arjan Singh admitted to me 70 years later*), but who had to call them Sir because he was not an officer, whom they could seek sanctuary from in the Officers Mess, suddenly appears as your equal or even your superior. These few laid-back lads displayed all the traits Harjinder despised, and he loathed to perceive them in 'his' Air Force, so he unleashed the full weight of his wrath on them. Mukerjee agreed to his request to act as the Squadron Adjutant Officer for one week.

From the first day, the whole Squadron was on drill parade every morning. The result was miraculous, everybody turned up on time. Half an hour's drill every day taught the young officers to obey orders without protest. This continued until they had mended their slovenly ways. Harjinder went through the Mess, and offices, like a whirlwind, and attitudes there soon changed too. After all, Harjinder knew that the Squadron would be back in combat at some point. He was not out to make friends with people, but return a Squadron to the peak efficiency, ready to face all odds, as they had been in Burma.

The war in Burma ebbed and flowed but the attempts to push the Japanese back had come to nothing. In North Africa, things were better, with the Germans being pushed back in the brilliantly executed Battle of El Alamein. The IAF clamoured to be in midst of the action, but their fearless leader felt that combat wasn't imminent for their squadron, and so, when he was given a chance at a promotion, he took it, moving up, and out, of Squadron life. Everybody was more than happy to serve under his replacement, Henry Runganadhan. Henry; the man who had won the air races, the man who had sheepishly called Harjinder when he felt unable to face his colleagues over lunch after crashing a Lysander, but a man who had grown in stature whilst in combat. He was recognised as a man of great courage, daring and enjoying the good life (*some thought too much!*). He had been in No. 1 Squadron nearly from the beginning, and was much admired by every man jack. They would all follow him, not just because of the man he was, but to continue to raise the reputation of the Jumbo Squadron.

Henry headed down to take command of *his* new squadron in a twin-engined, Lockeed Hudson transport aircraft. He hated flying as a passenger, but it was to be a treat for him this time as *his* pilots from *his* Squadron wanted to welcome him in style by escorting him to their base, in their new Hurricanes. The Hurricanes bobbed up next to Henry as he looked out of the aircraft's side window, proud to be taking the responsibility of the Jumbo Squadron. In one of the Hurricanes was Homi Shapur Ratnagar, the Burma veteran who'd arrived on the battlefield with a case full of civilian clothes, and sports gear, because nobody had told him otherwise. The story told to Harjinder at the time was that as they were passing near Karachi, Ratnagar's Hurricane engine started to leak fumes from around the exhaust. The odourless carbon monoxide seeped inside the engine cowling and further back into his cockpit. Ratnagar felt relaxed, pleasant, just like after a few drinks, but, so very tired, too. As he slid gently into a happy unconsciousness, his Hurricane drifted around the sky. The Hurricane wasn't known to leak fumes and after the war Ratnagar was removed from flying duties after he suffered dizzy spells. The truth of the matter is the Hurricane was probably not to blame, but the carnage was inevitable all the same.

The gunner in the top turret of the Hudson was seen furiously waving the Hurricane away from his glass bubble, but there just wasn't time enough to shout a warning to his own pilot as the Hurricane slide sideways between the twin tail-fins of the Hudson. The propeller turning at over 2,000 revolutions a minute chewed through the thin aluminium fuselage and the turret's glass and metal, in a heartbeat. The entire tail section was ripped away from the fuselage and fluttered downwards, strips of aluminium filling the air like confetti. It can only be imagined what it was like inside the transport aircraft when it suddenly, and savagely, pitched up, pinning all the occupants to their seats, snapping their heads down onto their laps. The crippled aircraft flipped on to its back, then rotated into a tight spin towards the ground. It took their new Commander, Henry Runganadhan to his death. Henry had always said, that to die as a passenger in a plane was a mean death. Henry Runganadhan survived Burma only to have that mean death.

Harjinder was heartbroken as his final link to the original No. 1 Squadron IAF died with Henry. Squadron Leader Goyal was rushed in to take over, but Harjinder felt that his time, with his beloved Squadron, the parent Squadron of the IAF, was at an end. Like Mukerjee before him, he also believed that there was no imminent chance of the Squadron going into action; he was not entirely correct. It would not be long before they went into combat, and by then, a tall, slender Sikh would take command. As a Squadron Leader, it was to be the first, of many, commands in Arjan Singh's long, illustrious service with the IAF. He would take No. 1 Squadron to fight the Japanese as they invaded India. When that moment came, it would be a desperate battle. In the Soviet Union, the Germans had failed to capture the city of Stalingrad in a gruesome battle. What would happen on Indian soil would not be on the same scale, but it was to earn the name of the Stalingrad of the East. The Germans had come to a crashing halt in Stalingrad, allowing a sliver of hope for the Allies, but that was not yet the case in India. The Japanese were still advancing.

Harjinder was ready to leave his No. 1 Squadron when the time came, and on 1st February 1943, after ten years continuous service he flew up to Air Headquarters to be interviewed by Air Commodore Proud, Inspector General of the IAF. He was to be appointed President of the Initial and Re-selection Board at the Recruits Training Centre at Walton, Lahore. It must have been difficult indeed for Harjinder to think of leaving a life in active combat and his family in No. 1 Squadron, for what was effectively a desk job, but Jumbo was one step ahead as always. He was straight on the phone with Harjinder:

'I have specially chosen you to go over to Lahore, because I have found very low-morale men coming into our Service. 30 per cent of them desert within a month of their arrival. I want you to see that we get more enthusiastic material. Our objective is to put as many Indians into uniform as we can, wherever they can be absorbed, so that we can readily form No. 10 Squadrons for the IAF when the time comes (*The idea of the No. 10 IAF Squadrons burned at the very heart of Jumbo*). I have impressed on Sir Richard Pierse the urgent need for a large number of Indian Airmen to work with the RAF. I have convinced him of this necessity by telling him that British Airmen may not stand up to the malarial climate of Burma where we will have to fight the Japs for a number of years to come. He has agreed with me and has decided to recruit twenty thousand Indian Airmen. In fact, my object is to train the main bulk of a future Indian Air Force in this guise. The war, when won, will bring in its wake a new awakening in our country. The soldiers who are fighting in the Middle East and Burma will not long be content with being a subjugated people

in India. We are on the eve of great political changes and during
the process we must have a strong Army and a strong air arm to
support it. This is my aim as much as to fight the war in Burma.'

Jumbo knew how to press Harjinder's buttons; by giving him a
challenge, and giving him the end goal. It worked:

'I left for Lahore inspired by his vision; determined to work for
him with missionary zeal.'

For Harjinder, it was good to be back in Lahore, and back in the
Punjab region. However, when he walked into Walton Base at Lahore he
was shocked at what he saw. The new recruits were made to rough it out in
tents just as he had done 10 years before. There had been no improvement
in that time, and the attitude towards the new recruits seemed so familiar
to him. The British Sergeants and Corporals seemed overly harsh with
their charges. Harjinder was a strict disciplinarian, but this was too much
even by his standards; he immediately set to work to sort things out. He
met the Officer Commanding, Recruits Training Wing, Flight Lieutenant
Cox, and was pleasantly surprised:

'An excellent type. He was one of those rare Englishmen who
genuinely liked India and everything Indian, at least, he is the first
Englishman who ever said so.'

Harjinder knew the Boss of the Station, Wing Commander Blandford.
He had been a Warrant Officer during Harjinder's time in Karachi, and
he knew him to be keen on discipline. He explained to Blandford that his
target was nothing less than to reduce the number of discharges to zero.

Two days later, he interviewed the first batch of recruits. He discovered
that all of them had one thing in common; they had been lured into
uniform by false promises made by the recruiting officers. During his
rounds, he came across a recruit called Jagdish Awasthi, who explained in
Hindustani, that he had been a tonga-walla (*a horse and cart man*) and could
not speak a word of English; that the Recruiting Officer had duped him,
and therefore, asked for a discharge on those grounds. He did look the
part, with an unshaven face and dirty clothes.

Harjinder wanted the best for his Air Force, and was deeply annoyed
over this man's story, and so sent out a telegram to the Recruiting Officer
asking for the man's original papers. When he received them, he was

thunderstruck to see that the man was, in fact, studying Science. It was clearly a pretence; he would soon settle that! Harjinder called the man in for an interview before the Board and spoke to him in Hindustani. He apologised to him for the conduct of the Recruiting Officer and promised to take action against him. Then he turned round and spoke to the members of the Board in English; 'Gentlemen, here is a very smart, physically fit recruit. He would make a good Infantryman. We should transfer him to the Army as a recruit. We need soldiers more than Airmen, because of the heavy casualties the Infantry has sustained in the Middle East.'

As he spoke these words, Harjinder noticed the recruit looking intently at him with raised eyebrows. All of a sudden he burst out in English; 'You can't do that, Sir, I have signed only for the IAF!'

The cat was out of the bag. He broke down and confessed. Harjinder then reasoned with him and appealed to his patriotic sentiments, which worked. He decided to stay on, and was allotted a Radar Operator's trade.

The 1st April 1943 was a very proud day for Harjinder, as he marched at the front of the local parade to celebrate the tenth anniversary of the IAF. Ten years ago, Harjinder had given up everything to become a Sepoy and now, as an Officer, he paraded 500 recruits, very smart in their uniform, and well-drilled in their marching. The damning words of Sir John Steele must have come to mind as he looked out over his men, the future of the ever expanding IAF. These men were no disgrace, no, not by a long shot.

Things were not smelling of roses, however. Fifteen days later, Harjinder did see the more unsavoury elements that had developed in the IAF. The local Air Force Recruiting Officer sent him his recommend list of ten new recruits for commissioning immediately as officers. It was a great power vested in Harjinder, the ability to pick out a new recruit and make him instantly into an officer. For the individual recruit it was a golden opportunity. Harjinder noticed that all these ten new recommended recruits were by no means the best of the bunch, but they all belonged to the same community that this particular Recruitment Officer hailed from originally. List denied! The Officer threatened Harjinder with dire consequences if he didn't pass the list, but was told in no uncertain terms that since Air Headquarters had so much confidence in him, Harjinder would be the last person on earth to abuse their trust.

Harjinder was to be tested again shortly afterwards, when the uncle of one of the recruits appeared and asked if he was looking for a small Austin car. Indeed, that was the case, but only a secondhand one. Harjinder simply assumed that this man must be a car dealer touting for trade. The man continued; 'But supposing you get a brand new one for the same price?'

This does seem a little naïve of Harjinder, but he thought that this man must be offering some money-lending scheme, common practice amongst the officer class in those days. Harjinder told him that he was an engineer, and would prefer a second-hand to a new car, because he liked tinkering with the engine. The next exchange left Harjinder in no doubt as to what was being offered, and rendered him almost speechless;

> 'Sahib, make hay while the sun shines. You are in this chair and you have great authority. You will not be here always. You have the power to discharge recruits. All I want is that you should discharge one of the men, my nephew. I will present you a brand new Austin plus a cheque for five thousand rupees.'

He qualified his statement by adding; 'My nephew is the son of an ex-minister of Kashmir State. His mother, who is a widow, will spend any amount to obtain his release.'

Corruption was commonplace in India, and while Harjinder had encountered it before, he had never seen it on this scale. He was taken aback, and it took him a second to regain his composure, as he tried to get this persistent man to leave. Then, finally, his brain caught up with the events and kicked into overdrive. An idea came to him to help root out this evil; he would arranged a trap. He finally gave in to this man's offer and told him to meet him again at the office at 9 o'clock the following morning. Just before leaving, the man produced an Air Force form for Airmen's discharge, duly completed and ready for a signature. He seemed to know all the procedures.

Harjinder promptly went to the Station Adjutant, where they put together the details of a police trap. They called in the magistrate and by the following morning, all was in place. It was a scene straight out of the cinema, a curtain hung dividing the office in two parts; behind the curtain lurked the magistrate and a police officer, ready to pounce. In fact, it felt like the whole morning's events should have been only in black and white, just like in the movies. The man in question, accompanied by a friend, arrived at 9 am sharp. He introduced the other man as the maternal uncle of the recruit. They got down to business straightaway. Harjinder repeated all the negotiations as loudly as he dared:

'I must repeat the terms that you have offered. If I sign the discharge certificate of your nephew, is it understood that in return you will give a cheque for five thousand rupees and a new Austin car?'

The man beamed all over and said; 'That is correct.'

'You do not want me to do anything else? In other words, this is the price just for one signature?'

He seemed delighted, nodding as he confirmed what was said once again. The form was signed and the cheque for five thousand rupees was duly handed over. Then came the registration book of the car, and a letter to the Regional Transport Officer requesting for the transfer of the car.

Harjinder had heard enough and, as pre-arranged he rang a bell to indicate the moment for the trap to be sprung. In the cinema the police would jump out, the guilty man would try and make a run for it but be caught by the gallant policeman, who wrestled him to the floor. That certainly didn't happen! What unfolded was completely bewildering. The police officer came forward from behind the curtain but instead of arresting the culprit, he stopped suddenly, rooted to the spot. He drew himself up to attention producing a smart salute. The magistrate looked at the policeman; he looked at Harjinder; he looked back at the policeman in complete confusion. The bewildered Harjinder lost his temper and shouted at the police officer; 'Well, why don't you arrest him?'

The so-called culprit beamed at Harjinder and said; 'Actually, we came to arrest *you* but now you want *us* to be arrested?'

It took a few seconds, but the penny finally tumbled to the floor. It had been a double-trap, to entangle Harjinder! The culprit was actually a very senior Crime Investigation Officer, and the man accompanying him was also a magistrate. They had picked a recruit's name at random from the list and concocted their story. They had wanted to prove that any recruit could be discharged provided the price was paid, and, additionally, they wanted to show that Harjinder Singh could be bribed. In a time and place where corruption was the norm, Harjinder proved himself incorruptible.

The senior officer from the crime unit warmly shook hands with Harjinder and congratulated him, apologising for the embarrassment. The surprises didn't stop there, because a few days later in Delhi, when Harjinder told the story to Jumbo, it seemed that Jumbo knew more about the events than Harjinder did. Jumbo laughed:

'Well done. I knew it all the time but I had to take up Tull's challenge. He is an Internal Crime type here and said that Selection Board officers were making a lot of money, and that you must be in it too. When I told him that I had as great confidence in you, as in myself, he said that he had heard differently. The Recruiting Officer (*who produced the list for fast commissions that Harjinder had turned down*) had sent in a report against you. So I agreed to let them try to trap you.'

In celebration, Harjinder went out, and bought his secondhand car, an old Austin 10, for one thousand rupees and, yes, he did tinker with it for a number of years!

Having proved his honesty, Harjinder now had to work on the desertion rate of the recruits. He had dramatically reduced desertions by treating them all with dignity, but that had not entirely stopped the rot. One day, two deserters were brought back by the police, but before they were placed under arrest, Harjinder took the chance to discover the 'whys' behind their actions. The main 'why' was surprising: they only were given two chapattis at each meal! It seemed that any recruit who asked for more was abused and sometimes even placed on a charge. When questioned about this, the Officer Commanding reacted violently to the 'allegation', and accused Harjinder of trying to defame the Station Administration. A junior officer was called in and asked if the statement could be true, but he denied it, staring daggers at Harjinder, so much so, that Harjinder did start to feel a little stupid bringing up the whole chapatti subject.

A month later, the head of the Qadiani Sect of Muslims wrote to the Officer Commanding making an identical allegation based on what some of his people in the camp were telling him. The Officer Commanding summoned Harjinder, and, when told about the fresh allegations, Harjinder offered to take over the running of the Mess to get to the bottom of it.

His first step was to seek out a reliable man to put in-charge. He chose a man with a flowing white beard, known to be very religious, telling him that he would be in-charge of the ration store. He then appointed a Messing Committee from amongst the Airmen. He calculated how much the messing allowance, and additional recruits' contributions, should purchase per day. A few days later, he carried out a surprise check on a Saturday afternoon, when rations for the next two days should have been in the store. Harjinder was shocked to see the real state of affairs. There were not sufficient rations in store for a single meal for these 6,600 men, so he called in his newly appointed head cook, took him to task and asked for an explanation. The bearded man broke into tears and the story came flooding out. The previous Messing Officer seemed as effective as a chocolate teapot, and had not bothered with any supervision over the stores. This had given the Flight Sergeant free reign to abuse his position, and to run a racket in collusion with the contractor, who supplied the rations. The amount was drawn in full only on paper; most of it never came into the Mess. For a man as principled as Harjinder, this was deeply offensive, but he had to have proof. The Station Security Officer, Flying Officer Deane, was an ex-policeman, so took to the task with relish. They raided a merchant's shop thought to be acting as the receiver, and, sure enough, sacks full of sugar and tins of ghee were found still with the Government seals intact! The owner followed the lead of the head cook and broke down in tears. With the tears came the confession that he had been dealing in the stolen Air Force rations since the Depot was opened. Acting on further information, the police raided a well-known house of dancing girls in Lahore and found a similar hoard of Air Force rations. The Flight Sergeant, with certain other friends, had been spending thousands of rupees a month on these dancing girls, while the Airmen recruits starved and deserted. He was tried by a General Court Martial and sentenced to 18 months rigorous imprisonment. Meanwhile, back at the Mess, the food was delivered as it should have been, with more than enough for all. Not a single complaint was heard again, and the desertions ceased.

Harjinder then set about re-allotting 5,000 men from clerical jobs, to ones of a technical nature. Many of these men had been cajoled into joining the clerical line by recruiting officers but, Harjinder also had his eye on building up the IAF's technical department. However, Harjinder was suddenly hauled up before Air Vice-Marshal Collier for having 'sabotaged' the war effort. It seemed his scheme had left Head Quarters desperately short of clerks, and how could they be expected to shuffle their paperwork without office workers! Harjinder defended his point by bringing attention to the drop from 30 per cent desertions to almost zero, claiming that the re-allocation had achieved that; failing to include the information on the improvement at meal times. The subterfuge worked: He was even complimented for his action.

Harjinder got involved with individual cases, which once again led him down a dangerous path. A young Bengali recruit, called Kapila

Chatterji, held a master's degree in arts and had been a teacher of history at Tagore's Shantiniketan University before he joined the IAF. He suddenly took it into his head that the armed forces of India were the tools of British Imperialism, and was asked to resign. In a discussion with Harjinder which lasted six hours, Chatterji told Harjinder all about his own ideology and his belief in the Indian National Congress. This was a matter close to Harjinder's heart so he argued that India must fight alongside the British, for the time being, and help them win the war, thus winning Dominion status. Before parting that evening, Harjinder assured him that one of them must convert the other, and so, the debate continued over the next fortnight. Although Chatterji was a good debater, Harjinder finally convinced him that he ought to stay in the Service, or at least that was what he thought. Perhaps what really decided it for him was a letter from his anxious mother urging him to remain in the Air Force. As she was a widow, and he the only child, he agreed to serve on.

On 1st August 1943, Harjinder was called in the Station Commander's office to be confronted by Air Commodore Proud, Inspector General of the Indian Air Force. Proud was cordial, almost friendly, as cups of tea were offered and they sat on a sofa together. However, he did not mince his words and revealed his real intent:

'What are your political views vis-à-vis the British in India and the war? Do you believe in the "Quit India" gospel?'

Harjinder had never been afraid to give his frank views:

'I joined the Indian Air Force for nationalistic reasons, to help form a strong Air Force of our own, so that we would not have to depend upon the RAF to defend us when we became a Dominion. This is what I still feel.'

He continued in that vein, including how his English Principal had showed him the Hunter Commission Report all those years ago in college. He talked about the 'Quit India campaign', pointing out that the Allied forces must win for a future Independent India:

'If after the war we are treated shabbily by the British, we will fight them, too, until we become a Dominion, which I believe is the next step for India.'

Expecting trouble, Harjinder was surprised when Proud got up and shook hands with him, saying:

'You are a real and true patriot. I am glad you practise what you preach. We do not want "Yes men" who say things to please us, and yet would garland the Japanese if they landed at Calcutta. We need men with principles who can be true to us and to their own country. Your anti-British remarks are understandable. We are to blame for the introduction of the Rowlatt Act even after the Indians' magnificent war effort in the 1914-18 war. But I assure you, it will be a different story after this war. Now I want to talk to you about this chap called Chatterji.'

Harjinder's heart leaped into his mouth when he read the sheaf of letters handed to him. They were Chatterji's intercepted letters to various contacts describing how he had joined the Air Force to spur other Airmen to anti-British activities. He had written about his conversation with Harjinder, reporting their discourse accurately, and about his mother's plea for him to remain in Service. However, he did have doubts and expressed his sense of betrayal by serving in uniform. If Harjinder had not been so frank, he would have been earmarked as an imposter, and a world of trouble could have been dropped from above.

As the year reached the halfway point, it was not trouble that came Harjinder's way, but praise from high above. In the King's Birthday Honours List of June 1943, Harjinder found that he had been awarded the MBE for his work in the Burma campaign. Jumbo was overjoyed by the news pointing out that with his Distinguished Flying Cross (DFC), they were the first two IAF officers to be decorated. A medal for distinguished flying was one thing, Harjinder, however, was being made a Member of the Order of the British Empire; an interesting concept after his conversation with Proud. Thinking back to Peshawar, Harjinder remembered how Warrant Officer Simms seemed to have reached an unattainable level with his MBE. Only two years later, he had his own MBE. His entrance into the Order of the British Empire.

Harjinder briefly teamed up again with Jumbo Majumdar, DFC, and they headed back to the North-West Frontier for the shooting of the propaganda film. At one point, Flying Officer Ranjan Dutt was supposed to zoom over the top of the two of them as they walked towards the camera, but he got a little carried away. The shot ended up with Jumbo and Harjinder face down in the dirt, with the Hurricane seemingly cutting their hair with its propeller. The finished film was taken to Sir Richard

Pierse, the Air Officer Commanding, India, who promptly hit the roof. He vehemently objected to the part where Harjinder was shown leading the strike in Lahore with banners that read 'Long Live Revolution'. 'What madness is this? Do you want to encourage students to revolt after seeing this film?'

So that part was deleted, but the rest was passed. However, for some inexplicable reason, they kept Harjinder's service number, but changed his name to 'Pawar' in the film.

Not only was Harjinder a 'film star', but he became a pin-up, too! The recruiting department produced a poster that was circulated throughout India. Someone in Delhi had a brainwave; Flight Sergeant Pring had shot down three Japanese aircraft over Calcutta, and his surname had a certain ring to it when combined with Harjinder's. Pring's name and Harjinder's were headlined in bold print; 'This is Pring and this is Singh!' Both their photos appeared side by side, the text complimenting Pring for his aerial success, his coolness under pressure; Harjinder as the man who gave up an engineering degree to become the first IAF technical officer. His face was now seen around India, but many of the readers didn't take time to read the text. For months he received letters of praise from all over congratulating him on his piloting skills and three downed Japanese aircraft!

The time running the recruiting centre was coming to an end, but the film and the MBE seemed to do some good, as later that year, Harjinder was told that he had been selected to undertake advanced technical training in the United Kingdom. He always wanted to remain as a 'hands-on' engineer, and this was the course that would take his skills to another level.

Harjinder sailed aboard the 'Strathmore' for England on 1 December, 1943. He left behind a country with the enemy beating at the door. Harjinder's No. 1 Squadron had been sent back up to the North-West Frontier to continue operations against the tribes. This seemed to be their fate, until mid-December saw a visit by the Commander in Chief of the Army in India, Field Marshal Sir Claude Auchinleck. Arjan Singh so impressed the Field Marshal during his visit, with the efficient operation and the deep burning desire to be back in the thick of the fighting, that within the week, the orders were issued for the Squadron's return to combat, and a move to Imphal on the Burma border. Harjinder's old No. 1 Squadron was going back to war, with Arjan Singh taking on the role Jumbo had made his own.

Harjinder was accompanied by another Knight of the Realm on his sea voyage. Sir Douglas Young, the retiring Chief Justice of India, departed from the Bombay docks amid the confusion of the bowing and scraping of a million yes men, ready to serve his every need. Sir Douglas was in for a rude shock when they landed at Liverpool. Air Vice-Marshal Hind received Harjinder, looked after his disembarkation, detailing an RAF Airman to look after his kit. Meanwhile, poor Sir Douglas – he was last seen alone at the docks, dragging his cabin trunk across the deck with nobody paying him a blind bit of attention. Welcome to wartime Britain and life without servants!

Throughout Harjinder's service life, he had pilots around him who had trained at the RAF College, Cranwell, in Lincolnshire. They had related stories, and descriptions, of the country they had trained in, so Britain was not a whole new world to Harjinder, but almost like being re-acquainted with distant memories. As always with secondhand stories, the bad bits are forgotten, and the only the best parts are told, and re-told. The England of these stories had been a land of green fields bathed in summer sunshine, but this was not the England Harjinder encountered. This was winter; and war time; so possibly not the best time to see the country at its finest! The night came at 4 o'clock in the evening, and stayed on until 8 o'clock in the morning. The sun, when it appeared, seemed to struggle into the sky, never reaching a great height. The trees were devoid of leaves, giving a much-drained look after the lush greens of Burma. Grey, more than green, seemed to be the overwhelming colour in the towns with the blacked-out windows and absence of light. Everything was rationed, and it seemed as if the majority of the population was in uniform of some description.

On 11 January 1944, Harjinder was interviewed by the grading board of the Air Ministry at Alexandra House, Kingsway, London. The Board consisted of two officers; Wing Commander Able and Squadron Leader Lancaster. The former was a very experienced officer with a long period of service in the practical field, and Lancaster was a graduate in Engineering from London University. Any Interview is supposed to be gruelling affair, but Harjinder found himself having 'a very enjoyable afternoon'.

They started on the basics he had learnt in his first year of engineer training, more a test of memory than one of knowledge. They then proceeded through every aspect of theoretical and practical engineering. The more in-depth the men ventured, the more it spurred Harjinder to provide prompt and accurate replies. They covered repair schemes and engine overhauls. Altogether four and a half hours flew by, rather a long time for one candidate when those preceding him had each been in for an hour at the most.

The verdict was the reward for his patience with the board.

'You do not need a (*advanced training*) course at Cosford. We have examined you fully. They should not have sent you all the way to us from India. There is no academic course in UK for you. You should return to India.'

Harjinder had assumed that in Britain, he could attend more RAF technical courses to take his skills to a higher level, but it seemed that he had reached the end of formal instruction. The additional comments were supposed to be a compliment, but Harjinder didn't like what he heard; 'You have given us a very good impression of Indian Engineers. In the past, we have met some of your countrymen who claimed to know everything on earth, but on discussion we found their knowledge limited and shallow. That was one reason why I start from the beginning.'

Harjinder replied; 'Perhaps you have not met an average Indian Engineer before. The class of people who usually come out to UK are the sons of the rich, who have plenty of money but very little brains. Real engineers have to work hard for a living.'

The next day Harjinder called on his old instructor, Newing, the man who had been such an influence on Harjinder, and whom Harjinder had made a point of seeing off on the ship before he left India all those years ago. Newing was now a Group Captain, and a senior staff officer at the Air Ministry. Harjinder was due to return to India, but Newing advised Harjinder to avail himself of the manufacturing courses run by defence companies in England.

After lunch, Flying Officer Harjinder Singh MBE was taken round to meet Group Captain Ardley, a face from the past. He was the first Officer to interview Harjinder back in 1931, and who had instructed his staff to escort Harjinder out of his office telling him 'You college boys are too soft and will not be able to last the pace'. Conveniently, he seemed to have forgotten the event!

Harjinder's first course was with Dowty, covering their hydraulics systems. It was the sort, of course, Harjinder could get his teeth into. Only four days long, but covering all the different aircraft systems, you needed to be on your toes, and work long and hard. He also got on well with Mr Hunt, the Chief Instructor. In the evening they had tea together, and talked at length about India. For Harjinder, Mr Hunt was the first Englishman he met who readily agreed that England, though the mother of democracy, did not practise it in India. When Harjinder told him how his countrymen behaved in India he replied;

> 'Yes. I know the type. We call them the "Poonahs". There is a whole colony of them here in Cheltenham, officers who have served in India. They have even forgotten basic and elementary etiquette.'

Harjinder and Jumbo had discussed setting up a wing of the Indian Air Force in UK. On 17th March 1944, he wrote to Jumbo back in India. In that letter he confessed to having come to England under the assumption that Jumbo too would come too and start the IAF Wing (*not entirely true, as Harjinder was also motivated by taking part in engineering courses he wrongly thought existed for him*). He wrote 'HURRY UP', as his new dream was to read in the newspapers about 'Indians over Berlin'. He expanded further; 'There is a very great bond between us, a very everlasting friendship; a unique one. We two are destined to do a lot in this war together as in years gone by, in years to come. We are lucky together, do not forget that. Anyway, what is there, a man is born and he must die, but very few die for a cause, so great as we want to fight for. Let them see that India can produce men like you.'

Germany would, indeed, see what India could produce, but it would be only in the shape of Jumbo, not Harjinder.

Harjinder didn't stay idle whilst waiting for Jumbo to arrive from India. The next company he visited was the Rotol factory where the General Manager was keen to hear about India. The next day, he visited the Gloster aircraft factory, where the new Typhoon fighter/bomber aircraft were being built on behalf of the Hawker Company. Little did Harjinder know that Jumbo would be strapping into one of these new machines in a few months' time. Harjinder was told he was the first foreigner allowed into the factory, a decision they started to regret when his inquisitive nature took him into areas he wasn't supposed to see. He saw a single strange-shaped aircraft lined up along one wall of the building. Harjinder noticed there were no propellers on the 2 engines buried in the wing. He was ushered past the nameless plane. That plane would appear in the war, this propeller-less aircraft; it would be called the Gloster Meteor and it was destined to become the RAF's first jet aircraft chasing rocket powered, flying bombs over the English Channel; the German V1 terror weapons.

Harjinder took a lot from these visits, and it helped change his opinion of the British in their own country;

'I could not help but admire the spirit of the British people at war. Young girls entered the factory looking very smart and attractive. In a few minutes they would put on their blue workshop-soiled overalls and begin their work on lathes, or cleaning the floors or spraying dope on the fabric. I also saw an old woman of seventy working on a ball-bearing sorting machine. Previously, I had seen girls washing locomotive engines, porting luggage at railway stations, sweeping platforms, unloading cargo and driving vehicles; but the most inspiring sight I saw that day was a woman pilot, who I was told was employed in ferrying Mosquito bombers to various theatres of war. My admiration for the British at war held no bounds thereafter. The whole nation seems to be acting as one team. War work appears to be their religion and the only aim in life. How different were the British in India!'

After a brief visit to Hatfield to study the manufacture of the Mosquito 'wooden wonder' aircraft, he returned to London to discover that he had been promoted to the job of 'Flight Engineer' which involved flying in the bomber aircraft, handling all the systems for the pilot. There was a message waiting for him from Jumbo, now also in UK, asking him to be ready to join an IAF Squadron that would be trained in Canada, but return to fly in the UK. The idea bumped along for a short while, but the IAF squadron in the UK never materialised, much to the frustration of Jumbo. When there was obviously no hope left for Jumbo's dream for the IAF, he presented himself in front of any senior officer he could find in the RAF. He pushed and pushed for a place on a fighter squadron and he finally got his wish; No. 268 RAF Squadron. So determined he was to serve, to show what Indians could do, that he took a drop in rank just to go back into combat. The Germans were going to get a taste of Jumbo's talents.

It seems a shame that both Jumbo and Harjinder were in England on the 20th February 1944. The event they had dreamt of for so long, the goal that burnt in Jumbo's heart, actually happened. Back in Lahore the last Indian Air Force Squadron to be raised during the World War II was formed and equipped with the Hawker Hurricane IIc fighters. It was

No. 10 Squadron IAF. It has to be said that the unit was not a pure Indian one, but more a 'Commonwealth' formation with a fair number of British pilots, as well as Australians and New Zealanders, all serving under an Englishman, Squadron Leader Bob Doe, DSO, DFC & Bar, but it was to be the tenth IAF Squadron.

Harjinder remained in the UK for a few more months, visiting more companies and installations to soak up information wherever he could. It was clear that Southern England was filling up to the brim with troops of all nationalities. Something big was going to happen, and happen soon.

Then in May, Harjinder received orders to board a ship for his move back to India. He was keen to get back. The news from the Russian front may have been good with the Germans being beaten and pushed back, but in India the news was shocking. The Japanese were on the offensive again, and this time, they had broken through. India had been invaded! The Japanese had crossed the border into the Indian state of Manipur, 440 miles North-East of Calcutta, between the Naga and Chin Hills. In what was originally an attempt to disrupt the allied planned offensive, the Japanese offensive went so well that they decided to push on and implement the long-held goal to take India! On the far Eastern border of India, the town of Imphal had proved a stubborn nut to crack, so the Japanese encircled the area, cutting off the Indian and British troops. On the 3rd April 1944, they had captured the ridge above the town of Kohima just a few miles from Imphal. They cut the main India-Burma road, and if they succeeded in pushing along this road, it would give them access to the town of Dimapur. Beyond there, they would be into the Brahmaputra valley, where the Bengal-Assam railway could be cut and the airfields used to supply China in the 'over-the-hump' operations could be taken. Once in that valley, the door would be open to the lower lying regions of India and her ports. The Indian and British troops were told to hold their position in Imphal and Kohima at all costs. The road behind them was cut, the Japanese held the high ground, and so started the Siege of Imphal and the Battle of Kohima.

Due to Arjan's Singh's persistence, No. 1 Squadron IAF were in a position to take the fight to the Japanese under his leadership. They led the air battle using their Hurricanes as dive bombers, and as fighters to escort the transport planes that brought in supplies to keep the inhabitants alive, and the troops fighting. Sitting in Marshal of the IAF, Arjan Singh's living room 70 years later, he talked very clearly about his time over Kohima. I wanted to know how many missions a day they were doing at the height of the battle, but I worded my question very badly. 'How often did you fly in Kohima?'

There was the pause, a smile, and once again the twinkle in the eye;

'We didn't get Sunday off. It was war, you know!'

Through April, May and into June, the battle continued. Some of the heaviest fighting took place at the North end of Kohima Ridge, around the Deputy Commissioner's bungalow and his tennis court. In what sounds like a hard fought match at Wimbledon, the reality of what became known as 'the Battle of the Tennis Court' was quite different. This tennis court became a no man's land, with the Japanese facing the defenders of Kohima, dug in on opposite sides, so close to each other that grenades were thrown between the trenches. By this point, Kohima resembled a battlefield from the World War I, with smashed trees, ruined buildings and the ground covered in craters.

Not only were there no Sundays off, but Squadron Leader Arjan Singh actually led No. 1 Squadron into combat several times a day, while the Indian and British troops assembled for the counter attack. Harjinder left the UK, bound for India as the battle reached its peak. The England he left behind was bursting at the seams with military personnel. June 1944 was to be a turning point in England and India.

Eleven

Spreading Wings, Clipping Wings

'You will not last long on this Station, Flying Officer Harjinder Singh.'

'You have a great part to play in India's future.'

As Harjinder travelled by boat to India, another armada of boats left the shores of the UK. It was the 6th June 1944, D-Day; when the British, American and Canadian forces fought their way ashore into France. In his Fighter Control Ship, organising all of the 104 different Fighter Squadrons operating over the French beaches, was Air Commodore Cecil Bouchier, the man who had first commanded the IAF with their 4 Wapitis. One of the Squadrons descending from the unseasonably heavy skies onto pre-arranged targets, was No. 268 Squadron, RAF. Normally, a new pilot would carry out weeks of training with a new Squadron, in a new aircraft, but Bouchier's apprentice, Karun Kanti 'Jumbo' Majumdar, DFC, flew his first operational mission over the deadly beaches of Normandy. In the same area, his countryman, Pilot Officer Sayanapuram Doraiswamy Thyagarajan, from Pondicherry, was flying daily strafing and bombing sorties in his Typhoon with No. 263 Squadron, RAF. Below them, in one of the landing craft on the angry, choppy sea, was Glen McBride. The Officer who'd destroyed Lashio as Harjinder and Jumbo retreated, had found his way from China to the UK, to become a part of RAF 101 Beach Squadron. He was the only man with a Royal Australian Air Force uniform to take part in D-Day. Jumbo and Glen both had their wish for action fulfilled, and they had it in spades.

Jumbo continued with No. 263 Squadron in to the next year, flying one of the mysterious aircraft types Harjinder had noticed lurking in the shadows, clouded in a veil of whispers, in the Hawker factory. The Typhoon, as the aircraft was known, is the aircraft that Jumbo took into the firestorm that was the Falaise Gap. They took their Typhoons down to low level, an area Jumbo thrived in, looking for German troop concentrations and military vehicles. Pierre Clostermann, one of the RAF's top-scoring aces, thought that the Typhoons were the stars of the RAF following the Normandy landings. He wrote; 'again and again, they rescued Allied units from situations of dire peril by taking on the German Panzers.'

The Typhoons' frantic attempt to minimise the terrifying effect of the German tanks on the Allied armour and infantry alike, attracted the full fury of the Wehrmacht's flak; Squadron losses in that world of flak, tracer rounds, explosions and obstacles, were horrific. Clostermann wrote of a whole Squadron diving into the attack, but only half, sometimes less, resurfacing. Jumbo not only survived this hell, but earned a bar for his DFC, the only Indian to do so, before he finally followed Harjinder's tracks and headed for home.

Pilot Officer Sayanapuram Doraiswamy Thyagarajan wasn't to make that journey home. He was killed on the 25th August 1944, the day Paris was liberated, shot down at La Lande St. Legere, where he is now buried.

The news of D-Day exploded all over the world with headlines heralding, very prematurely, the beginning of the end of the war. However, the pilots and crew of the IAF's No. 1 Squadron overhead Kohima, were a little pre-occupied to pay much attention to the blood spilt on the sands of France. The Battle of Kohima and the Siege of Imphal were nearing their own bloody climaxes. The order was to hold the position at all cost, to stop the Japanese pouring through the valley and into the open plains beyond. Hold they did, but at a terrible cost. D-Day rightly grabbed the world's headlines but it consigned this immense achievement of human endurance to a mere footnote of the World War II.

News on board the ship was patchy, but the information grabbed from the HF radio was all positive. The news from the combat zone was pouring in through the IAF grapevine. The Japanese had been stopped; did it mean that India was safe? The Japanese had actually been pushed back from

Kohima and Imphal by the very troops they'd tried to surround there, and on the 22nd June 1944, the leading troops of the British 2nd Division fought their way down the Valley. Constantly operating overhead were Arjan Singh's Hurricanes, flying in pairs, pinpointing and often "softening up" the enemy in front of them with their four lethal 20mm Hispano cannon. Those Hurricanes reported back on the historic meeting between the drawn faces of the 5th Indian Infantry Division breaking out from Imphal and the relieving force of the 2nd Division. The 79-day Siege of Imphal ended just 48 km South of Kohima. 79 days of continuous fighting in the shattered landscape, kept alive by the pilots above them. The unstoppable Japanese had been stopped through grim determination, by constant supply and attack from the air, and the most basic of desires; to survive.

Today, 60 years on, the green slopes around Kohima and Imphal are once again lush with trees, its terraced fields bow under the staggering weight of another season's bountiful yield. Garrison Hill is covered with ever spreading urban sprawl, but the scene of the Battle of the Tennis Court in Kohima, remains tranquil, now an Allied cemetery, it is untouched by time, a gentle reminder of the ravages wrecked on this haven by the war. The Epitaph carved on the memorial has become world-famous; the Kohima Epitaph.

'When you go home, tell them of us and say,
For their tomorrow, we gave our today.'

During the battle, the British and Indian forces had lost 4,064 men – dead, missing and wounded, in the most appalling of conditions. Against this, the Japanese had lost 5,764 men in battle casualties. India drew breath; but only those at the top knew how close it had been. If the Japanese had fought through to the more open ground beyond Kohima, the outcome might have been vastly different. The astounding execution of D-Day captured the imagination of the world, so the eyes of the world hardly rested on Kohima.

Lieutenant General Renya Mutaguchi's grandiose plans for taking Kohima, and, thereafter, India, were obliterated.

Harjinder's No. 1 Squadron IAF had been in the major part of the battle. Without the constant air attacks and air re-supply, the battle would have been lost. Admiral Lord Louis Mountbatten, Supreme Commander of all Allied Forces in South-East Asia, flew into Imphal to meet up with

No. 1 Squadron. In dramatic fashion, he climbed onto the wing of Arjan Singh's Hurricane to give a speech to the assembled personnel. When he jumped down, a hollow square was formed by the men, and Arjan Singh was called forward. Mountbatten pinned the Distinguished Flying Cross (DFC) medal on to the chest of Squadron Leader Arjan Singh's working jungle uniform, which he was still wearing, ready to fly again later that day. This was only the beginning for No. 1 Squadron, as they continued chasing the Japanese back through Burma until Arjan and his men had been on operations for a continuous, record-breaking, 14 months. A British military publication, 'An Account of the Air Operations in South-East Asia', called No. 1 Squadron; 'outstanding amongst all the Allied Squadrons in South-East Asia for its fighter reconnaissance work and its high standard of aircraft maintenance.'

The Officer Commanding the Air Group went even further; 'Ground crew have set a record for serviceability of aircraft, averaging 99 per cent, which is second to none in any Air Force in the world.'

The ethos cultivated by Harjinder obviously continued throughout the wartime operations of the engineers. The pilots had the foundations laid by Jumbo, and cultivated by Arjan Singh. However, that reputation, forged in war, was at great an expense of the 20 pilots who originally went with Arjan Singh in No. 1 Squadron to Imphal, only 4 came back. Of them two, B.R. Reddy, and Nanda Kariappa, were killed shortly thereafter in Civil aircraft crashes. It was a bloody time to be involved in aviation.

However, for Harjinder, it was not the long yearned-for return to No. 1 Squadron and combat operations in Burma. In July 1944, he was posted to Kohat, his old stomping ground in the lawless North-West Frontier, but it was not the Royal Air Force Station Kohat he had left. It was now called Indian Air Force Station, Kohat. All air operations against the tribal warriors had been handed over to the IAF, with the RAF personnel now working for the IAF. Were the tribes going to stop 'being troublesome', just because a World War was on? Quite the contrary! Understandably, the tribes attempted to take advantage of the British pre-occupation with the war. And so, it was back to policing the North-Eastern wasteland from age-old forts, using the basic, rocky, dirt landing strips; back to the barren brown landscape and back in the old atmosphere of rivalry and obstructionism from the increasingly reluctant RAF personnel based in India. Here, Harjinder still found some examples of the British at their worst.

On arriving at Indian Air Force Station Kohat, with its stunning backdrop of mountains, like enormous brown shards of glass thrust into the ground, Harjinder was greeted by the Station Commander. It was not only a reunion with harsh conditions, but it was also a reunion with the now Wing Commander, Subroto Mukerjee, in that landscape so well-known to the both of them. However, their first exchange about Kohat was not one he had expected. Harjinder's opinion of the British had changed following his time in the UK; the IAF had more than proved how capable they were, and the war was turning in the Allied's favour on all fronts, but, however, back here in the North-West Frontier, it seemed that little had changed. Mukerjee was the Station Commander, technically in-charge of the whole base, but Harjinder was the only other Indian in the Wing Headquarters. All the others were British. Mukerjee suspected that instead of working for, and with him, they were all actually reporting directly to the Group Headquarters at Peshawar. They seemed to be making decisions over his head, circumventing him and leaving him out of the policy-making. Mukerjee's parting comment on that first meeting was not encouraging; 'So, Harjinder, watch your anti-British talk. What you do will reflect not only on you, but also on my capability as an Indian Station Commander and, therefore, the future of the IAF.'

Harjinder hated this defeatist attitude; he always tackled issues head on, leaving the politics to others. He did, however, promise Mukerjee that he would be tactful. Harjinder; tactful? How long do you think Harjinder could be tactful?

Squadron Leader Kennenworthy was responsible for that promise lasting for less than one day. Kennenworthy was actually the Station Adjutant Officer, there to sort out the day-to-day running of the Station for Mukerjee, but he had elevated himself into the self-proclaimed position of 'Deputy Station Commander'.

The next morning, Harjinder went to see Mukerjee in his office. He found Kennenworthy standing in front of the Commander's desk, one foot on a chair and his hands clasping his knee, in an informal, patronising, attitude. When Kennenworthy walked out of the office with a casual 'Righty-ho' tossed over his shoulder, Harjinder's blood was boiling. 'Sir, this officer's manners are preposterous. If *we* do not put the British Officers in their correct place, who else will?'

Mukerjee's mild and conciliatory tones didn't satisfy Harjinder, so he went straight into Kennenworthy's office. He stood outside for a moment to compose himself, then deliberately sauntered in, placed his foot on a vacant chair, and took up the pose. At once, Kennenworthy shouted, 'Flying Officer Harjinder Singh, stand to attention before a Senior Officer. Where the hell did you learn this un-officer-like behaviour?'

You can see where Harjinder was going with this!

'Squadron Leader Kennenworthy, I am an officer always willing to learn from his seniors. You taught me only a few minutes ago how to stand in a Senior Officer's office.'

With that he walked out without saluting, as Kennenworthy exploded; 'I shall put you under close arrest.'

Over his shoulder Harjinder retorted, 'Righty-ho!'

Seconds later, Harjinder was summoned into the Commander's office where Mukerjee tried his utmost to convince Harjinder to demonstrate the respect for an Officer of a higher rank. Harjinder would not relent, 'If a British Officer does not respect his Indian Commanding Officer, I would rather face a Court Martial and give him his dues in his turn.'

Mukerjee was not convinced, and looked miserable, knowing that his hitherto calm life was at an end. Luckily, Kennenworthy decided to stomach the insult, rather than make an issue of it this time.

Kohat; welcome to Harjinder Singh!

Naturally, that was not an end to it. Every Saturday, the Station used to carry out a parade drill, but Harjinder noticed that the British Officers of Station Headquarters did not attend the parade. Harjinder decided to keep away too. He knew full well that it would be noted, and trouble would ensue. Sure enough, it was the self-appointed Deputy Station Commander, Kennenworthy, who once again met him the following morning and asked, 'Why were you not on parade when all other IAF Officers were there?'

Harjinder was ready and waiting, and, pulling himself up to his full height, he replied, 'Why were you not on parade as well as the others? Is it a Station Parade or is it confined only to Indian Air Force personnel? Moreover, my predecessor, the British Station Engineer Officer, never attended it either (*a guess from Harjinder, but a correct one*).'

Kennenworthy's face turned an interesting shade of red. 'You will not last long on this Station, Flying Officer Harjinder Singh', and with that, he stalked away fuming.

Kennenworthy was in Harjinder's office the next morning, looking for revenge. 'Why did you drive in through the Aerodrome Gate instead of the Main Gate? Don't you know your Standing Orders?'

Harjinder looked up from his desk; 'Because it leads straight into my office and I save half a mile that way. I have indeed not read the Standing Orders, for the simple reason that there aren't any.'

Kennenworthy went out of his way to never cross paths with Harjinder again. To give him a modicum of credit, he did take what Harjinder said on board. After a month of serious hard work he produced, the first ever, Kohat Station Standing Orders, including orders prohibiting the use of the Aerodrome Gate. Was Kennenworthy motivated a sense of duty or revenge?

Harjinder was aware that these clashes were petty and ridiculous when, in the wider world, people were fighting, and dying. The Germans troops were being pushed back towards the borders of Germany, and the IAF were helping to push the Japanese back, through Burma. There was now an end in sight to the war, so perhaps, this was reflected through the attitude of some of the British in India. It had been a long, hard, fight, and the British were war-weary, longed for home, and for a normal life; whatever 'normal' would now mean. It was now clear that the Brits on the Station considered Harjinder to be a 'bolshie', and who can blame them, when only a few years earlier, the IAF was openly discussed at the most senior levels by the British in India, as being inferior and incapable.

Trouble continued when he investigated why his phone was never being routed through the exchange. When summoned, the Sergeant in-charge casually wandered into Harjinder's office and informed him, 'I have strict instructions from the Station Signals Officer not to worry about what you may, or may not, wish to do.'

Harjinder gave the Sergeant a piece of his mind and wanted to take it further, but once again, Mukerjee counselled patience and forbearance, believing that discretion was the better part of valour. Harjinder felt let down by Mukerjee. Was this really an Indian Station, or just a puppet show?

The telephone incident escalated when the Station Signals Officer, Flight Lieutenant Bruce, followed the Sergeant's lead by wandering into Harjinder's office without the customary formalities. 'What do you mean by threatening a Sergeant of my Section? You must not forget that they are British Airmen of the Royal Air Force.'

Harjinder had anger, but mixed in with amusement, at this comment. He assumed that this Officer must be new in country, and so, pointed out, for his benefit, that a King's Commissioned Officer, irrespective of his nationality, exercised authority over all ranks working under him.

Bruce wasn't new; 'I am a regular Royal Air Force Officer, and I will not tolerate any Indians bossing it over my Airmen.'

Harjinder felt his amusement drain away, replaced by anger rising from the pit of his stomach. He stood, and once again pulled himself up to his full height like a cobra about to strike; 'I have worked with RAF Officers in peacetime, and seen them at war, here, and in England. You are a very poor copy of an Officer of the RAF. Why did you not salute when you entered my office?'

'Salute you! I feel like punching your nose.'

That did it! Harjinder strode over to him so they were face to face, a few paces apart:

'I give you exactly one second to get out of my sight, or it is *I* who will punch *your* nose.'

Instead of turning tail, Bruce menacingly advanced one pace closer. For the first, and only, time in Harjinder's life as an officer, he put to good use the noble art of boxing, taught to him by Henry Runganadhan at Drigh Road. His fist shot up from his side, taking the Officer completely by surprise. He had told Bruce the target, and the target was duly struck. His nose bleeding, Bruce ran out of the office saying, 'I will see you before the Station Commander.'

This example of inter-service love and harmony could easily have proved the undoing of Harjinder's career, and a very black mark against the IAF. Harjinder knew he had done wrong and saw that the only way to limit the damage would be to avoid the fast-approaching political explosion. He quickly rang through to Mukerjee; Harjinder's phone was working for a change!

'Sir, I have just had a dust-up with the Station Signals Officer. His nose is bleeding and he is walking, over to see you. Please leave your office immediately to save yourself the embarrassment.'

Naturally, Mukerjee was most disturbed, but he knew what was good for all, and so he got up and left.

On finding the Commanding Officer out, Bruce barged into the Adjutant's office, and there, met Flying Officer Bose, the Orderly Officer for the day. When he told Bose what had happened, Bose 'refused' to see the blood. He patted the Signals Officer on the back and said; 'There! There! You must have been to a late party last night. You are all right. I can't see any blood on your nose.'

Bruce had nowhere to go, and you would like to think that he could see the fault of his comments, but that does, alas, seem doubtful. He reported sick and applied for two weeks leave, using the time to get posted to Air Headquarters. One can only imagine the stories he told around the Corridors of Power about the 'useless Foreign Officers'. Back at Kohat, Harjinder received a tongue-lashing of biblical proportions, and quite rightly so. Harjinder knew that he deserved it, and felt that he had let Mukerjee down. However, no British Officer ever tried to elevate himself above the Indian Officers at Kohat after the boxing lesson. He had won a small battle, but Harjinder was drained, disheartened, and at the end of his tether.

Matters in Kohat seemed to go from bad to worse. The good news from Europe, with the Germans pushed out of Greece, the Soviets entering Yugoslavia, and Strasbourg falling, was of little consolation in the Badlands of the North-West Frontier. Harjinder was to encounter a challenge that would take his mind off the internal conflict, and it would involve the tea urns at full pressure again. On the 15th November 1944, Flying Officer Akhtar, of No. 3 Squadron IAF, slowed his Hurricane down, dropping the flaps and undercarriage, ready to land. He still had too much speed as he crossed the airfield fence, so, instead of touching down, he floated just above the runway, the camouflaged fighter still not ready to give up its lift and land. Even with the canopy slid back for landing, you can't see around the nose of a Hurricane. With his peripheral vison, Akhtar saw the runway edges disappearing at speed on either side, but he seemed determined to land from this approach. There was no burst from the engine to take the Hurricane back into the air for another attempt, just runway distance being eaten up very quickly as the speed slowly bled away. When the wheels finally touched down, kicking up a spurt of dust from the runway, he had no chance to stop before crossing the track that ran around the perimeter beyond. On that track was transport from another age, unchanged for centuries, a rough wooden cart being pulled by a bullock. The modern world and ancient world collided. The poor beast of burden didn't have a chance as the Hurricane slammed into it. The death of the ox saved Akhtar, slowing his machine, before it went on to hit the steel perimeter fence. Akhtar was alive but the aircraft was badly damaged, looking like a scene from a horror movie, with bullock blood and flesh draped over it. The cart was shattered, tucked underneath the aircraft belly.

The RAF pilots faced no charges if a machine was repaired within four days, no matter what the damage, so Harjinder stepped forward to once again save the reputation of his pilots. The usual high pressure repair routine was activated, with the men working day and night, in three shifts, powered by steaming hot tea. By 10:00 hours on the 18th November 1944, the bloodied, battered Hurricane was repaired, cleaned, and back on its wheels; all that was needed was a pilot. There was an army exercise on about 30 miles outside Kohat, where Mukerjee and Squadron Leader Prithipal Singh had gone to participate, and talk Army/Air Force cooperation. It was Prithipal who, as a young Pilot Officer, had crashed his Wapiti in Sandeman, sitting in the wreck with the engine still running.

So D.S. 'Dipi' Majithia, the Flight Commander, stepped up, with a plan to fly low enough for the number on the side of the aircraft to been seen by the Station, and the Squadron, Commander. It was a simple idea. When the senior officers saw the Hurricane flying within the 4-day time window, the damage would not have gone on record, and Akhtar would be saved. The plan was a good one except… Dipi really, really enjoyed low flying. After circling overhead to get their initial attention, he disappeared out of sight, pushing the spade grip on the control column forward to take his solid Hurricane down to tree top level. Jinking left and right around the obstacles, he came screaming in. The senior officers were his target, and he headed straight for them as he eased even lower. They were forced to throw themselves to the ground, believing that their heads were in danger of being removed by the thrashing propeller, a not-unfounded belief. Mukerjee had certainly seen the Hurricane's LD 486 side number from his position spread-eagled on the floor! Mukerjee's message was not one of congratulations, but instructions to arrest the pilot. Poor Dipi! Harjinder admitted he did not have the moral courage to face Dipi, he was only trying to save the other pilot's career, and the good name of the IAF. Harjinder had done his magic with the spanner, and now he did his magic with Mukerjee. It took a while for Harjinder to soothe his commander, but he finally talked him out of arresting Dipi. The incident could not be kept quiet though, and so it was not long before the period of grace following a crash was reduced from four days to two. That did not stop Harjinder, of course. Even within this new time limit, they repaired every crash that occurred at Kohat. Two days was enough to replace an engine, fit a new wing, or replace a propeller. Eventually, the IAF Squadron received the trophy for the most accident-free Squadron in India!

Harjinder and Subroto Mukerjee had different approaches to achieving the long-term goal of an independent IAF. Mukerjee was more political, and therefore, often more tolerant; concerned that pushing too hard would result in the loss of his command, which would mean an end to their progress. In comparison, Harjinder was more in-your-face and uncompromising. Mukerjee was constantly reprimanding Harjinder in private for his 'bloody-mindedness', an accusation he could not deny. When Harjinder found out that Field Marshal Auchinleck was personally planning to invest him with his MBE medal, he told Mukerjee he would return it, as it was a political, and not a military decoration. Harjinder had been thrilled at first with his MBE, but his opinion changed when he heard of another officer being awarded the same decoration. Harjinder considered this man a crook with no outstanding service, and so it devalued the award in his mind. As usual, Subroto talked him out of his resolve by saying that his action would be considered as an insult to the King Emperor and would affect Indianisation.

'All our efforts and sufferings of the past eleven years will have been in vain.'

Harjinder avoided the issue by taking leave when the Field Marshal visited, an action that wouldn't have been missed by Auchinleck, but the MBE remained in place. Later in his career, when Harjinder returned to England, he realised just how much the respect the MBE commanded. In several shops, still under supply restrictions, he would get the standard 'not in stock' reply to his requests. When they spotted the distinctive red ribbon on his uniform tunic they would apologise for not initially seeing he was a Member of the Order, and the under-the-counter supplies would appear. He came to be very proud of his MBE, even if it was not a passport to heaven, and he continued to use the letters after his name throughout his life as a matter of principle, even when the Government of the Independent India ordered the removal of these awards because they were viewed as part of the old Raj.

However, back in Kohat, the issues with the RAF continued.

While Mukerjee and Harjinder's history went back to the earliest days of the IAF, their personal relationship became even stronger now that they were brother officers. Even though Harjinder held Mukerjee in high regard, they were two very different individuals – this was perhaps the wrong time in the history of the IAF for a fruitful partnership to develop between these two men.

Harjinder felt that he could no longer take this tip-toe approach, so he took the difficult step to appeal for a posting to Lahore on compassionate grounds, not entirely an untruth, as his wife had still not recovered completely from her surgery. Mukerjee forwarded the application with a strong recommendation, making no bones about his sense of relief at being rid of a black sheep, at what he saw as a delicate time for the IAF. Harjinder wrote; 'I can't say I blame him; he was always the mild, middle-of-the-road professional. Who knows, perhaps he was the one who was wiser. But wisdom or no, I had had enough of pandering to the British Officers. I had seen them in England; the RAF, the Army and the civilian. There they were a sterling people. But only the dregs seemed to come out to India; either that or they come here and then sink to the bottom as dregs.'

So it would seem strange that later, Harjinder would write of the next twelve months in Kohat as the happiest of his service career. That was because the day after requesting his posting, a signal arrived from Air Headquarters announcing a change at Kohat. Mukerjee was moved further up the chain. His tip-toe approach had been successful, for both him, and the IAF base.

His move up made room for Aspy Engineer to take over as the new Officer Commanding, Kohat. Engineer, one of Bouchier's original musketeers from the IAF's early days, the pioneering 17-year-old who won the Aga Khan trophy for his solo flight, was a very different man from Mukerjee. Harjinder 'jumped with joy, unashamedly'. He promptly withdrew his application, and life changed for the better.

Aspy Engineer took over the Command in the middle of December 1944. This officer's reputation had travelled ahead of him, so much so that the RAF officers, with a look of fear in their eyes, started asking Harjinder what was he like; how strict was he? All the other IAF officers took malicious pleasure in spreading exaggerated stories about the tyrant that was Aspy Engineer. Offices were soon being tidied up, and backlogs cleared. The station was getting additional coats of whitewash paint, and there was a whiff of fear everywhere. Even Kennenworthy started paying Harjinder courtesy, with fear in his eyes, if not friendliness. When Harjinder tried to paint a realistic picture of the man, he was not readily

believed, as all seemed to think that he was trying to lull them into a false
sense of security. Harjinder did have disagreements with Aspy Engineer
later in their careers, and much was made of it. However, Harjinder
described Aspy; 'as the finest pilot I had ever come across, and I had come
across many, both in the IAF and the RAF. I had never seen him making a
heavy landing. He was a very, very, strict disciplinarian and he would not
tolerate a "no" to any of his orders.'

Aspy Engineer soon made his presence felt in Kohat. He didn't tread
softly like Mukerjee. He was in charge, and all those around would
serve under him as per the recognised chain of command. This was not
management by committee. Ideas and suggestions were listened to, and
deliberated, but Aspy would make the final decisions. He was of the
same mould as Harjinder, and upsetting the norm was fine with him.
He particularly wished to explore ways by which they could increase the
efficiency of the Station. He planned a unified servicing/maintenance
system, which suited Harjinder, and the two of them took to the task
with zeal.

Working with Aspy was a dream come true for Harjinder but his fate
was telling him something.

The combat role in the North-West Frontier had provided Harjinder
and Aspy with a focus to keep the Squadron sharp, but it also served to
keep them distracted, as they both felt that the war was being won without
them. The IAF was fully involved in the closing scenes of the World War
II, now flying Spitfires, as they continued the big push back through Asia
that had begun in Kohima. During the first two months of 1945, the news
reels gushed with the successes in Europe, with films of troops heading
for Berlin. The Americans were taking island after island in the Pacific,
although the terrible cost of lives on both sides wasn't being released to
the public.

Jumbo Majumdar visited Kohat with stories of flying the state-of-the-
art Typhoon aircraft in operations over Europe, but also of the terrible cost
in lives. He sported the bar to the DFC medal on his uniform and his rank
stripes showed him to be back at his original rank of Wing Commander,
but it was clear that the events in Europe had had a deep effect on him. He
should have been destined for a desk job, but that was not for Jumbo. As
the darling of the IAF he was thrust, against his will, into the public eye
with lectures and broadcasts all over India. This took him away from the
family that he had missed so much during his time in Europe. There was

no time to experience some sort of normal life, to relax after such intense experiences. Jumbo was famous, appearing in a Life Magazine article that listed him as one of the twelve best pilots in all the Allied Air Forces. The IAF wanted to cash in on his fame, to encourage more recruitment, and so he was to be the Officer in Charge of the newly formed 'Display Flight'. They were to fly some of the Hurricane aircraft that were being discarded by the front-line Squadrons, as they re-equipped with the sleek Spitfires. The Hurricane, that had seemed so modern when they first took delivery of them after the Lysander, now seemed very old and dated next to the much developed Spitfire.

The start of what came to be known as 'Jumbo's Circus' was not a good one. Prithipal Singh, who owed Harjinder his career after the Wapiti debacle, who we last perceived ducking for cover after the assault of Dipi's low flypast, was now back under Jumbo. On the second day of training, he took a Hurricane up to practice his part of the Jumbo Circus display.

The report soon came of a crash nearby. Jumbo grabbed a vehicle and headed up to the telltale black, oily, spiralling smoke. He found his close friend scattered about the hillside 'like butcher's meat'. Karun had lost squadron friends in Europe but the loss of Prithipal Singh hit him hard. His demeanour changed and his usual zeal for all things IAF began to wane. The situation worsened with a further two accidents in rapid succession and suddenly, the 'Circus' seemed jinxed, and Jumbo seemed to feel tired of life in general.

The show must go on, and so the Display Flight, with their mascot commander, moved around India, drawing the crowds in their thousands. The public had spent five years hearing about the daring exploits of their Air Force, but here were the Hurricanes up close, with that beautiful, sighing-howling Merlin engine noise as they swooped overhead. When they arrived at Lahore to display to some old friends from the Chinese Air Force, stationed nearby at Walton, Harjinder found an excuse to join them for their display. Also arriving at the airfield on that day was Wing Commander Arjan Singh DFC. His desk job had been driving him mad, and his stress relief of flying a Harvard down Delhi Golf Course at exceedingly low level had produced a reprimand, followed a week later, with a posting to Jumbo's Display Flight!

Harjinder watched the display by the team. It was an impressive spectacle, and he could see how the general public were lapping it up, but he was concerned when he saw one of the undercarriage legs of these tired, 'old' aircraft half pop out from the retracted position, when it was still taking part in the display. Harjinder knew the Hurricane well, and his diagnosis was that the up-lock pin in the wing, that held the wheels in the 'up' position, was worn, so he tackled Jumbo about the condition of these aircraft. It was fine as a fighter taking on the Germans, or bombing the Japanese in Burma, but doing aerobatics, low level, in effectively discarded planes, wasn't a good idea, in his view. Even Mrs Majumdar showed uncharacteristic concern when she heard of Harjinder's reservations, so she asked him to try speaking with Jumbo again. The next morning was the 17th February 1945, an important day at the Majumdar household. Jumbo's son, Bambi, turned two that day, and Jumbo had been given explicit instructions to be home in time for the party.

When Harjinder got the chance in the morning to talk with Jumbo, he merely replied that if all senior officers took to 'safe' flying, the younger officers would lose respect for their elders. There was time enough for him to be chair-borne later in his career. He added; 'Harjinder, promise me that you will propagate the spirit of flying even if I get killed in the next flight.'

Jumbo did another couple of unusual things that morning. He only ordered 10 meals for lunch even though there were 11 Officers on the team. As they walked to their aircraft, he handed over the small soft toy to another pilot saying, 'It's for Bambi. Take it back with you.'

As Jumbo pulled the Hurricane's nose up into a loop, the smooth lines of the underside were rudely interrupted as one undercarriage leg and wheel unlocked completely. This time, it didn't just move out a few inches, but snapped out, fully extended, into the airflow. Who knows if there was a red light that came on in the cockpit to show an unlocked undercarriage leg, but the airspeed indicator would have started to move rapidly anti-clockwise. The extra drag on the aircraft destroyed the energy gained in the previous dive, and the momentum was quickly draining away. In a horrific replay of the RAF pilot over Calcutta three years earlier, Jumbo was left in an aircraft with not enough speed to complete the loop, and not enough height to gain more energy, or speed. When Jumbo still had the nose pointing vertically up, the final energy was being expended; the heavy engine in the nose came swinging down, pointing it directly at the ground. The aircraft yawed as it swung down so the Hurricane flicked into a spin. In front of Harjinder's eyes, Jumbo's aircraft rotated into the ground. He stared at the burning crumpled wreckage that was the funeral pyre of his hero, his role model, his closest friend.

When Harjinder reached the scene of the crash, he picked up the metal remnants of Jumbo's flying goggles and his harness locking-pin, from the burnt-out debris. He took a solemn oath at the site to carry out his friend's last wish as long as he lived. Certainly, much of his subsequent enthusiasm for the Service, his single-minded zeal to promote the cause of flying, aircraft maintenance and aircraft manufacture, stemmed from his long and memorable friendship with Karun Kanti 'Jumbo' Majumdar DFC and bar, that good-looking, larger-than-life man, and aviator par excellence. In Harjinder's meticulously kept diary, there was absolutely no mention of Jumbo's death. Was it disbelief that he was gone, or an inability to accept the fact? It was only when he subsequently wrote an obituary about Jumbo that we know that he was there, he saw it, and that a part of him died that day.

Bambi Majumdar was getting tired, so the two candles on his birthday cake were lit. He had already been tucked into bed when four pilots arrived, ashen-faced, at the door. Jumbo would not be coming that evening, but the bunny soft toy did. It is still with Bambi in his house in the UK.

Arjan Singh stepped into Jumbo's shoes to lead the Display Flight, replacing the man who was surely destined to be the first Chief of the Indian Air Force. What would Jumbo have made of the announcement a month later, on 12th March 1945? A signal from the Viceroy was issued informing the world that the IAF would now become the Royal Indian Air Force. The signal recognised the massive growth of the IAF from 200 people at the start of the war, to 27,000 as the war drew to an end. Jumbo's vision had been achieved with the No. 10 IAF Squadron being formed. The Viceroy continued, 'Your squadrons engaged against the Japanese in Burma have done splendid work and earned the confidence and respect of all. Now take your place as one of the tried fighting services of India and the British Commonwealth.' The final comment was the most telling one; 'You have a great part to play in India's future.' That future probably came much sooner than even the Viceroy could have anticipated.

As the months clicked over, the end was finally in sight, but there was still plenty more blood to be shed. The news of Hitler's death on 30th April 1945, was greeted with more relief than celebration. Victory in Europe, or VE Day, on 8th May 1945, was naturally welcome, but the Japanese were still fighting viciously, and the RIAF Spitfires were still in action forcing them out of Burma. The final chapter promised to involve huge losses, on both sides, when the inevitable invasion of the Japanese mainland kicked off. All Japanese citizens were ordered to carry a weapon at all times, if even just a stick, to be ready for that invasion. The Indian trainee pilot enlisted in the Azad Hind Fauj, the young Ramesh Sakharam Benegal, who Harjinder had passed in the retreat from Burma, was billeted in his Japanese training establishment outside Tokyo. He saw the fire-bombing of that city, which resulted in the death of 100,000 people, but still the Emperor had decreed that there would be no surrender. Every adult would fight to the death when the invasion came. However, the Emperor knew nothing about the most secret of American plans – Project Manhattan. On the 6th August 1945, the first atomic bomb was dropped on Hiroshima. On the 9th August, the city of Kokura was to follow Hiroshima. In one of those twists of fate that are difficult to comprehend, the people of Kokura survived because of the most basic of Mother Nature's offerings; clouds. The bomb aimer had orders not to release his bombs without actual sight of the city, and so, Kokura was saved. Nagasaki was the alternative target; a small break in the cloud sealed the future of that city. With two cities devastated, and the prospect of many more, the Emperor had no option. The Royal Indian Air Force, carried out the last bombing sortie on 11th August, destroying a command post, but just three days later, the unconditional surrender came. The 15th August 1945, was officially Victory in Japan, or VJ Day. The World War II had come to an end.

On the 23rd August, the Senior Air Force Officer in Rangoon received a radio message that representatives of the Japanese forces in South-East Asia wished to come to the city to surrender. At 1400 hours, on the 26th August 1945, the Japanese aircraft, painted white on the insistence of the Allied Commander, were met overhead Rangoon by a Squadron of Spitfires including two from No. 8 Squadron IAF. One of the escorting pilots was Pilot Officer Dougie King-Lee, now Air Marshal King-Lee, settled in Bangalore. At Rangoon's Mingaladon airfield, Lieutenant General Numata surrendered to Air Vice-Marshal Cecil Bouchier. The man who had started the IAF, with Harjinder as one of his Sepoys, took the surrender. The victory was achieved in part by the IAF, and by 'his' No. 1 Squadron.

When Burma fell in 1941, the Government of Burma, and the recently escaped British Governor of Burma, Sir Reginald Dorman-Smith, had taken up residence in the beautiful mountain retreat of Simla, the very same place where the IAF had been gazetted. The town had long been the Summer Capital of British India, a place for the British Government Officials to escape the Delhi heat. Fashioned to resemble a hamlet in Sussex, it seemed like a little bit of home, combined with the best of India.

Motor vehicles were banned in Simla, so rickshaws the preferred mode of transport. These were not the small two-seater rickshaws seen throughout India, but grand, ornate affairs pulled by four men, a fifth running alongside, as relief. Men in the uniform of their employer pulled these rickshaws, many bearing a coat of arms proudly on the side, passed the tea shops of the main broad Mall. However, it was time for the Burmese Government to leave their tranquil haven in the shadow of the Himalayas and take back the reigns at Rangoon. Mr Nanda owned the Imperial Rickshaw Works, turning out these fine machines for the Viceroy himself. His son and daughter-in-law were both practising doctors in Simla. Mrs Nanda was the first woman permitted by the British to practise as a Doctor, and had been appointed Chief Medical Officer to the Burmese. They developed such great relations with the Burmese that the head of the government in exile, Sithu U Tin, invited them to shift to Rangoon and set up a practice. Driven by their love for Simla, and for India, they decided to stay, a decision that would, unwittingly, affect Harjinder's story as well. One son of Simla would not be returning home. Wing Commander Guy Gibson VC, the leader of the famous Dambuster raid, killed in his Mosquito over the Netherlands.

The world took a huge, collective, sigh of relief as the official end of the war unfolded, but back at Kohat, there were still operational duties to be done. Harjinder and Aspy felt that they'd missed the end of the war but they were still fighting their own small war; little had changed in Kohat since 1939. It was now No. 6 Squadron, RIAF, with their Hurricanes who were posted in. If the new Squadron Commanding Officer thought that he could stretch his wings in his new role, he was sadly mistaken. It was 'Jangoo' Engineer, Aspy's younger brother. If Aspy had high standard of discipline for IAF, and RAF alike, he had impossible standards where his own brother was concerned. Poor Jangoo was chased from pillar to post as Aspy watched him like a hawk, and pounced on him for the slightest misdemeanour. One afternoon, there was a knock at Harjinder's door and there was Jangoo Engineer standing in his dressing gown. He put a finger on his lips for silence and was asked to come in. He whispered,

'Harjinder, no one must know about my visit, least of all, my brother. Flying Officer Jolly has just force-landed 40 miles West of Kohat near a river bed. The cause, as usual, was that he failed to switch to the main fuel tank. But we must save him. The poor chap is worried enough as it is because of domestic anxieties. No one knows about the accident yet; you must recover the aircraft and repair it. Don't say "no", please.'

The old Hurricanes still being used in the region had a snag that had existed throughout their long sterling service. If the pilot forgot to switch to the main fuel tanks after the takeoff, the engine would cut after 45 minutes of flying. When that happened, all attempts to restart the engine in the air were usually in vain, and a number of aircraft saw an untimely end that way. Air Headquarters issued an order that any pilot force-landing a Hurricane within 45 minutes of takeoff would be court martialled. One would hope that the jury would at least check to see if fuel had any part in the accident, otherwise it does seem a little harsh!

Harjinder assured Jangoo that he would not report the forced landing, but that he felt bound to inform the Station Commander. Jangoo's reply was brief and mournful, 'Impossible! I know my brother better than you do. Unfortunately, it happens to be one of my aircraft. He will never agree.'

Harjinder's heart fell through his boots when he saw one of the sycophantic Squadron Leaders at Aspy Engineer's bungalow. Harjinder spoke with Aspy about the incident. His response was understandable, 'How can you undertake such a mad thing, Harjinder? Don't you know that ever since I have arrived here the British Officers are waiting for a chance to report me to Group Headquarters? They find themselves under a hard taskmaster who does not allow them special privileges just because they are RAF. I don't let them budge an inch. So how can I allow this?'

Naturally, the Squadron Leader Flying nodded along, like a lively puppy. Harjinder kept his temper under control and asked to be alone with Aspy before explaining to him, 'If anyone is going to be court martialled, it will have to be me. I have promised the pilots that as long as I am present on a Station, no IAF pilot will be court martialled, not if I can repair the aircraft. This one I certainly can (*brave since he had not actually seen it!*). Today is a Sunday. No British Officer will see the crashed aircraft being towed into the camp. We have to do this, not just to save the officer, but as a matter of IAF pride.'

It must have touched a nerve, because, after what seemed like an eternity holding Harjinder's gaze, the normally unyielding Aspy gave him the go-ahead and agreed to take the responsibility, should he fail. Aspy gave Harjinder 24 hours, but let him know he would have his hide before he himself was dragged off to face a court martial.

Harjinder put a team together and headed straight out, without even stopping for tea. But of course, the hangar would have been issued strict instructions to get the brew ready once they returned! The area of the crash was surrounded by hills. The tribesmen who lurked in those hills were known to appear at a crash site to collect the ammunition and the guns. Harjinder was so intent on not drawing the attention of the British, he left without an armed escort; their only defence was crossed fingers. When Harjinder was told to stop the vehicle because they had arrived at the crash site, he thought there was some mistake. He looked at the deep and sandy riverbed between them and the damaged wreck with horror. He looked up at the hill sides where it was easy to imagine tribesmen shuffling into position, making him feel suddenly naked and wanting that armed escort, RAF or not. He shook that thought from his mind, and started to negotiate the riverbed, just to get a closer look at the damaged Hurricane. Suffice it to say that the prognosis did not look very good. The riverbed showed the furrows the powerless Hurricane had made on its violent, unscheduled stop. The wings had taken a very savage blow and the bolts attaching them to the fuselage had been bent. Harjinder and team had only managed to dismantle one wing as the sun set. To add to his discomfit, Aspy also arrived in his staff car to see if he was looking into the face of a court martial.

'Sir, it will be only five minutes more before the bolts come off', was repeated time and again as the hammers pounded against the bolts. Amazingly these repeated thunderclaps of hammer on metal, echoing off the valley sides, didn't bring any tribesmen. As that fear subsided, Harjinder started to see the darkness as his friend – he could sneak the wreck away from this godforsaken corner of the valley and back to base, right under the noses of the sleeping RAF. At 0130 the bolts finally gave up their fight and they all paused briefly to catch their breath and gather their thoughts. The men had taken turns at beating the bolts with the hammer, but now it was all hands to the pumps. They gathered around each wing, in turn, to push them across the river bed. When it was time to move the grubby fuselage, the aircraft's design came to their rescue. The wings of the Hurricane bolt on to a centre wing section, upon which sits the fuselage. The wheels are fixed to this 9 foot-wide centre section, so the men could push, heave, cajole and swear at the fuselage, get it over the river bed on its own wheels and then on to the waiting lorry. Even Aspy had to get his hands dirty, pushing with the rest of them, to get this final job done. It was four in the morning when the team stole back to base with aircraft parts crudely covered with tarpaulins. No thought to sleep, it was straight to work. Breakfast, lunch and dinner were taken in the hangar, and those in shifts, too. The following morning, the herculean task of repairing the wings was complete, so along came Flying Officer Sharma to do his preflight inspection. For once, Harjinder had committed a basic error. He had assumed too much. He had assumed the fuselage, being a rugged and strong structure would be fine, and had not given it more than a glance in the darkened river bed. Sharma pointed out the creasing and crinkles in the fuselage fabric behind the cockpit. Now, in the light, with the dust removed, it was easy to see that the fuselage was bent. The damage illustrated that Flying Officer Jolly could thank the strength of the Hurricane's construction for saving him a broken back, but it did also seemed to imply that all the efforts to save his career had been in vain.

So, did Harjinder give in – Never! Think. Think. Think. They could never carry out the complex repairs to the fuselage. This was no more than junk. Junk! That was the answer. There was a Hurricane in the salvage yard and Harjinder recalled that the fuselage was OK, albeit stripped of everything. He immediately sent for it and a sense of hope, or was that relief, spread over him as he made his inspection and realised that it was serviceable. The engine, wings and every other fitting from the original aircraft's fuselage was transferred across into the spare. By mid-day, the mass of men stood back – the aircraft was ready. Sharma was summoned again, and the sight of his heels lifting off the ground, saved both Jolly's and Aspy's careers, along with the IAF's reputation.

Jolly's Hurricane was not the only crash. Several of the new young guns caused damage to the aircrafts in varying degrees, but Harjinder always stepped forward to work his magic. In one incident, a pilot, belonging to another Command, crashed an aircraft at night, while flying in weather conditions he shouldn't have been sent up in by his Flight Commander. When Harjinder rang up a Senior Air Officer and told him there would be a delay before the aircraft returned, he was quizzed on the circumstances, and the present condition of the aircraft. Harjinder pleaded with him to not go too deep into the matter, but his pleas were not well-received. The conversation took a different turn when Harjinder's led him down a different avenue, 'It is all right you telling me that the young officer must be taught a lesson; but have you forgotten your own irresponsible days when you and Janjua were flying low over Clifton Beach in Karachi, vying with each other to see who could splash the water with their propellers?'

'The senior officer was stunned, 'How in hell did you know about that?'

'Because I was in the rear cockpit of the aircraft!'

The case against the pilot was dropped and the aircraft returned when fully repaired. Another pilot saved.

These events were endearing Harjinder to the new generation of pilots who now saw what their senior colleagues already knew. A special deputation, led by Flight Lieutenant O.P. Sanghi, one of the 24 Indian pilots who'd gone to the UK in October 1940 and survived the war, met Harjinder and another important part of his life began.

'What can we, in our turn, do for you, Harjinder? Whatever you want us to do, it will be a real pleasure.'

Harjinder was thrilled at this magnificent offer, but there was nothing he wanted in his life. However, when pressed he casually mentioned, 'I have always wanted to learn flying, but that is an impossible wish.'

'Nonsense, if that's what you want that's what we'll give you. I have been an instructor. I will teach you flying.'

And so, Harjinder stretched his own wings for the first time and started his flying 'career'. It was a new chapter that would soon take over his life. Having flown as a rear gunner around some of the most stunning, barren, dangerous and spectacular scenery on the planet, the thrill of cruising high above the trees, or zooming in at low level over the moonscape ground was not new. However there is definitely a bug that gets under your skin when you pilot an aeroplane, when you control it, when it does what you tell it to do (*on those occasions when they do as they are told!*). That moment when you take the collection of rivets, bolts, panels, cables, push-rods, pistons, con-rods, oil and fuel into the air and, more importantly, bring them back onto the ground with some vague degree of control, is a life-changing event.

Harjinder flew the Harvard. This two-seat, American-designed aircraft was the main Allied advanced flying trainer throughout the war, produced in the thousands. The large round, radial engine didn't look too dissimilar to that of the old Wapiti, but it had the power to spin the metal propeller at speeds where the tips went supersonic. The trainee pilots flew the Harvard before progressing on to Spitfires, Hurricanes, Typhoons, or any other of the different types of fighters that were rolling out of the factories. Harjinder loved that aircraft and the flying bug well and truly burrowed under his skin;

> 'I started flying from the front cockpit (*the main pilot's seat*) and enjoyed it immensely. I felt the independence and elation of going out there at the controls, which, as a passenger, I had never experienced.'

It didn't all go smoothly, 'I swerved on takeoff and once nearly went into the Flying Control building at Kohat. However, the zealousness with which the pilots took turns to teach me flying made me a very proud man.'

The favourite run was between Kohat and Lahore. In fact, the number of flights to Lahore became so great, that the Station Commander ribbed Harjinder that he had a girlfriend there. The pilots queued up to, in Harjinder's words; 'risk their necks sitting in the rear cockpit', and the two Air Traffic Control Officers also looked the other way as Harjinder climbed into the front seat and spoke with them on the radio. They all kept the flying lessons a secret from the Station authorities. They all wanted to do it for Harjinder.

Of course, it could not stay that way. Harjinder had been flying the Harvards for a number of months when the cat was, inadvertently, let out of the bag by Ganguly. He asked a senior pilot to authorise a flight for him 'just like Harjinder' and was overheard by someone outside the group. Within minutes the call came from Aspy, and when Harjinder was welcomed so warmly he knew it spelt trouble, 'How long have we worked together, Harjinder?'

'About 14 years, Sir.'

'We have achieved a lot, wouldn't you say?'

'We certainly have, Sir. Why don't you come to the point?'

'OK I will. Tell me truthfully, have you been flying from the front cockpit of a Harvard?'

'I have.'

'Why?'

'Because I love flying.' (*Not much of an excuse but straight-forward honesty!*)

'Well, it has got to stop. I know you meant well, but we do not want to lose our senior-most engineer. Promise you will not fly again from the front cockpit.'

'All right, Sir, if you insist. I promise I will not fly from the front cockpit at IAF Station, Kohat.'

This conversation was followed by a long sermon from Jangoo Engineer telling him all about the strict rules of flying training. However, when the station pilots heard about it, they held a hurried conference amongst themselves, where a fresh scheme for Harjinder's training was hatched. It was unanimously decided that henceforth, he should go to the Fort and airstrip at Miranshah and fly. His promise to the Commanding Officer would thus be honoured in the letter, if not in the spirit! No flying at Kohat.

Harjinder held Aspy in very high regard, so it shows how strong his draw to flying was, if he was willing to bend the meaning of Aspy's instructions, if not actually break them. Also, Harjinder had been around military aviation for fourteen years, and he knew that accidents were part of the scenery. The inevitable happened on 18th October 1945, when Harjinder arrived at Miranshah in Harvard FE-372. With the whole weekend available and his instructor, Flight Lieutenant Sanghi, now in Command of the Detachment at Miranshah, he thought he could get plenty of flying time. At 0900 Harjinder went through the routine of an experienced Harvard pilot: Climb onto the wing walk way; turn to face the tail; place one foot on the projecting foot rest half way up the fuselage; swing the other leg over and on to the front cockpit seat, to end up facing the front; drop down into the seat and start the strapping in sequence. Once he was firmly attached to the aircraft, he operated the hand fuel pump watching the fuel pressure gauge. Then he moved that hand up to the magnetos (*ignition*) switch. He pushed the starter switch and heard the flywheel spinning up in front of him. The noise transported him back to the Wapiti days when he had to be joined by another airman to hand-crank the flywheel for that big, cumbersome engine. Here he was, now as the pilot, a battery replacing the labours of two sweating Airmen. He then moved the start switch in the other direction to connect flywheel to engine. The propeller turned over and first one, then the rest of the cylinders, fired to bring the engine to life.

Meanwhile, in the rear cockpit, Sanghi was still strapping in. They were in a rush to get going. As Harjinder taxied a little faster than he should have, he noticed all officers of the Detachment were out watching, and little did he know, they were about to watch a real show. They watched the bright yellow aircraft lift off from the dusty strip and the undercarriage legs, and wheels, tuck up into the centre section, much like the Hurricane. Harjinder brought the Harvard around in a large circuit to do some practice landings. He lowered the flaps to slow the machine down. He lowered the wheels again and lined up perfectly on the runway. As the wheels gently bumped onto the ground Sanghi announced on the intercom that his first approach was marvellous and the landing good too, however, the devil with these aircraft with a tail-wheel is what can happen after the touch down. Having the main-wheels in the front, and a small wheel on the tail, is just like pushing a two-wheeled luggage case in front of you instead of dragging it behind; the luggage, or the aircraft, wants to spin around to swap the front end with the back end. The Harvard tried to do this and Sanghi shouted, 'I have got it.' He stopped the swinging aircraft by opening up the throttle to full takeoff power, thereby, blasting additional air over the rudder control surface on the tail. Harjinder noticed that the engine was not responding to the full throttle as it should. Here they were stuck in a dilemma. The aircraft was increasing in speed and now couldn't stop before the fast approaching fence, but neither was it gaining speed as fast as it should to start flying. Sanghi yanked the stick back to try and get the Harvard back in the air which it did with the help of a hump on the rough runway. The nose was high in the air with the tail only inches off the ground. There was not enough airflow over the wings to keep them in the air, so they stalled and the Harvard dropped. The wheels slammed into the ground followed by the starboard wing tip. The undercarriage legs compressed and then sprang the aircraft back into the air. The good news was that it hopped over the big drainage ditch, but the bad news was it slammed down once again. Back up into the air again, this time, the Harvard staggered and waffled, but stayed flying with the propeller clawing at the air. Elated with his recovery from this potential disaster, Harjinder was completely oblivious to the danger ahead, until, shaken out of his dream-like stupor, he saw the large wall of the firing range up ahead. The engine wasn't producing enough power to take the aircraft clear so Harjinder pushed the stick forward and switched the ignition off without any great plan, or knowledge of where they were heading. The aircraft dropped like a stone, from an even greater height this time, into the circle used for practice bombing, luckily piled high with sand.

Inside the aircraft there was a large bang and both heads were thrust down towards the cockpit floor by the impact. From the outside, the aircraft was seen to flop to the ground and come to an immediate halt amid an ever-increasing column of smoke. All those watching assumed that the aircraft had caught fire, and felt sure that the two coffin boxes which were always kept in reserve in Miranshah Fort would now need replenishing.

Harjinder dragged his head up as the shuddering stopped, his mind still reeling. Time slowed as he forced his hands to do what his brain instructed. Flick the catch on the aircraft straps, turn the buckle on the parachute, unplug the helmet, grab the canopy lever on the left-hand side, pull it inwards to unlock and drag it back. It all seemed to take an eternity, but eventually he put his hands on the cockpit side and dragged his body up so he could stand on his seat. As he swung his leg over the side he pivoted around to face backwards, and there in the back was Sanghi, frozen in his seat and shouting, 'Fire, Fire.'

Harjinder jumped down onto the wing and back up onto the small step alongside Sanghi's rear cockpit. He pushed down the outside catch and dragged his canopy forward. Harjinder could smell no fire and correctly identified the billowing cloud around them as the brown dust of airfield dirt. He told Sanghi to shut up and get out, there was no fire. However, the ghostlike face in the back just stared ahead. Just because there was no immediate fire didn't mean the whole thing couldn't still go up like a torch, so Harjinder unstrapped Sanghi and dragged him out. As Sanghi regained control of his senses, he finally uttered his first coherent words, 'Never again in the rear-cockpit of any aircraft, and no more instructing.'

The dust settled and Harjinder looked around. It seemed the aircraft had picked the only safe spot around. They were surrounded by piles of stones and boulders, and to one side was the 12 foot-wide ditch that the Harvard, as if a sentient being itself, had so expertly circumvented. A miracle had happened, but more miracles would be needed if careers weren't to end. Understandably, the shaken Sanghi kept talking about court martials, but Harjinder tried to reassure him that he would not allow the machine to lie there for long and that no harm would come to him.

Harjinder reviewed the damage and approached Flying Officer Bose, asking if he would risk flying the aircraft with him. Harjinder pointed out, probably unnecessarily, that the undercarriage legs were bent, so not only would his takeoff and landing have to be the sweetest of his career, but the flight would have to be done with the undercarriage left down and not retracted. Most pilots would tell you, in no uncertain terms, where to go with an 'offer' like that, but Bose said, 'If you can risk your neck flying with me, I don't mind flying anything, whether it has legs or not.'

Such was Harjinder's reputation as an engineer, if not so much as a pilot at this stage!

Records don't show if he thought of changing his mind when Harjinder set to work on the propeller. These finely balanced pieces of machinery whizz around at 2800 RPM, they require not only a specialist, but an artisan to work on them with their small files to remove any small nicks or dents to get the balance perfect. That day, the specialist was Harjinder, with a large hammer and a wooden block. You can only assume that Bose wasn't in the vicinity when Harjinder's hammer rang out, as he battered the bent tips back into position. That said, when he fired the engine up he found it 'reasonably vibration-less' (*it is the term 'reasonably' that concerns me!*) and the original engine problem was cured. Next, he removed the wing tips and patched up the wing's aileron control edges with red dope and fabric, leaving the machine looking tattered and semi-abandoned.

While they were carrying out these repairs, the sound of an approaching Harvard caused them all to tense and search the skies for the approaching machine. If this was the Commanding Officer from Kohat coming to see what was cooking then the game was over. As the aircraft taxied to a halt, the canopy slid back to reveal Flight Lieutenant Killick, the new Adjutant Officer. He was quickly whisked away for a welcome drink in the Officers' Mess. Around him, four pilots gathered, offering him glasses of beer and asking for news from Kohat. The drinking and chat kept him clear of Harjinder's work outside and left him under the impression that these were the friendliest pilots ever!

The tea kept the technicians at work through the night, but the Militia guardsmen had also been hard at work completing a causeway over the ditch by filling it up with stones. Meanwhile, Harjinder strategically avoided a number of telephonic calls from Kohat enquiring about his whereabouts and requesting an estimate of his return. Aspy even called the Air Traffic Control Officer, enquiring sarcastically whether some pilot had crashed and if the Station Engineer was busy repairing it on the quiet. How close to the mark he was, little did he know it *was* the Station Engineer himself who was the culprit on this unauthorised flight!

In the morning the bent, tattered and forlorn looking Harvard took to the sky, timed perfectly to arrive when the boss, and his sly Squadron

Leader Flying, would be at their tables having lunch. The next day was Saturday, and Harjinder took the whole weekend, with his supply of spares, to bring the aircraft back into service for the Monday morning operations.

They got away with it, but his flying instruction had to pause for a while with Sanghi badly shaken and more than a few suspicious glances back at base. The time had come for Harjinder to move away from Aspy and his other IAF colleagues. Harjinder wanted to serve in the IAF but that couldn't continue indefinitely. He was now flying up the ranks and had been promoted, briefly through Flight Lieutenant, to Squadron Leader. The year in Kohat with Aspy had been a dream for Harjinder. He felt that they had pushed the IAF further along the road to being the self-sustaining force he had dreamt about with Jumbo. But in January 1946, he was posted to Peshawar as Chief Technical Officer of the RAF Operational Training Unit. They trained IAF pilots, but the ranks were made up of 800 British, and only 250 IAF Airmen. All the officers were British except two Junior Officers.

Harjinder was willing to make the most of his new posting but, as seemed to be the standard pattern for him when he arrived at a new base, he was disappointed. The British Airmen were not on his side, but this time, there was a reason for their gripe, beyond xenophobia. He heard the rumours of discontent among the Airmen because of the number of Indian pilots who had left the IAF directly after training to go straight into the civil airlines on fat salaries. They felt that these officers had not really played the game. Naturally, another major factor for the British men was that they wanted to go home. The war was over, and every man was anxious to return to England. Some had been away for the entire duration, and the expected repatriation after victory in Japan was not the instant affair many had thought, and dreamt of. The process was painfully slow, and so morale was low, this was reflected in a shockingly low standard of maintenance.

In the first week, Harjinder took the bull by the horns, as was his way. He assembled the 1,100 Officers and men and introduced himself. As soon as he mentioned the lack of interest shown in the training of IAF pilots, a voice piped up from the parade, 'Of course not! They run away to earn big money elsewhere.'

He thanked them for their honest and frank remarks; then offered some of his own. He talked about how his Squadron had fought in the outdated Lysander in Burma when, in his opinion, the RAF were quick to leave. He continued, pointing out the huge expansion the IAF had carried

out, going from one, to ten squadrons, all through volunteers joining the
military, conscription was not required. They won more decorations,
squadron for squadron, than the RAF, and the King offered the IAF the
title Royal. 'Had I, or my compatriots, known that after the war the RAF
would repay this debt in the manner you are doing, I assure you, I would
have been the last person to do what I did. (*A murmur of approval rumbled
through the ranks*). I am very happy to note that most of you agree with me.
Let me, therefore, appeal to you to start afresh. We have 90 aeroplanes.
Serviceability has been only 30 per cent against 75 per cent in the IAF
Station at Kohat. I expect every man to work hard so that we can reach
the same 75 per cent figure.'

He message was received, and the men certainly knew who Harjinder
was now! The next Saturday a weekly conference was held in the Station
Commander's office with more medals around the table than you could
shake a stick at. Enter Harjinder:

> Group Captain Campbell Vallaine opened the proceedings,
> talking about the low serviceability of aircraft, which seemed to be
> accepted by all in the room. Harjinder could not contain himself
> any further, and so interrupted the meeting to point out that in
> Burma they achieved over 90 per cent serviceability continuously
> whilst being shot at and bombed. He finished by stating that at
> Kohat, he didn't accept anything less than 75 per cent. It was not
> awe, or respect, that greeted his outburst, but a wave of laughter;
> the officers shook their heads, some even turned to each other
> and winked. The boss had to quieten the room down before he
> could address Harjinder; 'Squadron Leader Harjinder Singh, an
> ounce of showing is equal to a pound of talking. If you can raise
> the serviceability to 50 per cent, I would be mighty pleased, but if
> you can go to 66 per cent, I would be staggered. If, however, you
> can go to 75 per cent, I would faint as that would be a miracle.'

All eyes turned to Harjinder. It will now come as no surprise to know
that he would take on this challenge, 'I will cross the "miraculous" line
and keep it there.'

Not only did he accept the challenge, he started accepting bets on
his ability to deliver. From the Commanding Officer he took a bet of
one thousand rupees that they would reach his target; the Chief Flying
Instructor added five hundred rupees into the bargain. Hardly had Harjinder

reached his office, when his Warrant Officer, Mr Simms, walked in with a mischievous twinkle in his eyes and threw his one hundred rupee bet into the ring. At the door a queue was forming, starting with a British Flight Sergeant. The money was stacking up! Such faith!

The bet with British Officers was only three days old when luck entered the fray; bad luck, of course. Two Harvards crashed on landing, followed by Pilot Officer Mehta hitting a labourer's handcart on the takeoff roll in his Spitfire. The labourer had run out of the way when he saw the Spitfire, the pilot saw the man clear out of the way and assumed he was the only obstacle. The long nose of the Spitfire pointing skywards in front of him completely blocked the view of the abandoned handcart. Harjinder asked a RAF Flight Lieutenant Engineer how long he needed to repair the machine. 'Repair?' he questioned, 'I would not attempt to repair this machine at all!'

When Harjinder pushed Warrant Officer Simms, he said, 'It will take a fortnight with all our men working flat out on it.'

What seemed like bad luck was actually a chance for Harjinder, with the aid of tea, naturally, to show what he, and his IAF technicians, could do, 'Give me two IAF Airmen and we will see this aircraft in the air in 24 hours.'

Once again it was laughter that greeted his statements. Warrant Officer Simms added: 'You can take *a hundred and four* hours, if you like, Sir. If at the end of that you succeed, I will relinquish my coat-of-arms (*Warrant Officer rank*) and revert back to being an airman.'

Harjinder took Cadet Officer, and trainee fighter pilot, Suranjan Das, as his Assistant, and they set about knocking out the hundreds of rivets to remove the panels that had pieces of handcart thrust through them. They worked the whole night and the following day, with tea running through their veins. It seemed as if Harjinder had discovered a secret weapon to add to his arsenal. Cadet Officer Suranjan Das's technical ability was as good as any technician's, and, he was willing to learn. Harjinder learnt more about Dasu, as Suranjan was known to his friends. He had also started with a degree in engineering, pushed into it by his parents who told him he wasn't clever enough to be a pilot! During the war, he was accepted into basic pilot training, completing it in Canada. On his return, proudly wearing his pilot wings, his parents and assorted aunts in the family jointly declared that if he could get his wings, they could not be very difficult for anybody to get! Luckily, his senior officers saw what his family couldn't.

Later in the decade, he was one of two pilots selected to attend the Empire Test Pilot School in Britain. He went on to become the Chief Test Pilot at Bangalore many years later, combining his pilot's skill and engineer's intelligence. His achievements were so well-respected, that the authorities in Bangalore named a road after him. Harjinder would call on his talents again, later in their careers.

The Spitfire was ready in exactly 22 hours. The Flight Commander was summoned, and asked to get airborne within the next two hours in order to beat the self-imposed deadline. He took a long look at the aircraft on the ground but could find no fault. As he climbed down from the cockpit after his test flight, smiling as he came, he reported it as good as any other aircraft on the station. Simms reported to Harjinder's office in his overalls, no rank badges on, and said; 'Sir, as long as you are the Chief Technical Officer, I am Airman Simms and will do anything you order.'

He kept his word and the story spread around the Station like wildfire. Any aircraft which Harjinder pointed at was serviced, ground tested, and flown. The Station Commander and Chief Instructor came to know about the serviceability shooting up, so sent for their Pilot Instructors to carry out mass formation practice to test how many aircraft could really fly. During the next few days, they flew hundreds of hours, but the serviceability remained at 80 per cent. Instead of the expected plummet as the aircraft were pushed, repeatedly, into the air, the serviceability rose to 90 per cent and Harjinder's reputation was sealed.

Then the British came to settle their debts. The Station Commander came to Harjinder's office with a cheque for a thousand rupees. Harjinder politely declined the cheque, but instead, asked him for an autographed ten rupee note. Right until the end of his days Harjinder held on to this note, along with signed ten rupee notes from all the others. It marked the change on the station. When the Station Adjutant started calling him by his first name, he knew that he had broken the barriers down.

The British were respecting Harjinder and his IAF technicians for their abilities, but something else was becoming obvious. The British Empire was finished, and the days of the British ruling India were coming to an end. India had fought in another World War for the British Empire, but the Empire was in its death throes. The dreams that Harjinder and his colleagues in the IAF – Jumbo, Mukerjee, Aspy – had nurtured for so long, were about to be turned to reality, but at what price?

The three men who emerged from the embers of the World War II to shape the future of India were Gandhi, Nehru and Jinnah. Mohandas Karamchand 'Mahatma' Gandhi stood above all, his unrivalled ability to communicate seemed to speak for the country's soul. However, the passage of the World War II had seen his influence diminish and he drifted apart from many of his followers in the Congress movement with his unswerving belief in nonviolence. As Churchill had broadcast his blood and guts speeches to the Free World during the height of the Blitz on London, Gandhi had suggested another course. 'Invite Hitler and Mussolini to take what they want of the countries you call your possessions. Let them take possession of your beautiful island.'

When Italy invaded Northern Africa he urged the Ethiopians to; 'allow themselves to be slaughtered'. He then followed this up with a plan for ranks of disciplined, nonviolent Indians to march forward onto the bayonets of the approaching Japanese until that catalytic point when the enormity of their sacrifice would overwhelm their foes. When it became clear how the Japanese press had been making celebrities from the swords of their officers, keeping a running total of the highest 'scoring' blade in terms of heads removed, it is difficult to believe that that point would have been reached, ever. On 8th August 1942, Gandhi suddenly had sent out the word 'I want freedom immediately, this very night, before dawn if it can be done... We shall either free India or die in the attempt.' What Gandhi and the leadership of the Congress party got before dawn was jail, where they crucially stayed for the duration of the World War II. It is at this point that many historians believe that Gandhi lost some of his influence. However, he was still a mighty figure in Indian politics.

Gandhi's choice of leader for the Congress Party was Jawaharlal Nehru. He was a product of seven happy years spent in the British learning establishments of Harrow and Cambridge, until he came to realise that the colour of his skin would keep him from the inner circles of British life. He turned against the system, a decision that cost him 9 years in prison, often in solitary confinement. His beliefs, while not concurrent with, were influenced by, Gandhi's teachings. However, Gandhi became his Guru, re-Indianising him on his return to India, and a father-son relationship built up between them.

Mohammed Ali Jinnah studied law in Britain just as Gandhi had done before him; he was even from the same Kathiawar peninsula as Gandhi.

If Jinnah's grandfather had not converted to Islam, they would have been from the same cast. However, Jinnah returned to India from Britain as an Englishman, complete with a monocle and clean-cut linen suits, a successful lawyer who naturally moved across into the world of politics. He had preached Muslim/Hindu unity, but would not entertain the idea of casting his fine clothes to one side for a loincloth as Gandhi preached. He also felt let down by the Indian Congress party in 1937, when they refused to share the spoils of the Indian provinces with a substantial Muslim minority. With Gandhi and the Congress party officials locked up during the war, the British Government turned to Jinnah's Muslim League to negotiate with. It raised their standing far beyond the minority status it had been, and placed Jinnah on the top table of talks about India's future. Now Jinnah only wanted one thing for this land; a separate Muslim state.

'Quit India' was still the cry, but it was no longer a question of would Independence come, but was only a question of when. Harjinder, Mukerjee and Engineer would see the Independence they strived for, but it was to come at an unimaginable price.

Twelve

Independence! But at What Cost?

Winston Churchill:

'Our Imperial mission in India is at an end: we must recognise that. Someday justice will be done by world opinion to our record there, but the chapter is closed... Sorrow may lie in our hearts but bitterness and malice must be purged from them.'

'If the RAF is withdrawn out of India, the RIAF cannot maintain their existing squadrons in the Air... The RIAF has not the technical personnel even to man one Squadron.'

India would become Independent, that seemed obvious; but it didn't stop the 'Quit India' campaign from continuing at full strength. Indians wanted results immediately; no more waiting. The dreams of Harjinder, Jumbo and the musketeers of the 1930s were of the country they called India being Independent. What had started from Jinnah, and the Muslim League, as a small subplot in the great thrust towards Independence had grown in favour with the war-weary British Government. Gandhi's idea of a transition to a one multicultural state was falling apart in front of him and he was spending more time in the troubled Muslim areas around Calcutta trying to quell the surge of religious violence.

Jinnah's goal of a separate Muslim state would not be realised without new lines being drawn on maps based on religious beliefs. To many, that seemed an impossible task, but Jinnah had said; 'We will have India divided or we shall have India destroyed.'

For Harjinder, and others in the Air Force, this was a cause for concern – what would happen to the IAF they had dedicated their lives to; if the country was to be divided, would the Air Force be broken up, too? Would they become a small unit under the Army; could they exist without British personnel? The struggle for Independence had gone on for years, but as the dream became a reality, it left so many unanswered questions, much nervousness and much unrest.

On 26th February 1946, Harjinder, erstwhile leader of the student revolt at Maclaghan Engineering College, had an interesting job to do; one that brought life full circle for him. He received a disturbing telephone call from Aspy Engineer, back in Kohat; the Indian Airmen of the Station had gone on strike. They had heard that the IAF might be used against the Indian Navy 'mutineers' in Bombay. The 'mutiny' had nationalist undertones, the Navy men sought redress for their grievances – lower grades of pay and unequal treatment, in comparison to their British colleagues. Aspy had already called in the Ghurkha troops to block the aerodrome gate, giving orders to open fire on the strikers, his own men, if they tried to force their way out. He was tackling the problem head-on, with no compromise.

Harjinder approached Group Captain Campbell Vallaine, his Station Commander, and without offering any explanation, he asked permission to fly to see Aspy immediately. With Harjinder hunched in the back seat, Flying Officer Glandstein managed to wrestle a Harvard through the dark, heavy rain clouds covering the entire area. As they popped out of the atrocious weather, Harjinder unfolded himself from the protective posture he had subconsciously taken to see that they were directly overhead Kohat. More importantly, looking down through the rain-streaked canopy, Harjinder could see the Airmen amassed in the open ground near the airstrip. There, in the middle of this ant swarm, stood a man in the midst of the clearing, clearly addressing the men. He assumed it was Aspy, but on his arrival, he discovered that it was one of the leaders whipping the men up into an emotional frenzy.

When Harjinder found Aspy in his office, it soon became apparent that they had very different views on the situation. Aspy said the men would not let an officer near the group, so the army were on standby; he was not tolerating any nonsense from his men. Harjinder felt the legacy of Kohat, as the first Indian Air Force station in Indian, would be ruined, if this situation wasn't resolved soon, and dealt with a sympathetic touch.

As he moved towards the group Aspy tried to stop him, 'I will not be responsible for your life, Harjinder.'

As Harjinder approached the strikers, someone among them shouted, 'Don't let this officer come near, because he will finish off the strike.'

Then another few voices called, 'No, no, it is Harjinder. He must come.'

An idea leapt into Harjinder's mind; a way to show the men that they were in control of their destiny at this precise moment. He called for those in favour of him remaining should raise their hand. It was a gamble, and he later admitted it surprised him when most hands flew up.

It was clear that the two very energetic and persuasive Airmen, in the centre of the circle of men, were the ring leaders, so Harjinder addressed them directly in front of the crowd, and let them speak. Emotions at fever pitch, they all started to speak at the same time. When they managed to quiet down a little, Harjinder was told the whole story – the strikers had requested the Station Commander to signal the Commander-in-Chief in Delhi to inform him that the Indian Air Force Station Kohat would not cooperate in the bombing and machine-gunning of fellow Indians. The men were lost for words when Harjinder paused, and said; 'Is that all?'

It seemed a reasonable request to Harjinder and he had the advantage of knowing that HQ in Delhi had no intentions to that effect. Crisis averted, Harjinder didn't hold back on his disappointment in their behaviour. They had disgraced themselves by striking and they should report back to work before it was too late. Sensing that he had regained control, he took a gamble and issued an order. When the two ring leaders immediately obeyed by forming up in parade ground order, the rest of the men smartly followed up. He marched them all to the Cinema hall where they were to await Aspy Engineer. He told them to accept, without hesitation, any punishment the Station Commander dished out, and when asked, they should say it had not been a strike. An eerie silence spread throughout the cinema, where the men collected, and Harjinder left to speak with Aspy. To be fair to Aspy, he did back away from the head-on tackling of the situation, and wrote the signal along the lines demanded by Harjinder before addressing the men. The men shouted 'No!' with one voice when asked by Aspy if they were striking, and all accepted the one month of afternoon parades without a murmur. The strike was over; Aspy received a sound dressing down from HQ over his signal and Harjinder, the scourge of Maclaghan College, suddenly acquired notoriety as a 'trouble shooter'.

His carrot and stick approach worked, the men listened to him, and his seniors had full confidence in him.

In Delhi, too, the Airmen staged a strike, but Mukerjee, who had shown his soft hand-approach at Kohat earlier, had done a fine job calming the waters until the RAF sent their intelligence branch. The intelligence branch demonstrated their lack of intelligence by arriving like bulls in a china shop. They drew up a 'discharge from Air Force' list of those involved, including Warrant Officer Verghese, who had been pivotal in settling the Airmen's fears! Trouble flared up, and Harjinder, on the back of his Kohat success, was sent for by Mukerjee. He arrived and soothed the beast that was the RAF Intelligence branch and brought the Airmen back into line.

Another station was Secunderabad, where the 'strikers' were Sergeants attending the School of Technical Training. They had been arbitrarily made to remove their Sergeants' stripes during their training course and were being treated as Airmen even though many were soon to be officers. Once again Harjinder spread calm. But these little rebellions, in tiny pockets, were not isolated incidents – the whole country was caught up in a storm of uncertainty, which fed these micro events

Harjinder's and Jumbo's dream of an Independent country and an Independent Air Force was going to come true. Both believed the degree of severance from the RAF would depend mainly upon the capability and quality of technical maintenance personnel. Harjinder felt that Delhi was the place to be to make this happen, and so went up to Delhi to urge the now Group Captain, Subroto Mukerjee, that it was time to start a separate RIAF Headquarters, and thus gradually become independent of the UK. Mukerjee's reply showed that not all were confident of the future; 'Don't you believe it. The British are far too clever and powerful to leave India.'

This did, however, illustrate Mukerjee's complete lack of understanding of their Imperial Masters – with industry crippled, their exchequer bankrupt, the Sterling on life support from the Americans and Canadians, the British were left with no appetite for further conflict. He may have had his doubts, but he agreed to have Harjinder attached to Air Headquarters, working directly under him again; but this time as head of Technical Training for the entire Air Force. Their difference in opinion, and in approach, seemed inconsequential in the face of the task ahead, and a strong bond was quickly established.

Their old friend from No. 1 Squadron's Burma days, Rup Chand, was now in politics, he showed Harjinder extracts from a paper written by Air Vice-Marshal Walmsely, who had taken over as Chief of the Indian Air Force in November 1946. It seemed to hark back to Sir John Steele's 'greatest disgrace' comments in 1924, doubting the Indians' ability to be involved in aviation. He had written, 'If the RAF is withdrawn out of India, the RIAF cannot maintain its existing squadrons in the air. As a matter of fact, the RIAF has not the technical personnel even to man one Squadron.'

Harjinder leapt from his seat, paper crumpling in his tightening grip as he read the report. He saw this as an attempt to sabotage their goal of setting up an independent Indian Air Force; to leave India defenceless. His response was predictable; 'If anything, the IAF maintenance is superior to that of the RAF as was amply proved during the war in the South East.'

As it would turn out, it was not just the British they were fighting. Indians, even at the highest level, regarded aircraft as an instrument of mystery, and assumed that only white men knew the art of aircraft maintenance. Rup Chand invited Harjinder to a lunch with Pandit Kunzru, a senior politician, a meeting that left Harjinder completely disillusioned. It seemed that the British had succeeded in producing a sense of inferiority in many politicians. Mukerjee, and even Aspy Engineer, counselled patience but Harjinder invoked the memory of Jumbo, the daring and dauntless leader who, were he alive, would have kicked the applecart over in his own inimitable way. He saw such allegations as an affront to Jumbo's legacy, and as an attempt to belittle the IAF's engineering capability; he wanted no part of it. He wrote out his letter of resignation, placed it on the table in front of Subroto Mukerjee and walked out.

When the newly promoted Group Captain Aspy Engineer heard about Harjinder's resignation, he claimed that Harjinder was playing into Walmsely's hands. Aspy said Walmsley would accept it in an instant, and with a smile on his face. They could not have been more wrong. Instead of being told to pack his bags, Walmsely asked for Harjinder's demands to remain in the Air Force. Harjinder replied, 'Since the Air Marshal has commented upon the inability of the RIAF to overhaul aircraft and aero-engines I would like to prove him wrong. I demand that the Maintenance Unit at Lahore should be completely nationalised and then you will see what we can do.'

To Harjinder's further surprise, this was agreed to immediately. This was an unimaginable step forward for Harjinder's dreams, so he wasted no time, despatching his technical Officers and men to Lahore, the moment the authorisation arrived. He withdrew his resignation with a happy heart. If only Harjinder had an inkling of how little time they had in Lahore. The assumption was that Lahore would be part of the new India, and any form of Independence was still several years away. When the partition did come, the majority at Lahore had to re-establish the nucleus of the RIAF at the Aircraft Repair Depot in Kanpur; a place Harjinder would get to know very well.

The year 1947 was going to a momentous one, but as the year began, few could have believed how it would unfold. On New Year's Day, a black Austin Princess drove down the drab, deserted streets of London, slipping past shops with messages scrawled on their windows; no coal, no logs, no potatoes, no cigarettes. As the car passed Buckingham Palace, the man in the back seat looked at the home of his great grandmother, Queen Victoria. The present King, George VI, still presided over the 560 million people of the Empire; over Africans and Australians, over Canadians and New Zealanders, over Indians and Chinese, over Arabs and Borneo headhunters. When the Austin arrived at its destination, Number 10 Downing Street, the man who pinned the DFC onto Arjan Singh's working shirt in Burma left the warmth of the car and rushed through the famous doorway. Viscount Louis Mountbatten of Burma was 46, and no stranger to this doorway. It would not be his close friend Churchill who waited to greet him on the other side. Clement Attlee, and his Labour Party, had come to office publicly committed to the dismantling of the Empire; Mountbatten knew why he was here.

The man who had recommended Mountbatten to Attlee was the outspoken, left wing Indian, Krishna Menon. In 1924, Menon had arrived in the UK, to attend the University of London, where he earned a First Class Honours degree. Professor Harold Laski described him as the best student he ever had. Menon became a passionate proponent of India's freedom, working as a journalist and, as secretary of the India League, he formed the very close friendship with Nehru that would flourish after Independence. Menon was notorious for his brilliance, and his arrogance, he was eloquent orator and possessed a razor sharp wit, which he put to regular use on friend and foe alike. When the novelist Brigid Brophy expressed surprise at the quality of his English, he immediately retorted: 'My English is better than yours. You merely picked it up; I learnt it.'

He was a member of Attlee's Labour party, and the Prime Minister sought his counsel on all matters Indian. He was yet to enter Harjinder's life, but when he did, it was with far-reaching consequences.

Mountbatten wanted no part in moving India towards Independence. Although he whole-heartedly endorsed the idea that Britain must leave India, during his time in South-East Asia, he had thrown himself into understanding the region, and so had no illusions about the magnitude of the task. He had, in his time commanding the troops in South-East Asia, requested an audience with the representative of India's various factions, including one with Nehru, then imprisoned in Ahmednagar, in January 1944, which was promptly denied. After the war, Mountbatten did meet with him in Singapore, ignoring his advisers' comments about the 'rebel whose shoes still bore the dust of a British prison'. The mutual affinity the two leaders struck up was immediate, they delighted in each other's company and sympathised with their adversary's position. To the horror of those advisers, Mountbatten spontaneously decided to ride through Singapore in an open car with Nehru. When told it would dignify the anti-British rebel, he retorted; 'Dignify him? It's he who will dignify me. One day this man will be Prime Minister of India!'

Mountbatten may have found he could relate to, and work with Nehru, the future Prime Minister, but he knew the task being discussed by Attlee had no solution. In the previous year, the Muslim League had held a Direct Action Day in Calcutta to protest the killing of Muslims by Hindus and Sikhs. Within 72 hours, more than 4,000 people lost their lives, and 100,000 people in the city of Calcutta were left homeless. These were no minor street skirmishes.

The age-old antagonism between the 300 million Hindus/Sikhs and 100 million Muslims had suited Britain's Divide and Rule; Keep the communities divided under the threat of the Empire's military umbrella. The Muslim leadership now demanded tearing through the British enforced unity, and thereafter to provide a separate Muslim state. An ultimatum was issued, if their demands were not met, the bloodiest civil war in Asia would be unleashed. Proof of the potential wreckage that religious violence could incur already seemed to exist, if the events in Calcutta were anything to go by. However, how could a country's borders be drawn up purely on religious grounds? Gandhi, the father figure that the majority of Hindus, and many Muslims, would turn to, insisted that India must remain whole. The people were Indian; religion should not enter the discussion.

Mountbatten laid out a set of minimum requirements to Attlee. He reasoned that without complete resolution of certain matters, the task could not be undertaken, let alone resolved. He wanted full powers without reference to London. He insisted on a public announcement of the date Britain would pull out, thereby forcing all the parties to take the negotiations seriously. He knew that no Prime Minister would agree to these conditions, and therefore, he wouldn't be handed the poison chalice; the role of Viceroy to India. One can only imagine his shock, as each one of his requests was complied with, right down to his request for his original private aeroplane from Asia, and his specified team of secretaries. He had been tasked with the impossible! As he drove back past Buckingham palace he realised it was 70 years to the hour when his Grandmother had been proclaimed Empress of India, on a plain outside Delhi. The princes of India had attended and publically requested for her 'power and sovereignty to remain steadfast forever', motivated no doubt by the knowledge that their own grasp of power depended upon British rule. Now, on the first day of 1947, he was going to put an expiration date on 'forever'. It wasn't just Gandhi, Nehru and Jinnah that he had to convince, there was also the minor issue of the 565 maharajas, nawabs, rajas and rulers holding hereditary sovereignty over one third of India. The Hindu Maharaja, Hari Singh, ruling over the mainly Muslim state of Kashmir was going to be a real problem.

On the 18th February 1947, Attlee rose from his green leather-clad bench in the House of Commons and stepped up to the Table of the House, in his hand he had a short text written by Mountbatten, replacing his own lengthy draft. He looked across the table to the seated opposition party and in particular their leader, Winston Churchill. 'His Majesty's Government wishes to make it clear that it is their definite intention to take the necessary steps to effect the transference of power into responsible Indian hands by a date not later than June 1948.'

A stunned silence followed, Attlee continued, introducing Mountbatten as the man who would make this happen, and the powers vested in him as Viceroy. Afterwards, Churchill spoke; 'It is with deep grief that I watch the clattering down of the British Empire with all its glories and all the services it has rendered to mankind. Many have defended Britain against her foes. None can defend her against herself.'

However, not even the words of the master orator could change the realities of the modern world, and Churchill knew it. His party still held power in the higher house, the House of Lords, but he urged his fellow Conservatives to support the Bill, believing it was too important to be the gift of one political party.

Now that the timetable to Independence was official, the enormity of the situation began to dawn on the Air Force. They were ten squadrons strong, but soon, much of the leadership was going to be ripped out and sent home to the UK. Talk of partition was in the air too, but it seemed unlikely that India would be split into several parts; undoable. However, if this eventuality were to occur, the carcass left behind by the RAF's sudden exit would be picked at further, until the Air Force was stripped to the bone.. A vast majority of bases were in the North, the area that might be lost if this partition happened. The Air Force was told to be prepared, and plan for this split if it came to pass. Every man was given a chit to indicate his choice; India, or this new state that was being called Pakistan. In real terms this meant an Air Force that was only 15 years old would lose a third of all the personnel, aircraft and equipment, and have no bases from which to run its operations.

With the British personnel being withdrawn, it would mean rapid promotion for some men in every department of the Air Force.

The thoughts of the husband and wife doctor team from Simla, who stayed behind when the Burmese Government left, were very much focused on the future of India and on their own family. Dr Nanda had a two-year-old son of his own, and was searching for the right suitor for his sister. He had heard about a talented man from Simla, Sergeant Saigal, the same man who had helped Harjinder load the bombs on to Jumbo's Lysander in Burma. The arrangements were made for 9th March 1947. A Sergeant would have seemed a poor choice a few years previously, but Dr Nanda was very progressive, and reasoned that this talented young man would be commissioned as an officer and shoot up the ranks once the British left.

Harjinder, too, was promoted to Wing Commander in early 1947, reaching the same rank as his hero Jumbo. With the rank came additional power and the chance to work with Mukerjee on establishing the technical back-up that any Air Force needs. Even with the gulf of Airman to

Officer, Harjinder had never held back with Mukerjee but now, as Wing
Commander to Air Commodore, they were closer in rank and closer as
friends and coworkers. Harjinder's first act, with Mukerjee's approval, was
to have the number of technical trainees increased to 2,250, and the school
shifted to Tambaram near Madras. He dissociated himself from the RAF,
setting up a new office with a signboard outside his door saying, 'Wing
Commander, Technical-RIAF'. There was no such appointment in Air
Headquarters, he made it up, but nobody seemed to notice!

It was not all desk work for Harjinder; he kept himself busy outside
of the RIAF business too. From his first faltering steps as a pilot, despite
the Harvard crash in the North-West Frontier, Harjinder was determined
to continue on and become a pilot. He began to take flying lessons at the
Delhi Flying Club. One day Wing Commander Narendra asked him to
come into the Flying Club hangar to inspect his L5 light aircraft that he
kept there. During his visit he noticed another L5 lying in a corner, it
looked positively toy-like when compared to the imposing Harvard he
was used to. Upon enquiry he was told that the little aircraft had been in a
crash, although it appeared to have escaped any major damage. Harjinder
preached to all who would listen, that it was a great pity that such national
assets were allowed to go to waste through lack of technical ability; he
hated to see aircraft idle, or even worse, abandoned. The Chief Engineer,
an Englishman named George Floate, mistook his comments as a personal
slur to his professional competence, and challenged Harjinder, 'If you
think you are a better engineer than us, you repair it.' When Narendra
tried to quieten him down and expand on Harjinder's legend, it only
served to infuriate Floate more. He said, 'I have heard that before. I have
met many boasters. Let us see what your friend can do to this aircraft.'

Harjinder took a different approach for a change, and instead made
an offer to the owner. The gentleman in question could hardly believe
his ears when Harjinder offered him two thousand rupees for what he
considered to be a wreck. The deal was done, and Harjinder became the
owner of an aircraft.

On the 24th March 1947, the land of ceremonial splendour, with
the blend of Victorian pomp and Moghul magnificence, provided the
backdrop for the last ceremony of its kind. Mountbatten proudly wore his
uniform tunic, weighted down by the Order of the Garter, the Order of
the Star of India, the Order of the Indian Empire, and the Grand Cross
of the Victorian Order. When he walked to the Durbar hall, the guard of

honour, sabres gleaming, included the Royal Indian Air Force for the first time. As he pronounced the concluding words of the Viceroy's oath, the cannons of the Royal Horse Artillery rumbled outside. From Landi Kotal on the Khyber Pass, to Cape Comorin in the South, from Fort William in Calcutta, to the Gateway of India in Bombay, the cannons fired their own salute in unison. It was not lost on anyone present at the proceedings that the fading of the echoing gunfire was signalling the fading of the British Empire. Mountbatten, now Viceroy of India, had already broken with tradition by being seen face to face with his predecessor, not, as protocol dictated, passing in their own ships in the waters off Bombay to save the locals the 'embarrassment' of having two versions of the same god in India at one time! He now broke another tradition by addressing the gathering, much against the advice of his staff. 'I am under no illusion about the difficulty of my task. I shall need the greatest goodwill of the greatest possible number, and I am asking India today for that goodwill.'

Five days later, that goodwill seemed in short supply, when news of the deaths of 99 Hindus and Muslims in Calcutta was received. Two days later, 41 mutilated bodies were left on the pavements of Bombay.

Life at Air Force Headquarters was hectic; trying to provide a plan, a platform, for an event they didn't know exactly when, or in what form, would happen. However, Harjinder was used to burning the candle at both ends, and RIAF duties didn't stop the engineer within him. Soon his new acquisition, the little L5, was repaired, and the whole of the Flying Club turned out to witness the flight of Harjinder's latest rebuilt plane. He had carried out all the tests imaginable on the previous evening and stepped up to carry out the first test flight himself. This little L5 had the wing running on top of the fuselage, with a pilot seat in the front and passenger seat directly behind, similar in layout to the Lysander. However in the Lysander, as with all the military aircraft he had flown, Harjinder scaled steps in the huge fuselages to get to the cockpits. With the small L5, he had to duck his tall frame under the wing, and fold himself into the front seat of his plane. The engine burst into life encouragingly and Harjinder taxied the short distance to the runway. After doing his power checks on the engine, he stopped the aircraft briefly to look down the length of the runway to focus on the task ahead. No point in delaying any further, he thought, and so opened up the engine to full power, and was rewarded with the small tail-wheel lifting off the ground almost immediately. The throb of the engine at full power reverberated throughout the aircraft, but the main-wheels had barely left the ground when the throbbing suddenly ceased as the engine stopped stone dead. Harjinder's focus flicked from the horizon in front of him to the remainder of the runway below him. Luckily, the engine had stopped soon enough for him to ease the machine on to the remaining runway and, just as importantly, to stop it before it entangled itself in the boundary fence at the far end! When the heart had slowed and the sweat had eased, Harjinder dived under the cowlings to discover that an insect in the vent pipe of the fuel tank had cut the flow to the engine. Ever the optimist, Harjinder saw this as a good omen, believing that success after failure is more worthwhile! This certainly seemed to hold true, as Harjinder flew over 300 hours in his small L5 during the years he owned it. When he sold it, the aircraft kept flying for 20 years with the Bombay Flying Club. Not bad for an old abandoned wreck.

The escalating violence that was spreading throughout the country made it clear to Mountbatten that a speedy resolution was required. Advised by George Abell, a man known for his brilliance and deep understanding of India, he was left in no doubt that India was heading for civil war. Mountbatten's Chief of Staff, General Lord Ismay, described India as; 'A ship on fire in mid-ocean with ammunition in her hold.'

Lord Ismay's question was, could they get the fire out before it reached the ammunition? Field Marshal Auchinleck, the man who should have pinned Harjinder's MBE to his uniform, was still in command of the Indian Army in cooperation with the police. He confirmed there was nothing the police and army could do to maintain law and order when faced by the sheer number of people. He also went on to say 'The partition of the RIAF into two forces... will lead to the disintegration of the RIAF as it now exists, to an extent which will leave India well-nigh defenceless against air attack for a period of years which cannot be estimated.'

Luckily, Harjinder, Mukerjee and Engineer would soon prove him wrong.

With civil war staring him in the face, Mountbatten knew he must work fast. He was already working a successful charm offensive over the Indian public by being more accessible than his predecessors, and now decided to scrap the conference table and meet each leader separately, with no staff present on either side. The first was Nehru, in his white congress cap, a fresh rose twisted through the third buttonhole of his waistcoat. They both slipped back into the warm undercurrent of relaxed, mutual sympathy and understanding. Mountbatten led the way, talking openly about the fears he had for the task ahead. His opening line to Nehru; 'View me not as the last Viceroy but as the first to lead the way to a new India.' Nehru's response was; 'Now I know what they mean when they speak of your charm as being so dangerous.'

The next man through the Viceregal door was Churchill's 'half-naked fakir'. Mountbatten thought 'he's rather like a little bird', but he was under no illusion of the importance of the man. He had already predicted that on his death; 'Mahatma Gandhi will go down in history on a par with Christ and Buddha.' They talked for two hours and the easy nature of the conversation led to a stroll through the grounds of the Viceroy's Palace. When they left the furnace-like Delhi temperatures to return to the air-conditioned room Gandhi started shaking uncontrollably from the sudden temperature change, Edwina Mountbatten thought her husband had killed India's icon. She turned the air-conditioning machine off, threw open a window and grabbed something to cover Gandhi up with. It would have seemed inappropriate, so unfortunately, the opportunity was missed to take a photograph of Mahatma Gandhi sitting in the Viceroy's study, wearing an old, tatty Royal Navy uniform sweater!

When they returned to the business at hand, Gandhi left Mountbatten in doubt over his thoughts on the future of the country they called India; 'Don't partition India' he begged, 'even if refusing to do so means shedding rivers of blood'.

He went further, raising an idea that had not even entered Mountbatten's thoughts. Give the Muslims the baby instead of cutting it in half. Give Jinnah all India. Mountbatten assured Gandhi he would take the suggestion seriously if Gandhi could assure him that the Congress party would accept. The press noted that when Gandhi left the palace he seemed to 'bubble with happiness'.

It was said that the air-conditioning that nearly did for the frail Gandhi, was not required for Jinnah, since the austere and distant leader of the Muslim league cooled the atmosphere sufficiently by his presence alone. Things were not helped when Jinnah's attempt to inject a degree of informality backfired. He knew he would be photographed with the Mountbattens, no doubt with Edwina in the middle. As they were shuffled around he ended up in between the two Mountbattens, but could not stop his prearranged lines from tumbling out; 'A rose between two thorns!'

It may not have been a good start, but the social gaffe did not stop the discussions between the two men. They had six crucial meeting throughout the month, but despite Mountbatten using 'every trick in the book', he could not get the steadfast Jinnah to relax his views on a separate Muslim state. With Jinnah's absolute control over the Muslim League, and the memories of the bloodshed in Calcutta still very raw, there was only one thing the men did agree upon; there must be a resolution as quickly as possible. Jinnah reassured Mountbatten over his concerns of bloodshed following partition by stating that once his surgical operation had taken place, all troubles would cease, and India's two halves would live in harmony.

Gandhi's attempts to convince Nehru and Vallabhbhai Patel, the driving force within the Congress party, of an India run by Jinnah naturally fell on rock-hard ground. They had a limit to the price they would pay for Independence, and handing power over to Jinnah crossed that line. Nehru was a torn and anguished man, caught between his deep love for Gandhi, and his new admiration and friendship for the Mountbattens. Nehru detested the idea of a partition, but his head told him that it was the only choice. Once Nehru voiced his agreement, the rest of the Congress party fell in line. He informed Mountbatten that, while Congress remained passionately attached to the idea of a United India, it would accept partition provided the great provinces of Punjab and Bengal were divided. One thing Nehru had in common with Jinnah is they both believed, unlike Gandhi, that the bloodshed would stop after partition. It seemed the cast was being set. Had Mountbatten, Nehru and Patel known about the existence of several carefully developed pictures lying in a safe belonging to Dr J.A.L. Patel in Bombay, their rush for Independence would have been reigned in, and possibly, the history of the region would have been very different. Standing out in the centre of the pictures were 2 dark circles ringed with a ragged white corona, looking like twin pictures of a celestial solar eclipse. The black circles on the X-ray pictures showed the extent of the advanced TB had destroyed whole sections of the lungs, and the spread of the corona indicated the patient had little time left. The lungs belonged to Jinnah; he was surviving on cigarettes and coffee. He was the unmovable rock for Pakistan's Independence, and his dictatorial style meant that those below him, with more flexible thoughts, could not challenge their leader. Mountbatten admitted, that had he known of Jinnah's condition, he would have slowed the train hurtling towards partition, if he knew there was a chance to deal with those behind Jinnah. How the region would have progressed if Gandhi had his wish of a single

India, can only be guessed at. However, the existence of the X-rays was known only to the Doctor, his patient and a few members of the family. Mountbatten had his last meeting with Jinnah on the 10th April where he begged, cajoled, and pleaded with him for a united India. When all his efforts were unsuccessfully spent, he sat alone in his study, meditating. It was becoming clear that the only way forward, was to give Jinnah what he wanted. The next day, he called Lord Ismay and told him to start drawing up the plans for partition. Mountbatten would look back on his failure to move Jinnah as the single greatest disappointment of his career. He wrote; 'It is sheer madness, and no one would ever induce me to agree to it, were it not for this fantastical communal madness that has seized everybody, and leaves no other course open.'

The next day, Mountbatten's aircraft left Palam Air Base in Delhi, just 40 days after it had arrived. This time it carried Lord Ismay with the plans for the division of India to be submitted to His Majesty's Government. The Mountbattens had a bumpy trip by air to Ambala and an equally uncomfortable four hour journey up the twisting mountain track to Simla for another meeting with Nehru. All the advisors told the Viceroy he was mad to meet with Nehru, but when he told them that he intended discussing the partition plan with Nehru, and not with Jinnah, they told him that he risked civil war right there and then. However, Mountbatten had taken his own path several times in his military career, and did so once again. Calmly, Mountbatten slid the document over the dinner table telling Nehru to read it later. When Nehru was alone, back in his room, he scrutinised the text. The effect was dramatic as he exploded with rage on seeing the clauses arranged by Mountbatten. Any state could claim Independent status if the inhabitants so wished for it through a vote. Nehru could see this was an attempt to let Bengal and Kashmir become a separate entity outside of India.

He stormed into the room of his friend staying next door. It was Krishna Menon, the man who had recommended Mountbatten to Attlee. Nehru exclaimed 'it is all over', but Menon preached calm. When Mountbatten heard the news in the morning of Nehru's explosive reception to his plan, he felt the whole plan was disintegrating before him, and this was just as Ismay was offering the plan to the British Prime Minister! However, a combination of Menon's counselling and the respect between Nehru and Mountbatten, led to an extra night at Simla which brought the two men back into discussions. Mountbatten gave all the ground to Nehru to keep the head of the Congress Party on his side. There, in Simla, described by Lady Mountbatten as 'a hideous house, bogus English Baronial, Hollywood's idea of a Viceregal Lodge', the final plan for the partition of India was set. The regions of the North that were of Muslim majority, together with parts of the Punjab, would become West Pakistan. Bengal would be split, with the areas of a Muslim majority becoming East Pakistan. The new country of Pakistan would have one head, but two bodies, with no land connections between the two. The issue that so enraged Nehru was removed; the Indian provinces and princes would only have two choices; India or Pakistan.

Harjinder had strived for a lifetime to achieve Independence, but he could never imagined the speed it would arrive at. The three party leaders announced on the 3rd June 1947, that India would be carved up into two sovereign states just two months hence. The unbelievable was happening in London as they watched Indian Independence moving from an unthinkable concept, to reality, in the blink of an eye. The Indian Independence Bill was drawn up in six weeks, incredibly thin, with just twenty clauses on sixteen pages; a model of conciseness and simplicity. Even Churchill labelled it 'a tidy little bill'. On the 18th July 1947 when the bill arrived in the House of Lords for the final act, it had to wait its turn. The Clerk of Parliament read out the title of the first bill to be considered; the South Metropolitan Gas Bill. The next bill he came to was the Felixstowe Pier Bill. Then, after a household utility and seaside tourist feature, it was the moment that would place the British Empire in the history books. The Clerk of Parliament read out, to a hushed chamber; 'The Indian Independence Bill'. The reply, with the ancient Norman phrase, seemed so innocuous; 'Le Roi le veult'. However, the words of ancient Britain sealed the end to the modern British Empire. The path to the dissection of one country, with the formation of two new sovereign states was now a reality. The dissection was not to be carried out with scalpels, however, but with a pencil.

This cartographical nightmare was to be the onus of one man, Sir Cyril Radcliffe, a man who had never before seen India. A potent combination of the New Delhi summer, and the dubious task of having to draw up a boundary that would determine the fates of million, drove Radcliffe to seek solace in the hills of Simla – he escaped his green shuttered bungalow in Delhi, and moved into the splendid Viceroy Palace at Simla.

The difference in accommodation was astounding, even if it wasn't to Lady Mountbatten's taste. The tall arches of the high ceilinged first floor were topped off by smaller arches on the second floor, which provided the balconies for the top floor, giving the building a whiff of Versailles. On one side, an octagonal turret jutted up a further level, topped with the ornate roof and splendid weather vane that called to mind Germanic great houses. The square, Norman-like tower on the opposite corner seemed like it belonged to a world of fairy tales and magical kingdoms, but Radcliffe felt no magic as he spent day after day hunched over his table. On top of the loathsome job of drawing lines on maps, he had suddenly been presented with an unbelievably short timescale. Every day he was drawing 30 miles of frontier, basing it on the few documents he had been provided with. At first, he tried to clear his mind by venturing out but he was constantly showered with requests to place this village in India or that area in Pakistan. Eventually, he locked himself away and lived with only his maps, his books and his pencil for company. There was no time to visit the villages whose names flashed past on the maps. There were no walks in the fields marked as open spaces on his maps. He knew, but could not see, how the lines would separate a farmer from his fields, a village from its well or the thousands of family members divided by a hitherto unseen border. Then there was the problem of Lahore. He was supposed to be splitting the country on religious grounds but Lahore was evenly split. It was surrounded in the immediate vicinity by mainly Muslim areas but with the solidly Sikh city of Amritsar only 20 miles away floating in a sea of Muslim townships and hamlets. Could he place Lahore as a separate enclave? The beautiful, and strategically important, state of Kashmir was an issue of even more immense proportions; was it to be part of India or Pakistan? Sir Cyril needed guidance.

Kashmir bordered China, Tibet, India and Pakistan, but with an overwhelmingly Muslim population, the obvious choice was that it be linked to Pakistan. All that was required was for the Maharaja, Hari Singh, a Hindu, to accede his principality to Pakistan, and all would be in order. Lord Mountbatten was now franticly trying to pull the thousands of untied ends together. He had known the Hindu Maharaja since they galloped together across the manicured polo field at Jammu during the Prince of Wales's visit. The Viceroy arrived with all the splendour of a state visit, in an attempt to sway the dithering leader. Mountbatten intended

to affix Kashmir to Pakistan and he brought Hari Singh the news from
Jinnah, that the Maharaja would be given an honoured place in the new
dominion. The dust from the horses' hooves was still to settle and notes
from the blaring trumpets yet to fade, before Mountbatten was brought
thumping back to earth. The Maharaja told him that he would not accede
to Pakistan. Mountbatten pleaded with Hari Singh to reconsider, since 90
per cent of his subjects were Muslim. With visions of bloodshed already
leaping into his mind, the Viceroy quickly promised Indian troops posted
in Kashmir for Hari Singh's protection if he did insist on acceding to
India. Mountbatten was briefly caught off guard, and then enraged, when
the Maharaja said he would not accede to India either, but wanted to be
independent. The Viceroy could have had no idea how quickly his words
would come true when he said, 'What I mind most is that your attitude is
bound to lead to strife between India and Pakistan. You're going to have
two rival countries at daggers drawn. You'll end up being a battlefield.'

The date fast approached for the birth of two new nations. What seems
almost inconceivable now is that Jinnah and Nehru would not know the
border of their countries, would not know what towns and cities they
would govern, until the day after Independence was granted. Radcliffe's
work would be revealed to them after the celebrations, the pomp and
ceremony, in Delhi and Karachi. Radcliffe knew from the very beginning
that whatever he did, there would be terrible bloodshed and slaughter
when his work became reality; 'I am going through this terrible job as
fast, as well as I can,' he wrote, 'and it makes no difference because, in the
end, when I finish, they are all going to start killing each other anyway.'

Already, stories were trickling in about frenzied attacks in Punjab.
With a sizeable population of both religions, it had the most to lose by the
twist and turn of Radcliffe's pencil. History would turn on the Viceroy,
Mountbatten, for his lack of understanding of the Punjab and Bengal, but
the reality was that all the main players, with the exclusion of Gandhi,
failed to see the magnitude of the forthcoming disaster. Nehru and Jinnah
assumed that their countrymen would have the same, tolerant, un-bigoted
views as them. They genuinely believed that partition would stamp out the
flaring of violence already taking hold, and therefore, speed was essential.
They assumed that all would react to the unfolding story with the same
reasoning, the same humanity as they would. They were grievously wrong.
Gandhi knew what was coming even as he found himself being attacked
by people infuriated by his opposition to partition. One particular Muslim

woman asked him, 'If two brothers were living together in the same house and wanted to separate and live in two different houses, would you object?'

'Ah' said Gandhi, 'if only we could separate as two brothers. But we will not. It will be an orgy of blood. We shall tear ourselves asunder in the womb of the mother who bears us.'

The military also prepared to break the deep bonds that comrades-in-arms share. Just three years earlier, they had fought alongside each other and spilt their blood for their Imperial master. In the Delhi Gymkhana Club, a party was held by the Officers of the Dominion of India as a 'Farewell to Comrades Reception, in honour of the Officers of the Dominion of Pakistan'. With arms around each-others' shoulders, the Cavalry officers discussed next September's polo matches. The Hindu Brigadier, Cariappa, called for silence before speaking to the various assembled military officers. 'We are here to say au revoir and only au revoir, because we shall meet again in the same spirit of friendship that has always bound us together.... We have been brothers. We will always remain brothers. And we shall never forget the great years we have lived together.'

To the senior Pakistani officer attending, he presented a silver statue of a Hindu and Muslim solider standing side by side. The band struck up Auld Lang Syne and spontaneously the officers reached for each other's hand. It is true; they would compete against each other soon, under circumstances more deadly than a game of polo.

The Air Force personnel were being shuffled around according to the country they had ticked on their chit. Arjan Singh was now a Group Captain and moved in to command the advanced flying training school just North of Delhi, in Ambala. He was assisted by the Station Commander, Erlic Pinto, who was already making a name for himself, and was vetted to follow Arjan Singh in the line towards IAF stardom. Arjan Singh was tasked with arranging the 18 Harvard aircraft that would spell out the word 'Jai' for the Independence flypast. He wanted the most experienced pilots he could get, so he thought nothing of including Flight Lieutenant Zafar A Chaudhry before releasing him to join his new Pakistan Air Force. So it came to pass that the Indian flypast would have a Pakistani flying in it, one who would go on to be the Chief of the Pakistani Air Force. With Arjan Singh destined to be Chief of the IAF, they would repeatedly cross swords on the orders of their political masters in the years to come.

Harjinder had spent his life striving for an Independent India. When he stood in the Principal's office at Maclaghan Engineering College in

Lahore, with Captain Whittaker's pistol placed in his hand, the Captain's reasoning had hit home; idealistic thoughts needed to be backed up by a position of strength. He had spent his adult life working with Jumbo, with Mukerjee, and with Engineer, to see a strong Air Force lead the way. When their wish became reality, they didn't have the luxury to sit and savour the moment. The rebuilding, reorganising and restructuring of their Air Force wouldn't allow them a moment's rest in the months to come. On the 14th August 1947, as the sun dipped below the horizon, the British Union Flag was lowered on every flagstaff, in every official building, throughout India. Under the direction of Mountbatten, there was no fanfare or ceremonial lowering of the colours. As the new day dawned on a new nation, the country would see a celebration as the Indian tricolour was raised for the first time. Gandhi spoke to the crowds; 'From tomorrow we shall be delivered from the bondage of British rule. But from midnight today India will be partitioned too. Tomorrow will be a day of rejoicing, but it will be a day of sorrow as well.'

In Lucknow, Major General Curtis could not bear the thought of another flag being run up the flag pole at the Residency where the Union Flag flew day and night, and had done since the siege of the city in 1857 by the Indian freedom fighters, or mutineers, depending upon which side of the fence you sat. That night, the British Sappers cut the steel flagstaff of the Residency from its base and pulled out its foundation. Then they re-cemented the base, leaving no trace whatsoever of the flag pole on which, for 190 years, the symbol of British Power had flown high without a break. The Union Flag which was removed from the Residency was sent to Field Marshal Auchinleck, who, in turn, sent it to Windsor Castle, where it still hangs.

At 17, York Road, in Delhi, Nehru was just about to finish his dinner, when he was summoned to the phone. He returned with tears in his eyes and was, for a time, unable to speak. The call had come from Lahore, to report that the water to the Hindu and Sikh quarter had been cut. People were going mad from thirst in the dreadful heat, but when the women and children came out to beg for water, they were being butchered by the mobs. Fires were raging out of control in several parts of the city. In an almost inaudible voice he said; 'How am I going to talk tonight. How am I going to pretend there's joy in my heart for India's independence when I know that Lahore, our beautiful Lahore, is burning?'

It wasn't just Muslims burning buildings in Lahore. In Nehru's India, the Sikhs and Hindus were burning Muslims in their homes. V.P. Menon, a talented bureaucrat, had redrafted Mountbatten's partition plans, and had been very influential in coaxing a majority of the Princes to the discussion table to ultimately throw their lot in with the new India. When his daughters heard the conch shells signalling midnight, they jumped about with delight. Menon brought them back down to earth. 'Now our nightmare really starts.'

Harjinder spent the last evening in British India with about 100 of his brother RIAF officers, including Subroto Mukerjee and Arjan Singh, in the Delhi Gymkhana Club. They enjoyed the good humour and banter at the 'farewell supper', whilst seated for the last time under the light blue flag; Union Jack in the top left corner, RAF roundel sitting over the Star of India at the centre.

Tomorrow was another day.

For years to come, the lasting memory for so many in the cities and major towns of India, would be the crowds, the sea of humanity, sweeping through the streets to celebrate the day they thought would never come. The rule book was briefly sent spinning out of the window. Hindus, Sikhs, Muslims, Brahmins, untouchables, Parsees, Anglo-Indians, rubbed shoulders, laughing, cheering and weeping with emotion. In Delhi, the outgoing Raj had estimated 30,000 people would come to see the official raising of the Indian tricolour. They were not wrong by a few thousand; they were wrong by well over half a million. This was not a crowd to look on curiously at some parade by their rulers. This was a crowd that insisted on witnessing the birth of their nation, so they could tell the next generations that 'I was there'. The seething mass of scarlet and gold swept away any attempt at order by the departing masters. In Delhi, the little wooden platform at the base of the flag pole looked like a raft bobbing on a stormy sea. Nehru and Mountbatten looked out at this torrent of people sweeping away guide-ropes, barriers, the bandstand, and any scrap of the original, carefully-choreographed plan. Mountbatten's daughter was stranded from her carriage by the crowd. Under Nehru's guidance, shoeless, she stepped out onto the carpet of humans below who happily offered shoulders, backs and heads for her to walk across to join her father. Mountbatten had to shout at Nehru to be heard; 'Let's just hoist the flag. The band is swamped. They can't play. The guard can't move.'

A metaphor for what was to come, the celebration of Independence happened in a chaotic, shambolic, but an exciting moment. As the Saffron, White and Green flag burst from the top of the flag pole, the noise from the crowd and the valiant, but already swamped, offerings of the band were blown away as nine RIAF Tempests thundered overhead only 400 feet, at 250 mph, above the flag and sea of heads. Squadron Leader Moolgavkar led the Tempest formation on this historic day with Arjan Singh. They were followed by the group of Indian and Pakistani pilots in their Harvards. Mountbatten and his wife made it back to their open carriage. Nehru was carried by the crowd and dumped alongside them. Then the Mountbattens heard what no other English ears had heard before. 'Mountbatten Ki Jai! Mountbatten Ki Jai!' – Long live Mountbatten.

Sergeant Saigal was leaving the smoking city of Lahore with his new bride, the sister of Doctor Nanda of Simla. With the Sikh quarters still burning and being ransacked, they boarded the train with only a revolver for company. The killings and destruction were most evident in Lahore, but the reality was that the whole of the Punjab, Harjinder's home state, was witnessing massacres on either side. Saigal's train travelled the 20 miles through the largely Muslim areas to pass into the safety of the Sikh city, Amritsar. The red-brick station at Amritsar had become a refugee camp for the Hindus fleeing from the regions of the Punjab, which most now believed, were heading for Pakistani rule. Every train passing through was swamped with people looking for relatives and friends, or any scrap of news concerning them. Nobody was ready for the arrival of the No. 10 Down Express that evening, but even as the puffing engine approached the station, the crowd sensed that something was wrong. When the station master saw the petrified driver being guarded by 4 soldiers, he too, knew that something was amiss. The constant chatter and wailing that was the established background noise at Amritsar station fell to a hush as the eight carriages came to a halt. It was the first time in many days that a silence descended, leaving a growing feeling of dread spreading within the Station Master's soul. He knew he had to enter that train, even though every sinew in his body was screaming not to. The floor of the compartment before him was a tangled jumble of bodies with throats cut and skulls smashed. Limbs and body parts that had been hacked off were strewn along the corridors. There didn't seem to be a single body intact, but he felt the need to call out, to tell them they were in Amritsar; they were safe. Incredibly a few bodies moved, as the ones trapped below, pushed their way to the top. One woman took her husband's severed head and cradled it as she left the train. Children clung to the bodies of their dead parents, and one man held the dead body of his child, unable to move from the spot in the middle of the carnage. The station master found the same scene in every carriage with just a pitiful few literally rising from the dead around them. When he got to the end, he found painted on the back of the corpse train: 'This is our Independence gift to Nehru and Patel.'

Perhaps because of the number of military personnel on the train of the newly-wedded Sergeant, and Mrs Saigal, or perhaps it was simply a stroke of good luck, they completed the 20 mile journey terrified, but unharmed.

In Simla, Dr Nanda was waiting for news of his sister and her new husband, when his father burst into the room shouting 'Lahore is lost. Lahore is lost.'

It seemed impossible that Lahore, the city where they had grown up, the city where their family house had been for generations, would no longer be a part of their India. The news coming from Lahore seemed just the tip of the iceberg; the stories of the savage bloodletting spreading throughout the Punjab grew from the isolated incidents of previous months. The whispers in Simla turned into shouts, concerning the gangs collecting at the only exit from the Simla valley, effectively controlling who came and went. No one remained untouched by the violence, even down to the three-year-old boy in the Nanda household who knew something terrible was happening. His friend Shaukat was suddenly not there for them to go playing on the hills together like they always did. On their last meeting, Shaukat had taken the young Nanda's stuffed penguin toy called Kuka, but his parents wouldn't tell him where either had gone. The whispers he heard still haunt him today; 'They didn't make it to the Railway Station.'

This town, the British Government's summer retreat, was to feel the terror along with the rest of the Northern India. Mr Nanda senior, the Royal Rickshaw builder, climbed onto the roof of the family house where he was to stay night after night for several months; he had an armour plate hung around his neck and a shotgun by his side. This was a common enough occurrence throughout the region – men standing guard over their families for nights on end, living in perpetual fear of the marauding gangs. Hindus, Sikhs and Muslims all turned against each other, the savagery by one side being magnified and handed back by the other. It was not an eye for an eye; it was a massacre for a massacre, a rape for a rape, and blind cruelty for the sake of blind cruelty.

The day after Independence, when the Pandora's Box was opened, Mr Nanda's prophecy about Lahore was confirmed. Mountbatten handed Nehru, and Pakistan's Prime Minister, Liaquat Ali Khan, a manila envelope each containing the fruits of Sir Cyril Radcliffe's hurried labours. They went into separate rooms to open and digest the news. Mountbatten was reassured by one observation; both men looked outraged as they emerged, so he knew that Radcliffe had been truly impartial. It was true, Lahore was now in Pakistan, and Amritsar was in India. The city that took Harjinder into adulthood, trained the engineer in him and formed his views and his goals, was now in a different country. Radcliffe's scalpel had also sliced through Jumbo's Bengal creating the Muslim enclave of East Pakistan, separated from the rest of the country by 970 miles of Himalayan peaks and Indian Territory. As much as possible, he had separated Bengal based on religious beliefs, this however, had created a conundrum of a different sort. East Pakistan would have 85 per cent of the world's jute growing within its borders, but not a single mill to process it with; they all lay in the city of Calcutta. The idea of complete religious separation was, of course, ridiculous. India still harboured 50 million Muslims spread throughout the country, leaving India still as the third-largest Muslim state in the world. The borders were now public, and so began the greatest migration in history.

For the next few months, there would be an unparalleled tide of misery flowing through Northern India, as people were ripped from homes held in the family for generations, forced to move because their religion differed from that of their neighbour. The Air Force flew from dawn to dusk to try and monitor the rivers of humanity. Flight Lieutenant Patwant Singh remembered seeing, 'whole ant-like herds of human beings walking over open country spread out like cattle in the cattle drives of the westerns I'd seen, slipping in droves past fires of the villages burning all around them.'

One such surging caravan of people in Punjab was estimated to contain 800,000 souls, unwilling participants in a record-breaking feat.

The sweep of Radcliffe's pencil was to cause a myriad of problems but there was one stroke that millions of Pakistanis would never forgive him for. Gurdaspur seemed inconsequential but despite being mainly Muslim, Radcliffe followed the natural boundary of the Ravi River to bring it under Indian control. To the North was Maharaja Hari Singh's beautiful

Kashmir. The Hindu Maharaja with his mainly Muslim population, desperately tried to remain neutral but, unintentionally, Radcliffe's scalpel had offered India a hope of retaining Kashmir through this gateway; through Gurdaspur.

So Harjinder's dream had come true, and suddenly he found himself in the Air Force of an Independent India. However, the Air Force he knew had been torn apart. All the permanent bases, bar one, were now in Pakistan. The majority of airstrips, hangars, offices, forts, barrack blocks and landing grounds were now in another country. A sizeable portion of his technical equipment was there, too. This was a twisted, butchered, version of the dream. Within the entire Indian military force, partition was an overwhelmingly sad experience for everyone, sapping away any euphoria of an independent India. Old and trusted friendships were abruptly ended as so many of their comrades left for Pakistan. Some friends they would perhaps never see again, some they would see on the battlefield. Tension quickly rose between both the new countries as the two Air Forces were dragged towards conflict.

The power in Delhi now rested with Nehru's Congress Party, but Nehru requested that Mountbatten remain as Governor-General. Krishna Menon was made the first Indian Ambassador to the UK. When criticised for the Rolls-Royces he kept as official vehicles, he retorted; 'I can scarcely hire a bullock cart to call on 10 Downing Street.'

Menon was using the iconic British car as a signal to the British Government that India was to be taken seriously on the political stage. The reality was that he preferred to use London's double-decker buses whenever possible, and his wage from the new Indian Government was a token one rupee. The handing over of power had caused a stir back at Air Force Headquarters. Air Vice-Marshal, Sir Thomas Elmhirst, RAF, was sent to India as the Commander-in-Chief of the RIAF. In Harjinder's opinion, the RAF seemed to be carrying out a 'scorched earth' policy on their equipment in India. He believed that because Pakistan was retaining a large number of RAF personnel, and not trying to stand on its own two feet like the IAF, it was getting preferential treatment. Other accounts by senior Indian Officers cast Elmhirst in a very good light, but it is easy to see why Harjinder came to his conclusions. Certainly in Delhi, many files, records, maintenance and overhaul books, made a fine bonfire. Spitfires were having concrete blocks dropped on to them from a height to render them useless. The large 4-engine American-built Liberator bombers were dangled from a crane, the wheels retracted, then dropped on their noses. The only repair depot that would still be in the new India was Kanpur, and that was stripped of much of the equipment which was then sent to Pakistan. Some specialist tools were found five years later in the main domestic water tank when it was drained! To Harjinder it felt as if a huge portion of his life's work was being torn apart in front of his eyes.

Knowing full well how the RAF had disposed of their Liberators, Elmhirst rang Harjinder up one day to demand his approval of the proposal to buy the famous, but very obsolete, RAF Lancaster bombers. Harjinder voiced the opinion that they were not suitable for the hot conditions in India. When he discovered they were proceeding with the deal despite his complete veto, he once again put in his resignation. When called up to the Elmhirst's office and grilled by the man running the RIAF, Harjinder forcefully pointed out that they had 50 Liberators in Kanpur; they could overhaul them in the RIAF and so Elmhirst's old Lancasters were not needed. A very bold statement!

Elmhirst was so sure that this was a flight of fancy that he challenged, oh yes, he challenged, Harjinder to go to Kanpur and do the job himself. Naturally, Harjinder did. Throughout India there were about 100 of these aircraft abandoned and packed into various airfields. Many had been damaged by the departing RAF, all had endured the hot temperatures and monsoon rains. Grass and shrubs had grown through them and birds and snakes had taken up residence in the crevices. However, as news of the IAF's intensions became known, spare parts and engines started to flood in from around the country. Harjinder set up camp in Kanpur, working with the Government-run Hindustan Aircraft Company, and the first Liberator was flying by the end of 1947. Eventually, the IAF bomber force was formed with more than 40 aircraft returning to active service, assembled using salvageable parts from all the available broken and smashed hulks. It was the use of the tea urn, and Harjinder's penchant for aircraft reconstruction, on an industrial scale. A few of the 'Frankenstein' Liberators were still going strong 20 years later.

There is no doubt Harjinder thought that Elmhirst had his own agenda, and not necessarily one for the benefit of the RIAF. Naturally, the British Government had an agenda of its own, but Harjinder's view of Elmhirst seems a little harsh. He certainly helped the new Indian Air Force take a massive step forward in terms of re-equipping, much of it coming from one phone call. Elmhirst's friend, Sam Elworthy, had been given the job of closing down an air base in Pakistan. Sam Elworthy called Elmhirst to ask him if he 'had a use for fifty new Spitfires in shipping containers there?'

That is the phone call dreams are made of! Elmhirst needed no time to deliberate; 'Pop them on the first ship to Bombay'. The Indian Air Force had just gained two squadrons and a flying school!

Harjinder felt that the RAF technical staff's attitude towards their task of cultivating technical ability in the RIAF was neglectful and borderline dangerous; 'not caring two hoots for our pilots' lives'. Harjinder's reactions were violent and bold. Pakistan was requesting many hundreds of RAF Technical Officers, but Harjinder decided not to retain a single RAF Officer or airman. It was a long cherished dream to see the RIAF as a complete unit without any outside help, and in this, he received the full moral support from Subroto Mukerjee and Aspy Engineer. In Engineer's recollections, he remembers the conversation with the British Chairman of the restructuring committee. The Chairman started by asking Mukerjee how many RAF officers he wanted. The Chairman was taken aback when Aspy replied, 'a few'. However, when he asked Aspy Engineer how many senior Airmen he wanted, the answer caused him to drop his pen, Aspy wanted none. The chairman was stunned, 'Engineer, I suggest you go get a cold shower and come back.' He paused and added, 'This is a serious matter and I give you 3 months before the IAF collapses and asks for the infusion of a large number of RAF NCO's.'

Aspy replied, 'Sir, as a matter of fact, I had to take a cold shower this morning as the heater packed up!'

Partition saw Wing Commander Janjua become the most senior officer in the Pakistan Air Force (PAF). He had been a great personal friend of Harjinder for some time, and despite the increasing hostility, it was still quite normal for Harjinder to pick up the phone that still linked the now HQ RIAF Delhi to the HQ PAF in Peshawar. Both sides had the 2,500 horsepower, single seat, brutish, Hawker Tempest fighter aircraft. The Tempest was the last word in piston engine aircraft, the fastest ever built, a development from the Typhoons Jumbo had flown, and capable of carrying large war loads. Harjinder's problem was that he had absolutely no specialist tools to work on the very complex Bristol Centaurus engines. So Harjinder rang up Janjua, who very sportingly invited him to go to Lahore and collect whatever engine overhaul tools he required. Towards the end of October, Harjinder flew to Lahore in a twin engine Dakota transport aircraft, piloted by an Englishman and accompanied by Wing Commander Rup Chand, who wanted to retrieve whatever he could from his house in Lahore. All other displaced Indians didn't have the option that Rup Chand did. The abandoned, looted city moved him deeply. Much of Lahore being placed under control of the authorities.

Small insurgent groups in Kashmir had been fighting since the partition, but they were becoming better organised, and better equipped, with the assistance of Pakistan. This three person team of Indians, landing in their Dakota aircraft, couldn't know of the Pakistan Government's plans to officially back and strengthen the forces with their own Army that very same day. The day Harjinder first stepped into Pakistan was the beginning of the First Kashmir war.

As soon as Harjinder landed at Lahore, Janjua ran towards him. His first words were a smack straight between the eyes, 'Harjinder, I hold myself responsible for your safety. Our countries may be at war soon over Kashmir. Please send your Dakota out of Lahore and recall it when you have collected your Centaurus tools.'

The friendship still ran deep enough for a war not to come between them. There was no question of sending Harjinder away without his tools for warfare. As suggested, Harjinder sent his Dakota off to Amritsar to await the recall. He knew that if they didn't collect the tools immediately, he would probably never be able to do so. Even though shots were being fired between the two armed forces, the PAF officers were extraordinarily generous and hospitable. Harjinder was locked inside the hangar, food was provided, and he was told to take half of what was there. They worked through the night and into the following day. The Dakota was recalled and the precious cargo flown out to India. The engines on their front-line Tempest aircraft could be overhauled and not a day too soon. They were just about to go into action in Kashmir, against those very same Pakistani forces who had so graciously hosted Harjinder. India, just a few months old, was at war with her neighbour. Just five years earlier, in his last war, Harjinder had been a Sergeant, converting spotter aircraft into bombers, borrowing steam trains and rebuilding discarded RAF aircraft. Now he was the senior-most engineering officer, and was to start his first war in the Independent Indian Air Force, prowling around in 'enemy territory' collecting tools from their hangars to fix the aircraft that were to be at the forefront of combat operations.

The Hindu Maharaja, Hari Singh, still sat on the fence, refusing to accede Kashmir to either country. This 'Standstill Agreement' had held for the first few months after Partition, even when Pakistan started an economic squeeze on the state. Pakistan had certainly offered no resistance when the fierce Pathan tribesmen crossed into Kashmir and started the slaughter, but now they were officially backing the claim on Kashmir. When the Pakistani troops took part in a full-scale push into Kashmir, the frightened Maharaja fled from his palace on 26th October 1947. Without hesitation, he went straight to Delhi where he signed the accession to the Indian Government, simultaneously requesting military assistance. Kashmir would be part of India, but first, they would have to fight over it.

The Pakistan–backed tribesmen pushed through Kashmir with relative ease. Action was needed fast, and it was the RIAF that was flexible enough to do this. At Palam, in Delhi, and surrounding airfields, the engines of the RIAF Spitfires and Tempests spluttered, and then roared, to life. They formed up in pairs, took off with the snub noses of the Tempest and long elegant noses of the Spitfires heading North. They dropped into Amritsar to refuel, before arriving at the various dusty, makeshift strips that were to be used as temporary bases; after a quick briefing, the pilots took off again, this time into battle. The silver painted machines glinted in the sunlight as they came in low, levelling their wings before the guns rattled into action and rockets leapt from the rails under the wings. Initially, with only small numbers of aircraft, they merely tried to intimidate the men on the ground. It worked, as their former colleagues stopped in their tracks and took cover as the rockets and bullets rained down wave, after increasing wave. A group of 3 Spitfires headed towards the battle zone as ordered, but one pilot, Ram, was separated after problems in starting his aircraft in Amritsar. As the sun began its descent, the visibility worsened. Ram gave up on the straight line navigation, and tried to follow the foothills, but it is notoriously difficult to distinguish one hill from another, one valley from the next. Sure enough, Ram had picked up the wrong group of hills and ravines, so he was now crawling around the Murree Hills, in Pakistan. His fuel finally ran out just as he was contemplating a landing in a football field; he had to take to his parachute instead. On the ground he was captured immediately by regular Pakistani troops, if he had fallen into Tribal hands he would not have survived for more than a gruesome, agony-filled hour. Instead, such were the relations between the two services at this point, that he was flown back to Ambala, just North of Delhi to rejoin the fight!

The sky over the battlefield soon filled up as Dakota transport aircraft flew the Indian Army into battle. An observer on the ground might have wondered just who was fighting this war – some of the aircraft still had the RAF World War II roundels of dark and light blue, other RIAF aircraft appeared with the new official roundel, the chakra wheel symbol from the centre of the Indian flag, and some had the more familiar red white and blue RAF markings, with their old RAF serial numbers crudely painted over. However, to add to the surreal quality of the battlefield, the commandeered civilian Dakota transport started to arrive, still sporting their bright colours, as they followed their military counterparts into virtually undefended airstrips. Bright white aircraft with the words Jupiter Airlines or Tata Airlines splashed down the sides were shot at as they too disgorged their cargo of soldiers. These men stepped off their transport and straight into the battle that was happening around the very fields they were landing in. One of the pilots leading from the front in his Dakota transport aircraft was another of the old guard from the days of flying Wapitis. It was 'Baba' Mehar Singh, the pilot who had his fuel pipe shot away and walked through the night only to be shot at by his own men from the fort. Now he was an Air Commodore, in-charge of the Kashmir air-lift operations, being shot at by men who were on his side only 6 months ago. Being shot at by friends was becoming a habit for Baba!

During the war, Mukerjee was only Deputy Chief of the RIAF as Air Vice-Marshal Thomas Elmhirst, RAF, was still the boss. In Pakistan, Elmhirst's contemporary was Air Vice-Marshal Perry Keene, a man of similar seniority, whose career had crossed several times with Elmhirst's. This put the two British Officers in an interesting position. They could either obey their new masters as per their orders from the British Government, or send a letter of resignation back to UK. They chose to go to war against each other. The phone line between the two remained open throughout the war, which must have been party to some interesting conversations. 'I say Perry, old chap, how are you getting on? Best you don't pop down to the front tomorrow at 0600!'

Harjinder reflected that those months were among the busiest in his career. As the senior technical officer of the RIAF, he had to hastily reorganise the entire maintenance cover for the Kashmir war and oversee the operations. This involved late night conferences with his old colleagues Mukerjee, now an Air Vice-Marshal, and Aspy Engineer, now an Air Commodore. The country was threatened, and a war was on, but this would not get in the way of Harjinder's flying training. Every morning, Harjinder was trying to attend classes at the Delhi Flying Club to get his commercial pilot's licence. He couldn't use the Harvard he had learnt to fly in Miranshah, because even these aircraft were in Kashmir, their bright yellow colour covered by household green and brown paint. They added what little firepower they had, but their main function was dropping supplies to the troops. They were also the early birds, the pilots taking off in the pre-dawn light with an observer in the rear seat taking pictures and making notes of troop locations to update the fighter boys. Harjinder was qualified to fly his little L5 civilian aeroplane, so he took that toy-like machine to war. He started to fly into Kashmir to watch proceedings from the air firsthand. As the silver Spitfires and Tempests zoomed down on the attack so Harjinder weaved the little L5 through them, and the chubby transport aircraft that festooned the skies above the battlefield. In the back seat was Neki Ram, his chaprasi, or office peon, but it is unclear whether he willingly volunteered to fly into a war zone in a slow, fabric covered aircraft, or on orders from Harjinder!

A few days earlier, the airstrip at Srinagar had been the private strip for the Hari Singh, and thought to be too small for military fighter aircraft. Now it was a hive of activity with maintenance crews swarming around Spitfires, Tempests and Harvards; the physical size of these aircraft seemed to take on enormous proportions given the limited area they had to operate out of. The pilots usually operated in pairs, a system used so successfully by Arjan Singh in the Battle of Kohima. As the Airmen refuelled and rearmed the aircraft, the pairs of pilots could be seen standing at the rear of an aircraft, maps spread over the tail as they discussed the next mission, no time until nightfall for thoughts of rest. The first person Harjinder met was Hrushikesh 'Arvind' Moolgavkar, the new Commanding Officer of No.1 Operations Wing, fresh from leading the Tempests on the Independence Day fly past. This gave some sense to the furious pace around him. Moolgavkar was the same mad keen Pilot Officer who had harangued Jumbo in Burma for not getting his fair share of missions, winking at Harjinder because he knew the opposite to be true. Now Moolgavkar, as a Wing Commander, was leading from the front again, flying the Tempest into combat, and taking his orders from the other dynamo, Aspy Engineer. When a Dakota touched down, it was not to disgorge further supplies, but to bring in the senior Army Officers to survey the battlefield. Aspy Engineer was pulling the strings of the IAF, but it was the tactical brain of Lieutenant-Colonel Sam Manekshaw MC, who controlled the Army on the ground. The seven Japanese bullets in his stomach, from the battle Pagoda Hill just outside Rangoon, had failed to kill this man.

The manoeuvrability of Moolgavkar's Tempest made it ideal to twist and turn through the valleys, the huge wing area grasping lift from the rarefied air of the high altitude battlefield. The Pakistani anti-aircraft guns were a constant threat on attack runs so, in a change of tactics, Moolgavkar took his bomb and rocket laden aircraft up to 18,000 feet with his Flight Commander tucked in alongside flying another Tempest. They pushed the noses of the aircraft over into a vertical dive to scream down on the target. Another important development incorporated into the Tempest design was the knife thin wing profile for the newly developing idea of laminar air flow. The air streamed smoothly on the surface, but since it offered considerably less drag than the wings of their previous fighters, the Tempest leapt forward towards the mountainous landscape below shrouded in the smoke of battle. Suddenly, Moolgavkar's aircraft started shuddering and shaking so violently that he ordered all bombs to be jettisoned. With the change of weight distribution the Tempest's nose shot up skywards, crushing him into the bucket seat with the G force causing a temporary loss of consciousness. Before he had fully regained his senses they were back in a vertical climb passing through 20,000 feet. They brought their aircraft back to Srinagar gingerly although everything seemed in order. On landing, the top surface of the wings were found to be wrinkled, like skin after soaking for too long in a bath or a swimming pool. In America, Chuck Yeager had only just broken the sound barrier in the rocket powered Bell X-1. Moolgavkar, the man who would be Chief of the Air Force one day, had nibbled the speed of sound encountering compressibility problems, and had only just got away with his life.

Harjinder repeatedly used the L5 to fly from base to base, collating firsthand knowledge on the serviceability of his force. There just weren't enough hours of daylight to complete his endless tasks, so he taught himself night flying. Officially, Harjinder was attached to a desk, but he was still one to get his hands covered in oil at every opportunity. When he went to Palam air base, outside Delhi, he saw a desperately-needed Tempest aircraft, lifeless, as it awaited a new engine. Rather than wait for a junior engineering officer, he gathered some technicians together, rolled up his sleeves, and got on with the job. By the time he was ready to fly home to Safdarjung, the airfield in central Delhi, it was getting late and also very windy. The petrol filled gooseneck flares were lined up to pick out the runway edge but the wind caused them to flicker, throwing dancing demon-like shadows on the runway. Harjinder positioned himself centrally between the jigging flares and opened the engine up to full power. As he started his takeoff roll, Harjinder didn't compensate for the wind soon enough with his rudder, and he was blown towards the downwind side of the runway. As his main-wheels skipped off the tarmac his tail-plane clipped one of the gooseneck flares, splashing petrol over the tail surfaces. The flames from the next flare came close enough to ignite the fuel soaked fabric. As soon as he settled in the climbing attitude, the ever-present Neki Ram tapped him on the shoulder, and with more than a touch of understatement, said; 'Sahib, there is a little fire on the tail.'

Harjinder struggled against his shoulder straps to pivot around. His efforts were greeted by the sight of Neki's head back-lit by his tail-plane, merrily burning. The flames, being fanned by their forward speed, were slowly devouring the aircraft's fabric covering. Harjinder reasoned that landing straight ahead might end in a minor crash that would escalate as they burnt out so he took the other option, kept the engine at full throttle and pointed the little smouldering aeroplane back towards the ground to build up speed. The extra air flow luckily did the job and the flames blew out, leaving only a faint glow at the tip; his gamble worked. Harjinder climbed the machine back up and set course. There was great activity on his arrival at Safdarjung airfield with fire engines and ambulances alerted by a radio call from Palam. Harjinder wondered what all the activity was in aid of, because the aircraft seemed to be handling OK, and all was fine with the landing. As the propeller came to a stop an airman ran up to the cockpit. Harjinder was ordered to present himself to the Aerodrome Officer. As Harjinder entered the official's room, slightly annoyed at the delay to get home, the Officer erupted with threats to have Harjinder's pilot's licence taken away. After giving the officer a good listening to Harjinder eventually got away with a stern lecture and probably a few reminders from his pilot friends in the RIAF that traditionally you land immediately when you are, or have been, on fire!

The 1st Kashmir war lasted 15 months with the RIAF learning fast as time progressed. They soon perfected operating from small landing grounds close to the fighting with Harjinder's engineers mirroring his own days in Burma, but without the stolen trains! Different fronts opened up throughout the soaring peaks, ridges and valleys of the region. Soon

Mehar Baba Singh found himself considering Dakota operations from tiny strips perched high up in the Himalayas. The villages of Leh and Poonch were surrounded by Pakistani troops. The Major in-charge at Leh reported that they would be overrun the next day, and was preparing for the final showdown with what precious little they had in the way of supplies. At 11,000 feet up, the airstrip was one of the highest in the world and had only seen small aircraft struggle up there in the thin air. Throughout the military, it was assumed that large aircraft could not fly in to support the surrounded soldiers at such a height, so all was lost. They didn't factor in Baba who decided the only way to find out if it could be done was to do it. He personally took command of a Dakota and placed that big aircraft at the very leading lip of the landing strip, pulling it up to a stop before the limited ground ran out. It was a massive morale boost to the Indian troops, and stunned the attacking soldiers. He then returned later in the day leading 6 Dakotas that brought the first of the Gurkha troops as reinforcements. Cariappa, now a Lieutenant General, was pushing towards Poonch to meet up with his old friends; now his new adversaries. In the speeches in the Delhi Gymkhana club party he had said that meeting again was inevitable but polo wasn't on the agenda as he had predicted.

The army, supported by the Air Force, stopped the invasion and re-established the borders. As the winter of 1948 arrived, the fighting went into hibernation until the UN cease-fire came into effect on 1st January 1949. There is little doubt that without the Air Force, the map of India would look different today. It had been a baptism of fire, but Air Vice-Marshal Elmhirst had an interesting view on the conflict on later reflection. 'The 1st Kashmir war, though regrettable in itself, certainly helped get the Indian Air Force into its stride. Sad as it was for the two new nations, it provided an immediate objective for the Indian Air Force. Pilots came under fire and had to fire their guns; leadership or failure showed itself. Regrettable as it all was in principle; in fact nothing could have been better for the morale and training of the new Air Force.'

Two events in 1948 helped bring about a halt to the sectarian killings in India. The ongoing fighting between Indian and Pakistani troops somehow seemed to make the conflict official, a formalisation of killing and therefore not something the individual should partake in. The other event happened on Friday, 30th January 1948, in Birla House in Delhi.

Gandhi held a vital meeting with Patel in an attempt to prevent his resignation. There had been the inevitable conflict between Patel, the tough-minded realist, and Nehru the socialist idealist. Mountbatten had pleaded with Gandhi to intervene since India needed both men to take the country into the future. On Friday 30th January, Gandhi had succeeded in his task, but his deep, intense conversation to safeguard India's immediate future had made him late for his 5 o'clock prayer meet; there was nothing Gandhi hated more than being late. Manu, Gandhi's great-niece, had spent an anxious 10 minutes trying to catch his eye, but now the old man placed a hand on her shoulder and shuffled as fast as he could out into the garden. It was the first time Gandhi had been able to walk unaided since finishing his fast, so he took the shoulder of Manu to try and speed his progress. The usual entourage that flowed around Gandhi was seriously depleted. His Doctor was still in Pakistan, and the police officer assigned to him was summoned to an urgent meeting in downtown Delhi.

As with every day, a group of followers had gathered on the lawn to partake in the 5 o'clock prayers. Nathuram Godse was amazed that nobody had searched him as he entered the inner sanctum of Gandhi's present location. His plans to disguise his pistol in a camera, or to dress as a woman using the sari to conceal the gun, had all been abandoned. He walked in bold as brass and suddenly, unexpectedly, here he now stood waiting for the arrival of Gandhi. His two fellow conspirators entered Birla House separately, but positioned themselves just behind his shoulder. Apte and Karkare knew the 35 foot shot through a milling crowd to Gandhi's small meeting platform would be a difficult task for the untrained Nathuram. The restlessness of the crowd was calmed when the small man, with the big aura, appeared behind them, stopping his speedy shuffle towards the platform just very briefly to place his palms together in a greeting. To try and make up for his uncharacteristic lateness, Gandhi dispensed with his usual route around the perimeter of the lawn and set off directly for the meeting platform. The crowd dutifully parted to form a narrow corridor to his destination. Karkare saw Nathuram pass the pistol from one hand to the other before slipping off the safety catch. As Gandhi approached, leaning on the shoulder of Manu, Nathuram took 2 steps forward into the ad-hoc corridor formed by well-wishers. Nathuram bowed slowly from the waist and said 'Namaste Gandhiji'.

Manu thought the man had come to kiss Gandhi's feet; 'Brother; Bapu is already ten minutes late.'

At that moment Nathuran's left arm whipped up to roughly shove Manu away. His right arm brought the small black Beretta pistol up to Gandhi's chest and three sharp cracks signalled the end to Mahatma Gandhi.

Mountbatten sped to Birla House. As he pushed his way through the crowd a man, his face contorted with hysteria, screamed, 'It was a Muslim.'

A sudden silence descended which held the crowd in a frozen moment of time. Mountbatten looked over the sea of faces and boomed back, 'You fool. Don't you know it was a Hindu.'

Seconds later his press secretary asked Mountbatten how he could possibly know the religion of the assassin. Mountbatten's answer was chilling. 'I don't, but if it really was a Muslim India is going to live through one of the ghastliest massacres the world has ever seen.'

The news soon broke that indeed Gandhi's murderers were Hindus and India was spared from further, unimaginable, bloodshed. Gandhi achieved in death what he had so desperately tried to achieve in the last months of his life. Naturally, the antagonism still remained, but individuals were so shocked by the violent end to Gandhi's life at the hands of their own kind, they collectively let the military work out their grievances on the battlefields in the conventional manner. Peace returned to the cities of the new India.

The task to arrange Gandhi's funeral fell to the British Commander of the Indian Army, Lieutenant-General Sir Roy Bucher. It was the second time for him to organise such an event. By a bizarre twist of fate, he had arranged Gandhi's funeral in 1942 in Yeravda prison following his famous 21-day fast. Gandhi had failed to attend that event, but now, as his ashes were carried away by Mother Ganges, his death brought calm to India.

Numbers concerning the weeks and months following partition have been tossed around ever since the chaotic events unfolded. There is the very real danger of any meaning being lost in the uncertainty. It was impossible to paint an accurate picture of the carnage with unknown numbers left to die at the side of the road, thrown down wells, cremated in their own homes or abandoned in fields. To give some comparison to the figures, during World War II, India had lost 87,000 troops. Mountbatten preferred to use the figure of 250,000 killed during partition, most probably driven more by wishful thinking then actual fact. Some historians now place the figure as high as 2 million dead. However, a figure a figure of 500,000 is generally agreed on. The numbers of refugees was on a scale hitherto unseen, with three quarters of a million flowing across borders weekly. Eventually ten and a half million people would be displaced in the North with a further million, in slightly more peaceful circumstances, forced to relocate in the divided Bengal. Terrible as the price was, it was being paid by the northerly one tenth of India's population. For their sacrifice India not only gained Independence, but was placed on a path to form a country that would come to epitomise tolerance. As the population spiralled up to 1.3 billion, the different religious, creeds and castes would live together with remarkably little friction. Harjinder's beginnings of an Air Force as a team, irrespective of beliefs, would become central.

Harjinder's dream of Independence was complete, but it also brought him great sorrow to see the people he felt such affection for, turning against one another just because of the religion they followed. From the moment he could influence the happenings within the Air Force, he had preached religious tolerance and he had found the willingness of his men to respect all others beliefs and backgrounds. With sad eyes he looked North to see every organ, bone, muscle, sinew, artery and vein of his Punjab torn in two. The full realisation of the British departure had not fully hit home before he was called to fight his old comrades. Elmhirst had said there was nothing better for training and a test of leadership; Harjinder had brought together a maintenance organisation shredded by partition; he had successfully supported the entire Air Force campaign in a war just months after setting out on the road to self-reliance. With the conflict resolved against Pakistan, for the time being, it was clear that the Indian Air Force needed to rapidly build up the supporting network that sits behind the more glamorous front-line flying of the aircraft. This was to be Harjinder's major challenge, and one he tackled with characteristic dedication. What had started as a visit to Kanpur to restore the Liberator bombers, soon became Harjinder's life for the next 6 years. Kanpur was to be the home of the RIAF Engineering, and so Harjinder was the obvious choice as Station Commander. Harjinder accepted the post even though he had always hoped that he would avoid being made a Station Commander. He considered it a waste of a senior technician and also throughout the war he had seen Station Commanders weighed down with mundane matters of administration, supply, technical, medical, welfare, security and the whole paraphernalia that goes to build up an Air Force Unit. He still liked to get his hands dirty and working on aeroplanes. Kanpur gave Harjinder plenty of opportunities and, as usual, most of them far beyond the normal duties expected of him as a Station Commander!

Thirteen

Command!

'Since when have I lost the confidence of the Air Force?!'

Aristotle:

'He who never learned to obey, cannot be a good commander.'

Once Harjinder accepted the new post as the Station Commander of Kanpur, he was suddenly in-charge of hundreds, and soon, thousands, of men. Promotion, that seemed so slow to come in his initial years in the fledgling IAF, now came at a pace and Harjinder received another with his new job. From Sepoy to Group Captain in 16 years! When he had first joined the Air Force, any Officer seemed a man of great importance, but a Group Captain was a demigod. Suddenly it was Harjinder who had the lives of these people in his hands; he now knew that the Group Captains hadn't been demigods, just men with far reaching responsibilities to cope with. Harjinder's future was not assured because on his departure from Delhi, Air Marshal Sir Thomas Elmhirst made it clear that he would be sacked immediately if he failed to deliver on his promise to reclaim the Liberator bombers. Bringing damaged aircraft back to life was Harjinder's forte, and this was a challenge he was more than ready for. The rebirth of the liberator bombers was just a fraction of the whole challenge, Harjinder intended to set up an entire self-sufficient Air Force maintenance facility.

The challenge for the IAF was to restructure the Air Force so that it could serve their sovereign nation without dependence on any external source. The RAF had set up the IAF to quell the troublesome tribes in the North-West Frontier and force the Pushtun population to submit to their Imperial system; the irony was that more Pushtuns now lived in India than Afghanistan! The area, now called India, had mainly been seen by the RAF as a staging post in support of Singapore; that was until the Japanese charged through the region. As a result the majority of the permanent air bases were in the North, in Pakistan. The IAF may have been given a greater number of front-line aircraft squadrons at Partition, but very few bases to keep them or maintain them in. They had fought the war in Kashmir in true IAF style-making do with whatever was available; small tactical landing grounds, the private airfields belonging to the Maharajas, and tools that Harjinder took from the Pakistan Air Force at Lahore on the opening day of the war, or discarded equipment gathered in Kanpur.

So Group Captain Harjinder Singh took command on 15ᵗʰ August 1948, as the war in Kashmir rumbled to a conclusion, with the border more or less restored to the original, drawn so hastily by Sir Cyril Radcliffe. Harjinder arrived at his new Command, but received a shock on his very first morning as he took a tour around the Base. He knew he had a large number of civilians working on the station, and that they would fall into his sphere of responsibility. However, when he found some of them lolling in the shade of a trailer, his first impressions were not encouraging. When he called to them, they ambled over and addressed him with the very informal 'Babuji' and while they seemed an intelligent enough lot, they always seemed to look slightly unkempt. So if this scruffy, ragtag bunch was going to be a part of his crew, part of his responsibility; he knew that something drastic was required to shake them all up.

Harjinder took fifty of the most promising men to one side, told them that their grubby *dhoti* was unsuitable as work clothing, and pointed out to them that they would actually save money if they switched to military issue. He started with some basic military drill and discipline, to show them the difference between a civilian and an airman. Harjinder's Warrant Officer, Mr Shirke, played a very significant role, never giving up on these men. The men took to their training, and over time they turned these fifty men into model workers.

The military was already a profession that was held in high regard in India, but the prestige and glamour of the armed forces, when combined with the wondrous, futuristic aircraft of the IAF, left many in open-mouthed awe. It was an interesting sight to watch these men, who only a few short weeks ago had been of a slovenly sort, march smartly to the military band, looking determined, their faces shining. This nurtured a feeling of belonging, and soon, others volunteered to join in, until more and more men began to take pride in their work and in their appearance. It gave the participants a very different status amongst their fellow workers, earning them the respect of their peers. Harjinder insisted that these parades were purely voluntary and in no way compulsory, but it was not long before a request came from the civilian technicians asking to be given some type of training. This sense of pride and prestige was infectious. Soon, all the civilians became physically fit, mentally alert, and efficient. They obeyed their superiors with a smile. A sense of order and organisation pervaded their work. The Kanpur station began to work like a well-oiled machine, each of its workers overwhelmed with pride, working to the best of their abilities.

The telephone girls and stenographers also volunteered. Within a matter of nine months, all civilians at the Air Force Station, Kanpur, numbering nearly a thousand, had been welded into one homogeneous organisation, even forming their own marching band. It was inevitable that onlookers would refer to the group as Group Captain Harjinder Singh's private army. Even the sweepers wanted to be a part of the new order. They grouped together and, after their daily cleaning chores were completed, to a new, higher standard, they began operations to reclaim fallow lands on the periphery of the Station. Soon, they had their own vegetable gardens bursting into production. Not only did Harjinder have Kanpur turning out Liberator bombers from abandoned wrecks, to form the IAF Bomber Squadrons, but the personnel were providing their own food to keep their bellies full.

Kanpur was a Heaven-sent for Harjinder. Not only could he lay the cornerstones of the IAF maintenance system, but he also had almost 100 wrecks of Liberator bombers to turn his attentions onto. The Government-run, HAL (then known as Hindustan Aircraft Ltd.), would do the refitting of the aircraft, but there was the small matter of getting these huge, damaged, bombers down to Bangalore from Kanpur, a distance of over a thousand miles. Road transport was out of the question, so the only solution was to fly them down. In two's, or three's, the aircraft were assembled by cherry picking the useable parts from all the available hulks. Harjinder's first priority was to get two Liberators flying and fitted out as cargo aircraft, not as bombers. These soon started a regular route back forth between Kanpur and Bangalore, feeding parts to their sister airframes arriving at HAL after their own ferry flight from Kanpur. In less than a year, 40 aircraft went from scrap metal shells in Kanpur, to front-line bombers leaving the Bangalore workshop. It only took the combined teams until 2nd November 1948, to form the first IAF bomber Squadron; No. 5 Squadron took the name 'The Tuskers,' and adopted the Elephant, standing on its hind legs with its trunk raised, as their mascot. The logical place to base this first bomber squadron was at Kanpur, so Harjinder's men would be on hand to help. Kanpur was soon throbbing with the sound of the four 1,200 horsepower Pratt and Whitney engines on each of the restored goliaths.

As the number of aircraft increased, two more squadrons were formed. Harjinder's experience of patching up individual Wapitis, had now led to squadrons of 4-engined bombers that were created from junk. The Americans actually suspected that the IAF had purchased these bombers clandestinely, but after a visit to Kanpur, they went away satisfied, and not a little impressed! The workmanship shown by Harjinder's teams, and the HAL personnel, stood the test of time over the two decades of additional service these Liberators provided, before the jet bombers replaced them. Most of the Liberators couldn't keep the scrap at bay any longer, but three did survive. The Royal Air Force, and the Royal Canadian Air Force, were both presented with an example of this aircraft from a different era, to display in their own museums where they can still be seen. The IAF's final example still sits in Delhi, next to the hangar where the Vintage Flight's Wapiti, Lysander, Tempest, Vampire, Hurricane and Spitfire are waiting for their own restoration process to start. It would be an enormous undertaking but could this old relic be rescued, a second time, to take to the air for a third reincarnation?

On the 19th April 1949, Harjinder found himself back at the Delhi Gymkhana Club, with old, familiar faces. No. 1 Squadron RIAF had a wonderful reunion dinner. As expected Mukerjee, Engineer, Arjan Singh, Mehr 'Baba' Singh, Narendra, Nanda were present, but it was another six members of the original No. 1 Squadron members who made the evening so perfect; those who now flew, and fought, for the Pakistan Air Force. From friends, to foe, and back to comrades, in just two years! More than anyone in the room, Harjinder missed the obvious absentee; Jumbo Majumdar.

News of the successes at Kanpur travelled to the very top of the political ladder in India. The bomber squadrons being formed from the scrap yards, after the departure of the RAF and USAF, had allowed what limited funds that were available, to be transferred to the acquisition of fighters. One day in 1950, Nehru, now Prime Minister, was invited to lunch in the Officers Mess at Kanpur. Mukerjee came with Nehru, and before the event he warned Harjinder not to lay out an elaborate lunch because the Prime Minister thought the armed forces were being overfed! So much for 'An *army marches on its stomach*'! Harjinder had a plan, and arranged what he considered a reasonable menu befitting the occasion. Mukerjee knew his man well, and, as he'd predicted, the Prime Minister did remark at the spread before him, telling Harjinder that he was lucky to get such good food. Mukerjee's eyes narrowed as he gave Harjinder a 'told-you-so' look over the meal table. Harjinder pounced; 'Sir, I would request you to see our cooperative vegetable garden, our poultry farm and our piggery, which are run by our class IV employees in their spare time. All these items on the table are a product of their efforts from here on the station. I encourage people to work hard, produce more, and eat more. Unfortunately, this is not the case in the rest of this state. There is so much land lying uncultivated, so many rivers flowing, yet people remain semi-starved. They are not used to hard work.'

The Prime Minister caught the twinkle in Harjinder's eye and probably knew he had just walked into a carefully laid ambush. He replied; 'Yes, I have visited the Punjab (*Harjinder's home state*) and found that every inch of land is under the plough. So the peasants eat well, dress well, and they look cheerful. Here, the reverse is true. You must show my aides your Air Force food-growing schemes. I congratulate you.'

Mukerjee's eyes widened, and his face split into a smile that ran ear-to-ear. 'Trust you to pull it off, Harjinder' he said, when he had Harjinder to himself.

Harjinder and his family settled into their new house outside the Air Force Compound. Harjinder's wife, Beant Kaur, now had the opportunity to shine. Her husband may have been in-charge of all the men working on the Station but Beant Kaur leapt headlong into organising the welfare of all the families, both military and civilian, who had their lives intertwined with her husband's Command. She introduced a Ladies' Arts and Crafts School, where hundreds of ladies learnt stitching, tailoring, and embroidery. The course she structured was six months long with a certificate to show for their efforts. This resulted in children being always smartly dressed in well-tailored clothes. The Ladies' Arts and Crafts School was so popular, that a double shift had to be organised. The ladies even adopted a sort of uniform of pink sarees, or pink shirts and white salwars. Much admiration was showered on Beant Kaur by visitors of ever-increasing importance, but her answer to their questions was the same to all; 'This is a necessity for Airmen's families. I should know, because I have passed through this stage – and I know where the shoe pinches.'

Harjinder made a point of meeting every new officer, and their family, when they arrived at his station. In 2014, I had the pleasure of sitting in the front room of a delightful lady, Mrs Vera Albuquerque, the wife of the late Air Vice-Marshal Albuquerque. When he was a newly qualified Flight Lieutenant Engineer, they arrived with great trepidation at Kanpur; but there was Harjinder, on their first evening, to show them around and introduce them to the other officers. Harjinder was certainly thoughtful, and kind when it came to those under his care but that didn't mean he had mellowed. When he walked into the room the men would stand to attention as etiquette demanded and the women found themselves hovering between sitting and standing. Etiquette said sit; but the aura that surrounded Harjinder said stand!

There was more to occupy Harjinder and his wife beyond the families under their protection. They had their own son to nurture. The illness Beant Kaur had endured on her own, while Harjinder had been facing the Japanese in Burma, had left her unable to bear children. However, her brother's family was suffering from a different problem, an ever-increasing family. So, together, they came up with the perfect solution. Harjinder and Beant Kaur adopted one of her brother's sons as their own. The house in Kanpur finally became a family home with the arrival of Manmohan Singh Bains, or Mohini for short, their four-year-old son.

Harjinder had a family, and was in command of his own growing station, but for the last few years there had been something gnawing at him constantly, even eclipsing his desire to form a successful Air Force. Since those first sneaky lessons in a Harvard on the North-West Frontier, he still yearned to be a pilot, and he would never forget Jumbo's last words, 'Harjinder, promise me you will propagate the spirit of flying even if I am killed in the next flight.'

Harjinder had come to hear about a more modern, small, light aircraft available in India, a Beech Bonanza, which had crashed, but was in a repairable condition. The owner was tracked down and the offer of Harjinder's little L5 light aircraft as a straight swap was accepted (this little L-5 now languishes as scrap at Mumbai's Juhu Flying Club – would that Harjinder were alive to work his magic on it now!). This was not the only aircraft Harjinder was getting his hands dirty on. Scouting through the salvage of India had become second nature, to help build up the supply of Liberator bombers. However, when he spotted the sleek thoroughbred lines of a Spitfire, abandoned under a heap of broken aircraft in the salvage dump at his own Base, he couldn't get it out of his mind. Just as he had brooded over the semi-abandoned RAF Lysander he had seen on the way to Calcutta before the war, he now started to make plans for this Spitfire.

That Calcutta Lysander was saved to become No. 1 Squadron's 13th aircraft, and Harjinder knew that he could find a role for this Spitfire. He sent his men down to carefully dismantle the wreck, and bring it into one of his aircraft workshops. He worked alongside his men to nurse this aircraft back to life, and when Rolls Royce stepped in to arrange the overhaul of the Merlin engine, Harjinder knew he would see the Spitfire fly again. However, there was a minor problem, the Spitfire was a single seat fighter, and Harjinder was an Engineering Officer in the IAF, not a pilot. Technically he wasn't allowed to take IAF aircraft up for a spin unless there was a pilot with him to officially Captain the machine. This Spitfire had been written off from the military inventory, but clearly, it wasn't a civilian aeroplane either, so it fell between two stones. The answer for Harjinder was just to ignore both sides. After filling it with IAF fuel there was only one man to invite to Kanpur to fly it; Suranjan 'Dasu' Das. The Officer Cadet, who in 1946 had shown that his Engineering skills matched his flying ability while assisting Harjinder rebuild the Spitfire in Peshawar, was now a RIAF test pilot. He knew any aircraft that had been worked on by Harjinder would be safe as houses, and so the test flight was done; the Spitfire was cleared to fly again and handed over to Harjinder.

Climbing on to the trailing edge of the Spitfire's wing, to walk up to the cockpit, you know this is something special; the rounded lines of the wing as they taper into the famous crescent shape at the wing tips, the smooth curves of the metal fuselage leading up to the flattened top cowl of that long nose, housing the 12 cylinder engine, the bubble canopy, the small door on the left side of the cockpit; all scream beauty and perfection. Harjinder had worked on Spitfires, had sat in the cockpits to do engine runs in Spitfires, but this time it was to *fly* a Spitfire. This was a completely different generation of aircraft from the open-cockpit, buffalo-like Wapiti. It was similar to the Harvard, but the Harvard's cockpit seemed vast compared to this snug, close fitting single-seater that you pull on like a jacket. The Merlin engine ran very smoothly, the sound from the exhaust stacks, and the vibration, transferred to the seat of the pants communicating a visceral power, almost a desire to be turned loose and hunt. His little fabric covered L5 seemed a child's toy in comparison, his present Beech Bonanza more like a family car. Harjinder strapped in and joined the elite ranks of Spitfire pilots. It is no surprise that this reclaimed machine soon became known as Harjinder's Spitfire, as he flew himself to meetings throughout India. A generic nickname for Engineers at the time was 'plumber' so Harjinder not only used a radio call sign of 'Plumber 11', he also fashioned a name plaque himself to affix to the engine cowling of this Spitfire, just below the jutting stub exhausts. The silver script 'Plumber' plaque is still firmly in place over five decades later.

Harjinder was an established civilian pilot, but now, more than ever, he wanted to be an Air Force pilot; the pride of having the innocuous winged brevet on a uniform with the deep meaning that lay behind them. This desire was further driven to new heights after an argument with Aspy Engineer. The New Pay Code had placed the pilots' pay on a scale higher than that of technical officers. Harjinder thought this most unfair and aired his opposition frequently. One day, Aspy said that Harjinder would never be able to appreciate the risks and responsibilities of a flying man; 'If you could fly, you would understand.'

This was a red rag to a bull, as Harjinder considered himself a pilot already, so he fired back; 'All right, I will learn to fly.'

Air Headquarters were considering a scheme to encourage technical officers to learn to fly, believing that it would help them appreciate a pilot's difficulties, mechanical restrictions, and the psychological limitations of the job. Harjinder nearly blew the door at HQ off its hinges when he got a whiff of the proposal. His persistence was already legendary, so any resistance was futile, anyone who thought to obstruct the man on his mission, quickly put the idea out of his head. It was to be a reunion for Harjinder and the Harvard advanced trainer, although his previous training never officially happened, did it?

The original letter ordering Harjinder to commence flying training still exists, in a safe, in an office in Delhi. He was instructed to travel from Kanpur to attend flying school in Ambala, where he would first start ground lessons, and take the exam on the theory of flight, and the rules of the air. Under the heading 'Transport' it simply says; 'by own Spitfire'! This must be the only example anywhere in the world where a trainee military pilot was 'ordered' to arrive by Spitfire to commence his pilots training course!

With or without recognition of his previous experience, there was never any doubt of the outcome. On the 15th April 1950, the young officers, all in their early twenties, prepared for a life defining moment. As the families gathered, it would be a day they would remember for the rest of their lives as the coveted wings were pinned to the chest of their pristine uniforms, and thoughts turned to the front-line Squadron they would be joining. Whether Harjinder had intended to make a statement, or the theatricality of it all eluded him and it was simply a matter of convenience, he certainly made a grand entrance on the day of the Parade. The young Pilot Officers formed up on the Parade Square for the Wings Parade, as the 41 year-old Group Captain Singh, MBE, landed from Kanpur. He taxied up in his own Spitfire, parking it next to his own Wings Parade. He left his flying helmet in the cockpit, climbed down off the wing and took his place in the parade.

As time went by, and Harjinder flew more as a military pilot as well as a civilian one, he became firmly convinced that the pilot faced more risks and accepted greater responsibility then his earth bound colleagues. Aspy ultimately won the argument over the addition pilots' pay. I wonder if the fact that Harjinder was now receiving the extra pay as an IAF pilot, may have softened his ideals!

From now on Harjinder would sport those coveted wings on his uniform, but it was not his flying abilities that would be examined by the military, it was his skill as a commander. The Brigadier who raised a toast in Delhi to his Muslim colleagues before partition, who as a Lieutenant General led his men against those same people in the relief of Poonch in the 1947-48 war, was now the first Commander-in-Chief of the Indian Army. However, General Cariappa had a poor opinion of the discipline in the Air Force after seeing Airmen in their working overalls as he flew around the country, courtesy of the RIAF. On Mukerjee's request Cariappa was invited to Kanpur. Cariappa's reaction to Mukerjee was, 'What can I see in the blue-eyed boys of the Government of India, except tilted caps and swaggering walks?' Nevertheless, he went, and Mukerjee chuckled inwardly, knowing the sort of reception Harjinder would provide.

On landing, Cariappa was taken on to the dais, from where he reviewed a parade of 2,000 men, Airmen and civilians, all smartly turn out. The young women who worked as secretaries, dressed in their smart blue uniforms, headed the march-past of the civilians, they were followed by the technicians, clerks, storekeepers and sweepers. Cariappa was quite taken aback by the discipline and smartness of this Air Force Station and said, 'Harjinder, you are in the wrong Service. If you had been in the Army, with your drive and administrative ability, you would have been a Major General by now.'

Harjinder didn't realise that it was in fact a compliment being paid and instead retorted, 'Sir, I would never exchange my blue uniform for khaki whatever the rank offered. I am proud to be a Group Captain in the Air Force.'

Cariappa rose to the occasion, smiled, and patted Harjinder's shoulders: 'Well done, you are a real airman.'

Cariappa was not put out by Harjinder's unintended rudeness, but his tall, Sikh, Army Staff Officer looked to have murder in his eyes with the perceived slander to his beloved Army.

Cariappa subsequently issued instructions ordering several senior Army Officers to go to the Air Force Station at Kanpur to study what he called 'Efficiency in Man-Management'. This included a gruff old Lieutenant-General. The gentleman in question was sure that he could be taught nothing by this upstart of a Group Captain, and he would not have the wool pulled over his eyes like the General before him. To prove he could not be fooled, he ordered the band to be assembled, and then he drove around the base, choosing men at random to assemble on the parade square. The hundred odd civilians comprised of clerks, technicians, servants and sweepers marched to the tune of the brass band as if they were a bunch of seasoned soldiers on a ceremonial parade. The stunned General started shaking Harjinder's hand even whilst the parade was on. Later he talked to many participants. His one common question was; were they *ordered* to wear uniform? 'No', they all replied. From then on he never ceased to praise the Air Force for having achieved something miraculous.

When the King bestowed the prefix 'Royal' to the Indian Air Force, it was meant as an honour, to show appreciation of a hard fought campaign in World War II, but now, as an Independent nation, divorced from the collapsing British Empire, the term 'Royal' seemed out of place; from another era. On the 26th January 1950, India became a Republic and it was the opportune moment to drop the 'Royal' prefix, and the Air Force returned to its original name coined in 1932. The IAF was back. It was time for more flypasts down the main Kings Way, now to be called Raj Path, in Delhi. Once again, it was Moolgavkar who led the formation in his silver aircraft. However, it was not the big, brutish, silver, propeller-driven Tempest that Moolgavkar was leading the formation in. Not only was the IAF back to their original name, they were back to achieving firsts. They were the first Asian country to use jet aircraft, the superb De Havilland Vampire, and the first silver examples of this propeller-less wonder celebrated India becoming a Republic.

The IAF were working towards establishing more permanent bases throughout India, especially in the North, where the threat from Pakistan seemed ever-present, but the IAF still only really had a few established stations to work from. Kanpur, with all the technical expertise, was the logical place to base these new jet aircraft, and Harjinder's arrival in Kanpur coincided with the arrival of the IAF's newest aircraft. The De Havilland Vampire was capable of speeds in excess of 500 mph, and operating at heights far beyond its propeller driven cousins. However, it had just missed out on front-line service in World War II, and then India's Kashmir war, by a few months. The fuselage was a small, egg-shaped pod just big enough to squeeze a single pilot's seat into. The pilot's head protruded out the top of the pod into the streamlined sliding canopy above. Without the cumbersome piston engine and propeller in front, as in the fighters before, the visibility was excellent. In this new piece of technology the jet engine was bolted on to the pod just behind the pilot. The metal wings sprung from the pod, starting with air intakes in the wing roots to feed the hungry engine. Then, two thin fuselage booms stretched back on either side of the engine. This allowed the hot exhaust gases to blast out of the fuselage in the shortest distance producing the thrust from the engine in the most efficient way. A slab-like tail-plane linked the two small fins at the end of each boom. It was a clever, compact design, and in the all-silver colour scheme, they looked very space age and futuristic. However, if you gave the fuselage pod a tap with a knuckle it wasn't the clang of metal you would hear but the supressed thump of wood. The wings and tail were all metal but the pod was constructed from a balsa and plywood sandwich, which was still covered in canvas; this machine's only link back to the venerable Wapiti. That fuselage design was taken directly from the incredibly versatile De Havilland Mosquito of the last war.

The first three Vampires were flown from the UK directly to Kanpur in 1948, to the newly-established Aircraft Testing Unit (ATU). Soon the distinctive sound of piston engines from the aircraft parking line was replaced by the crack, crack, crack of fuel igniters in combustion tubes leading to the thump, then roar, of the Vampires' jet engines as the fuel ignited. Occasionally too much fuel would cause a twelve foot long tongue of orange flame to blast under the tail on start-up. Initially it caused Airmen to dive for fire extinguishers, but they soon realised these flames would soon disappear into the shimmering heat haze behind the jet exhaust. The roar of the jets, even at idle power, left the observer in no doubt of their potential.

After the first three were delivered, the subsequent Vampires were shipped in component form to be assembled in Bangalore. Life Magazine ran a series of pictures showing the jarring collision of old and new. The new, sleek, silver Vampires, with their lovely rounded features and futuristic twin fuselages, sat outside the hangar as they came off the production line. The oil, fuel, final fittings and ground equipment was brought up to the aircraft by two-wheeled carts drawn by oxen. When the final assembly was completed in this way, they were then flown up to Harjinder in Kanpur, to be tested in the ATU.

In January 1949, the battle weary No. 7 Squadron IAF left their tents in the sub-zero temperatures of the Kashmir region to move to the more temperate climes of Delhi. As the Commander of Kanpur, Harjinder had supervised the training of the pilots and Engineers at his base on this new, cutting edge aircraft. When the training was complete, No. 7 Squadron became the first jet fighter unit in India, and in Asia. In February, Wing Commander Moolgavkar had also left his duties in Kashmir and formed a display flight of three Vampires. He travelled around India to show the public their new deterrent, with the highlight being the first Republic Day flypast. The county-wide tour also gave Harjinder's maintenance personnel the opportunity to practice working on unfamiliar airfields in a wide variety of climates. After all, the Vampire could get from one end of India to the other in a few short hours.

This was all very interesting for Harjinder, but, having seen these aircraft at his station for two years, he now wanted to start the new decade by getting his hands on this new jet fighter. He couldn't hold himself back one day after a 'daring test pilot' from the ATU came to see him. The pilot was testing his newly assembled Vampire when he taxied it into a barbed wire fence. He tried to tell Harjinder that this new jet was not easy to handle, harder than Harjinder's own Spitfire (*he clearly didn't know the technical details of both aircraft since they both used the same braking system; compressed air, controlled by a lever on the control column, which inflates a bag in the wheel hub to push pads onto the wheel*). Harjinder knew he was bluffing, trying to cover up his error. Harjinder just held out his hand, telling him to hand over the aircraft checklist. Half an hour later the pilot was standing next to his machine as Harjinder snapped shut the harness buckles of the brand new jet. The cockpit sides curved in around the shoulders not dissimilar to his Spitfire. With the nose curling down around the feet there was nothing of the aircraft to see beyond the front windscreen. Harjinder completed the checks and pressed the button to start the engine. When the engine RPM was sufficient, he moved the fuel cock to the open position and he heard the familiar thump as the engine roared to life. He turned the handle above the throttle on the left side of the cockpit. The bicycle chain moved over the cogged wheel to slide the slender Perspex canopy shut. With no big propeller on the front there was no need to have the plane sitting on a small tail-wheel to give the necessary clearance. The Vampire had a nose wheel and sat in the flying attitude. For the first time, Harjinder could actually see down the runway as he lined up for takeoff. He gingerly pushed the throttle forward, not too fast, otherwise, too much fuel would pour into the combustion chamber and extinguish the flame in the engine. Just before reaching 100 mph on the runway Harjinder gave the control stick a gentle pull rearward, and, as he tucked the undercarriage up into the wings, he started his first flight in the Vampire, his first flight in a jet. From rear gunner in the back of a silver Wapiti biplane, to the pilot in the silver streamline jet fighter.

He left a stunned test pilot back on the ground. It is not the recommended military technique of converting onto a new aircraft; take the Pilots Notes, wander out to the jet – your first ever jet – strap in, start the engine and get flying! Aspy Engineer, understandably, once again flew off the handle on hearing what Harjinder had been up to. Harjinder tried the old excuse of, 'I was testing the brakes when it just leapt of the ground,' but Aspy wasn't having any of it; he knew Harjinder too well. He warned him that the Ministry would have him hung, drawn, and quartered, if he crashed their expensive new machines. It will be no surprise that Harjinder continued flying the Vampire with his theory being; if he did crash a Vampire he wouldn't be alive to hear what the

Ministry thought. However, when he once used a Vampire to fly to his meeting with Mukerjee, blatantly disregarding the orders issued by his superiors, Mukerjee launched at him, but Harjinder batted the comments straight back at him. He said that all senior officers with pilots' wings should fly a Vampire otherwise the younger pilots would not respect their bosses. Mukerjee was stung by his remarks, and off he went, quietly, to give the Vampire a go.

India's need for the small, fast, agile Vampire jets and the lumbering, leviathan Liberators, had increasing urgency. The eyes of the world had turned away from Kashmir, when on 25th June 1950, North Korean forces stormed across the 38th parallel to drag the United Nation forces into the Korean War. Western forces streamed into the region, and they wanted bases, and general political stability in the Asian region. Pakistan was happy to provide bases and accept military aid from the USA but they made it clear that they wanted a conclusion to the Kashmir issue, no prizes for guessing what that conclusion that should be.

The Pakistan Government made a big play of promising that there would be no fighting on Indian soil, but quietly, in a move not unnoticed by the Indian Government, they refused to recognise Kashmir as Indian Territory, thus keeping the door open to move into the disputed region. Throughout 1951 and into 1952, it appeared that invasion was looming once again. Pakistan was taking delivery of American F-86 Sabre jets, and yet, Harjinder was spending day after day supervising the patching together of increasingly obsolete propeller aircraft like the Tempest, and even the Spitfire. The Vampires were now being built by HAL under a licence agreement, and Harjinder saw these aircraft as they passed through his hands en-route to the Squadrons. However, even the Vampire was a generation behind the Pakistan Sabre aircraft, and the British were restricting the supply of engines to the IAF because of the political situation. The Indian Government turned to France who, as usual, had no issues about supplying arms to anyone with the requisite cash. In 1952, Moolgavkar was part of the IAF team that flew the latest French fighter, the Dassault Mystere, a plane he flew in a dive beyond the speed of sound whilst testing it. Negotiations in France soon concluded, and India was provided with a second avenue for combat aircraft procurement, which reduced the IAF's reliance on a single country. India was taking a step up on to the world stage, through the United Nations, and the world would soon know all about it. Krishnan Menon had left his post as Ambassador in

London, to take command of the Indian delegation to the United Nations, a position he would hold until 1962. Both superpowers, the USA and the USSR, initially courted Menon, but they soon came to understand the stubborn, quick-witted orator. India stayed firmly placed between the two Superpowers and Menon coined a new term; non-alliance.

In the UK, 1952 was time for a change. King George VI died, leaving the 25-year-old Princess Elizabeth to become Queen of the United Kingdom, Canada, Australia, New Zealand, South Africa and she was still the Monarch of Pakistan and Ceylon. India however, had already become a Republic, so she was not to inherit the title 'Empress of India', like Queen Victoria before her. On the day of her Coronation, Edmund Hilary finally conquered the roof of the world just beyond Simla; Mount Everest had been climbed. The pictures he used to plan his route were taken from those modified Wapiti aircraft that had lifted off from India as Harjinder joined the IAF. The Wapitis were gone, and the IAF was now in the jet age. One of the first tasks for the new Monarch was to send a senior RAF man to India to take control of the IAF for the final time.

Sir Ronald 'Ronnie' Ivelaw-Chapman became the new Indian Air Force Chief, just as the Indian Government recognised the need for a larger Air Force. The IAF was to grow, and so Kanpur would expand massively, flourishing as it did. Chapman decided to pay Harjinder a visit. He had heard about Harjinder's private army, but what he witnessed far exceeded anything he had previously come across in India or the UK. Harjinder had not just a military unit under him; he had created a complete community. Chapman was so pleased with the running of Kanpur, that later, in Harjinder's office over a cup of tea, he said, 'Harjinder, you have done an excellent job here, really first class. Ask of me anything you will; I will grant it, if it is in my power.'

Harjinder wasn't expecting such a request, but knew exactly what to ask for; 'Sir, please give me permission to fly any IAF aircraft I want.'

Chapman kept his word and put the instructions in writing; Harjinder could fly the Vampire whenever, and in front of whosoever he wanted. If such an offer was unforeseen, the next turn of the conversation came as an even bigger surprise. Chapman offered Harjinder the rank of Air Commodore. However, with one thick string attached, he would have to leave the IAF to become the Chairman of the Government run aircraft manufacturing company, HAL. Harjinder immediately dismissed the idea, explaining that he would not leave his IAF. There is no doubt that the offer of such a position in the Government was meant as a compliment, but Harjinder instead wondered if people back in Headquarters were losing faith in him. Not one to tiptoe around an issue, he marched into the office of Air Vice-Marshal Mukerjee. 'Since when have I lost the confidence of the Air Force?'

Mukerjee laughed and said, 'I know what you mean. I told the Chief that nothing would induce you to leave the IAF, but he would not believe me, and you are going to stay. When it is time for us to leave the Service, I would like to go out hand in hand with you. We have stuck together through thick and thin so far, so we will stick together all the way.'

There can, perhaps, be no greater compliment.

On the 4th February 1952, Mukerjee summoned Harjinder to Delhi. The Defence Secretary, Patel, wanted to see him most urgently. That urgent call was nearly the end of Harjinder Singh. The only way to get there for the 11 o'clock appointment was by air and the only aircraft available at short notice was the good old Harvard. The weather man said that Delhi was completely overcast with low, grey, threatening cloud. Rain was forecast at the Air Force Station Palam, Delhi, but the circumstances, the urgent call from Patel, and Harjinder's overconfidence in his flying abilities, combined and soon he was airborne in awful weather.

He climbed higher and higher through the grey filth in an attempt to break into that burning blue that bores into your eyes when you first burst through the blanket of cloud. Harjinder stared over the round nose of his Harvard, just occasionally flicking his eyes down to check that he had the best climb speed, and that all the engine temperatures and pressures continued to stay nailed in the green 'all-is-well' arcs. Several times, a lighter patch of cloud would zip past, but it was a false sign. In reality, the clouds were becoming increasingly dense, with no sign of the sun-filled world above. The sound of the rain beating on the Harvard was deafening, the water streaming in from the top and sides of the canopy. Little rivulets were getting past the rubber seal and spitting into the cockpit.

Agra Control answered Harjinder's radio call, but their report of cloud down to 200 feet, lashing rain, and winds at 30 miles an hour, was not what he was hoping to hear. Soon, he could raise Delhi on the radio, but they passed on a similar report with winds even stronger, at 35 miles an hour. That made up his mind, he would try to return to Kanpur, where, at least, he knew every tree and building around the airfield. After an hour he was in radio range, but Kanpur had even worse news for him;

they were effectively closed, the weather had worsened since he'd left for
Delhi. He turned again for Palam, which, at least had proper Air Traffic
control facilities to try and talk him down to terra firma. Had there been a
life before the start of this flight? Time seemed to be suspended, except for
the fuel gauges which seemed to be playing with him as they sped towards
zero. His personal history seemed to just involve this grey gloom and the
endless wisps of cloud. Visions of Beant Kaur and his son seemed from
another life. Working only with estimates of wind speed and direction,
knowing by flying back and forth multiplying any errors, Harjinder hoped,
more than assumed he was near Delhi.

A voice came through the headphones. For a moment it felt as if he
was communing with someone from the beyond, it was so surreal, for the
whole world seemed to convene into the cockpit, the glass canopy spitting
raindrops at him, a thick, swirling greyness making him feel like he was
floating in a dream. He had somebody to speak to; somebody to share his
existence with. The voice was a welcome comfort, but they had no words
of comfort for him – he was not given permission to land. He had no
alternative but to bailout, and hope that his men in the parachute section
had packed his parachute with meticulous care.

The plan was to estimate a position where he would pop out of the
cloud cover, away from any buildings, as he dangled under his parachute.
He could only hope that his aircraft would find a convenient place for its
last, and most spectacular arrival. As he tightened his parachute and his
hands moved towards the top of the canopy, and the canopy jettison lever,
he heard an American accent crackle through on the radio. It was a Flying
Fortress bomber talking to Palam control. They were seasoned pilots and
moreover, carried the equipment that might help him get through this
dark, totally enveloping hell. Adrenaline coursing through his veins, he
shouted his problems into the radio and requested for help, this was no
time to observe radio discipline.

Any pilot, anywhere in the world, would have offered to help a brother
aviator in distress, especially under the given circumstance. The Americans
told him what height they were at, they estimated that they were directly
over Palam, right at that moment. They commenced flying in lazy circles
over the airfield in the cloud. Harjinder climbed the Harvard to the height
the Americans had reported, and headed to where he thought they were
now circling. He knew he was running the massive risk of hitting the
Americans before seeing them but the thought of plunging out of the

Harvard into the swirling maelstrom outside drove him to grasp at this slim hope.

Harjinder saw the sky in front of him begin to glow, as a soft beam of light pierced through the rain and clouds. Somehow, he had ended up close enough to see them and with enough time to pick out the source of the light; it was passing from right to left. He hauled the nose of the Harvard onto a similar path to slow the rate that he was closing in on the glow. A shape formed around the glow, and that form took on the shape of a silver fuselage. Harjinder flew his Harvard as close as he dare to nestle alongside that fuselage, wings overlapping. Sweat added to the seeping rain, replacing the cold grip of the terror from only minutes earlier.

Now his fate was in his own hands; he could use his own skill to remedy his own poor decision-making. The Americans brought their aircraft down through the gloom as smoothly as they could in the conditions. Harjinder's Harvard bobbed around in the air currents, but he kept his eyes glued to the side of the Flying Fortress. The Americans saw the runway lights at about 200 feet from the ground and wrestled the 4-engine bomber onto the concrete. Harjinder finally tore his eyes from his saviours and focused on the bubble of ground, runway, now distinct from the all-pervading greyness. The American pilots let their bomber roll to the end of the runway giving Harjinder the room he needed to drop behind them and slide over the runway in their wake. The Harvard tyres splashed through the puddles of water to give the most gorgeous sensation of firm land under the wheels as the speed dropped to zero. As he cleared the runway Harjinder had to prise his death-like grip from the control column before parking the aircraft and opening the canopy to let the full force of the weather in. Flying control demanded to know how the area control had cleared Harjinder's takeoff in the conditions, but he told them to obtain that information from Air Vice-Marshal Mukerjee. This silenced their queries, which was fortunate because Harjinder knew that the whole close brush with death had been down to his own poor judgement.

So what was the urgent call from the Defence Secretary that had nearly resulted in Harjinder's death? It was Patel who had originally wanted Harjinder to become the Chairman at HAL, and he now wanted to speak with Harjinder in person, to try and convince him to take the job. Adrenaline still pumping through his veins, and still flooded with relief at still being alive, Harjinder had no patience for pleasantries. Diplomacy went out the window, and he gave Patel short shrift. 'Neither rank nor pay will ever induce me to leave the IAF. I am quite definite about that, Sir.'

The blunt approach failed, so Patel's next move was to butter him up. 'You are the first IAF officer to have won my deepest respect. You are a patriotic Indian, an aircraft Engineer with an unparalleled record and now you have won your wings (*but had just nearly died using them!*). You have reclaimed fifty Liberator bombers out of the junk yard in Kanpur. What is more, your administrative ability is outstanding, as I have seen for myself in Kanpur.'

These were all flattering comments, and under normal circumstances, it would have been a delight to hear them, but flattery never sat well with Harjinder. After his experiences over the last few hours, Harjinder just wanted an end to this discussion, so off the top of his head he told Patel that his application to return to Engineering within the IAF had been submitted, and that he was moving away from Administration. Mukerjee was in the room, and his eyes widened when he heard this, but he picked up on Harjinder's exit strategy. He added that Harjinder's replacement was being sought. That ended the matter.

Harjinder's 'replacement' couldn't be found for another 3 years, so life continued in Kanpur, but with one great addition, one that would influence the rest of his life, and beyond. Harjinder was given a Staff Officer to help with his increasing workload in Kanpur. While it would be wonderful to imagine that the IAF Personnel Department took time to carefully select the man for the job, but their perfect selection was most likely down to luck. The officer selected would very quickly become something more than an assistant. Amrit Saigal had started as a Sepoy, just as Harjinder had done. He had loaded the bombs on to the Lysanders in Burma as part of Harjinder's team. As Dr Nanda had predicted, the husband he had chosen for his sister was now racing up the ranks, he had already reached the rank of a Squadron Leader. Later, Dr Nanda even sent his own son to live with Squadron Leader Amrit Saigal, so he could finish his education. The relationship between Amrit and Harjinder was very much like the one Harjinder had shared with Jumbo Majumdar ten years earlier. Now, Harjinder was the senior man, but just like Jumbo before him, he largely ignored the rank difference, regarding Amrit as a close friend, and the main port of call to seek advice and discuss the thorny issues at hand. Harjinder had looked up to Jumbo with an unsurpassed level of respect. Amrit now offered that same respect to Harjinder and could not do enough for him. He made sure Harjinder's drive from his family house into the camp would pass smoothly every day, even if it did mean holding up the train that used the railway crossing bisecting his route. Amrit was always with Harjinder, and when the young Nanda boy arrived, he spent as much time as was possible with his Uncle. Harjinder was to make a great impression on the young boy as he grew up in the long, barracked accommodation on the Kanpur base.

Harjinder used his rebuilt Bonanza 4-seater aircraft to fly around the county when not using IAF aircraft. His wife had witnessed firsthand how the flying bug had crawled under Harjinder's skin and she now decided to put to test the old adage – if you can't beat them, join them. So in 1952, she completed her own flying training to become one of the first women to be issued an Indian pilot's license. She went on to fly regularly, when with Harjinder they took turns to fly the aircraft, or occasionally she headed out on her own. She not only spent her life encouraging women to fly, but promoting the idea that women should have a place in traditional male spheres of employment.

The list of aircraft Harjinder had brought back to life was long and impressive. It seemed as if there was something deep in Harjinder's psyche that wouldn't let him walk away from an abandoned aircraft. The Czech built Aero 45 could never be described as a good-looking aeroplane; with a big, bulbous front to the fuselage, it resembled a tadpole with wings. On each wing an engine, similar to that in a Tiger Moth, was bolted on. In 1951, this particular aircraft had crashed on landing nearby, and, as soon as Harjinder saw the wreck he was transported back to the North-West Frontier and his days with the Wapitis. The Aero 45 was a mess, having turned upside down in the crash landing, its nose, cockpit and tail were all crumpled, one engine had been ripped off and the other smashed under the wreck.

Anyone one else looking at this mangled mass of metal would have consigned it to another life as kitchenware, but not Harjinder. He set his men onto the task of a complete rebuild, without plans or diagrams to fall back on. When news of this rebuild reached the Czech Automobile and Aircraft Works (*later to be known as Skoda*) they felt compelled to write a letter to Harjinder:

'We hear with what energy and skill you and your staff are endeavouring to repair Mr de San's damaged Aero 45 and how ingeniously you are rebuilding those parts which have been completely destroyed. Being quite conscious of how difficult a task you have undertaken, more so as the Aero 45 is a design hitherto surely not known to you, we wish to tell you how much we appreciate your readiness to give help even under most adverse circumstances and how we admire the spirit which enables you and your staff to tackle successfully all the problems that necessary must arise thereof.'

It was clear that they thought Harjinder was in for a tough job. The task was completed, and the aircraft tested, before the owner, Mr de San, returned to the aircraft he thought he would never fly again. Mr de San lost no time, and, after reassuring himself that it was a job well done, he set out for Europe. When he arrived in Belgium in the repaired machine, it seemed as if Harjinder had lost none of his aircraft resurrection skills.

'I made Belgium in 4 days, alone, without a single trouble. This aircraft flies better than when I bought it from the factory. The Certificate of Airworthiness has been immediately granted by the Belgium Directorate of Aviation, who praised the work; they found it an unbelievable feat.'

With his family established, and the personnel under him feeling like an extended family, life at Kanpur was idyllic for Harjinder, but all good things must come to an end. The Korean War had finished with a very uneasy ceasefire in place; with troops staring down the barrels of their guns over the border, as they still do to this day. In the early 1950's, with hostilities at an end on the Korean Peninsula, world attention turned to the world's other flash points. India-Pakistan was high on the list. The Indian Government wanted military expansion, and the British wanted no further part in the region, taking this opportunity to finally pull out their last influence over the IAF and hand over all responsibility to India. Air Marshal Gibbs of the RAF stepped down as Chief of the IAF on the 31st March 1954. The next day, on the 1st April 1954, the twenty first anniversary of the Indian Air Force, nearly a hundred aircraft flew over Delhi, as Gibbs handed over complete control of the IAF to Air Marshal Subroto Mukerjee OBE. Subroto Mukerjee had come a long way from his early days of chasing pilotless Wapitis through the dust in Afghanistan. He would now lead the IAF into the jet age. Another of the original musketeers and Harjinder's good friend, Aspy Engineer, was promoted to become the Deputy Chief. Arjan Singh too was in Headquarters, close to finishing his time as Head of Personnel. He would soon be taking over the complete Western sector; the defence of the disputed borders would fall in his domain. As these three men took control, the IAF took a great leap forward. They knew that if they had a solid support structure behind the Operational Squadrons, they could push for an increase to fifteen Squadrons and exceed the size of the World War II RIAF. After all, India's own sovereign Air Force had already been called into combat, and the rising tension with Pakistan indicated that they would be required again soon. The IAF needed a Maintenance Command, gathered together in a single place with a single point of contact. The men at the top knew that single point was Harjinder.

Due to Harjinder's new role in the IAF, a new role *model* was set to walk into Harjinder's life. That person would destroy his legacy.

Fourteen

Kindred Spirit or Dangerous Liaison?

'Why not lay by something against your old age? I can arrange
it. A numbered account in Switzerland, so that the law can never
catch up with you. If you play ball with us, we will look after you.'

Harjinder was summoned back to Delhi in January 1955 for another
important meeting. Harjinder had come to know the Headquarters
intimately now. Those leaky, H-shaped huts that had been thrown
together as temporary accommodation during the build-up to World War
II, were still the nerve centre of the IAF. Harjinder had seen the various
Chiefs come and go through these doors. His first Chief had called him,
and all his colleagues, 'The Greatest Disgrace.' Sir Edgar Ludlow-Hewitt
had come next, and spoken directly to (acting) Corporal Harjinder Singh
as he stood to attention in front of his Wapiti. As the World War II came to
an end, Harjinder had walked into the Chief's office, now occupied by Air
Vice-Marshal Sir Hugh Walmsely, to offer his resignation, then he crossed
swords with Sir Thomas Elmhirst. He had sat in the Chief's office with
Sir Ronald Ivelaw Chapman, and then, Air Marshal Gerald Gibbs, on the
opposite side of this same desk to discuss his progress in Kanpur. This day
he walked into that same basic office, with the ill-fitting windows, and the
ornate table, to meet a new Chief. This time he was greeted by his friend
Subroto Mukerjee; Chief of the IAF.

The Air Force that Mukerjee now commanded was still operating in
the original RAF format. Maintenance units were scattered all over the

country, each running independently of the others. This visit to see the Chief was to arrange a radical shake up. It was immensely logical to form a brand new Maintenance Command; bring all the workshops, supply points, repair depots and other maintenance units under one functional command. There was only one choice of who would sit at the helm. The madness of the duplicated effort was pointed out to all the relevant Officers around the country, but the plan from Headquarters would require those men to lose some of the power from their own small fiefdoms; that didn't go down too well...

Harjinder had his friends at the summit of the IAF, but a number of men, who sat in offices at Headquarters, or at the individual bases, saw Harjinder as an upstart, and a possible threat to their own advancement. Harjinder was only a Group Captain when he took over command of the whole maintenance of the IAF and he was 'stealing' from the mini empires of more senior officers. Normally, a Command Officer has a Staff Officer to assist him in HQ and, as Harjinder shuttled back and forth from Kanpur to Delhi, he brought Amrit Saigal with him. Those senior officers who felt they were losing out to this Group Captain even raised objections to Amrit Saigal wearing a Staff Officer's armband. They wanted to deny Harjinder the staff car, and other privileges normally lavished on a Command Officer.

They hadn't taken into account that the trappings of such a position meant nothing to Harjinder. Kanpur was made the home of Maintenance Command, and remained Harjinder's home for the rest of his time in the IAF. The flight from Kanpur to Delhi became a well-known route for Harjinder, Amrit, and sometimes, Beant Kaur, but it was soon time to start venturing further afield.

In 1955, the cold war between the East and West was at full chill, with fingers hovering over the launch buttons of nuclear weapons. In the United Nations, Krishna Menon had introduced the term 'non-alignment'; India would deal with the East and the West. It was partly a desire to remain on trading terms with both sides, but also out of geographical necessity. When the Soviets paid a high profile visit to India they endorsed India's claim to Kashmir. There was little doubt they were thinking more about future military hardware sales than seeing fair play in the region. A return visit was hastily organised, and it was to be an interesting group who represented the IAF. Mukerjee, the ultimate politician with the disarming smile, was to lead the team. He was accompanied by the charming Arjan

Singh, DFC, who wooed people wherever he went. Group Captain Erlic Wilmot Pinto, the man who had run the station at Ambala with Arjan Singh, one of the 24 pilots trained in England in 1940, was back by his side. If Arjan Singh was already being considered for Chief, Pinto would perhaps be his successor. Also on the team was the powerful frame of Group Captain Moolgavkar, who had the look of a powerful wrestler, capable of taking on any Russian bear. His stature was partly the result of a terrible Spitfire crash, where he'd overturned and broken his back. His father, a surgeon in Bombay, had saved his life. Then there were the broad shoulders and booming voice of Harjinder, whose presence filled the room when he entered. The drab colours and grey faces of Moscow were suddenly lifted by the arrival of the colours, characters and charm of the IAF at its best. The blue uniforms, indistinguishable at a distance from the British Royal Air Force, caused great confusion, some of those who caught a glimpse of the visitors, feared an invasion. However, this distinguished group of Indians left the Soviets in awe when they led a parade to lay a wreath at Lenin's tomb.

Back in Kanpur, the base continued to grow; and as the number of aircraft increased, so did Harjinder's responsibilities. The only Spitfire left flying in IAF colours, if not technically part of the IAF, was Harjinder's own Spitfire. The Hawker Tempests that sprang into action in the Kashmir war were also being retired. The next three years were going to see some massive expansion, with the Government agreeing to increase the size of the IAF to sixteen squadrons by 1957. These squadrons were filled by foreign aircraft, mainly British. The IAF fighter squadron were becoming an all-jet operation. Harjinder also received the responsibility for the first aircraft to be designed in India, which required a whole new maintenance regime to be set up. In 1948, the Indian Government had requested designs for a basic trainer, so HAL took the De Havilland Chipmunk, the successor to the De Havilland Tiger Moth trainer, and designed a simplified version to ease production in India. It was the same tail-wheel design as a Chipmunk – the pilots still in tandem, and the square, lines of the machine may have made building simpler. The military test pilot assigned to the project was Harjinder's old friend, the talented flying cadet from Hurricane days, Suranjan 'Dasu' Das. Harjinder also knew HAL's test pilot, Mr Jamshed K. Munshi, who had ferried the Liberator bombers out of Kanpur during those hectic early days. The HT2 must have felt toy-like to Munshi, and he only thought it necessary to fly the prototype for 45 minutes before declaring the new aeroplane fit for military service. After a demonstration flight in Bangalore he handing it over to Dasu, and the IAF, and washed his hands of the project. After the HT2 had the old Tigermoth engine replaced by a more powerful, but heavier, Cirrus Major engine, he still thought it unnecessary to fly again.

Over 50 years later, when I broke into the IAF hangar containing the abandoned Vintage Flight aircraft, I had my first chance to get up-close and personal with a complete HT2. Having flown many hours in the delightful Chipmunk (fondly known as the 'poor man's Spitfire') and knowing its flowing lines very well, there was something that instantly struck me about the HT2; the fin and rudder at the back were tiny! In any tail-wheel aircraft, you need a large fin area on the tail to keep the aircraft running straight when it is in that tricky phase of changing from a flying machine into a ground-based machine. I thought, 'this is going to be a handful on landing'. Dasu saw the rear of the HT2 in 1952 and had a slightly different reaction, he thought, 'getting this aircraft out of a spin is going to be interesting!' He was told by Munshi that spinning was no problem, although Dasu had suspicions that it had never been spun. He then requested for an anti-spin parachute to be fitted, like those he had used during his time as a student in the British Empire Test Pilots School in Boscombe Down, UK; this request was denied. The test flying had to go ahead, so he set out his own set of limits for his first test flight: At a suitable height, he would put the aircraft into a deliberate spin; after it had rotated twice, he would do the standard spin recovery of full opposite rudder to the spin rotation and then control stick fully forward. If the HT2 failed to stop, and continued to spin for another 4 turns, he would bale out: And that is exactly what happened! The prototype was lost, Munshi left HAL soon after, and the project didn't come into Harjinder's hands, and wasn't ready for IAF service until 1955. Throughout its career, the spin remained an issue, recovery depending upon the various weights of the two pilots and the amount of fuel being carried. Despite reservations, there were 169 HT2s built, and they flew in IAF service for nearly three decades. The strength of the machine was never in doubt. This strength was to do a great service and save one young man's life on 8th March 1972, and this young man was to be a key player in the rebirth of Harjinder's Vintage Flight.

There were more aircraft types to prepare for, but Harjinder was not one to stay in his office and orchestrate things from an ivory tower. He would regularly pounce into areas of the Kanpur base, unannounced. Whilst the civilians may have voluntarily lined up to form their own quasi-military units, there should be no mistaking the fear that Group Captain Harjinder Singh's visit could induce. Harjinder had seen life in the Air Force from the very bottom, so there was no opportunity to pull the wool over his eyes. He set himself very high standards and an impossible work rate, which he expected his men to strive for. Cat-like stealth was not one of his attributes. The men would hear of his approach and scatter around the unit shouting a warning to all working there. The thump, thump, thump of his purposeful, striding feet would be the final signal of the impending whirlwind. Some of the junior men were known to shake with fear as Harjinder seemingly blocked out the sun. The fear was well-founded. If anything was found amiss, his verbal avalanche left the individual quaking. It was that feeling of a pent-up volcano inside Harjinder that gave him the aura when he was in the room with you. However, there was not a man in Kanpur who would not tell you about Harjinder's deeply caring side. If Harjinder left a man shredded after one of his tongue lashings, he would often meet up with him in the evening for a drink. If Harjinder came to know of a compassionate case, or found a project in which he saw merit, he would work tirelessly until there was a happy conclusion; just like the crashed Wapitis and Hurricanes of his early years. Those men who worked hard, and showed promise, found that they had the backing of their boss, pushing them up through the system to further their careers.

Harjinder had already seen talent in Parashar far beyond his role as Harjinder's personal driver. When Harjinder's aircraft burst a tyre, sending him careering, harmlessly, off the runway, the news filtered down to Parashar of a terrible crash. When Harjinder strode into the medical bay Parashar was already there, fearing the worse. When he saw Harjinder he passed out on the spot thinking he had seen a ghost. Seeing his unswerving loyalty, Harjinder commissioned Parashar as an officer on the spot. No other officer would have been able to push through an instant commission through Headquarters like that. Parashar went on to become a well-respected Wing Commander.

Harjinder had enough to keep him busy in Kanpur, but that didn't stop him from keeping an eye on global politics. In 1955 the Soviet Union brought all their Communist neighbours into a single political club, which they called the Warsaw Pact, in order to face the NATO forces in the West. Egypt was very much in the same boat as India; an ex-British colony with feet in both East and West camps. Their leader, Gamal Abdel Nasser, had swept into power as the charismatic champion on a wave of post British-rule nationalism, but had become increasingly dictatorial. He was doing a fine job in playing the Americans off against the Russians to enrage the global superpowers, when he stepped over the line. On 26th July 1956, during a speech in Alexandria, Nasser deliberately pronounced the name of Ferdinand de Lesseps, the builder of the Suez Canal – it was a codeword for Egyptian forces to seize control of the Suez Canal. That stretch of water, linking the Mediterranean to the Arabian Gulf, was vital to Britain's ability to move troops and materials into Asia. France also felt the pinch on her Asian colonies, and the two countries joined together, mobilising their military in the old colonial style, and on the old colonial lines.

It was Nehru, and Krishna Menon who led the call for calm and remained even-handed with the two sides. As the British and French troops moved into Egypt, it was Mountbatten, now in-charge of the British Royal Navy, who wrote to Eden, the British Prime Minister. It is clear Mountbatten's opinion on the situation was in close alignment with Nehru's – a military invasion was politically unsound, it was an endeavour that was doomed to fail.

The spectator nations watched the flexing of the old Imperial muscles, until the Americans finally stepped forward to agree with Nehru. Political pressure increased, with increasingly severe sanctions threatened, until Britain had no choice but to bring an end to their military action. Eden lost his job, and the New World Order was confirmed.

The Americans only had one year to sit back and preen themselves as holders of the balance of power, as they surged ahead with their political and technological lead over the Soviets. In October 1957, they received a rude shock. The uninspiring ping, ping, ping sounding around the world on radio sets didn't come from American hardware. The Soviets had taken the first steps into space with Sputnik. Non-alignment suddenly seemed a very good idea.

If the Government of India were taking their place in the new World Order, the IAF too had to develop into a world class operation. Any country worth their salt should be close to being self-sufficient, in military terms. It was to become Harjinder's role in life.

Amrit Saigal and Harjinder formed an unbreakable team; moulded into a single piece of machinery as they operated, and thought, as one, to achieve that self-sufficiency. That is, except for one particular occasion after a summons back to Headquarters in Delhi.

They flew down together, assuming that it was another meeting on the routine events of Maintenance Command. The first surprise was a second offer for Harjinder to go to HAL as the Chairman; the second surprise was that it came from Mukerjee, who should have known better.

Mukerjee knew that neither rank, nor pay, would tempt Harjinder, so he tried a different strategy. 'Harjinder, you are a visionary. I have often heard you say that you would like to see the day when India begins to export aircraft. Well, now you have a chance to get India started along that road. Government has suggested that you take over at HAL. You would not only be helping the IAF by strengthening its repair and overhaul base, but you would also start India on the road to aircraft production.'

Decades of friendship had indeed schooled Mukerjee in the ways of Harjinder, he certainly knew how to push his maintenance commander's buttons. Harjinder became more and more excited about the opportunities being presented to him. As morning turned to afternoon, he found himself agreeing to the Air Chief's suggestion. It was only then that he was told that it would involve promotion to Air Commodore, and a salary of three thousand rupees per month, far more than the actual pay of that rank.

Harjinder was taken into the Defence Secretary's office, where another speech on self-reliance to achieve the nation's goals was designed to further stoke his enthusiasm for the venture. Amrit Saigal was not with Harjinder during these meetings, and received the message to arrange the return flight to Kanpur. Harjinder was not piloting the aircraft, for a change, which gave him the chance to sit back and ponder the swirling emotions of the day. After some contemplation, Harjinder spoke. He told Amrit that he had agreed to take over the running of HAL. There was no response from his friend, so Harjinder pushed him for his thoughts. The answer was typically short and terse; 'Sir, when you have already accepted the post, there is nothing left to discuss.'

Harjinder told him that doubts were now bubbling inside, and he was quite willing to be persuaded to change his mind. It was clear from Amrit's reply that he strongly opposed this idea.

'In that case, Sir, I can honestly say that I do not think you would be happy in HAL. I have always heard you say that we can create a HAL in Kanpur. Why not do just that, if you want to manufacture aircraft?'

Amrit's words brought Harjinder to his senses, he could now see clearly through power play that was used to massage his own ego. Harjinder was an Air Force man, and that is where he belonged. They were still 30 minutes out of Kanpur, but he sent a message to be relayed to Mukerjee; he would refuel and return to seek another interview with him and the Defence Secretary, that very same evening. The second attempt to get Harjinder into HAL was foiled thanks to the man who knew Harjinder better than he knew himself; Amrit Saigal.

There was no doubt that this was the right decision for Harjinder, but there was to be an unforeseen consequence. That decision was the first step in a series of events that started to divide opinion about Harjinder, within the IAF; one that prevailed right into the 21st century. When Harjinder refused to take the job at HAL, another Senior Officer had to be selected; the 'honour' fell to Aspy Engineer. Aspy was not happy about having to leave the IAF for a job he believed that Harjinder should have been made to take. This started the early heat of friction between the two comrades from the North-West Frontier. The public view of this friction was blown out of all proportion with some individuals seemingly enjoying the opportunity of making more from it than actually existed. Behind closed doors, their friendship continued, with great respect flowing both ways, albeit with a slight frosty coating.

In April 1957, Krishna Menon became the Minister for Defence in Nehru's cabinet. Following his earlier, record-breaking, eight-hour speech defending India's stand on Kashmir, he'd earned the nickname 'Hero of Kashmir,' and was expected to be the darling of the armed forces. Harjinder and Menon soon met in an official capacity. Both men were outspoken, driven, uncompromising, but above all, yearned with all their heart for India to take great strides forward in self-reliance. From that very first meeting, a new friendship was formed, and Harjinder felt he had found a kindred spirit, someone who not only listened, but also helped him develop his own ideas. There had not been anyone in Harjinder's life to fill the huge void that Jumbo had left; that of mentor and role model. There had been a natural power gradient between Harjinder, the Sepoy, and Jumbo, the Officer and pilot. Now as a Senior Officer, Harjinder could look up to Menon, his Defence Minister, in the same manner.

There were a considerable number of similarities between the two men. Their thoughts, and their goals, all revolved around making India a better country, and to increase its standing on the world stage. Both men worked tirelessly on projects they believed in, requiring little sleep. They had both begun their education in college but from that point their paths in life diverged. Harjinder had then taken on the lowest position available in the new Air Force; Menon continued to climb upward from his early education. He was even adding a third degree to his portfolio. Menon's colourful side was carefully calculated and designed to boost his not-inconsiderable ego. Apart from his arrival at his own Wings Parade in his Spitfire, flamboyance was not a trait that was found in Harjinder. Menon had been in the background, steering his close friend Nehru's public image into a position where he became the natural replacement for Gandhi, for quite some time. He had suggested Mountbatten's appointment as Governor General to India during Independence, and now he took the post in Nehru's Government which was the most heavily scrutinised, second only perhaps, to Finance. Due to his close friendship with Nehru, Menon's tenure as Defence Minister brought him more power, and a higher-profile, than his predecessors.

Menon's experience brought a degree of governmental, public, and international attention that India's military had not previously known. Soon after his arrival, Menon abolished the seniority system within the military; nepotism was thrown out, replaced by a merit-based system of promotion. His restructuring of India's military command system surprised some within the old guard, and gained him many enemies; the Chief of the Army Staff resigned in disgust. Whether Menon's fingers were tweaking the strings behind the scenes or not, remains unclear, but March 1958 saw Harjinder promoted to the rank of Air Commodore without the need for jumping ship to HAL. His elevated rank brought him into regular contact with Menon. After several trips to visit Harjinder's work in Kanpur they become ever closer friends with a meeting of minds.

To those that had to arrange an arrival committee for Menon, often at short notice, it seemed as if he were there every few weeks. The young Mr Nanda would see his uncle launch into action when he heard the cries, 'Menon is coming! Menon is coming!'

As Harjinder's Staff Officer, Amrit Saigal soon knew the routine; get a pot of really strong, freshly-ground, coffee on the boil, with a good supply of cashew nuts at hand. The two men would be seen striding around the base as they discussed matters far beyond the perimeter wire of Kanpur. If they could be thought of as twins in their outlook in life, physically they couldn't be more different. Menon was tall, with a slim frame topped with a shock of white, unruly, hair swept backwards to give him that professorial look. Despite Harjinder's solid frame and intimidating presence, Menon's own bearing and poise left the observer in no doubt where the ultimate power lay. Both men carried a stick, but for different reasons. For Harjinder, it was the baton that went with his rank, for Menon, it was an old fashioned shepherd's stick. When the young Nanda was in the office with his Uncle, awaiting the return of the two men from their wanderings, it was the tap-tap-tap of Menon's walking stick that announced their imminent arrival.

Not all meetings took place in Kanpur. Menon called a meeting in April 1958, with all three military Chiefs; the heads of the Army, the Navy, and the Air Force. Eyebrows were raised when the fourth person to be included was Harjinder. Menon's thrust in that meeting was how one-third of the central financial budget was being lost on defence expenditure. The military was his empire, but he knew that the resources that came to him would leave so many vital aspects such as basic education, agriculture and irrigation, all neglected. He reasoned that the Armed Forces could reduce the burden on the state by producing some of their own weapons and equipment, and by reclaiming the maximum possible from salvage still left from World War II. Many of the ideas brought forth were from talks with Harjinder held the day before. All in the Government knew of Harjinder's reclaimed Liberator bombers, and naturally deduced these new ideas came, at least in part, from Harjinder. From that point onwards, in the minds of many in authority, there became little difference between Menon and Harjinder. If insults were hurled from military and Government personnel at Menon's reputation, Harjinder was lumped in with him.

However, from this early meeting, things *did* move forward, and progress was made. Menon continued to preach self-reliance, and with this ringing in his ears, a small seed of an idea started to take root in Harjinder's mind. He had spent much of his adult life rebuilding aircraft, so why not design and build a light aircraft at Kanpur, for military and civilian use? He had built a Frankenstein of an aircraft from various aircraft parts, when he was in based in Kohat, but this would be a brand new machine. Harjinder saw this project as the impetus needed to start the indigenous production of defence equipment. Menon constituted a number of committees, and Harjinder was appointed Chairman of two of them; the Disposals Committee, and the Ground Equipment Committee, whose task it was to reclaim as much equipment as possible. The Sepoy who bolted damaged Wapitis back together in 1930s was now starting with a blank piece of paper. Harjinder still had all his Maintenance Command responsibilities but manufactured time to sit down and design a brand new utility aeroplane for India, with Menon nodding approval in the background.

Throughout Harjinder's life, he went full tilt into new ventures and this was no different. His enthusiasm was infectious, and inspired all his fellow Committee members to do their utmost to complete their allotted tasks within the time frame. Meetings with Krishna Menon really did become a weekly event, their discussions moved beyond the basic mechanics of the project in hand, and roamed far and wide. It was inevitable that a certain amount of talk would start about Harjinder becoming the Defence Minister's 'blue-eyed boy'. The goal of self-reliance in Defence was an obsession with both of these men, but others eyed the relationship as something more sinister, accusing Harjinder of motives less than noble, that the relationship he had cultivated with Menon was purely for personal benefit. Those people certainly didn't know Harjinder!

The combination of Harjinder's drive, and Menon's encouragement, saw a completely new 4-seater, light communications aircraft, designed, and built, in less than a year. The high wing design, with an enclosed cabin, was in no way revolutionary, but it was perfect for India. The plan was to make the maximum use of parts and material available in country. It was simple to build, and tough enough for the harsh operating conditions. The concept of 'keep it simple' was continued with the choice of engine; the widely used American Lycoming 180 horsepower engine. The people in Maintenance Command may have been calling it 'Harjinder's plane' but it was officially called the Kanpur-I. As you would expect, it was Harjinder who strapped into the machine for the first test flight alongside the test pilot. Menon was on the ground with a huge grin, waiting to present Harjinder with a garland when he touched down. The significance of this moment was not lost on Menon – the country's first homegrown/ domestically manufactured aircraft, designed and developed by its own Air Force, had taken to the air for the very first time – and he immediately used Harjinder's success to taunt HAL in Bangalore.

Relations were already strained, and this further enraged the management team in HAL, including Harjinder's friend Aspy Engineer, who was serving as Chairman. Menon was happy to point out to all who would listen, that despite HAL being the only aircraft factory in the country, they had yet to achieve anything as impressive as the team in Kanpur.

The Director of Development & Production at HAL, Mr Jagan Chawla, was not going to take this attack on HAL lying down, and had weapons of his own to call on for revenge. He refused to accord the Kanpur-I an Airworthiness Certificate, blaming poor welding. Harjinder's baby would never progress beyond the one example his men in Kanpur had built. It was by no means a wasted effort, because it did achieve one thing – stung by the Defence Minister's comments, HAL quickly made the Pushpak aircraft by copying the American, fabric covered, light aircraft called the Aeronca Chief, with a Rolls-Royce engine. The first Pushpak was ready within just sixteen weeks after being given the go ahead by Aspy Engineer. India was now manufacturing a new aircraft, even if the Pushpak was inferior to Harjinder's aircraft, only a small step forward from the HT2 trainer aircraft. Once the Pushpak was confirmed as the Government's choice of aircraft, the Kanpur-I prototype received permission to fly beyond the testing phase and it continued to operate on the Kanpur base for many years, fulfilling a role very close to Harjinder's heart. Over the years, the students of Kanpur Technical Institute experienced the pleasure of flight for the very first time in Kanpur-I, some catching the flying bug for life.

Without official backing, the aircraft could not live forever. They continued to beg, borrow, steal, and manufacture parts for Harjinder's Kanpur-I, but eventually, the Air Force Station, Kanpur lost the use of the aircraft carrying its name; it was reported as broken up. In 2011, I arranged a visit to the Punjab Engineering College in Chandigarh to survey a number of airframes in their aeronautical department. I was taken around the facility, which was full of surprises at every turn. The complete Spitfire, still in IAF colours, albeit dismantled, was quite a sight, and a perfect addition to the Vintage Flight. Finding a Spitfire, and parts of 2 others, would normally be the highlight of any day's work, but I found something else that day. I was taken into a windowless room where the seldom-used neon strips, dangling on chains from the ceiling, were to be our only source of light. When they were turned on, flickering and clicking, they illuminated the room's only other occupant – another aircraft. The harsh light reflected off the dust covered, silver painted, fabric of a high wing plane, snuggled in amongst tables of discarded engine parts. The lightning flash painted in red, that ran down the length of the fuselage ended in the IAF roundel, and tail number, BR570, confirmed that it was Harjinder's Kanpur-I, fully rigged for flight; if a little tatty around the edges.

Through the Kanpur-I Menon had seen further into Harjinder's abilities, and so now it was Menon's turn to try and push Harjinder into HAL, this time as General Manager. Harjinder left Menon in no doubt of the utmost respect he held for Aspy Engineer, he would never consider himself to be Aspy's equal, and so, insisted that the only way he would contemplate a move to HAL was as an ordinary Engineer. When Menon changed tack and asked how he could be compensated for the additional responsibilities of aircraft design and possible production, Harjinder's reply was, 'Sir, the best way to compensate me would be to reduce my rank by one; I would then be clear of all the petty jealousies that have been created in the Air Force.'

On 8th May, during a discussion on the future transport project, Krishna Menon brought up the subject of Harjinder's rank. It was not as Harjinder had requested, to bring him down a level, it was to raise him further up, to that of Air Vice-Marshal. He had alluded to this before, hinting that since Harjinder was head of a Command, he should also be an Air Vice-Marshal. Harjinder, of course, considered himself already promoted above his colleagues in the Engineering Branch, so he did not expect an out-of-turn promotion. On 15th May, Harjinder listened to the 9 pm news broadcast on All India Radio, as was his custom, work permitting. He had that classic delayed reaction to hearing your own name being mentioned in conversation, at a time and place you don't expect it. He had to replay the last few seconds of the broadcast over in his mind. Did they just announce his promotion to Air Vice-Marshal with immediate effect? He was shaken out of his confusion by the ring of the telephone. On answering, he was greeted by the familiar voice of Menon on the other end, 'Normally a Defence Minister does not personally congratulate promoted officers no matter how senior they may be, but you are an exception.'

The Deputy Air Chief rang up the next morning to offer congratulations, but also had to 'wonder' if the Chief, Mukerjee, knew about the proposal for promotion. He was obviously saying what many thought then, and many still think today; was Menon pushing his 'blue-eyed boy' through to the top? Harjinder could take a hint and so put pen to paper immediately. His concerns poured onto the page. In his letter to Mukerjee he voiced his concerns at the prospect of the promotion, pointing out that he did not wish to be promoted beyond Group Captain until those he thought worthy went before him.

He also stated that he had made several attempts to leave the IAF, but had been persuaded to stay; on one occasion, by Mukerjee himself. There are several insights into their close relationship in that letter, besides Mukerjee's own threat to resign if Harjinder were to leave the Air Force, he also recounts his earlier refusal of the job at HAL on the understanding that Mukerjee would stay on as Chief, so that the two men could retire at the same time. He finished by stating, categorically, that if Mukerjee had not recommended this promotion, he would refuse to accept it.

Subroto Mukerjee had always been an astute politician, and would not have been unaware of the talk around the corridors of power. He asked Harjinder to fly to Delhi straightway. Harjinder walked through the shabby H block and into that familiar Chief's office. Before he could draw breath for the speech he had been mentally preparing over and over again, Mukerjee sprang out of his seat and was holding Harjinder firmly by the shoulders. Harjinder, still dazed, didn't comprehend what was happening as Mukerjee removed the old strips from his shoulder epaulets, and slid the Air Vice-Marshal's strips on. He guided Harjinder into the chair facing the desk before he sat down opposite him. Mukerjee looked directly into the still-confused face of Harjinder, as he slid an open file across the desk. Harjinder looked into that file and the letter within. It was Mukerjee's original recommendation to the Defence Secretary for Harjinder's promotion. That kind of consideration was typical of Subroto Mukerjee.

The decade was drawing to a close. The world was changing; India had been Independent for over ten years. The Air Force that had been torn apart at Partition was functioning well, and trying to keep pace with the political, economic and technical changes happening all around. Harjinder's Liberator bombers were moved onto a maritime role, patrolling the vast Indian coastline, and the seas beyond. Their bomber role was being carried out by Canberra jet bombers recently purchased from Britain. Negotiations were also underway with the company that had supplied the wartime RIAF with their Hurricanes, the Hawker aircraft company, from Kingston-upon-Thames, in Surrey. The new bullet-like Hawker Hunter was in a league of its own and soon became known by Air Forces throughout the world for the light, agile, harmonised, controls that made it the ultimate pilot's airplane.

Also on the shopping list from UK, were the tiny fighter aircraft from the Folland Company. The suitably named, Midge, was originally designed as a lightweight, single-seat aeroplane; when armed and turned into a full-fledged fighter, it was rechristened, the Gnat. The RAF turned their back on this fighter, but eventually made the two-seat version of the Gnat their main advanced trainer wherein it became a legend as the aircraft that started the premier RAF aerobatic team; the Red Arrows. By the early part of 1959, HAL were tooling up to licence build their own fighter version of the Gnat, but it was also becoming obvious to the IAF that their old Dakota transport fleet, that brought all the troops right into the battle zone in Kashmir in 1948, was also creaking at the seams.

Talks about a replacement cargo and troop carrying aircraft made the round of Government and military offices, with Menon's enthusiasm for self-reliance and domestically built aircraft becoming infectious. The aircraft types offered by the American Lockheed, and Dutch Fokker companies were eventually dismissed, despite the best efforts of certain members of the Government and military trying to shoehorn these two aircraft into the top slot. Some very dubious claims were made about the capabilities of those aircraft which brought doubts on the motivation of the individuals concerned. In spite of their best efforts, the British Avro company (which would soon become Hawker Siddeley) was finding its way to the top of the list. They were willing to hand over the rights to manufacture the prototype in India as well as allowing export of the manufactured aircraft to other countries. The construction of the Avro aircraft lent itself to manufacture in India, more than the other contenders. The particular type on offer, the Avro 748, had a pressurised cabin with two Rolls Royce Dart jet engines driving enormous propellers. It was strong enough to cope with rough airfield surfaces and had an excellent short takeoff and landing performance, allowing it to operate in and out of the airfields in India's mountainous regions. This was the aircraft for India, it could serve as both military transport, and small regional airliner.

Menon, true to his style, stepped into the fray and squashed all the arguments, fair or foul, on behalf of all the other aircraft options. On 27th June 1959, the decision was taken to manufacture the Avro 748 in India, but with Menon at the helm nothing was going to be easy. The British design was now in India, and the UK, with both sides to start manufacturing at the same time. Menon's competitive edge came to the fore and he wanted the first Indian-made prototype aircraft to fly before the designers back in UK could. Even that tall order was not enough for Menon; he wanted it flying at the next Republic Day Parade; in other words, in less than seven months' time! What was Harjinder thinking when Menon gently threw his idea of time scales into their conversation? Did his mind drift back to the days when he repaired Wapitis and Lysanders? Best we get the tea flowing and let's see what we can do! This particular time scale was one challenge too far, even for Harjinder, but it was also an indication of Menon's lack of appreciation of the task ahead.

Then started the battle of where to build the Avro 748. The obvious destination was HAL and, with a whole raft of people who had their own personal agendas, the pressure was intense. Harjinder, Menon and Mukerjee all wanted to take a radical direction and let the IAF do the work; no prizes for guessing where that would be, and who would be in-charge. Harjinder told Menon that he only required an additional 1,000 men to be posted in to Kanpur. He finished his pitch with a request for all the moral support the military and Government could muster! The Defence Secretary, the Navy Chief; in fact all the men, bar one, with an interest in the project, gathered together in one room to thrash the issue out. The destination for the manufacturing was batted back and forth in a verbal tennis game. The conversation seemed to tie itself around and around in knots, and Harjinder's frustration bubbled to the surface at the lack of progress. He cut through the conversation to bring a moment of quiet before suggesting that Mukerjee, as IAF Chief, call the man who was not present in the meeting; Aspy Engineer, the Chairman of HAL. The call was made; the call was short. Without hesitation, Aspy sided with Harjinder and so the issue was closed. Harjinder and his men were to build a brand new aircraft for India. India would now manufacture its very first large plane, and it was Harjinder's Maintenance Command that would do it.

On the 10th August 1959, a delegation of six officers, under Harjinder's leadership, flew to the UK. He was met by a familiar face. Moolgavkar, appointed the Indian Air Attaché, had arrived in London in April. Menon had called Moolgavkar to inform him of Harjinder's arrival, or 'Kanpur Singh' as he now called Harjinder.

Stepping into a British summer's day was a total contrast to Harjinder's earlier wartime visit with the greyness of winter, and war, being replaced by colour and the promises of a new decade. However, Harjinder had an unpleasant reintroduction to something he thought he had left behind years ago; how poorly a few of the British Officers who had served in India, could behave. His contact man in Avro was a retired Group Captain who had held an important instructional post in an Indian Air Force Training College. Soon after Harjinder arrived in London, his contact appeared in his room at the Cumberland Hotel in Marble Arch. He began by sneering at the £ 4 room, in what he considered a second class hotel. Harjinder told him that he was wrong; he was staying at the Cumberland rather than at the Savoy at his own request, so that he could be with his team. This officer continued in the same vein but a little more cryptically, 'You Servicemen can't look after yourselves. You yourself remain what you always were; just a good airman.'

'That's all right with me', Harjinder replied, his blood starting to simmer.

'Now come on Harjinder! You know what I am getting at. You are nearing retiring age. I know that your pension rates are pretty meagre. Why not lay by something against your old age? I can arrange it; a numbered account in Switzerland. If you play ball with us we will look after you. What the Ministry of Defence wants, is that besides the right to manufacture, you should also order 30 British-made 748s from us to get you started. This is not an unreasonable proposal, and I know that one word from you, and the order will be through. We shall, of course, credit you with our 2 per cent commission on the deal.'

Harjinder's blood should have boiled over, but instead, he started to find the whole event very amusing. 'I look at India's requirements from a different angle to yours. I am on India's side, not Britain's. We want to save exchange; so we will not buy a single aircraft from you. We will produce even the fuselage in India. So let's forget about it.'

'You are a fool. Think it over. Your future will be secure if you take my advice.'

Harjinder's closing comment left no room for doubt, 'My future is secure even if I retire today. Look at my rank. From an airman I have risen to the second highest rank in our Air Force. What more do I want?'

Harjinder had come into contact with many RAF Officers from Indian Service, in ever-increasing seniority, and knew that they were not all like this. In his capacity as Chief of the IAF, Mukerjee attended the Farnbourgh air show which coincided with Harjinder's visit. Harjinder caught up with him and they dropped into the Savoy to meet with the now retired Air Vice-Marshal Sir Cecil Bouchier. When the three men had last met, Bouchier had been the boss of the tiny, four aircraft IAF, Mukerjee was a brand new Pilot Officer, and Harjinder was Bouchier's tail gunner as a lowly Sepoy. Here they were, with Sir Cecil and Harjinder on the same rank, and Mukerjee heading the entire Air Force in India as Chief. The letter Sir Cecil wrote to Harjinder before their meeting was heartfelt enough;

'I am delighted beyond words that you should remember me and our early struggles at Karachi to found, and build up, an Indian Air Force on a firm basis of high standards.

Yours must be one of the most romantic careers of any man in any service anywhere in the world.'

The letter after their meeting, dated 14th September 1959, went further.

'My Dear Harjinder,

I am writing direct to India to thank you so much for your most kind and generous hospitality at the Savoy, and to say how immensely I enjoyed it, particularly the thrill and joy it was for me to see you and Mukerjee again, after so many years. You both looked so well and not a day older. Throughout lunch, I kept looking at you and thinking it is just not possible that this young man is Harjinder Singh; the first airman, the No. 1 rigger, the first Naik (Corporal), at the very beginning of the Indian Air Force! What a wonderful life yours has been, full of endeavour and achievement and crowned with success as few men achieve entirely by their own efforts. Words cannot describe my joy to see and talk with you again and to find, old friend, that you were still the same old Harjinder I knew 27 years ago, not a whit changed by success-still the same loyal, upright, humble and kindly person, which is the hallmark of all great men.

Most of all, I want to thank you from my heart for your unbelievable kindness in remembering us and wanting to see us again; the one or two of us who, over a quarter of a century ago, were privileged to form part of that happy band of brothers who, at Drigh Road, set out on the great adventure of forming and training the spearhead of a great new Fighting Service...

Like all big men, in the best sense of the word, it was also like your generous nature to give so much credit for the success of the Indian Air Force to the insignificant efforts of a few of us in those early far-off days...

I shall never forget your kindly words, old friend, over lunch– however undeserved, they warmed my heart as few words have ever done and made me still feel a part of your great Service in which, when I left you, I left behind in Karachi a little of my own heart.

No, old friend, the Indian Air Force is what it is today because of one thing – the imagination, the courage, the loyalty and the great quality of that first little pioneer band of Indian Officers and Airmen, for they were the salt of the earth. By your own efforts alone, by teamwork and hard work, by adopting the right standards in all things, by determination, loyalty and by devotedly putting your whole hearts into the job, you and they have built up a great Fighting Service and I'm terribly proud to have been associated with you in this wonderful achievement if only for a little while in your early days.

When I look back to those early Karachi days, I recall that there always seemed to be a star shining above the head of Mukerjee pointing the way; and how wonderfully over the years he has trodden that path, fulfilling his appointed destiny as the leader and creator of this great Service. But there was no bright star shining above your head, old friend. You made your own, and followed it to your everlasting credit. Your career is a poetic one, an epic one shining bright as any star for all young men in your country to see and to follow...

What a lovely face does loyalty bare? I shall always retain that of the meeting with Mukerjee and you a few days ago, which was your close and real regard of friendship for each other; to have travelled the long road together; completely unchanged and unchangeable. What a world of difference it makes. Truly, real friendship and loyalty bears a lovely face. I'm sure that is why, in spite of all the problems you have faced and continue to face, neither of you look a day older; still the same charming, simple and unaffected men that once I knew so many years ago, with warmth in their hearts, and a smile never very far from their eyes and lips. How sweet a thing, old friend, is success and, in finding it, never to have changed.

Bless you again, dear friend, my kindest wishes and thoughts will always be with you.'

Harjinder's would have to get back to India to read those words. There was work still to be done in the UK. The team spent six weeks in England to familiarise themselves with the manufacturing schedule of the 748 at A.V. Roe & Co of Manchester, the makers of the world-famous World War II Lancaster bomber. Even then, in the midst of all this, Harjinder had a visit from a Vice President of the Lockheed Corporation, a Mr Chapman, with a very lucrative offer if he changed his mind on the aircraft type.

It was still not until 23rd January 1960 that the foundation stone of the Aircraft Manufacturing Depot at Kanpur was laid by Mukerjee. Later, when they walked round the hangars, all more or less empty, Mukerjee remarked, 'Harjinder! How do you think you can produce an aircraft here in two years? There isn't so much as a bench or a tool box in these hangars. I have believed whatever you have said during these last 28 years; but now I am beginning to have my doubts.'

Mukerjee returned to Delhi for an official function where Nehru would be in attendance. Delhi was growing at a phenomenal rate, and taking its place as a capital city of world status. The Rajpath, the Kings Way, is the ceremonial centrepiece of New Delhi. The tree-lined boulevard, flanked by canals and lawns, runs from India Gate, which arches over the tomb of the Unknown Soldier to the former Viceroy's Residence, now the Rashtrapati Bhavan, The President's Estate. In Mountbatten's time the land surrounding Rajpath was almost clear of buildings, except for a few important Government buildings nestled close to the Viceroy's Residence. In 1959, the city of Delhi was encroaching on the ceremonial splendour, and more and more of the area directly adjacent to Rajpath was being eaten up by the same red sandstone used in building the Edwardian Baroque Palace. An increasing number of Ministry buildings were springing up in a huddle around the central Government district. The first few new buildings replicated their predecessors' splendour, Agriculture and Commerce both securing magnificent buildings, as did the Railway Headquarters, close to Rashtrapati Bhavan. K Block, which stands to the

South of Rajpath, lacks the grandeur of its contemporaries. It would be entirely unremarkable, were it not for the red sandstone, clad around the windows, making them seemingly stand out from the red brick work.

In 1960, this building still had not been allocated to any ministry. As the conversation flowed between Mukerjee and Nehru, the Air Force Chief brought up the dilapidated state of his HQ to the Prime Minister. In a very offhand comment, Nehru suggested that Mukerjee take the top floors of K Block. Mukerjee made sure some of the Prime Minister's aides had heard that comment before he launched into action; within two weeks, he had a skeleton staff working out of the building. The IAF now had a Headquarters to be proud of, in a prime location overlooking the Presidential Palace, looking onto Rajpath. It didn't take long for the IAF to take over the floors below them, until the whole building became Vayu Bhawan, Air Headquarters; a building I would get to know very well, and that top floor is where the rebirth of Harjinder's Vintage Flight would be first discussed in the office of Air Vice-Marshal Kumaria, Assistant Chief of the Air Staff, Operations.

The acquisition of impressive buildings as offices were not top of Menon's list, and his exasperation began to show. As delays on the Avro started to build up, he suggested that they order three complete aircraft from the UK. Harjinder met Mr Egerton of the design staff from the UK, who informed him Avro had three aircraft on the production line ready to be sent to India. It was then that Harjinder realised that Avro were still pushing hard for some complete aircraft to be purchased directly from the UK, and, therefore, he surmised that Avro had been slowing the dispatch of raw materials and other components required for the IAF production line. Whether this was true or not, Harjinder would cast Menon's suggestion aside. They would manufacture every single Avro in India.

On 12th May 1960, they started manufacturing the first aircraft, and Harjinder was photographed by the press putting the first four rivets into one of the bulkheads. Some parts like undercarriage legs and propellers could not be built in India, so they were airlifted from Chadderton, Manchester and Woodford Airfield, Cheshire. Harjinder could hardly contain his excitement, another of his dreams was being fulfilled; it was admittedly only a small beginning for a very big adventure, but they had started upon a unique project. They must have been one of the few, if not the only, Air Force in the world to have turned to aircraft manufacturing; they were creating history.

On 17th October 1960, Mukerjee paid a visit to Kanpur to see how the project was progressing. His visit was an occasion to discuss the progress of the project at hand, and also to reminisce about old times. As they toured the workshops, he bubbled over with enthusiasm to see their progress. The teams in Kanpur were working round the clock to get the production line formed, just as Harjinder spent every possible moment ensuring each tentacle of the project, every aspect of the supply chain, operated smoothly together. Harjinder wasn't beyond a bit of showmanship though. When they passed a Sergeant having problems with a screw, Harjinder asked him to step aside and took the screwdriver from him. With the screw firmly driven home in a flash, the group moved on. Only when the Sergeant returned to his work did he notice that Harjinder had screwed in an adjacent screw to the one causing the problem.

On a visit by Menon, later on in the process, Harjinder was concerned that they were behind schedule, and so, ordered the men to hammer at metal pieces in the background for all they were worth. Confronted by the cacophony of noise, Menon hardly paused for breath in the assembly workshop.

The visit on the 17th October 1960 was an absolute pinnacle for Harjinder and Mukerjee's relationship. They had started their careers together in the IAF, their goal to form a strong Air Force to lead India into Independence, and then to find its feet. This goal realised, their next joint ambition was to achieve a certain degree of self-reliance. It was all coming together.

Less than a month later, Mukerjee was on hand to publicise another big event for India. Along with many journalists, he took Air India's Boeing 707 inaugural flight to Tokyo. On the evening of 8th November 1960, he dined out in Tokyo with a friend from the Indian Navy.

The 1960s had started well. Harjinder had an even closer friendship, and working partnership, with his old friend Mukerjee, and a new, blossoming, friendship with Menon. The IAF was firmly in the jet age, and they were now manufacturing modern aircraft. All seemed right with the world on 8th November 1960. Life seemed to stop the next day.

Fifteen

Reuniting Old Friends

'Mr Harjinder, you have had honour in the Air Force. Here in the Punjab you will have affection.'

On the afternoon of the 9th November 1960, Harjinder was travelling from Nagpur to Amla. The train rattled through open country, small collections of dwellings appearing at regular intervals clumped around the track. The rhythmic sway of the train lulled some into a ragged sleep, their slumber punctuated by the regular, sharp, sideways jolt, as wheels passed over a set of points, or an ill-fitting rail. Harjinder used this time to look through the various papers he had assembled for the journey, not for him the luxuriant half-sleep of railway travel. The brakes squealed as the train slowed, not an unusual event in the rural areas where livestock, vegetation or any manner of obstacle could impede progress. Looking out of the window, Harjinder could see the train slowing down at a small, insignificant, station. It really only consisted of a small platform with a makeshift shack that functioned as the Station Master's office but the train was definitely drawing to a halt. This was not a scheduled stop, and the mystery deepened when the Station Master, in his well-worn uniform, came down the line banging on all the carriage doors, shouting up to each window in turn. Harjinder's mild interest changed to concern when the Station Master approached his door, and he realised it was his name being called out. The Station Master repeatedly mumbled apologies for stopping the train, as he placed a message into Harjinder's hands. The message was short, but it took Harjinder a while to fully comprehend its contents.

Mukerjee was dead He had survived years of flying military aircraft to their limit, and beyond, in those early days when crashes, and death, were your constant companions. But now, the star described by Sir Cecil Bouchier as shining above Mukerjee, was snuffed out. The yin to Harjinder's yang was dead, and in such a wasteful, ridiculous way. The great man had been killed by a small piece of food; he'd choked to death on a fish bone in a Tokyo restaurant, with his colleagues unable to help him.

Harjinder had lost Jumbo when their vision of the future was close to being realised, and now he lost Mukerjee during a similar time of promise and euphoria. Once again, Harjinder's loss plunged him into the dark abyss of despair. He had certainly not always agreed with Mukerjee's methods in the 1940s, but he saw him as a great man. Mukerjee had been a very keen, energetic, and daring flier during his earlier career, and had retained that enthusiasm throughout his life. He was called upon to be the guardian of the IAF when he was still a young man, and he had acquitted himself admirably. Jumbo may have made the world take notice of the IAF, but it was Mukerjee who steered them through turbulent times. He was one of a few people without whom the future of the IAF could have been in jeopardy. He had the qualities of a diplomat, peace-maker and outstanding pilot, all rolled into one. He was also a great psychologist; his disarming smile could melt anger, and opposition, in most situations. However, it seemed fate was determined to take the best officers, and Harjinder's closest friends, before their time; Jumbo Majumdar, and Subroto Mukerjee, were gone.

Harjinder was in Delhi the very next day. It fell to him to carry out the mournful duty of receiving the Air Chief's remains. The urgent summons to attend to these official duties was not the problem. It was the urgent message to report to Menon's office that led to Harjinder's legacy being shredded by a version of history being written that is still widely believed today.

At Kanpur, the young Mr Nanda heard the rumours that resounded throughout the community, as news of Harjinder's departure to the Defence Minister's office spread like wildfire.

'Harjinder will be taking over the IAF.'

'Our Harjinder is going to see Menon to be made the next Chief.'

There is no record of what was actually discussed between those two men, those two friends, but there is little doubt that the leadership of the IAF was discussed. Either Harjinder was offered the position there and then, or Menon expressed a wish to see Harjinder as Chief. The fact remained, that Harjinder was the youngest of the nine IAF Air Vice-Marshals.

Mukerjee's remains were cremated at 11 am the next morning on 11th November 1960. Normally, a large flypast takes months of preparation – the timings need to be coordinated, to ensure safety, as well as a mighty spectacle. However, as the funeral pyre was lit, forty-nine aircraft of the Indian Air Force flew past with perfect precision and dipped in salute; one aircraft for each year of Subroto's life. It was a day to reflect and reminisce. Mukerjee had been involved with almost all of the senior officers of the IAF, right from the beginning of their careers. This was an occasion to consider just how far they had all come.

However, each of the individuals attending this sad occasion would fit into the reshuffle of the IAF. If Harjinder had perhaps talked to his fellow Air Vice-Marshals about the conversation with Menon, things might have taken a different turn. There was no such discussion, and soon the rumours were rife, and not just within the military, about Menon's favourite. The newspapers were happy to debate the contest for the Chair vacated by Mukerjee. They put three men in the ring together. Aspy Engineer and Nanda were the natural successors, based on seniority, and both were fighter pilots. Harjinder wore IAF wings, but was not a combat pilot, and his career had begun as a lowly Sepoy. The papers love an underdog – and Harjinder's meteoric rise from Sepoy to the most junior of the nine Air Vice-Marshals in the IAF, was exactly what they needed to spark public interest in the story. They stoked the rumours floating throughout the country, and they were keen to offer an opinion for or against Harjinder's appointment. Meanwhile, Harjinder found himself in a very dark place, the loss of Mukerjee, and the media frenzy swirling around, seemed to frustrate and suffocate him. The man who was quite happy to operate in the shadow, working hard for other people's gain, suddenly found his name being plastered across newspapers, and his career being picked through with a fine toothed comb. In his diary, he expressed his wish to leave *his* Air Force immediately, to have no further part in this circus. He harked back to the conversations with Mukerjee, and how, when he was in reflective mood, he would say; 'Harjinder, we joined the Air

Force together as the pioneers. We will go out together, you and I, at the same time.'

Mukerjee had gone; therefore it must be time for him to go.

There can only be one way that Harjinder was so sure he wasn't going to be offered the job of Air Force Chief, and that was if he had already removed himself from the equation in that meeting with Menon. Why didn't Harjinder tell the others he was not interested in taking the job? Perhaps, as a military man, he felt that any private conversations with Menon were not for wider broadcast. Perhaps he did tell them, but they suspected it was a subtle political manoeuver. The other eight Air Vice-Marshals believed promotion went with seniority and that only a fighter pilot could fill the boots as Chief. All eight men offered their resignation to the Defence Minister, thinking he was preparing to anoint Harjinder as the next Chief. Harjinder wanted no part of this elaborate political drama, and the more he thought about Mukerjee's words, the more confident he felt that it was indeed time for him to leave the IAF.

The other officers swiftly withdrew their resignations when it became clear that Harjinder was not in the running and, whatever happened, it would be a fighter pilot who would take over as Chief. The belief that the IAF Chief must be an ex-fighter pilot continued on into the next millennium. The first pilot to make the highest rank, who was not a fighter pilot, was Air Chief Marshal Fali Major, a helicopter pilot. It was he who occupied the Chief's office in 2008 when Air Vice-Marshal 'Tiny' Kumaria introduced my proposal for the IAF Vintage Flight.

Rumours abound that there was bad blood between Aspy Engineer and Harjinder, and the letters of resignation further re-enforced this misconception; the press were having a field day. However, the press, as usual, had got it completely wrong. It is not the action of an enemy to repeatedly phone their alleged nemesis, three times in one day, asking them to withdraw their resignation. Aspy said he could not imagine the Air Force without Harjinder. It was his consistent badgering that persuaded Harjinder to re-consider his parting from the IAF. The agreement the two men reached was that if Aspy became Chief, Harjinder would withdraw his resignation to serve under him.

Since the choice of new Chief was still a complete mystery to all IAF members, Harjinder spent the next two or three days visiting Delhi to sort out his retirement papers. Then, on the 19th November 1960, Menon invited Harjinder to lunch. As they sat to a simple meal, Menon let Harjinder settle before taking the very unusual step of revealing the decisions of the Defence Department ahead of time. He watched Harjinder's face as he informed him that Aspy Engineer would be appointed as the new Air Chief. As he watched relief spread over Harjinder's face, Menon jumped in with his concerns about Aspy, citing the gossip about Aspy's alleged underhand deal with the Daimler Company in France. Harjinder instantly came to Aspy's defence, he told Menon that this sort of mud-slinging by jealous rivals should not be credited; there was no doubt over Aspy's honesty. Furthermore, if Aspy were to become Chief, Harjinder wanted his resignation to be quietly turned down. Menon nodded his grey-haired head in satisfaction. Not only did he receive the reassurance about Aspy he needed, it also came with the extra benefit of keeping Harjinder.

On the 1st December, Harjinder flew to Delhi and walked the length of the 5th floor corridor in the new Headquarters building to get to the office of the newly appointed Chief. The man behind the desk looked so different from Subroto Mukerjee. Thick set, and a good deal shorter, it was easy to forget that this man had not only been a pilot in the war, but still strapped into the modern jet fighters to keep his pilot skills current. Harjinder saluted as he walked through the door, but it wasn't long before smiles broke out on the faces of both men. It was time for Harjinder, and Aspy, to work together again, but things had changed since the joyous days they spent at Kohat.

The political turmoil in Delhi may have been a drain on Harjinder's time, and energies, but back at Kanpur things were still striding forward. The first Avro 748 to be assembled in India was ready, just a few weeks after the second prototype made its maiden flight in the UK. On the 1st November 1961, the IAF made history with Kapil Bhargava at the controls of the aircraft. Harjinder had his wish granted, the first 748 carried the name Subroto in large letters down the side as a mark of respect for Mukerjee. As he watched Kapil take this new flagship aircraft into the air, Harjinder saw one of the last pieces of his life's ambitions realised. Amrit Saigal, his Staff Officer, was with him, as always, and he had brought along his nephew, the young Master Nanda; totally enthralled, as always. It wasn't just young Mr Nanda who stood in awe, the new aircraft wowed the throngs of people who had gathered to see this marvellous new technology. It marked the Air Force's ability to make, if not design, its own complex aircraft. Menon was there to place the garland of flowers around Harjinder's neck, and firmly shake his hand, when the aircraft landed and taxied up to the waiting dignitaries.

There is little doubt that Menon saw great possibilities in this success story to help his own election campaign. He was keen to have a proper, full ceremonial inauguration into the IAF, with all the press coverage that would go with it. The aeroplane was dedicated to the nation on 26th November 1961, at Palam, with Nehru present, and ranks of IAF Airmen marching past. The significance of this milestone for India was not lost on anyone, and Harjinder even received a personal telegram of congratulations from the United Nations. In 2013, I met Kapil Bhargava, one of India's foremost test pilots, who had test-flown the Avro 748, after the talk I gave at the Tata Institute in Bangalore. He spoke with great clarity of how he flew the demonstration routine for that inauguration. He decided he would show how safe the plane was by shutting one engine down just as he was about to leave the ground on the takeoff run. When his colleagues heard about these plans, they lined the taxiways, assuming they would see a spectacular end to Kapil's life, and Harjinder's dreams! Naturally, the aircraft climbed easily away, and Roy Dobson, Chairman of the Hawker Siddley Group, remarked to the Prime Minister that it was the best demo of the aircraft he had ever seen. After the troops had marched past, and the pictures were taken, Nehru came on board. Despite watching an engine stop on the demonstration, Nehru still asked to be taken up for a flight. Kapil pointed to test equipment in the cabin and politely turned his request down. To take this icon of Indian politics, in a three week-old aircraft seemed just a little rash.

Another of his goals realised, Harjinder thought it was time to take stock of his future. It had been 30 years since he had been a rebellious student at Maclaghan Engineering College, and had joined as one of the first IAF Hawai Sepoys. He was concerned that his health was not as it should be, and became obsessed with recording his daily health readings, writing them down in a separate diary. Harjinder had achieved more than he could really have believed possible when he had placed that pistol back on his Principal's desk in Lahore. His considerations of retirement had been emotionally motivated, but now he started to take a more serious, view of his future. Harjinder, and his wife, lived modestly and frugally, so he was adamant that once he left the IAF, he would not accept another paid job, but instead, work towards achieving what he and Jumbo believed in; to promote the cause of flying, and the aircraft industry. The house at

Kanpur had already lost one of its occupants after Harjinder's son departed
to make his own way in the world. From the moment the boy had entered
Harjinder's life, he had been exposed to military life, so it was no surprise
that he should also become a military man. What is surprising is that he
did not choose the IAF, but the Indian Army. Was it a small rebellious act
against his parents?

Harjinder was happy to see Aspy as Mukerjee's replacement but,
as time passed, Harjinder became more critical of him. He found him
indecisive, and too cautious, now that he held the top post. Aspy's opinion
of Harjinder was still coloured by his apparent closeness to Menon, the
Defence Secretary. Harjinder and Menon may have been similar in many
respects, but they differed in their respect shown to others. Harjinder was
known to rip into someone if they were not pulling their weight, but he
would always keep the utmost respect for the individual. That was not
Menon's way. He publically ridiculed Aspy, using his surname to make a
childish pun, 'He is neither an engineer, nor a pilot.'

Aspy's stature was not of the dashing fighter pilot of comic books and
films, but Menon seemed to forget that he flew the modern fighter aircraft
with as much spirit as the young guns under his command. Harjinder
and Aspy clashed frequently, often finding their way on to the front pages
of newspapers.

Things came to a head over Harjinder's pension. Since he was now
actively planning his departure from the Air Force, understandably, he
wanted an Air Vice-Marshal's pension. He had calculated that this would
be sufficient to cover their basic needs, and he would be able to carry out
new work in an honorary role. The problem was that he had been an acting
Air Vice-Marshal since the radio announcement of his promotion; his
rank was not yet confirmed. Subroto Mukerjee had been dealing with the
issue, but he was gone. Aspy was sympathetic to Harjinder's situation, but
told him that since he was Menon's 'favourite', then the Defence Minister,
should be the one to deal with the situation. Harjinder was saddened by
Aspy's reaction, but on no account would he ever approach Menon on a
personal matter.

Shrewd and perceptive as he was, Krishna Menon didn't handle this
situation as well as he ought to have. He began by playing a cat-and-mouse
game by offering a civilian job to Harjinder to top up the pension, but
that had never been what Harjinder was about. The damage was done
when Menon finally spoke directly with Aspy telling him, 'If you can't

get Harjinder's rank and pension sorted out, I shall have to do it myself, over your head.'

Naturally, this did not endear Harjinder to Aspy, and when Menon did start getting directly involved some of the other officers took offence at this perceived favouritism. In the end, the case was solved by Aspy, when he backdated Harjinder's Air Commodore's rank, so that he could pick up enough time as a full Air Vice-Marshal to qualify for the pension. It came with a warning from Aspy that this had stoked further resentment from their brother officers, in non-flying positions. It also left Krishna Menon and Aspy barely on speaking terms.

Aspy and Harjinder crossed swords over many subjects, adding to the hangover after Aspy's posting to HAL in Harjinder's place. The close-knit team at the top, from Mukerjee's time, was gone, and Aspy started to cut a lonely figure at the top. The about turn for their relationship, and cracks in the Harjinder/Menon's relationship, appeared during the purchase of the next generation supersonic fighter. Pakistan had been gifted the supersonic American F104 Starfighter, and India were forced into a situation where they had to play technological catch-up. The IAF were considering aircraft from the British, the French, and then Menon threw the Russian MiG 21 into the ring. The Russians had agreed to let India manufacture the fighters; they were not only cheaper, but they would buy them against rupee payments.

These were strong arguments in favour of the MiG 21, but there was one crucial one against it – it was not considered a particularly good aircraft! Krishna Menon had an altogether different approach to the problem. His enthusiasm for self-sufficiency, home manufacture, and technological advancement for India, made the MiG deal the obvious choice for him. Harjinder said he would not express any opinion about the MiG until he had an opportunity to assess the aircraft himself. On 31st July 1962, Harjinder returned to the USSR as part of a team led by Dr S. Bhagwantam, the Scientific Adviser to the Ministry of Defence, for the express purpose of finding out if the aircraft was fit for the IAF's use. They had hardly stepped off their aircraft when, on 1st August, at a meeting with members of the Russian Committee of State, Bhagwantam made the unexpected statement that he was ready to sign the contract.

At an Embassy meeting later that day, Harjinder lost his temper, and Harjinder in full fury was impossible to ignore. He called Bhagwantam Menon's stooge. The events of the visit had obviously been planned beforehand by Menon – Harjinder was not given clearance to visit all the equipment factories, but what little he saw hadn't impressed him. Harjinder had recently visited Britain to study the brutish Lightning fighter aircraft on offer from English Electric, the same company which had provided the Canberra jet bomber to India. The MiG just didn't match up. Moolgavkar was on hand to back Harjinder's argument. He got his hands on one of these MiGs, but he was told not to use the afterburner, which produced an extra kick of power when the fuel sprayed into the jet exhaust ignited with a plume of fire. Naturally, as soon as the wheels were tucked up, he pushed the throttle all the way forward into full afterburner. Within two and a half minutes, the aircraft was at 36,000 feet, the normal cruise altitude for a modern airliner. It was impressive, but still not on par with what he had experienced in Britain. With the Lightning's ability to go twice the speed of sound, and its superior build quality, it left the MiG physically, and metaphorically, in its wake.

Harjinder flew back to India prematurely on the 4th August, went directly from the airport to the fifth floor at Vayu Bhawan, and burst into Aspy Engineer's office. He didn't bother with pleasantries beyond the formality of a salute, and told Aspy that the MiG was 'unacceptable' to the IAF. Harjinder didn't have the reaction he expected from the cautious Aspy. When he paused, awaiting Aspy's expected insistence to toe the line, he saw instead tears come into the Chief's eyes. It had suddenly dawned on Aspy that Harjinder was not 'Menon's man', and that he still acted according to his own judgment. He saw clearly that the man before him had not changed from the friend he had known all these years. The fog of mistrust lifted, and the atmosphere instantly changed. The two ageing soldiers had a far more pleasurable, and successful, relationship, in the final years of their service together. This didn't imply that they saw eye to eye on every subject, like their time together at Kohat, the discussions could be heated, but mutual respect between the two men was restored.

As soon as the news of Harjinder's return from the USSR reached Menon, he had men hunting all over Delhi for Harjinder. When his men finally tracked him down, he was ushered up to Minister's office. Menon tried several ways to get Harjinder on to his side. Initially, he tried pleading with him, waving in his hand the approval notice that only required Harjinder's signature. He then turned to Amrit Saigal, assuming that Saigal, once convinced, would help convince Harjinder in turn – but Amrit was having none of it. Eventually, Menon pinned his hopes on the handsome, and dashing, Erlic Pinto, who was still with the delegation in the USSR. Pinto had been Menon's Air Attaché in London, during Menon's time as Ambassador, so he thought he had some control over him through that earlier relationship. Pinto prospects were looking up, he was slated to be a future Chief; surely, he would want to ingratiate himself further with his Defence Minister. Menon eagerly awaited his return, so the contract could be signed. He didn't get it; Pinto returned and also designated the MiG unsuitable, much to Menon's disgust. However, Menon was unstoppable; he had no thought for how the aircraft was to operate, or how suitable it was for the country as a combat aircraft. He refused to consider any counterarguments as valid, and bulldozed the issue through Parliament. The MiG deal was signed and the long India/Russia relationship with fighter aircraft started. What's more, in 2016 the MiG 21 was still in service with the IAF, far outliving the Lightening!

Even before Radcliffe had put pen to map, Simla had been the venue for the haphazard definition of another of India's borders. In 1804, Sir Henry McMahon had inked in India's Northern borders. India flowed into the Himalayas, butting up against Tibet, but the Chinese seemed indifferent to the British cartographers. The British feared that the Russians would take advantage of the void that was Tibet, and move into India, so McMahon was charged with formalising India's North-Eastern border, and consequently the outer reaches of the Empire. Where no obvious watershed existed he used 'a thick broad pen'.

In 1947, India inherited their political relationship with China from the British. The ambiguity to the mainly barren areas suited India, and, with instability rocking their newly-drawn boundaries to the North-West, it seemed sensible to keep this particular neighbour sweet. In 1950, India was one of the first countries to officially recognise the Peoples' Republic of China (PRC). In return, India was slapped in the face when, a few days later, the PRC Government announced its plan for 'the liberating of three million Tibetans from imperialistic aggression.'

The Chinese army moved into Tibet, and there followed nine years of political wrangling alongside the ebb and flow of Chinese troop movements within the country. Any plans China may have had in the early part of the decade were interrupted by the Korean War. India continued to extend the hand of friendship but, in 1959, tension broke in Tibet with a widespread anti-Chinese rebellion. The Dalai Lama was finally forced to flee, and chose to seek refuge in India. The rebellion was brutally crushed

by the Chinese Army, and, for the first time, the Government of the
Peoples' Republic of China questioned the validity of borders drawn over
the accepted map of the world; India was in trouble.

Menon preached calm, and despite the increasing number of border
clashes, he insisted that a political solution was possible. He reasoned that
the Chinese had enough on their plate with their own internal problems.
In October 1962, all of Menon's assumptions came crashing down around
him. Chinese troops moved into India, smashing through the line
McMahon had smudged on the map. The exact happenings of the conflict
will never be known since the military never formally declared war and
so their record keeping was still carried out in the peace-time mode. Also,
Menon took the very unusual decision for a defence minister in a country
in conflict, forbidding any minutes to be taken during meetings, a decision
that would cost him dear.

The news broke that the army was short of ammunition, and it really
seemed that Menon was intent on destroying his career. The Ordnance
Corps were not rolling out bullets and shells from their factories, but
were producing the coffee percolators much loved by Menon! Subsequent
inquiries were not made public, the Henderson-Brookes report only
seeing the light of day in 2014.

Harjinder's IAF were restricted to a transportation and reconnaissance
role. Even as his Army was being cut down, Menon refused to use the Air
Force in an offensive role. Any number of factors could have contributed
to his fateful error.

The Defence Minister certainly had no time for Aspy Engineer, so he
dismissed any advice from him out of hand. The American Ambassador
to India, J.K. Galbraith, had feared a war that would drag his country
into another conflict. Galbraith warned the government that the Chinese
would retaliate to any Indian bombing by launching aircraft against Delhi,
Calcutta, and even Madras in the South. Nehru accepted this absurd
suggestion, and requested the Americans to send their Air Force to protect
Indian cities. So began a most bizarre period in Indian military history,
India was trying to fight an invading army, but desperately trying to avoid
enraging them. Menon claimed that he was trying to control the intensity
of combat, and there is no doubt that his thinking was flawed, especially
his perception of the Chinese Air Force as superior to India's.

Harjinder and the Maintenance Command found themselves, for the
first time ever, bringing helicopters into operations, and in double quick

time. The helicopters arrived for assembly at Maintenance Command and were hurriedly dispatched to the front. This is how a newly arrived small Bell C-47 helicopter, ended up in the mountains, with Indian pilots, but still with Mexican markings! Soon Harjinder was in Canada placing emergency orders for the De Havilland Caribou transport aircraft to increase their transport capacity; Avro were still dragging their heels to deliver vital materials, still hoping for some direct aircraft orders.

When Harjinder returned to India he found Moolgavkar beating down his door. Moolgavkar only had to have a whiff of action before he wanted to be part of it. He remembered their wartime escapades in the jungles of Burma, how Harjinder had converted obsolete Lysanders into bombers. As Moolgavkar stood in his office, he found himself reminiscing, and saw Moolgavkar as a young man, always complaining that he wasn't getting his fair share of combat missions. He implored Harjinder to modify the now obsolete Tempests to carry napalm, so he could use them as bombers in the tight valleys of the Himalayas. Harjinder assured him it was possible, but this was a war being fought based on political, not military decisions. Menon continued to decree that the IAF would not go on the offensive.

The war was short, swift, and traumatic for India. Nehru forgot his policy of non-alignment and went directly to the Americans for help. On 7th November 1962, All Indian Radio announced that the Prime Minister had accepted Menon's resignation. It was inevitable; the Army was suffering a string of humiliating defeats. Harjinder called Menon, and in all honesty, said to him, 'You have done far better than any Defence Minister ever did.'

He must have been referring to the Defence Minister's string of victories in his time in office before the conflict began, because Menon had completely misjudged the Chinese Government in this war.

India was united in a way she never had been before, travelling roadshows, put together to raise funds, were being showered with donations from across the religious, and sectarian, divide. On 17th November, the Indian position at Se La was overrun. In 1944, Arjan Singh had flown in support of the troops in Kohima, who refused to let the Japanese pass. Now Air HQ was ordered to evacuate that area just to the North of Kohima, leaving Assam and Nagaland to the Chinese without a fight. As the Chinese troops approached the Indian airfield of Tezpur, all serviceable fighters were flown out, and those in maintenance were prepared for demolition. The invaders captured the nearby town of Chaku, and, with characteristic Chinese drama, they unexpectedly declared a unilateral cease fire. The war ended on China's terms. The IAF had been forced to remain silent throughout.

American defence analysts put pen to paper, and when those documents became public years later, they left little doubt; if the IAF had gone on the offensive it would have produced a resounding victory for India, with long term repercussions for India-China relations. In their limited capacity, the IAF had once again acquitted themselves admirably, within the limited scope they were given. They used rudimentary airstrips for takeoffs and landings, at heights up to 16,000 feet, breaking world records; and demonstrated expert use of helicopters in combat. These records, however, meant nothing to an utterly humiliated India.

Menon had been moved to the post of Minister of Defence Production, with Nehru himself taking on the Defence Ministry for a few weeks. Menon's new appointment was just a stay of execution; his career was finished. Once again Menon called Harjinder, but this time to say that he was no longer in the Government. There was too much opposition to him in Parliament, among his colleagues, and in the Armed Forces. His abrasive, and aggressive manner, had made friends, and enemies, in equal measure. However, the blame for China's resounding victory had been laid squarely with him, he had nowhere to hide, and any friends he still had were reluctant to come out in his support. It was inevitable that after Krishna Menon's departure, many of his pet schemes would come under attack as the new broom swept through the ministry. On the 27th November, less than a fortnight after Menon left the Government, Harjinder got a call from Aspy. It had been decided by the Cabinet that the manufacture of Avro 748 would be taken out of Harjinder's hands, and handed over lock, stock, and barrel, to HAL in Bangalore.

Harjinder's team finished the second Avro 748 and as it rolled down the runway, again with Kapil Bhargava at the controls, it had different name painted on the side. This Avro was called Jumbo. It was Harjinder's final nod to his old friend; his role model. The plane was handed over to the IAF where it served in the VIP role for many years.

Harjinder had only one goal left to fulfil; not bad when you look back at the almost impossible dreams of a young, idealistic, Engineering student. He still wanted the IAF to design, as well as build, aircraft. Harjinder was losing control of the 748, but he had been designing a bigger version of the

Kanpur-I. This new design was with a bigger, 250 horsepower, engine; perfect for the contract to provide an Army Air Observation aircraft. HAL had already announced their plan to build the Aeronca Sedan under licence, calling it the Krishak. Harjinder's design was once again built by the technicians under his control, and it was Kapil who was chosen as test pilot for Kanpur-II.

The pilot designated to carry out the evaluation testing for the Government was Group Captain Ramachandran, AFC. This Indian pilot had not joined the IAF, but he was one of the few Indian's to join the Royal Air Force during the war, where he served as a test pilot before coming back to his home country. He had attained notoriety as a test pilot after a particularly interesting incident occurred while he was test flying a brand new twin engine aircraft in UK. After takeoff, he made a split-second diagnosis that the ailerons, controlling the roll of the aircraft from left to right, were connected the wrong way. Many a pilot before had, and has since, died in these circumstances. The moment the pilot tried to lower a wing, caught by the first air current, makes the roll worse. The pilot would put in bigger, and bigger, control inputs to counter the situation, until, in a flash the aircraft is on its back, at low level. A fiery end to aircraft and pilot is guaranteed. It is possibly the only time in history when a pilot was not only quick enough to realise what was happening, but then fly the aircraft in the most unnatural way, by putting the stick over to the left to go right, and right to go left! Ramachandran's skills were put to the test by the ailerons in Harjinder's machine as well, when the linkage in the plane snapped, leaving him with no roll control. This time, he kicked the rudder pedals hard to slew the aircraft uncomfortably around the sky and eventually brought it down onto the runway. The problem was fixed, and the testing continued. Harjinder's Kanpur-II had a higher ceiling, as well as a higher cruising speed, than the Krishak. When the Evaluation Committee visited Kanpur on 13th March, Harjinder's plane was shown off to the esteemed team led by the legendary JRD Tata. Not only was JRD well on the way to forming the Tata empire that would stretch around the world, but he was also a record breaking pilot responsible for the first commercial flights within India, that led to the formation of Air India. He had even been hot on the heels of the 17-year-old Aspy Engineer during the race to claim the Aga Khan Trophy. JRD had an eye for aircraft and sure enough, he fell for the Kanpur-II after he insisted on taking her up and testing it out. Thereafter, he raved about it but to no avail. Aspy once again cornered Harjinder in Delhi to tell him that the evaluation team had pronounced HAL's Krishak superior to his Kanpur-II.

The IAF had manufactured four of the 748s, Harjinder's Kanpur-I, and Kanpur-II, prototypes, but it was the end of building aircraft for the Air Force. The equipment, manpower, and experience, however, did not go to waste. In the hands of HAL, the 748 production line continued to churn out more aircraft. In total 85 were made, including 17 for Indian Airlines. The IAF aircraft are still carrying out their duties today, and the trusty machines take their place in the flypast for the Air Force Day Parade every year. As I looked over my shoulder in 2012, once the Tigermoth engine had kicked into life, it was two examples of Harjinder's handiwork that were trundling past, before the thundering crashing of jet fighter engines.

Another blow came when Aspy finally had his way and the Aircraft Manufacturing Depot was moved out completely. Harjinder had been fighting against it, but he was a lone voice in a sea of indifference. He knew what was next on the horizon, and, as expected, the decision to move the whole of Maintenance Command was announced on 26th April 1963. It had been discussed for many years and illustrated the respect, or perhaps fear, so many people had for Harjinder. Nobody wanted to confront him directly on the matter, so the general consensus was, to let Harjinder be on his way, before implementing the change. Harjinder surprised his colleagues when he made no fuss about the future plans for Maintenance Command. In some ways, he could see the logic. The Command was headed for Nagpur, where there was some excellent Government accommodation. However, it also had to do with the fight ebbing from Harjinder after 30 years of endlessly fighting the system.

There was one bright, little, episode amid these depressing developments. Kanpur had a visit from the senior politician, Pandit Kunzru. It was the same gentleman Harjinder had met in Rup Chand's house, some 17 years earlier. Harjinder caught Pandit Kunzru at a quiet moment, and reminded him of the derogatory remarks he had made concerning Indian's technical capabilities, in comparison to their old British masters. Full marks to the old war horse; he apologised handsomely, and asked to take back what he had said, even after nearly twenty years. As they shook hands, Harjinder was filled with pride.

Looking through Harjinder's mountain of carefully-preserved documents, it seems he had one last step back into his early days of spanners, hammers, and rivets. A single letter, almost lost, in the reams of correspondence collected and preserved religiously, was a letter from the United States Air Force dated April 1963. It was to thank Harjinder, and his team, for the tireless two weeks of work they dedicated to the repair of the American C130 Hercules, which was stranded with structural damage. It was an aircraft type unknown to Harjinder, or the IAF; in fact the IAF would not have that aircraft in their inventory for another 45 years. Perhaps the team powered through one last time, fuelled by an unending supply of tea and confection.

There were a number of changes in Air HQ during 1963. A new post was created for a Vice Chief of the Air Staff, and the Deputy Chief was to report to him. Nanda was appointed the first Vice Chief, and Arjan Singh was to report to him as Deputy Chief. Arjan Singh was on his way to taking up the post of Chief, a position he would hold for five years before he became the only Marshal of the Indian Air Force. . It would still be another 50 years before I would sit with him in his front room, his hair and beard now snow white, as he reminisced about Sergeant Harjinder Singh and his Wapitis; memories brought on after witnessing the Vintage Flight's Tigermoth return to the sky.

In 1963, as Harjinder's date of retirement approached, Aspy and Harjinder were to complete the healing process of their friendship, returning to something more akin to their pioneer days. During one of their final days in the IAF together, Aspy sat Harjinder down and told him that regardless of all that had happened over the last few years, he had always liked him, and that the Air Force would never forget him. As Aspy and Harjinder spoke, Harjinder was overwhelmed with memories from all their years of friendship. In his diary, he confessed that there were tears in his eyes as a thousand different recollections ran through his mind. Aspy's remarks were heartfelt, but they were wrong. His assumption that the Air Force would never forget Harjinder was sadly misplaced.

The final days saw a flurry of activity, aimed at trying to hold on to Harjinder. Aspy wanted Harjinder to take on the mantle of Controller, General Aircraft Production. Harjinder went to see Aspy, and left him with no doubt that he would do anything in an honorary capacity, based in Chandigarh, but would not take up a paid position. Even as late as 17th June 1963, the Prime Minister wrote to the Punjab Chief Minister;

'I have a very high opinion of Harjinder Singh, and I do not want him to retire from Government Service. I should like him to continue for some more years...'

As Harjinder wrote in his diary;

'What greater reward can any man desire? What greater testimonial to pack in your bag when finally you wend your way homewards?'

On 27th July 1963, Aspy was once again on the phone with Harjinder. This time, the Ministry of Defence wanted him to accept a further extension of service. This was a nice parting gift, but Harjinder had made up his mind. The envelope containing his heartfelt regret at not being able to accept the offer, was duly sealed and sent off by Express Delivery, and thus signalled the end of his 30 year long, illustrious, bottom to top, career in the IAF.

Harjinder entered into a very reflective period, and he looked back on the man he had known as the teenage prodigy from back in 1930. Of Aspy he wrote; 'he was the one person in the whole of the IAF who has gone up the ladder demanding the very best from himself and other people around him. He drove his subordinates hard, but drove himself harder. I can confidently state that the IAF owes a lot to his love for the Service and his hard work. Being an excellent pilot, an officer and a leader, he won admiration from all and sundry. He was acknowledged as one of the finest officers that ever stepped into Air Force uniform. If there is one pilot in the IAF who has never made a heavy landing in his life, Aspy is that man.'

While there had been friction between the men, it was clear that there was no lasting rift between them.

When he was well into his 80s, Aspy wrote about his relationship with Harjinder, referring to him as the remarkable Hawai Sepoy who later rose to the rank of Air Vice-Marshal. He said Harjinder Singh was indeed a dedicated and energetic soul; the IAF was fortunate to have him.

By 2nd August 1963, messages of congratulation poured into his office. His final day in Kanpur arrived; the whole station was on parade that day. As is customary in the IAF, Harjinder was placed, standing, in the back of an open jeep. Ropes were attached, and lines of officers and men took the strain to physically pull Harjinder from his Headquarters building. However, the men took things a step further. Harjinder wasn't allowed to climb down from his jeep. He was hoisted onto the shoulders of the men, and passed from person to person, above their heads. It was a display of unabashed affection from those who had worked with Harjinder. He took the final parade before making his exit in the only way he knew how. Fifteen years previously Harjinder had flown his private aircraft into Kanpur to start his term there, and now, on the 3rd August 1963, he climbed on to the wing of his Bonanza to give a final salute to the parade before him. As he strapped in, and took off from Kanpur for the last time, he looked back to see the hundreds of men still lined up perfectly on the parade square.

Harjinder left behind his personal Spitfire; the one he had rebuilt; the one he flew to his Wings Parade, the one with his callsign 'Plumber' on the side. Harjinder, over time, almost by chance, had brought together a collection of aging aircraft. He knew the youth of India were the future but he wanted them to know about the past and the machines in which men went to war; some paying the ultimate price. Harjinder had formed the Indian Air Force Vintage Flight.

Amrit Saigal had left Kanpur a little before Harjinder, promoted, and sent on a career independent from his mentor. He would reach the rank of Air Commodore, and win wide respect from his colleagues. His replacement had continued the tradition of stopping the local trains to ensure Harjinder's swift passage to work. That disruption to the public transport system would no longer be required. Air Vice-Marshal Harjinder Singh had left Kanpur, but he would leave his name there. The local authorities decided to rename the area he had driven in every day. Nagpur still has an entire colony named Harjinder Nagar.

On the evening of the 3rd August 1963, he was the guest of honour at his final formal dinner at the Central Vista Officers' Mess in Delhi; his 'dinning out' of the IAF. A silver model of a Wapiti aircraft was presented to him on behalf of all ranks of the IAF; a fitting memento for an ex-Hawai Sepoy turned Air Officer Commanding. Harjinder was overcome with emotion. The IAF was his whole life, it was everything to him. Here he had made friends, and nurtured lifelong relationships, he had found mentors and guides, and had guided so many others in their careers. He had known unbearable sadness, and seen corruption, racism and bigotry, but also unconditional kindness, he had known joy and pride. As he looked back at his career now, the urge to stay was overwhelming, but the time had come for him to bid the IAF adieu. On the 4th August

1963, Air Vice-Marshal Harjinder Singh, MBE, the original Hawai Sepoy, officially left Delhi, and left *his* IAF. Aspy very kindly offered to fly him to Chandigarh in a Service aircraft, but he preferred to end his journey in his own aircraft. As he pushed the throttle forward, and the wheels left the Indian Air Force runway.

On 6th August 1963, Mr Pratap Singh Kairon, the Chief Minister of Punjab, invited Harjinder to lunch. During the meal, quite spontaneously, Mrs Kairon said, 'Mr Harjinder, you have had honour in the Air Force. Here in the Punjab you will have affection.'

Harjinder was given use of the Deputy Minister's house in Chandigarh. Things had certainly changed from the days when the orphaned child had been schooled just a few miles to the North. Back then, a small temple was the only structure in the area but now, with French styling, the new city of Chandigarh emerged from nothingness. In the middle of Corbusier's masterwork lay a prime plot of land, which was to be Harjinder's family home, a house that should have brought ultimate happiness to his family.

On the 22nd November 1963, the world stopped. A shock wave rippled out from Dallas in the USA. The next day, the world's newspapers carried the headlines of JFK's assassination; India was the exception. The smashed remains of a helicopter in Kashmir were splashed across the front page of newspapers across India. The broad, dashing smile, of Erlic Pinto was gone. With him were 4 high ranking Generals in the Indian Army. Another of Harjinder's friends was gone. Aspy was seen with tears in his eyes again. Bad weather had done more damage than the Chinese, or Pakistani, army could have done.

It seemed to some that there was another victim of the 1962 war against the Chinese. Nehru's health began to decline; it seemed he had absorbed all the humiliation of defeat. He saw the whole unfortunate episode as a betrayal of trust. On the 27th May 1964, he died, and India's First Prime Minister, the talisman who emerged from behind Gandhi to become the ultimate statesman, was gone. The papers carried the same quote they had used when Gandhi was assassinated; 'The Light has gone out of our lives and there is darkness everywhere.'

India's economy was taking a serious beating with levels of poverty, and disease, out of control. The nation as a whole, and the IAF in particular, had morale at rock bottom. The man for the job as Chief, to drag the IAF out of this slump, was none other than Arjan Singh. His leadership, and charisma, arrived just in time to plug into the soul of the IAF, and electrify them because as 1965 drew to a close, the Pakistanis came once again; the IAF went to war, but for the first time without Harjinder.

The attack began over the Rann of Kutch. Pakistan claimed that since Rann was flooded in the monsoon, it should be regarded as part of the sea; therefore, the border should pass down the centre of the area. They backed their claim by driving tanks into Indian Territory by claiming it was sea! Kashmir was also on the Pakistani shopping list, and when their army's infiltration units failed to take ground as hoped, they pressed the button for a full scale push over the border.

Harjinder had brought the IAF into the jet age. The Vampires were already antiquated and suffered terribly. The tiny Gnats caught the Pakistani Sabre fighter pilots by surprise and earned themselves the gory nickname of 'Sabre Slayers'. The modern Hunter fighters and Canberra bombers operated with great distinction and much of the gloom from the '62 war was swept away. Harjinder's attention was drawn to how his Maintenance Command performed. Writing over 40 years later, historian Air Commodore Jasjit Singh wrote; 'Our support organisations, especially the maintenance crews, from the lowest rank, all the way to the Air Officer Commander-in-Chief, Maintenance Command, ensured that the combat would not be affected by technical difficulties. The Air Force did not experience the type of disorderly unserviceability that the Pakistani Air Force displayed on the very first day's strike.'

Harjinder had left a robust system behind him. During the war, the Deputy Commander of Maintenance Command was Moolgavkar, no doubt wishing that he was in one of the fighters' cockpits.

Harjinder did the only thing he could do; he kept himself busy. He received more requests than he could cope with to attend colleges and deliver his inspiring speeches to India's youth. Motivational seminars may be a New Millennium phenomena, but Harjinder fell into that role in the 1960s. Only when sifting through the mass of correspondence he's left behind, does the true picture come into focus; President of the newly formed Air Force Veterans League of India; Adviser to the Government of Punjab for technical education, industrial training, general education, civil aviation and even child protection. He was an adviser to the American company General Electric, the Indian company Himalayan Helicopters, and to Sir Roy Dobson of AVRO. The company, Electronic

Ltd, in Faridabad, saw such a tremendous rise in production in the month following Harjinder's input, that the Managing Director felt compelled to vacate his chair.

After the 1965 war, the peace between India and Pakistan was uneasy at best, but this was due to the politicians, not the men leading the opposing militaries. Arjan Singh paid a visit to his Pakistani counterpart, and ex-colleague, Air Marshal Nur Khan. However, this was not to be a strained meeting over the desk in a war room. They met in Peshwar, where they had served together as young men, Arjan in Wapitis, and Nur in the Audax. For the entire duration of his visit, Arjan stayed in Nur's house, and they even found time to play a round of golf together.

The IAF had arguably finished the 1965 war with the upper hand, with little doubt that had the conflict continued, it would have seen the IAF in complete control of the skies, mirroring their colleagues on the ground. The Government knew it was down to the drive of Arjan Singh, and they took the long overdue step of reinstating the rank Chief of the Air Staff that had not been used since the departure of the last RAF Chief. Chief of the Air Staff, Arjan Singh, DFC, continued in that role until 16th July 1969. For a brief time, Arjan Singh controlled the Air Force whilst Field Marshal General Sam Manekshaw, MC, the man who could not even be stopped by seven Japanese bullets, was Chief of Staff of the Indian Army. When the time came, Arjan Singh handed over his responsibilities to Air Marshal PC Lal, DFC. The IAF was in good hands, but tensions continued to spiral upwards with Pakistan. The new decade started with a new Chief and, as the monsoon rains began to die down in 1971, the border clashes became an everyday occurrence.

Harjinder kept up his punishing schedule; he continued serving as an advisor to companies, but what he loved best was to interact with students and young people. He was always overwhelmed by requests from colleges and universities countrywide to come in for lectures and talk; the requests from the Punjab always took priority. In November 1971, he stood at the lectern at the DAV College in Chandigarh, his hair had turned white, and his frame refused to fill his suit as before, but his booming voice, and presence held the room in thrall, just as it had done all those years ago, when he was still a student. This time, his words were not to whip up support for student strikes, or to ask his peers to follow him into the Air Force, or even to persuade Airmen in protest, to return to duty. This time it was a 62-year-old war veteran, telling the next generation that anything was possible, but you had to work for it. Harjinder stood behind the lectern, on the raised stage area, with the sea of young faces listening to stories of biplanes flying over warring tribes, of obsolete aircraft becoming bombers, of rebuilding broken aircraft under impossible deadlines, of never giving up. He finished one sentence, paused, but the next sentence never came. His knees buckled, and the tall figure of Harjinder Singh sank to the ground. On that stage, in Chandigarh, Harjinder was reunited with his two friends; Jumbo Majumdar and Subroto Mukerjee. The musketeers were reunited.

Amrit Saigal was working at the Western Air Command Headquarters building in Delhi when he heard the news. He dropped everything and raced to Chandigarh, but there was nothing he could do for his hero. Harjinder's heart had powered him through physical feats of exertion, and endless nights of hard labour with no sleep, but when it gave up, it gave up completely. Harjinder was most probably with Jumbo and Subroto before he reached the ground; his heart just finally had had enough. It was obvious from the weekly letters between Amrit and Harjinder that their relationship had grown even stronger since Harjinder's retirement, but there was nothing for Amrit to do except to ensure that Harjinder's wife was comforted, and to prepare for Harjinder's funeral.

Air Marshals, Air Vice-Marshals, and Air Commodores, all gathered to carry Harjinder's open coffin. Beant Kaur conducted herself with utmost dignity, as she always had. She had been in step with Harjinder on every path they followed, even learning to fly when she was 34-year-old. In his diaries, Harjinder had written that Beant Kaur's demeanour had remained the same no matter what their circumstances – she conducted herself with grace both as the wife of an airman as she interacted with her husband's colleague's wives, and as the wife of the Commanding Officer who regularly interacted with world leaders. She should have gone on to have a peaceful retirement befitting someone who had stood as a rock by her husband's side. With Harjinder gone, it was a time when his legend should have been established as one of the cornerstones of the IAF.

Neither was to happen.

Epilogue
The Greatest Disgrace?

March 1934: Air Marshal Sir John Steele, Air Officer Commanding-in-Chief, India to Sepoy Harjinder Singh, pilots Subroto Mukerjee and Aspy Engineer, and to the entire 200 men of the IAF:

'Indians will not be able to fly and maintain military aeroplanes. It's a man's job; and all you have done is bring the greatest disgrace on yourselves.'

It is afternoon in the UK, evening time in Delhi, when my final call to Woody, from Reflight Ltd, finalises the hastily made plans during the day. It has been a busy day, as usual, in Delhi, so despite the rising excitement sleep is no problem. Still in the dark of night, we take 250 passengers into the air from Delhi's Indira Gandhi International Airport. They sit in supreme comfort sipping drinks, choosing their food and making their selection of films from a huge catalogue. The inscription on the side of the Boeing 777 may say British Airways but when Harjinder entered Lahore College in 1929, the forerunner of this very airline started the London-Delhi route with the name Imperial Airways written on their lumbering biplane. The speed has increased unrecognisably but in one way air travel has come full circle. Imperial Airways was the height of luxury and once again business passengers are offered flat beds to sleep in, and a choice of good food and wine. The Empire that Imperial Airways served no longer has a say on the land I look down on in the early dawn light. The brown/grey lands, viciously folded by mother nature is where Harjinder sat in the cockpit of a Wapiti, behind Jumbo, outside the walls of ancient forts; where Subroto Mukerjee chased his runaway aircraft in the dust; where Arjan Singh had a bullet pass through his biplane's fuel pipe.

Only seven hours later I am at London's Heathrow Airport and climbing onto my motorbike to start the sprint, via my house, to collect my flying equipment and head to Leicester Airport. The fresh air revives me, as I cut through the early morning traffic. There is no time to waste as I arrive at Leicester Airport, so I ride down the footpath that leads to the front of the hangar. Parked outside the hangar, shimmering with the droplets of light rain from the previous night, is the bright yellow Harvard; saffron, white and green roundels down the side, followed by the large IAF registration mark HT 291.

I have waited for this moment for many years, but the reality, as always, is very different. We're running short on time, so, after a brief chat with Tony, the other pilot, I change into my flying suit, still with the Indian flag on the shoulder from flying the Tiger Moth in 2012. I have seen this plane change from a dusty, faded, abandoned machine in the corner of an ignored hangar, into this gleaming aircraft poised to leap skywards. I have sat in the cockpit many times as it was built back up from its basic tubular frame, into this better-than-new beast. This time, when I occupy the pilot's seat, it will be very different, we will go flying.

I step up onto the wing, using the front foothold to pull on. Standing on the wing I realise that Harjinder would have gone through this process many times, perhaps in this very aircraft. Face backwards, inside foot on the step, pivot around so that the other foot swings over the cockpit side, and on to the seat. Both feet in and then I lower myself in. I strap in before I have time to stop and properly look ahead at the original black and white instruments facing me in the spring-mounted instrument panel. I am surrounded by the green gloss of the levers, push rods, frame tubes and side panels, that disappear into the cavernous bowels of the aircraft's belly under my seat. Did Harjinder work on this aircraft; did Harjinder sit on this seat; did Harjinder fly this aeroplane? This aircraft is from that era, but the early log books are long lost, not that Harjinder's name would have appeared in them until his official flying training: his early flying in the North-West Frontier never happened did it?

A few minutes later the wheels leave the runway and the patchwork of Leicestershire fields move away from underneath us. Flying in formation, I tuck in close alongside a chase aircraft for some air to air pictures. Looking along our gleaming yellow wing, past the small IAF roundel and over the white wing tip, there is little time to daydream about Harjinder sitting in this, or similar cockpits, as he battled through the clouds over Delhi, or bounced down the dusty strips around Kohat. We are on our way to RAF Brize Norton.

Our chase plane falls away, heading towards the Brize Norton runway. I can't resist the temptation, so with the permission of Air Traffic control, we keep a little height until the runway's starting threshold has long since disappeared under the nose. I push the control column forward until the black and white 'piano keys' of the runway are back in sight. The Harvard quickly accelerates as we gallop earthwards. As I level off, the runway zips underneath us until we are halfway down its length. As we pass the control tower I warn Tony of the approaching, gentle, G force, just before pulling the yellow machine up, around, and into the landing pattern.

Eyes flick in to check the speed; left hand finds the hydraulic pump actuator. One push forward to activate it followed by another flick of the eyes over the hydraulic gauge. Moving the undercarriage lever forward is rewarded with the satisfying thump as the legs swing out and lock in place: two green lights. Then left hand back slightly to find the flap lever, eyes once again flicking in, to check the progress of the flap indicator; out to check the runway; in to check the fuel gauges and out to keep tracking the runway.

Approaching the touchdown zone I bring the nose up into the landing altitude, losing sight of the runway ahead of me behind that large round nose, but the runway sides are in my peripheral vision rising slowly up to meet me. I keep the nose coming gently up, aiming to touch all three wheels at the same time as the speed bleeds away.

We taxi to the small group awaiting our arrival in front of the small hangar. This will be the home of the Harvard for two weeks before the RAF help to load it into the enormous hold of the Indian Air Force Boeing C-17 transport in the presence of the Indian High Commissioner. My grin could challenge the size of that C-17's belly when the business of flying is complete, and there is a moment to suck up the feelings of past, present and future. Maybe, just maybe, Harjinder sat in this seat. After unbuckling the seat harness, then the parachute harness, I step up on the seat, out

onto the step, down onto the wing and then a hop onto the tarmac of
Brize Norton. Woody, from the restoration company is there, along with
Will from the UK Ministry of Defence and members of the Brize Norton
team. My grin is reflected on their faces too. The Harvard will be going
home soon, but not before two of the RAF Battle of Britain Memorial
Flight's Spitfires pay us a visit for a unique photo shoot.

My meetings back in Delhi, over the past few months, have not only
been to arrange for this Harvard to go home to India, but also discuss
the next aircraft for restorations. The Spitfire that Harjinder rescued, that
Harjinder flew to his own Wings Parade, that still carries the Plumber
call-sign as a plaque on the nose, is the next candidate. The questions that
crowd my brain now, 'Did Harjinder sit in this plane? Did he help repair
it? Did he take it into the air?' will become a certainty with his Spitfire.

In Delhi, that imposing, five storey red sandstone building, just off the
Raj Path, is still Vayu Bhawan, the Headquarters of the Indian Air Force.
Since 2007, I have been leaving the noise and frantic traffic of the street
outside to enter the hushed corridors of the top floor, beautifully finished
in Air Force Blue Marble. The first three years involved a squeeze between
hoardings to reach the reception room in Headquarters to get my entry
pass issued. If it wasn't raining, I would still get wet from the chuntering
air-conditioning units overhead dripping water onto the unsuspecting
below. The hoardings gave the building an unfortunate, shabby visage,
but, it was all for a good cause. The ambitious metro underground system
was passing directly underneath the building with promises to provide a
real solution to the traffic gridlock that clogs Delhi's streets every day.

After signing another entry log, I entered through the main doors.
The bright, white, marble floor looked positively opulent after the basic,
paint-peeling, reception room, but the rest of the grand entrance also
looked a little tired. I walk to the left of the staircase that dominates the
entrance foyer, and come to the two beaten – up lifts that groan as they
grudgingly open their doors to let out their captives. Waiting for the lift
to arrive became a moment of trepidation for me, the small box could take
six people, but eight or nine would regularly pile in. On a previous visit
the power flicked on and off several times before leaving the small box
stranded between floors, with little air getting through, not the best way
to prepare for a meeting! Finally the doors were prised open and a hand
offered from above to pull us one by one up to the floor level which started
about half way up the door opening.

Since that incident, as a distraction while waiting for my lift, I took to examining the faces in the pictures on the wall. They were names and faces that I was becoming more, and more, familiar with as I dived into the history of the IAF. Naturally, Marshal of the Indian Air Force, Arjan Singh, took pride of place. There, was Subroto Mukerjee as the first Chief, and Aspy Engineer, the second. There was the grinning face of Jumbo Majumdar, sitting in his Hurricane, moments before his death. Next to him, a picture of Sekhon, who took off in his Gnat fighter when six Sabres attacked his airbase. He had taken off with Ghuman, but, in the misty, early, winter morning, found himself battling the Sabres alone, before he fell to their guns. For his gallantry, he became the only IAF person to be awarded India's highest gallantry award, the Param Vir Chakra. The obvious absence was Harjinder Singh; whose meteoric rise from Sepoy to the first Corporal, the first Sergeant, the first Flight Sergeant, the first Engineering Officer, the father of Maintenance Command and the Vintage Flight, should have earned him a place of honour on these walls. I first learnt of him when I asked why the word 'Plumber' was mounted with obvious pride on the side of the aircraft that was 99 per cent Spitfire and 1 per cent MiG 21. The Commanding Officer of the Vintage Flight I had revived, Wing Commander Mukesh Sharma, explained how Harjinder had found, and rebuilt, the Spitfire he'd found in a rubbish dump. The pneumatic system for the undercarriage was missing, so just as Harjinder had done throughout his career, he had found a way around the problem by fitting a system from the MiG 21. Mukesh's enthusiasm for the Vintage Flight knew no bounds, and there is no doubt that without his drive and dedication, we would never have seen it reborn. His interest in this man, Harjinder Singh, was also infectious, but he explained to me that Harjinder was out of favour, because of his friendship with the then Defence Minister, Menon, and his apparent clashes with Aspy Engineer. I had no reason not to take these facts on face value.

In 2014, the metro glides under the still gridlocked streets of Delhi. Until three months previous, I used the new metro to get me to Udyog Bhawan, the station facing Air Headquarters. It not only halved the time of a taxi, but I no longer had the regular battles with drivers who set off, saying they knew exactly where I was going, only to stop five, six, or seven times to ask for directions. The hoardings are down, and the building is back to its former glory, it finally looked like the building that Subroto Mukerjee knew when he first 'captured' the top two floors, before descending to take the whole building. The three dusty, and shabby, Gnat aircraft, that had lay abandoned in the corner of the Vintage Flight aircraft hangar I use in Palam Air Base, had been reunited with their wings, repainted to a fabulous silver shine, and now sit in perfect formation on their plinth, endlessly climbing into the hazy Delhi sky, the grass around them luscious green. The walk to the main doors of the building has reclaimed its rightful grandeur. The retina scan security check perhaps has more to do with too many James Bond films, rather than a real need, but through the routine we go. Then it is back into the white marble entrance hall, but now the walls are gleaming white in competition, huge models of IAF aircraft sit on their stands, and even the lifts have been smartened up inside. The size of the lift stays the same, as does the number of people squeezing in; and when I do get in, I idle away the short trip to the fifth floor wondering if the winding machinery is still the same. As I wait for the lift, I notice that the pictures have also reappeared after the building work. They are properly framed to a uniform size, backlit, and the faces have a small written piece underneath to explain, to those who might not know, what amazing deeds these men did. And, at the front of the line of pictures, the first one your eyes drift to, is an officer few people know about; Air Vice-Marshal Harjinder Singh, MBE. He is back. Is this a sign that he is being brought back into the brotherhood of the IAF? Has he been remembered in his true light, or have the rumours just been put to one side, temporarily?

My usual routine is to come to Headquarters on my newly-purchased Royal Enfield Bullet motorbike after visiting the Head Office of Avi-Oil. The lifts in the Surikiran towerblock have the luxury of a fan to stir the air as they bringing me down from the 6th floor. The office of Avi-Oil was cooler again and there is always a cup of tea waiting for me. The Chairman, Mr Nanda, sits behind his desk with photographs of his grandchildren standing, or sitting, in various aircraft. Behind him, on a table, are intricate, handmade model aircraft. These are Mr Nanda's prized possessions, having been made by Harjinder Singh from scrap metal pieces. Mr Nanda was the young boy who remembered the turbulent arrival of Independence, with his father sitting on the roof with a shotgun. The same young man who went to live with his Aunt, and her husband, Amrit Saigal, during the time Amrit served as Harjinder's Staff Officer. On one side of his office is the large safe. It is now a normal event to see him open the safe to retrieve items from within, but the first time was a surprise. There is no gold, or money, inside that safe but instead, endless piles of files and documents. Since the death of his uncle, Mr Nanda has become the custodian of Harjinder's life and his memories. It seems Harjinder threw nothing out. Original letters from the 1930s, including papers from his time as an engineering student, right through to the actual correspondence between him and his two Chiefs, Subroto Mukerjee and Aspy Engineer, are the treasures that are protected here, and these are just the most precious of his documents and photographs. Harjinder's personal belongings and papers line the shelves in this office, and reveal the stunning life he'd led; more lie in Mr Nanda's house. Time, with Mr Nanda, when discussing the life of Harjinder, vanishes in a flash, and he is responsible for more than one late arrival for meetings at Vayu Bhawan. The amount of information he retains in his head is staggering, and any question is either greeted with an old paper withdrawn from the safe, or a message on e-mail waiting for me by the evening. Without Mr Nanda much of the IAF history would have been lost; the chance to tell the story of Harjinder Singh would have been lost.

One visit in July 2014, I sat in his office, noticing two red-covered books by his elbow. After a brief catch up, he passed these old books to me, explaining they had been in possession of Jumbo's daughter until now. The red covers are embossed with the words 'Lion's Diary'. One is from 1944 and the other, 1945. I sat there staring at the inside cover of the first book, where, in Jumbo's own hand is 'Wing Commander Karun Krishna Majumdar, Indian Air Force: No IND/1555' in his neat handwriting. The obvious place to start is D-Day, 6th June 1944. All his entries are so matter of fact, listing the missions with calm comments like 'enemy seen and engaged' or descriptions of the intensity of flak. Just four days after the cauldron of D-Day, he notes, 'Feel I can cope all night. Burma was tougher.'

Having spent some time looking at the missions in Europe during 1944, I pick up the next book. Mr Nanda with a little nod of his head; 'Look at 17th February.'

It is a peculiar feeling; I am curious but also wary, do I really want to know what this page holds? I open the yellowing book to approximately half way but there are no entries. I flick backwards until I arrive at the last entry, 17th February 1945. Jumbo has details of the arrival at Lahore at 11:30 am and then his shopping trip to buy the birthday present for his son's birthday party that evening, and scent for Kooiee, his wife. Then he writes:

'1600 Walton fly past'

'1605. Lord, lettest now thy servant, depart in peace.'

Just five minutes later he was dead.

The hairs on the back of my neck are standing to attention. I look up, and get a knowing nod from Mr Nanda. He answers my question before I can even ask them; there are no other religious comments in Jumbo's diaries, apart from one the year before, when his son was born. Somehow, it seemed as if Jumbo knew.

One week later, the air-conditioning of the Delhi hotel lobby breaks over me like an icy wave as I climb off my motorcycle and venture indoors. The ride from Vayu Bhawan is always tiring. Already warm from the sweltering heat of the Delhi summer, the slow revving engine of the bike pushes my body temperature further up. Today's journey also involved juggling another heavy, precious cargo – I had brought with me, Harjinder's papers in an Avi-Oil bag. Once again, time raced by in Mr Nanda's office, as we dived headlong into another collection of yellowing correspondence. I knew that Harjinder had been busy after retirement, but it was this consignment of papers that revealed just how broad his involvement in all aspects of life was.

Having been separated from my phone by security regulations at HQ, followed by the noisy ride to Saket district in Delhi, it is the first time to check messages as I give the nod of a sweat-soaked head to my long-term friend Rajesh, the hotel concierge. I call Woody at the UK restoration company, Reflight. The timetable is tight to get it into RAF Brize Norton to await collection by the IAF C-17 transport aircraft. Before I turn in for the night, to get some rest, before flying back to London, I speak with Air Marshal Kumaria; he is still fiercely supportive of the project. Retirement caught him up before I could bring the Harvard back to India, but we did have our time together when I flew the Tigermoth in the 80th Anniversary Parade. After the parade rehearsal, his staff car flying his flag as the Vice Chief of the IAF, arrived at the hangar. He had a flying suit with him, it seemed after years of planning we were finally going to fly together. He was unaware of the leaking fuel drain I was trying to fix when he arrived. It was time for make one of those split second decisions, knowing that this would be our only chance to fly together in an IAF Vintage Flight aircraft. I decided it was worth the small risk. With a rag wrapped around the fuel drain, I taxied out having promised myself that if the fuel soaked through before takeoff, I would cancel the flight. I knew that once we

were airborne, the hot Delhi air, would just evaporate the occasional fuel
drip in an instant. It was a short flight. Both of us knew the importance of
this old-lady-of-the-skies being seen on parade. Air Marshal Kumaria was
concerned about hitting a bird, and I knew we were, albeit very slowly,
leaking fuel! I don't know who had the biggest grin when we landed.
Those few minutes above Delhi are one of the most significant in my
pilot's log book.

After finishing my telephone update with the now retired Air Marshal
Kumaria, I get back on the phone with Woody, and finalise my plans to
fly the Harvard down to Brize Norton. And then it hits me, in July 2014,
I am going to fly in one of Harjinder's aircraft.

In 1971, the death of a retired Air Vice-Marshal was not big news
in India, distracted as the public were by the war with Pakistan. The
Pakistani offensive was spearheaded by the tanks of their Armoured
Brigade. The attack along the entire length of the border was stopped by
the IAF's Hunters at a place called Longewala in the Rajasthan desert.
Pictures of the desert battlefield show endless spirals as the tanks fruitlessly
tried to escape the rocket and cannon fire from the IAF aircraft. It was
perhaps the most dramatic example, anywhere in the world, of the use of
stand-alone air power, but the IAF's deeds remain largely unheard of in, or
outside, India.

In East Pakistan the MiG 21s of No. 28 Squadron, IAF, launched
pin-point attacks on Government House where the Pakistani military
leadership had set up their base. They used a tourist map of Dacca as a
guide for identifying targets! Imagine how helpless these men would have
felt as rockets came through the window. The unconditional surrender of
the Pakistani troops was offered immediately. East Pakistan was liberated,
and Bangladesh was formed. As the forlorn Pakistani General, Lieutenant
General Amir Abdulla Khan Niazi, MC, signed the ceasefire agreement,
the senior most officials of the three Indian Services stood behind him.
When he was asked why he gave in with such little resistance, despite the
number of troops he had available, he pointed his pen at the Air Force
Officer behind him, Air Vice-Marshal H.K. Dewan, and said, 'Because
of them'.

What would Harjinder have made of this declaration? His beloved
Air Force had performed beyond even the wildest expectations in 1947.
Simultaneously, they had crushed the opposition on two fronts, but for
Harjinder it would have torn at his soul, for they were once again at war

with people he had called his own twenty five years before, and over the land that had been his country. Lord Mountbatten took no satisfaction in seeing his two-headed state fail as he had predicted, and the autonomous state he first suggested to Nehru, in Simla, come into existence.

In Delhi, one particular teenager had his own personal battle on 8th March 1972. DC 'Tiny' Kumaria had spent months at the Sadfarjung airfield in the centre of Delhi watching the aircraft from the flying club land and takeoff again.

After talking himself into any spare joy rides that were available for a flight, his enthusiasm was rewarded with a scholarship to learn to fly. Tiny Kumaria had completed his first, solo, takeoff and landing, but whilst it was fresh in his mind, he was sent up again for a second time with instructions to fly around the landing pattern, practicing his landings and takeoffs. After his second takeoff, the young man turned his plane to parallel the runway, the downwind position, and set up for another landing. He settled his silver HT2 at the correct height when his small world, in that narrow cockpit, exploded. All that the youngster knew was the world had erupted in a storm of Perspex shards and wind noise as his head was thrust into his lap, with just a blurred, dark view of the cockpit floor. When Tiny pulled his head up into the maelstrom of wind, he saw the needle of the engine RPM gauge threatening to bend over the stop pin that marked the maximum. The young and inexperienced mind still diagnosed, in that fraction of a second, that he no longer had a propeller attached. That had caused the engine to scream far beyond the designed RPM limits with the threat of the whole engine ripping free too. He flicked the engine ignition off and hauled back on the stick to recover from the screaming dive he found himself in. This fresh-faced pilot, with a grand total of ten minutes solo flying, showed what natural skill he possessed. Not only did he recover the twisted aircraft from a death-dive and into a glide, he steered it for the only open space available, down a dirt bank to slither to its final resting place.

When the instructor, in another HT2, had incorrectly descended into the same traffic pattern, he had done so right on top of Tiny's HT2. The wheel of his aircraft not only crashed through Tiny's canopy, but actually struck him on the back of the head, continuing on to tear the propeller off. It was a fatal mistake for the pilots of that second aircraft. Tiny Kumaria lived that day; if he hadn't, the Vintage Flight would have not been reborn and this story of Harjinder Singh would have not been told.

On the 25th June 1979, Lord Mountbatten celebrated his birthday. He became 79-year-old, surpassing, by one year, the man he had come to respect so much; Mahatma Gandhi. Two months later, on 27th August 1979, he too was assassinated. Just off the coast of a small Irish seaside village, the Irish Republican Army detonated the bomb they had planted on his boat. He was targeted not because he was the last Viceroy, or the first Governor General of India; or even for his life in the military. He was targeted purely because he was related, distantly, to the Royal family.

As the 1970's moved onto the 80's, senior IAF men either didn't know who Harjinder Singh was, or they felt it unwise to admit to any knowledge of him.

'Harjinder Singh? Not sure I know of him, or are you referring to Menon's man in the IAF?'

The nephew of Amrit Saigal proved to have absorbed many of Harjinder's traits as he had seen him in action. He added these to his own exceptional intelligence during his time in Kanpur, living with Amrit. Just like Harjinder, he drove himself tirelessly to excel in college to such an extent he was asked to take up an immediate teaching post after graduating. When he moved on from teaching he found himself in the petrochemical industry, but Mr J.R. Nanda had aviation running through his veins. Harjinder worked tirelessly to achieve self-reliance for India, so, when Mr Nanda discovered that all the various oils used throughout the IAF had to be imported, he set out on a long road to form his own company that would produce the IAF's every need from within the country. He had to use the same tenacity as Harjinder to fight bureaucracy to achieve this, but achieve it he did, with the very successful company, Avi-Oil. He remained very close to his uncle and kept Harjinder's legacy as close to his heart as his uncle had.

The Air Force Day Parade became the main event in the IAF calendar to celebrate the past, present and the future. In the 1980s, it was held every year at Palam, in Delhi, with the IAF Vintage Flight taking part without, however, any reference to the man responsible for its inception. In 1989, the Vintage Flight performed as usual with Harjinder's Spitfire, still with his call sign, 'Plumber' scrawled down the left engine cowl, leading the growing fleet which included a Tigermoth, a Harvard, a Vampire and the only HT2 left still flying. The brand new fighter in the IAF's 1989 fleet was the dart shaped, French Mirage 2000 fighter that would still be on display in the 2012 parade, but as the old girl herself.

So how did these airplanes find themselves locked up in a hanger for over three decades? There are of course, several versions of what happened next. Historian, and pilot instructor, Mukund Murty, saw the display, and said that Joe zoom climbed his machine heavenwards, rolling as he went. He then pushing the nose down into a spiralling dive, but crucially holding it in for one extra turn compared to the practised routine. But no matter who tells the story, the end is always the same, Joe Bakshi found himself with the nose of his aircraft pointing directly at the ground in front of the Chief, standing on his dais. A jet pointing earthward, gobbles up the sky in a fraction of a second. Joe Bakshi would have hauled the control column back into the pit of his stomach. The nose of the aircraft was pointing up, but the momentum was still dragging it down (what is known as 'mushing', in aviation parlance), as it smashed into the ground producing the awful, greasy, oil-laden fireball that marks all air crashes. Shrapnel from the engine sizzled and zipped over the heads of the crowd, and through the doors of a hangar nearby. By some miracle, all the opened mouthed spectators escaped any major injury from the metal shards slicing through the air in all directions, but three people in the servants' area behind were not as lucky. The Chief knew that by all rights his children should have been orphaned at that moment. His reaction, when he returned to his office, was to order all unnecessary flying to cease. Harjinder's Vintage Flight was deemed unnecessary, and was pushed into the same hangar that the shrapnel from the crash had slashed through, where it would remain , gathering dust, until the next millennium.

The work Mr Nanda had done in his industry brought him in direct, and close, contact with the upper echelons of the IAF, resulting in invitations to all the parades. At the Air Force Day Parade in 2005, he met the then Chief, Air Chief Marshal Tyagi. Mr Nanda's uncle had come into possession of the typewriter that Jumbo had kept with him during the war in Burma, and his time in England, as he flew missions over the D-Day beaches. Mr Nanda's offer of Jumbo's typewriter, as an exhibit, was accepted by the Chief, so a date was arranged to drop it off personally to the Chief's office.

Mr Nanda had kept in close contact with Harjinder's wife, and was a frequent visitor to their house in Chandigarh. Harjinder's son then moved into the house. Not long after his arrival, all contact with Harjinder's wife was severed, and this greatly troubled Mr Nanda. There had been persistent rumours within the Nanda family, which seemed too extreme to be true, but Mr Nanda felt he could no longer ignore them. He took the opportunity of his time with Air Chief Marshal Tyagi to discuss his concerns.

There had also been a number of pleas to the local military police from residents who lived near the Singh's house, and knew Beant Kaur, but now with Air Chief Marshal Tyagi taking a personal interest, these were taken seriously.

Early one morning, the military police moved down the high green hedge that kept all but the flat roof of the single storey house hidden. They kept low as they gathered at the white painted brick pillars supporting the large, arched metal gates and the gold-coloured plaque announcing the name of the inhabitant, and the house number. The men opened the locked gate with ease to make their way to the front door of what had been Harjinder's house. They rang the bell and waited. The door was cracked open and the military police pushed against it, then poured in. The police found, and released two women from the house; Beant Kaur and her sister Satwant Kaur. Harjinder and Beant's adopted son had reached the rank of Colonel in the Indian army before moving into the house that Harjinder had helped build. It is alleged that he had held the two women captive; fearful that they would sell the house which he regarded as rightfully his. He denied all the allegations levelled against him, but the fact is that, once released, the women went to live with a cousin and arranged for the sale of Harjinder's house, the home he had helped build after a life he had devoted to his country and his Air Force. The press gathered when Beant Kaur handed the Congress President, Sonia Gandhi, a cheque for the Rajiv Gandhi Foundation. Beant's sister Satwant Kaur told The Tribune newspaper that they were feeling relieved, and free of tension, after donating the cheque to the Foundation. In words that could have been written by Harjinder, she told the reporters 'It is better not to have money if it brings so much misery and pain. What is the use of having a house, carpets, money, jewellery, if they bring so much unhappiness? We went through hell for 25 years because of all these.'

Sonia Gandhi was visibly shocked when she was told of what the women had been through. She said that while it was true that older people were not cared for in Western societies, that such a thing had happened in India was shocking.

I knew nothing of these events; it is fair to say that I had the stereotypical view of India held by most of the British population. Even if

I had heard about a woman being rescued from alleged imprisonment by her own adopted son, it would have had little effect; I had concerns closer to home at the time. My youngest daughter, Gracie, was just 2-year-old as my oldest daughter, Ella, was celebrating her fourth birthday in 2005, and it certainly was an event worth celebrating. We had got Ella this far but we still had 18 months of chemotherapy to complete if she was going to beat leukaemia. She was home for her birthday, but the intensive chemotherapy, and any infection, would mean days of our own little imprisonment in the isolation ward. The reality was hours, flowing into days, of boredom interspersed with moments of terror; just like flying! In the days spent with a listless child in bed, or a happy child putting jigsaws together on the hospital floor, I filled my spare time doing research on my laptop. With my father having been a display pilot, I had grown up in the world of air shows and old aircraft. My search for possible gems left in abandoned hangars, or sheds, took me into 1940's India, and their squadrons of Spitfires and Hurricanes. The image search for 'Indian Spitfires' kept throwing up an unusual colour picture; a lone aircraft buzzing very low over the heads of a crowd. I found out this was a picture from 1989, at the IAF Parade held every year. So they did have a vintage flight! As I followed the links, I stumbled upon pictures of a Harvard, a Vampire, a Tigermoth and a chipmunk-like little trainer called an HT2. Strange how there was no mention of this vintage flight in more recent times, I thought. There were mentions of an Air Force Museum in Delhi, so I bundled all the info together on my laptop, just in case my job, as a long haul pilot, took me to Delhi.

It was just as Ella finished her treatment that I finally arrived in Delhi. Tempted as I was to sleep through the day after the long flight, then head to the bar for an early beer, I forced myself up after just a few hours of sleep, a routine that would become the norm! I thought I would take a hotel car as the driver would know the whereabouts of the IAF Museum. He didn't! We roamed around the International Airport, to the more obscure military side, but even the people we stopped to ask for directions seemed to know nothing. It was by chance we saw a sign, half obscured by an unruly bush, which took us down the road where the nose of an aircraft, on a plinth, jutted over the high wall; we had found the Museum.

The aircraft in this hangar, for that was all the Museum was, were interesting in their own right, but there was no sign of a vintage flight. Out of the far doors was an aircraft parking area with an identical hangar

visible in the distance. If I had a vintage operation, I thought, I would keep
it close to my Museum, so I crossed the parking area at a pace that I hoped
wouldn't look too suspicious, but would get me to the door expeditiously.
When I got there, the hangar doors were padlocked together. I would
have left it there but hangar doors never meet perfectly and it is possible
to peer through the gap right to the equally poor-fitting door at the other
side. The light from one end to the other was obstructed by a wing tip; a
crescent shaped wing tip – a Spitfire's wing tip. This must be the Vintage
Flight. I pushed through a side door to get down the side of the hangar
but there was still no way in. The far doors were also locked. I trudged
back and took one last look through the doors. In frustration, and disgust,
I rattled the lock, throwing some strong Anglo Saxon words at it. As I held
it in my hand it popped open; somebody hadn't pushed the metal loop
fully home to lock it. Hangar doors are heavy, but I don't recall having
any trouble moving one, because my next memory is that of standing in
the gloom after the harsh light outside, and, as my eyes adjusted, the shapes
around me took form.

There, in this single hangar, were the aircraft of Harjinder's Vintage
Flight, covered in a layer of dust, but all complete. The Spitfire I spied
through the door was perfect, if painted with a strange choice of colours,
and had this metal plate with 'Plumber' down the side. My camera clicked
into action before the shout, the scamper of feet, and the uniformed figure
of an IAF Sergeant was running at me. He wasn't happy, and I was bustled
to the front gate and expelled. A year later he was working with me!

People I knew in India started to take my idea of resurrecting the
Vintage Flight seriously, and I was introduced to retired officers of
ever-rising seniority, in particular, Air Vice-Marshal B.A.K. Shetty.
On my days off in Bangalore, we would meet for a lunchtime beer, and
swap stories of flying deeds, and narrow escapes. At first, he dismissed
my idea of the Vintage Flight, but on a subsequent meeting, he revisited
the subject, my enthusiasm rubbed off on him, he suggested that I write
a proposal and he would see that made it as far as the desk of a man who
had been his student at the Air Force Academy. So it came to pass that Air
Vice-Marshal Tiny Kumaria received my carefully drafted proposal,
delivered, courtesy of my new found friend. The young man, whose
natural flair for aviation had saved his life, went on to become a Jaguar
pilot. Having done his conversion on to the Jaguar aircraft, courtesy of
the RAF in Scotland, he understood better than most how the RAF used

their Memorial Flight to great acclaim. He was, perhaps, the only senior officer within the hierarchy who would have grasped the concept, let alone done something about it.

It was shortly after I flew the restored Tigermoth, with Air Marshal Kumaria, and then, on the 80th Anniversary Parade, that I started my meetings with Mr Nanda, and my interest was pricked about this man Harjinder Singh, MBE. My interest had come just a few months too late. In May 2012, Beant Kaur finally joined Harjinder and his musketeers. Harjinder's widow showed that she too shared her husband's principles and was not concerned with material things, giving all of the money from the sale of her family home, to charity. Despite allegedly being held a prisoner by her own adopted son, Beant kept her dignity intact and lived the final years of her life simply. She was 95-year-old when she died. In 1932, when Harjinder had been there at the beginning of the IAF, he had been one of two hundred men, with just four Wapiti aircraft. When his widow finally passed away, the Air Force had grown to over 127,000 personnel and 1,500 aircraft. Harjinder's influence threaded all the way from those first few days of the IAF, right up to present day. By many twists of fate this Gora, this white face, this Welshman, came to pick up what Harjinder had started, in Kanpur, with the Vintage Flight and through these old pieces of machinery to learn about the man behind it. In 1932, Air Vice-Marshal Sir John Steele had gathered Harjinder, and his 200 colleagues, to tell them that they had brought nothing but the greatest disgrace to themselves, to the Air Force and to India. But nothing could be further from the truth. Harjinder had already turned his back on a lucrative engineering career in the British Raj to dedicate himself to the Air Force, and through that to an Independent India. He drove himself, and those around him, to serve to their best ability. Harjinder never wavered from being the most upstanding, incorruptible, fair, conscientious person with a life of relentless adventure. Disgrace is not a word to be used for Harjinder or Beant Kaur Singh.

Acknowledgements

After discovering Harjinder's dust covered aircraft in the Delhi hangar, it took a conversation with Danny Phillips, a British Airways Engineer, to get the ball rolling. We became good friends and his introduction to a close family friend, retired Wing Commander Pradeep Karvinkop, started the chain reaction up the IAF ranks.

Without Air Marshal Tiny Kumaria, there would have been no mentor to revisit Harjinder's Vintage Flight. Without the endless support, and tireless work of Group Captain Mukesh Sharma, there would have been no rebirth of Harjinder's Flight, or an introduction to Mr Nanda. Without the enthusiasm of Air Commodore Maheshwar, and then the knowledge and drive of Air Vice-Marshal Vikram Singh, there would have been no progress of Harjinder's Vintage Flight. There has been a stream of IAF officers and technicians who have thrown themselves behind the Vintage Flight project. Air Chief Marshal Major took the decision to back my idea to reform the Vintage Flight and his successors, Air Chief Marshal Naik and Air Chief Marshal Browne carried that forward. The present Chief, Air Marshal Raha is a strong supporter of the whole project and I have never seen a smile bigger than the one he wore as he sat in the RAF Battle of Britain Memorial Flight's Spitfire.

Without Mr Nanda's love of the IAF, and dedication to Harjinder's memories, there would not have been the material to write this story. Without the assistance of historian, Mukund Murty, there would have been no punctuation in this story; but plenty of historical, or is that hysterical, errors. Jagan Pillarisetti was a constant source of information and he, and his friends, supplied the photographs to add to those of Mr Nanda.

It has not just been a succession of Air Force Chiefs that have been behind my project. Air Vice-Marshal GS Bedi served as India's Air Attaché in London, always on hand to keep the momentum of the Vintage Flight moving forward with a smile. There has also been the line of UK Air and Naval Advisors in the British High Commission. Ian Draper was there at the start and remained, in a different role, throughout. He has always been on hand to ensure I am fed and watered during my Indian visits, but much more too. A thanks to Charles Ashcroft, especially for my medal, and to Andrew McAuley and Stuart Borland.

Another team there from the beginning has been the staff at the ITC Sheraton hotel, especially the concierges led by my friend, and co-owner of my Royal Enfield Bullet motorbike, Rajesh Mitharwal.

The team at Bloomsbury have been outstanding. It is just a shame the gentleman who started my association with Bloomsbury, Suresh Gopal, is not around to see the final result.

The biggest thank you must go to my family and friends for encouraging me to keep at, what must have seemed like, this crazy idea for a Welshman to write the story of a forgotten Indian military man from a different age. Extra thanks to my brother Paul and to Norman Rhodes for being additional editors for me.

The final 'thank you' must go to Harjinder for having such an outstanding life and keeping such comprehensive notes. I just wish we could have met!